Cape T

DayNight Guide
Cape Town

The insider's guide to the Mother City

DayNight *Publications*

Editorial

Editor: Pnina Fenster

Original photography: Ronnie Levitan

Map design: Vernon John Designs

Contributors: Adelle Baletta (*Theatre, Film*); Brian Berkman (*Gay Cape Town, Clubs, Late Night & Early Morning*); Haydn Ellis (*Cape Town Architecture*); Shellee-Kim Gold (*Children's Cape Town*); Owen Kinahan (*History, Introduction to Museums*); John Linnegar (*Art Deco Walk*); Gill Lord (*Dance*); Basil Rubin and Vaughan Johnson (*Cape Wines*)

Researchers: Brian Berkman (*Cape and South African Cuisine*); Tweet Gainsborough-Waring (*Sport, Fitness & The Great Outdoors, Survival*); Shellee-Kim Gold (*Townships, Vegetarian, Students & Budget Travellers*)

Editorial assistants: Shellee-Kim Gold, Lynne Crossley

Thanks to: John Boehler, Capab, The Castle, Mervyn Gers, Lisa Karp, Rose Korber, John Linnegar, Basil Rubin, Lester Venter, Andrew Jardine, Bartolomeu Dias

Copyright © 1995 by DayNight Publications (Pty) Ltd

All rights reserved. No part of this publication may be reproduced or transmitted in any form or by any means without prior permission from the publisher.

ISBN 0 95840 571 9

First edition, first impression 1995

Published by
DayNight, PO Box 2981, Parklands 2121, South Africa. Telefax (011) 484-1014.

Distributed by Southern Book Publishers, PO Box 3103, Halfway House 1685

Cover design by Alix Gracie
Cover photograph by Photo Library Mark van Aardt
Set in Garamond and Neue Helvetica
Typesetting and origination by Positive Proof cc
Printed and bound by Colorgraphic, Durban

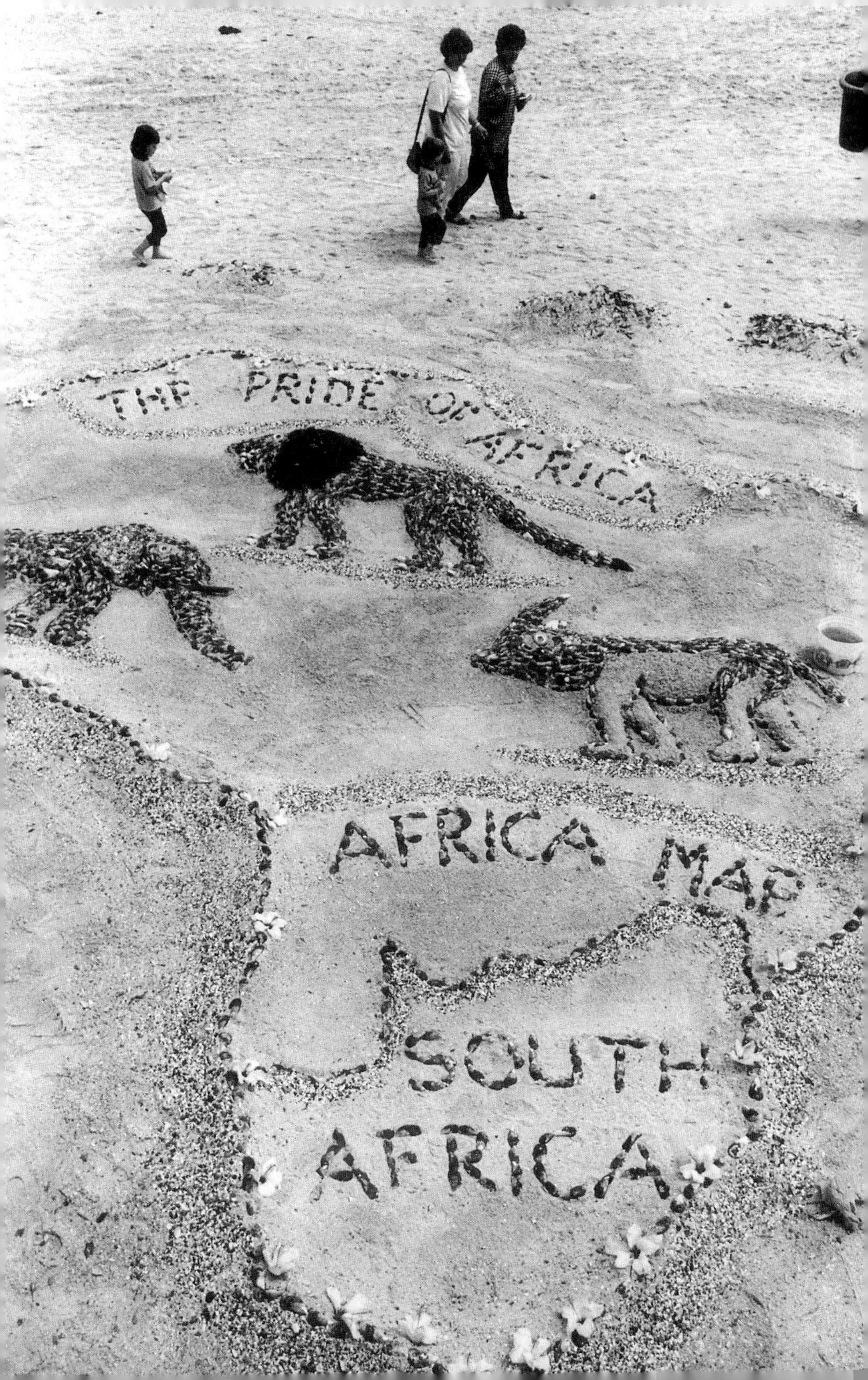
THE PRIDE OF AFRICA
AFRICA MAP
SOUTH AFRICA

TOBACCO IS ADDICTIVE

15 mg tar 1,4 mg nicotine As per Government agreed method

Peter Stuyvesant
The International Passport®
to Smoking Pleasure
Rich choice tobaccos
Miracle Filter King Size

...so much more to enjoy!

Made in South Africa. Also in Germany, United Kingdom, Australia, Netherlands, Malaysia, Canada, Switzerland, Austria, New Zealand, Singapore, Zambia and Ireland.
AMERICAN CIGARETTE COMPANY

CONTENTS

Introduction	ix
Essential Information	1
Getting Around	6
Accommodation	12
Cape Town by Season	27
History	32
Sightseeing	41
The Sights	45
Museums	66
Art Galleries	69
Cape Town Architecture	76
Eating & Drinking	79
Cape and South African Cuisine	80
Cape Wines	83
Where to Eat	85
Shopping & Services	115
Shopping	116
Services	141
Arts & Entertainment	149
Media	151
Theatre	154
Film	158
Dance	161
Music	164
Clubs	172
Late Night & Early Morning	175
Special Interests	179
Children's Cape Town	180
Students & Budget Travellers	192
Business	197
Gay Cape Town	204
Women's Cape Town	208
Wet, Wet, Wet	213
Day Trips	227
Sport, Fitness & The Great Outdoors	236
Survival	250
Maps	255
Index	263

$\mathcal{W}$here the world meets at the water's edge

To all who pass its way, the Victoria & Alfred Waterfront reflects the true spirit and vitality of the Cape. Experience the ambience of a working harbour, enjoy the diversity of shops, markets, restaurants and theatres or simply stroll along the promenade as mime artists and street musicians entertain you. Cape Town's Waterfront holds its own special memories for everyone.

For further information contact Waterfront Visitors Centre on (021) 418 2369.

waterfront

INTRODUCTION

'This Cape is the most stately thing and the fairest Cape we saw in the entire circumference of the earth,' wrote Sir Francis Drake in his journal of 1580.

Cape of Good Hope, Tavern of the Seas, Cape of Storms, Fairest Cape, Mother City and Escape Town ... welcome to a place of many moods, views, histories and peoples. Founded as a supply station in 1652 by Jan van Riebeeck, this city has been the destination of slaves, refugees, prisoners, jet setters and adventurers. It's been colonised by the Dutch and the British, symbolised by both Robben Island and Table Mountain, swept by winds and kissed by the summer. Now, as part of the new South Africa, it's a hot tourist destination – even when the sun isn't shining.

The *DayNight Guide to Cape Town* doesn't pretend to be an encyclopedia of this multi-layered city. Its aim is to accompany you to the best beaches and boutiques, point you in the direction of the wines, food, arts, sights and raves. It's designed to add depth to your experience, to reveal hidden corners of the city that you might otherwise have ignored, and to ensure you don't discover too late that you missed something unmissable.

Cities, like people, have their moods, and Cape Town is changeable as well as charming. High season heralds in new venues and trends. Restaurants and hotels that were marvellous yesterday may go out of fashion, or out of business, tomorrow. The phone numbers and listings details were correct at the time of going to press, but, alas, those too are subject to change. We welcome your suggestions, comments and recommendations.

That said, we're delighted to have your company. So let's open a bottle of wine, pack the picnic hamper, the aesthetic insights or the beach bag, put on our walking shoes or our most entrance-making gear. Urban delights, great escapes, shopping and soul food are just around the corner.

K 94.5 FM

Addictive Radio

ESSENTIAL INFORMATION

The lowdown on visas, money, phone calls, tourist info, public holidays, time, tipping and local lingo.

For transport, see chapter **Getting Around**. *For emergency information, see chapter* **Survival**.

WESTERN CAPE STATISTICS

Area: 129 386 km^2
Population (1993): 3 620 000
Population growth (1985-1993): 1,7%
Density (people per km^2): 28
Literacy rate: 71,9%
Life expectancy (1991): 64,8 years
Statistics supplied by Wesgro.

VISAS

American, Canadian, British and European Community nationals don't need visas for holidays of up to three months. Other nationals should check at South African consulates or embassies before departure.

For visa information in South Africa, contact the Department of Home Affairs, Visa Section, 462-4970.

INSURANCE

It is best to take out travel, accident or medical insurance before leaving for South Africa. Sophisticated health care does exist but is mainly in the hands of private clinics and as a result is expensive.

Travellers arriving in South Africa without insurance can contact Travel Assistance, part of Europ Assistance and endorsed by ASATA. The Cape Town branch is on the 9th Floor, Parkade Mall, Strand, tel. 21-6906, fax 21-1800.

MONEY

The South African currency is the Rand (symbolised by R before amounts). One hundred cents equal one rand. There are same-size notes in different colours for R10, R20, R50, R100 and R200. Copper coins are for 1, 2 and 5 cents. Yellow coins are for 10, 20 and 50 cents. Silver coins are for R1, R2 and R5.

Although most international credit cards are accepted at restaurants and shops, petrol can't be bought on credit card.

AUTOBANKS

There are internationally linked autobanks that accept foreign cards with PIN numbers, with the exception of American Express. These are found in major areas, but they can be problematic, so take travellers cheques with you if you're heading for a day of conspicuous consumption. Cash withdrawn is debited to your account on the day that the transaction information reaches your home bank.

Beware of thieves who check out your PIN number, create a distraction or ask for help, then swap or grab your card.

Cancel stolen credit or bank cards at:
American Express, foreign and South African cards: *418-5600 or 080-953-4300 (tollfree).*
Diners Club: *686-7880 (Mon-Fri) or (011) 33-5151.*
First National Bank: *0800-11-0132 (tollfree).*
Standard Bank (Autobank, Visa and Master Card): *0800 020-600 (tollfree).*

FOREIGN EXCHANGE & BANKS

Very few shops and restaurants accept payment in foreign currency. Foreign currency can be exchanged or cash withdrawn on credit card at banks. You'll need positive ID.

Hours at major banks: 9am-3.30pm weekdays, 9am-11am Sat. The exception is Trust Bank whose office hours are: 8.30am-3.30pm weekdays, 8am-11am Sat.

FOREIGN EXCHANGE SERVICES

Rennies Travel, *Tyger Valley, Upper Shopping Mall, tel. 949-7474.* **Open:** 9am-5pm Mon-Thu, 9am-7pm Fri, 9am-1pm Sat.
Trust Bank, *International Arrivals, Customs Hall, Cape Town International Airport, tel. 934-4270.* **Open:** when flights arrive.
Trust Bank, *International Departures, Cape Town International Airport, tel. 934-8435 or Domestic Departures, tel. 934-0223.* **Open:** according to international flights.
American Express, *Thibault Square, City Centre, tel. 419-3085.* **Open:** 8.30am-5pm weekdays, 9am-noon Sat.
American Express Bureau de Change, *City Centre, tel. 418-5202 (ext. 219).* **Open:** 9am-7pm weekdays, 8.30am-5pm Sat, 9am-5pm Sun.

SEVEN-DAYS-A-WEEK FOREIGN EXCHANGE BUREAUX

American Express, *11a Victoria and Alfred Building, Waterfront, tel. 21-6021.* **Hours:** 9am-7pm weekdays, 9am-5pm weekends.
Rennies Travel, *Victoria Wharf, Waterfront, tel. 418-3744/5.* **Hours:** 9am-7pm weekdays, 9am-5pm Sat, 10am-5pm Sun and public holidays. (International facility for all cards except American Express.)

PHONING HOME

Cape Town's area code is 021. Don't use it for inner-city calls. Phone numbers in this book are for Cape Town unless indicated by a prefix in brackets.

Electronic Yellow Pages: *418-5000.*
Local number enquiries: *1023.*
International number enquiries: *0903.*

Green public phones take phone cards and blue ones take coins. Phone cards are sold at post offices, Telkom offices and the Tourist Information Centre, 3 Adderley St, City Centre.

INTERNATIONAL CASH PHONE/FAX

Main Post Office, *Parliament St, City Centre, tel. 461-5710 or 461-5670. Tollfree Customer Careline: 0800-11-4488.* A poste restante and enquiry desk is situated in the main hall. **Open:** 8am-4.30pm weekdays, 8am-noon Sat.
Pronto Phone, *Tourist Rendezvous Travel Centre, 3 Adderley St, City Centre, tel. 25-3897.* **Open:** 8am-5pm weekdays (extended hours during peak season). Also at *Thibault Square, City Centre, tel. 419-2959.* **Open:** 8am-5pm weekdays.
Telinternational, *263c Main Rd, Sea Point, tel. 434-2162.* **Open:** 9am-11pm daily. A strange but workable combination of a gift-cum-phone shop, these public phone booths offer cheaper phone services than ordinary phone booths. Fax and phone message services also offered.

The solution to your foreign exchange needs

- Travellers Cheques and Foreign Banknotes.
- Exchange Control Assistance and Advice.
- Spot and Forward Exchange Transactions and Rate Quotations.
- Import and Export Documentary Collections.
- Import and Export Documentary Credits.
- Offshore Finance.
- Finance and Electronic Transfers

The above products and many more are placed at your disposal through the largest network of commercial banking branches in South Africa under the brand names of **Allied Bank, TrustBank, United Bank** and **Volkskas Bank.**

ABSA Bank will provide you with the solution to your foreign exchange needs. **International Offices: Frankfurt, Hong Kong, Singapore, London. For further information contact Johannesburg Tel (011) 330 4170, Fax (011) 337 7918.**

ABSA BANK

ABSA BANK LIMITED (REG. NO. 86/04794/06)

International Banking

YOUR INTERNATIONAL BANKING PARTNER IN THE NEW SOUTH AFRICA

RAPP COLLINS SA 7797

SOUTH AFRICAN TIME

South African Standard Time is two hours ahead of Greenwich Mean Time, one hour ahead of Central European Winter Time and seven hours ahead of Eastern Standard Winter Time. Telephone directories carry rates and time zones.

CAPE TOWN TIME

Cape Town doesn't operate at Johannesburg's furious pace. Thank goodness. But since the 17th century, Capetonians have had a booming local time reminder courtesy of the **Noon Day Gun** which is fired on the slopes of Signal Hill at noon every day except Sunday. Originally fired to signal the beginning and end of workdays, the gun also marked daily prayer pauses during World War I. It's an 18th century muzzle-loading cannon, best heard from the City Centre where it startles pigeons and reminds everyone about another venerable Cape institution – lunch.

PUBLIC HOLIDAYS

January 1:	New Year's Day
March 21:	Human Rights Day
April:	Good Friday – Friday before Easter
April:	Family Day – Monday after Good Friday
April 27:	Freedom Day
May 1:	Workers' Day
June 16:	Youth Day
August 9:	National Women's Day
September 24:	Heritage Day
December 16:	Day of Reconciliation
December 25:	Christmas Day
December 26:	Day of Goodwill

If a public holiday falls on a Sunday, the Monday is generally a public holiday.

TOURIST INFORMATION CENTRES

For maps, travel advice, brochures, accommodation assistance ...

CAPTOUR AND SATOUR

Captour Information Office, *3 Adderley St, Cape Town, tel. 418-5214/5 or 418-5202, fax 418-5227.* **Open:** 8am-7pm weekdays, 8.30am-5pm Sat, 9am-5pm Sun. Closed Christmas Day.

Captour Bellville, *Shop 007, Tyger Valley Centre, tel. 948-4993, fax 949-1449.* **Open:** 9am-5.30pm weekdays, 9am-1.30pm Sat. Closed public holidays.

Simon's Town Information Centre, *Simon's Town Museum, Court Rd, Simon's Town, tel. 786-3046.* **Open:** 9am-4pm weekdays, 10am-1pm Sat. Closed Sun and public holidays.

Satour Information Office (for general tourist info on South Africa), *3 Adderley St, Cape Town, tel. 21-6274, fax 419-4875.* **Open:** 8am-4.30pm Mon-Thu, 8am-4pm Fri, 10am-12.30pm Sat. Closed Sun and public holidays.

Captour Muizenberg, *Atlantic Rd, Muizenberg (next to library), tel. 788-1898, fax 788-2269.* **Open:** 8.30am-5pm weekdays, 8.30am-1pm Sat, 9am-noon public holidays. Closed Christmas Day. Sunday hours vary; check by phone.

WATERFRONT INFORMATION BUREAUX

For information on Waterfront events, shops, maps. Videos on Cape Town (in English and German). Prints, postcards, phone cards, gift vouchers ...

Waterfront Information Centre, *Old Harbour, Market Square, Waterfront, tel. 418-2369.* **Open:** 9.30am-5pm weekdays. **Bonus:** Booking for Table Mountain cable car.

Waterfront Information Kiosk, *Victoria Wharf Shopping Centre, Waterfront, tel. 418-2369.* **Open:** 9am-7pm Mon, Tue, Thu and Fri, 9am-9pm Wed, 9am-7pm weekends.

AIRPORT INFORMATION

Plane arrival and departure times: 934-0407.

OPENING HOURS

Normal shopping hours are 8.30am-5pm weekdays and 8.30am-1pm Sat, but some stores have longer hours. Shops at the Waterfront open seven days a week: 9am-7pm weekdays, 9am-6pm Sat, 10am-5pm Sun. During high season, shops generally extend hours.

ELECTRIC PLUGS

220/380 V-50 Hz. Three-pronged plugs are the norm and most hotel rooms have 110-V outlets for electric razors. American appliances need a transformer.

DRIVING

Capetonian drivers are notorious for ignoring indicators and pulling over without warning. They also like watching the scenery instead of the road. Nevertheless, traffic regulations do apply.

Drive on the left-hand side of the road and overtake from the right. Speed restrictions are 60 km/h in urban areas and 120 km/h where signposted on highways. There are speedtraps, especially during holiday seasons, and ticketing for overdrawn parking meters and illegal parking is efficient. Wearing a seatbelt is required by law and it's advisable to lock car doors as protection against hijackings.

SAFETY

Don't let the salt air go to your brain. Lock car doors while driving. Don't explore the townships without a reliable guide. Watch your wallet, avoid dark alleys and don't wear the family fortune around your neck. Even if your ego is the size of Madonna's, Table Mountain is bigger than you are, so hike on paths, take good equipment and don't hike alone.

VAT

14% Value Added Tax (VAT) is added to goods and services except for some basic foods. Foreign visitors can reclaim VAT on purchases with a total value exceeding R250. Do this at the airport of departure, harbour or customs offices. You'll need your passport and original tax invoice from the shop and you may be asked to show items on which refunds are claimed.

DUTY-FREE SHOPPING

Some accredited jewellers sell duty-free diamonds and jewellery to foreign tourists on production of a valid passport.

TIPPING

Unless indicated on the restaurant tab, service isn't included and the standard tip is 10-15%. Tip hotel porters 50c-R1 per item.

LINGO

While English is the *lingua franca*, Afrikaans, Xhosa and Zulu are among the 11 national languages you'll find here. And that's to say nothing of the colourful, unprintable swearwords indigenous to the city streets.

You'll find expressions like these creeping into the lingo:

Bagel – Male, wealthy, superficial, the bagel is, as his name suggests, lots of image around lots of useless air. His favourite Cape Town turf: Clifton and Bantry Bay. His female equivalent: the *kugel*.

Gauties – Inhabitants of Gauteng (Johannesburg and surrounding areas), *Gauties* flood the city during holidays and locals greet them with a mixture of scorn (they're so crass) and relief (they spend so much).

Howzit – A general greeting which intertwines 'hello, how you doing?' and general *bonhomie*. The correct response is not 'great' but 'howzit' in return.

Lekker – Afrikaans for nice tasting, this is applied to everything from weather to wine.
Ja – Afrikaans for yes.
Ja-nee – Literally translated from Afrikaans, this means yes-no. It could mean yes and it could mean no, but it usually means – I'm not sure, look at it both ways, on the other hand ...
Jol – Rave, good time. Can be used as a verb as in 'we're *jolling* at that *lekker* new place'.
Just now – It says something about African time that, contrary to what you might suppose, this popular phrase doesn't mean immediately. It simply indicates anything from 'this minute' to 'maybe next Tuesday (or in the foreseeable future at any rate)'.

Kugel – The South African equivalent of a Jewish American Princess, a *kugel* is literally Yiddish for sweet noodle pudding, and that pretty much says it. You don't have to be Jewish to be one, but you do have to be spoiled, superficial and an Olympic-standard shopper. *Kugels* talk in nasal drones and their standard greeting is *howzit!*
Nee – Afrikaans for no.
Now-now – Unlike *just now*, *now-now* means pronto (sort of).
Shame – Shame expresses anything from deep sympathy (in the case of a broken leg or heart, for example) to adoration (as in 'Shame, what a gorgeous baby!').

HELPFUL XHOSA PHRASES

Hello/good morning.
Molo.

How are you?
Unjani?

I'm very well.
Ndisapila.

Where are you going?
Uya phi?

What's your name?
Ngubani igama lakho?

Can you show me the way to ...?
Ungadibonisa indelela ...?

How much is this?
Yimalini?

I'm going now.
Ndiya hamba.

Excuse me.
Uxolo.

Please.
Nceda.

Thank you very much.
Enkosi kakuhlu.

What do you want?
Ofuna ntoni?

Do you speak English?
Uyakwazi ukuthetha iSingesi?

Good bye.
Hamba kakuhle.

NOTE: Throughout this guide, the following abbreviations have been used for credit cards: **AmEx** American Express; **Mc** Mastercard; and **V** Visa.

GETTING AROUND

How to find your way around the city – from arriving at the airport to taxis and topless buses to cycle hire and helicopters.

Because the flat-topped, 1 000-m-high Table Mountain is such a visible landmark, Cape Town is an easy city to negotiate. To the west of Table Mountain are the City Centre and Atlantic Seaboard suburbs. To the east are the Cape Flats townships. To the north are the municipalities of Goodwood, Parow, Durbanville and Bellville. To the south are the suburbs of Woodstock, Salt River, Observatory, Mowbray, Rondebosch, Newlands, Claremont, Kenilworth and Wynberg. Constantia links the southern suburbs with the False Bay coast, which extends to the Cape of Good Hope Nature Reserve. The City Centre is situated in the heart of a natural amphitheatre formed by Devil's Peak, Table Mountain, Lion's Head and Signal Hill.

The main arterial roads are the N1, which heads out to the northern towns (Bellville and others), and continues to the winelands of Paarl and Wellington. The N7 turns off the N1 and takes you up the west coast past Milnerton, Table View and Blouberg. The N2, heading east, is the main airport route, with off-ramps to the townships of Nyanga, Crossroads and Guguletu. To reach the Stellenbosch winelands, continue along the N2 until the Stellenbosch turn-off. If you keep going straight, you'll hit the turn-offs to Somerset West and the Strand.

The main routes to the south of Cape Town are the M5, which heads for the suburbs of Athlone, Crawford, Ottery and Lansdowne, and the M3, which goes around Devil's Peak, skirting Claremont and Bishopscourt before joining the Blue Route freeway to Muizenberg. Off-ramps along the M3 lead to the suburbs of Mowbray, Rondebosch, Newlands, Claremont, Wynberg, Plumstead and Constantia.

A slower, but more spectacularly scenic drive is the M6, a continuation of Victoria Road (which passes through Clifton). And no visit to Cape Town would be complete without a trip along Chapman's Peak Drive.

Detailed maps of the city are available from bookshops and tourist bureaux and, although you'll find Capetonians a helpful bunch, if you're staying for longer than a few days, it's worth having a map.

ARRIVING IN CAPE TOWN

Cape Town International Airport is 22 km from the City Centre. The international and domestic lounges are about five minutes' walk apart and both contain car hire services, public phones and Western Cape Tourism Board kiosks where you can buy phone cards and obtain maps, pamphlets and information about accommodation and tours. They're open 9am-4pm. Wheelchairs are available at both lounges. Lock up your luggage in the domestic lounge. For airport info and arrival and departure times, call 934-0407.

TO AND FROM THE AIRPORT

The drive to and from Cape Town International Airport to the City Centre takes about 25 minutes, and rush hour is around 7am-8.30am in to town and 4.15pm-5.30pm out of town; it's worst on Fridays. Be warned – peak traffic can add at least 15 minutes to your travelling time.

There are no trains into the city from the airport and, although you can haggle with the taxi drivers, your cheapest option is the airport bus – the service is pleasant, efficient and convenient, and it deposits you at Cape Town Station in the City Centre. From here you can take a taxi (there are plenty on the spot) or a train to the suburbs (remember that it's not always easy to find taxis at suburban train stations).

Cape Town Station is a block's walk from the Tourist Information Centre where you can book accommodation, find out about tours and collect tourist info.

See also listing **Chauffeur services** *later in this chapter.*

Intercape Airport Shuttle Bus
Tel. 934-4400 or 386-4414.
A minibus leaves Cape Town Station (at the Intercape office) one hour to half-an-hour before flights and you can book by phone or on the spot. Cost: R20 one way. There's also a door-to-door service at an extra charge, depending on distance. Help with wheelchairs, pets and luggage is provided. The service from the City Centre to the airport starts at around 5.15am and runs until the last flight of the day.

Welcome Shuttle
Tel. 26-2134.
Daily scheduled, air-conditioned pick-up from major hotels. Price determined by number of passengers. R50 per person one way.

TAXI SERVICES

Taxi rates from the airport to the City Centre vary. The average is around R90, but Cape Town's taxi service is largely unregulated and you can find better deals if you ask around. The taxi drivers generally don't object to cab-sharing.

AIRPORT PARKING

Unless you're dropping someone off at the airport and leaving immediately, *don't* park in no-parking areas – your car will be clamped. Your only choice is to park in the paid-for areas.

Cape Executive Parking
Tel. 934-2240 or 934-2245 or 934-2258.
Leave your car keys with the office in the departure hall and your car will be parked under cover and, if you want, cleaned and serviced. Cost: R30 per vehicle for the first 24 hours or part thereof. Thereafter R15 per 15 hours or part thereof. Monthly contracts are R480 plus VAT. R25 for cleaning and valet service.

TRANSPORT IN THE CITY

Trains, taxis, buses and more interesting options ...

BUS SERVICES

Citywide buses
The main bus terminals are outside the Golden Acre, Adderley St and at the Grand Parade. Buses depart around every half hour during peak hours and timetables are available from Captour (Tourist Rendezvous Travel Centre, Adderley St). Golden Arrow buses leave Adderley St for Kloof Nek, Sea Point and Camps Bay.

Those from the Grand Parade depart for Sea Point, Hout Bay and the southern suburbs going as far as Retreat Station or Simon's Town. Tickets are bought as you board, and you can carry luggage, but not bicycles or surfboards, onto the bus.

For information about bus timetables and routes, call Golden Arrow: 45-5482.

Intercity buses
For information on buses between Cape Town and Johannesburg, Bloemfontein, Port Elizabeth, Durban and Windhoek contact:

Greyhound, *tel. 418-4310.*
Intercape Mainliner, *tel. 934-4400 or 934-8380/1.*
Transcity and Translux, *tel. 405-3333.*

Waterfront buses
Buses to and from the Waterfront run seven days a week from 6.30am-11pm. There are two routes, one that operates every 10 minutes, and goes as far as Adderley St, City Centre, and a second that runs every 20 minutes as far as Sea Point's Peninsula Hotel.

Fares to the City Centre are R1,20 a ride and to Sea Point R1,50.

Catch the Waterfront bus outside the Tourist Information Centre (next to the train station in Adderley St), along Sea Point Main Rd and outside the Victoria Wharf shopping centre, Waterfront. Besides the convenience, the route's very pleasant.

BICYCLE HIRE

With outstanding scenic rides, around Chapman's Peak and in Hout Bay, for example, Cape Town is ideally suited to cycling. For info on cycle races, see chapter **Sport**. To buy or hire a bike and equipment, try the following:

Mike Hopkins
133a Bree St, City Centre, tel. 23-2527.
Mountain and road bikes for hire at daily, weekly and weekend rates, plus advice on good routes. Mountain bikes are R45 per day to hire and a R350 deposit is required. ID not essential.

Rent 'n Ride Cycle & Blade Hire
1 Park Rd, Mouille Point, tel. 434-1122.
Bicycles, rollerblades and cycling equipment for hire. Deposit required. Cheques accepted by arrangement only.

CAR RENTAL

Stiff competition between car rental companies means that you can get good deals by shopping around. To rent, you'll need a current South African, overseas or international driver's licence, and you must be over 21 (some companies stipulate over 23 or 25).

Third party and collision damage are usually part of the deal and there's a kilometre charge as well as a daily rate, except with really good deals (Stallion Car Hire, for example, offers an all-inclusive charge). If you're hiring for an extended length of time, investigate sliding scale rates – some companies offer them.

Most car rentals, even some cheaper ones, offer a drop-and-collect service and if you're budgeting, go for the second-hand car rentals – they may not look grand, but they're generally reliable. (Most second-hand hire companies require ID and a holding deposit.)

Credit cards and cheques are accepted by the majority of car hire firms.

New cars at good prices
Adelphi, tel. 439-6144.
Alisa, tel. 22-1515.
Avis, tel. 0800-2-1111 (tollfree) or 61-9104 or 24-1177. Chauffeur service also available.
Dolphin, tel. 439-9696.
Eezy Rent A Car, tel. 23-3834 or 24-3951.
Holiday, tel. 45-3229.
Imperial, tel. 21-5190 or 23-3300 or 419-3897.
Marine, tel. 434-0343.
The Pavilion, tel. 419-7362. BMWs – from manuals to convertibles.
Stallion, tel. 45-5872 or 45-4334.
Tempest, tel. 24-5000 or 0800-031-666 (toll-free).

Competitively priced car hire
Ace, tel. 782-6804 or 21-7332.
Budget Rent A Car, tel. 23-4290/7.
Cab Car Hire, tel. 683-1932.
Cape Car Hire, tel. 683-2441.
Cruise, tel. 696-3743.
Economy, tel. 434-8304. VW 10-seater buses and 10-seater Ventures also available.
Kenings, tel. 25-2629 or 25-2645. Range includes convertible VW Beetles.
Vineyard, tel. 64-1994.

4x4 and minibus hire
Safari Rentals, tel. 64-4895.
Wheelrent Car, Bakkie and Truck Hire, tel. 419-7750 or 946-3980 or 854-7700.

CHAUFFEUR SERVICES

Nono's Chauffeur Service
Tel. 081-211-1566
BMWs and Mercedes, complete with car phones. Price is determined by distance, but R95 should get you between the City Centre and airport.

Rendezvous Cape
Tel. 683-2503.
Mercedes with driver at R150 per person to or from the airport.

HELICOPTER

Civair
East Pier, Waterfront, tel. 419-5182.
Open: *9am-sunset.*
Flights to or from the airport and Waterfront in a four-seater are R650. Scenic flights and tours, of which the shortest is 20 minutes, start at R195 p/p or an hourly R550 p/p.

Court

East Pier, Waterfront, tel. 25-2966.
Open: *8am-6pm.*
The shortest helicopter tour, a 10-minute view of the City Bowl, Table Mountain and Signal Hill, is R400 for four passengers and R500 for six passengers. A one-hour trip to the Cape of Good Hope Nature Reserve is around R2 390 for four passengers and R2 990 for six. Flights to or from the airport and the Waterfront are R550.

HITCHING

You can hitch around the city, but at your own risk.

MINIBUS TAXIS

Considerably cheaper, if less sedate than conventional taxis, minibus taxis are crowded and fast, and they cover major Cape Town routes, all around the city and suburbs. The main rank is at the top of Cape Town Station, Strand St. Other major pick-up points are in Adderley St (outside the Golden Acre, the Groote Kerk and KFC), at the Grand Parade, outside the Cape Sun Hotel in Strand St or along Sea Point and Green Point Main roads. But you can just as easily stand at a bus stop or along a main road. Simply lift your arm to signal that you want a ride. Average fare: R1-R3. Expect a frequently jostling, sociable trip.

MOTORBIKE HIRE

Le Cap Motorcycle Hire

3 Carisbrook St (top of Bree St), tel. 23-0823. Le Cap hires out and sells motorbikes, helmets and gloves. Hired bikes come with a puncture kit. Hirer must be over 23 and in possession of a full motorcycle licence.

ON FOOT

Cape Town is a wonderful walking city. Apart from the mountain hikes, forest and beach walks (*for info see chapters* **Wet, Wet, Wet** *and* **Sport, Fitness & The Great Outdoors**), the City Centre is best explored on foot. Strolling around is extremely pleasant, and besides parking is difficult and traffic cops are efficient. Try the café and people-watching territory around Greenmarket Square, Long St, and for a shot of soothing, elegant greenery, take in Government Ave (between Orange and Adderley streets). At night, the area around Waterkant St hums, but watch your belongings and your back.

The Waterfront is extremely safe both day and night and it's crammed with shops and eateries. And obviously you're too sensible to wander down dark alleys with the family fortune and a precious collection of camera equipment strung around your neck.

For mountain and forest walks, see chapter **Sport, Fitness & The Great Outdoors**.

RIKKIS

Tel. 23-4888 or 23-4892 or 21-4871. Simon's Town, 786-2136. Stellenbosch, 887-2203.
A hop-on service in scooter-cum-minivans which take up to nine people, rikkis are an excellent way to get around the city – you get some fresh air and you're more involved in what's going on around you than you would be in a taxi. At R1 upwards (depending on the distance and number of passengers), they're also a good deal. Board along the main roads in the City Centre and along Orange and Kloof streets or outside the Golden Acre, Adderley St, on Kloof Nek and Kloof St or outside Texies Fish Shop, cnr Plein and Darling streets (opposite the Post Office). Private hire for trips to Clifton or further afield can be arranged.

TAXIS

Unlike cities like New York and London, Cape Town's streets aren't crawling with cabs and, apart from main taxi ranks and tourist spots like the Waterfront, in Adderley St and next to the Post Office in Darling St, it's best to phone for a taxi. Despite attempts to regulate fares, you'll find that prices vary, so call around for a good price. (Fares from the City Centre to the Waterfront start around the R14 mark.) Tip around 10%.

Taxi services include the following:
Marine Taxis, *tel. 434-0434.*
Sea Point Taxis, *tel. 434-4444.* One of the best-priced services around.
Unicab, *tel. 448-1720.*

Wild ones: the Harley Davidson Club.

TRAINS

A good network of trains links the City Centre to the southern and northern suburbs, but there are only buses to the Atlantic coast side. Train timetables are available from the Cape Town Station ticket offices (in the main hall of the station).

Tickets are reasonable – the single trip from Cape Town Station to Muizenberg, for example, is R4,60 first class and R2,20 third class.

Railway tickets are sold at stations, and if you don't buy yours from the ticket office, you could be obliged to buy it from the conductor – with a penalty surcharge (unless you're boarding the train when the station ticket office is closed). Most stations are open on Saturday mornings and some on Sunday.

There are two main lines: the Cape Town-Bellville-Wellington-Stellenbosch-Strand line and the Cape Town-Simon's Town line.

During peak hours (6am-9am and 3pm-6pm weekdays and 6am-8.30am and 11.30am-1pm Sat) trains on the Simon's Town line (to the suburbs) run every 5-10 minutes. Between 12am and 3pm, they run approximately every 20 minutes. For the rest, they're around half-hourly and they run from 5.10am-10.30pm.

It's inadvisable to travel third or second class after dark.

All stations, with the exception of very small ones, have timetables on display and conductors help passengers in wheelchairs. No bicycles or animals are allowed on trains and there's an extra charge for surfboards. Luggage is carried free.

For train information: 405-2991/2.

For train arrival and departure times:
Muizenberg: 507-2603.
Fish Hock: 507-2581.
Simon's Town: 507-2586.
Mainline reservations: 405-3871 or 405-3018.
Prices only: 405-2847.
Blue Train reservations: 405-2672.

TRAVELLING AT NIGHT

Most trains stop running after 9.30pm and third class can be dangerous, especially after dark when first class is recommended. Station security is being stepped up, but don't stand alone and watch your belongings. Even if you're on a tight budget, it's best to take a cab at night.

TRAVEL FOR DISABLED PEOPLE

Cape Town has plenty to learn about being wheelchair-friendly. Taxis are generally helpful (it helps if you advise that you'll need assistance when you phone to book), but public transport like trains, buses and minibus taxis don't generally have disabled facilities, although other passengers and conductors will usually provide help.

Check beforehand on cinemas – the older ones, Sea Point Metro, for example, are difficult for wheelchairs.

Major shopping centres have disabled parking bays, but the award for exemplary planning goes to the Waterfront, which is easily negotiated by wheelchair. Apart from 18 disabled bays in the Waterfront parking area, temporary disabled parking discs are available from the Information Centre and Kiosk, and ramps allow for easy access to buildings, all of which have disabled toilets. Wheelchairs are available from the Information Centre and Kiosk daily at a donation of R10 per day.

Museums and art galleries are making efforts to provide wheelchair facilities, but the older historic buildings can be difficult. Call beforehand. The Infoguide Kiosk, Waterkant St, City Centre, provides information on business and disabled access.

City Centre parking garages which are wheelchair-friendly include: Sanlam Golden Acre Parking Garage, Picbel Parkade, Strand St, Plein Park and BP Centre.

Audible devices at traffic lights are not the norm in Cape Town, but they're installed at the request of disabled rights organisations and facilities are being increased. A buzzing sound is emitted when it's safe to walk, except at parallel pedestrian phase traffic lights where there's a continuous buzzer across the main road if there's an exclusive phase, meaning that traffic on all sides is standing still.

You'll find audible-device traffic lights at:
Adderley and Riebeeck St, City Centre (across Adderley St on the fountain side).
Darling and Parliament streets, City Centre (across Darling St on the Adderley St side).
Long and Hout streets, City Centre.
Shortmarket and Long streets, City Centre (operates 7am-7pm).
Beach Rd, Mouille Point and Beach Rd, Sea Point.
Beach Rd and Three Anchor Rd, Three Anchor Bay.
Main and Glengariff roads, Sea Point.
At the lighthouse on Beach Rd, Mouille Point.
Liesbeek Parkway and Alma Rd, Mowbray.
Victoria and Mountain roads, Woodstock.
Main and Klipper roads, Rondebosch.
Main and Wetton roads, Wynberg.
Main Rd and Church St, Wynberg.
Main and Maynard streets, Wynberg.
Main and Gabriel roads, Plumstead.

For useful numbers, see chapter **Survival**.

Want a ride? Taxis are in plentiful supply at the Waterfront and the City Centre.

ACCOMMODATION

Looking for a cheap place to hang your hat? Or an exclusive suite with service and price tags to match? Here's the range – from camping to hostels to movie-star hideouts.

Prices and demand rise considerably in season, but you'll find a wide range of accommodation in Cape Town and its surrounds, much of it with excellent location and magnificent views. Some original Cape Dutch homes and national monuments have been turned into hotels. It's also worth exploring the guest-house option as you'll frequently find that these provide good value for money, a sense of home and, in some cases, as much luxury and care as you'd find in a good hotel.

Captour's Hotel and Accommodation Booking Centre *at 3 Adderley St, City Centre, tel. 418-5214 or 418-5216,* provides accommodation advice and reservations. For detailed info, you can also try specialised books like *A Guide to Guest Farms and Country Lodges in Southern Africa* and *A Guide to Bed and Breakfast and Guest Houses* both published by Struik and available from shops like CNA and Exclusive Books.

Shared accommodation in hostels with communal bathrooms and self-catering facilities starts at around the R20 mark. Permanent rentals are advertised in the daily newspaper classifieds or you can approach letting agents, who also advertise in the papers. Rent is paid monthly in advance and a deposit of at least one month's rent is the norm. The lessee is generally responsible for electricity and phone bills. The landlord pays rates and taxes. Leases are generally drawn up for a year with one month's notice, at a total fee of about R250.

Some of the larger Cape Town estate agents and property brokers are: Aida Real Estate, tel. 762-1106; Durr Estates, tel. 761-9910; Pam Golding, tel. 797-5300; Bill Rawson Estates, tel. 64-1093; Rourke and Gilmour Homenet, tel. 797-5150; Seeff, tel. 419-0920; and Steer and Co, tel. 26-1026.

GUEST-HOUSE HOTLINE

Available at both the domestic and the international airport lounges, this excellent freephone service provides bookings and advice on suitable guest-house accommodation. The choice includes 40 establishments in Cape Town and along the Garden Route, ranging from top-class to budget and backpackers' hostels. *For further info, tel. (0283) 70-0823, fax 2-1772.*

BOOKING AGENCIES

Captour Hotel and Accommodation Booking Centre
3 Adderley St, City Centre, tel. 418-5214 or 418-5216.
Same-day hotel reservations if accommodation is available. There's no booking commission charged, but you must go into the offices to book.

B & B ASSOCIATIONS

Bed and Breakfast (Pty) Ltd
17 Talana Rd, Claremont, tel. 683-3505, fax 683-5159.
These national operators represent about 100 bed and breakfast stops in the Peninsula. All rooms have bathrooms en suite, ranging from Quality Commended (in good areas with superior furnishings) to Highly Commended (rooms with TV and phones). Rates are R80-R150 p/p per night. No commission charged.

The Home Accommodation Hotline
Tel. 75-7130, fax 72-3340.
This is a reservations service for home-based bed and breakfast and self-catering accommodation.

LETTING AGENTS

Although you'll pay an agency fee in some cases, the reduced hassle of working through these well-established agents is worth the money.

A-Z Holiday Accommodation
11 Elgin Rd, Milnerton, tel. 551-2785, fax 551-1450.
This popular and established business applies standard commissions to its extensive list of bed and breakfast establishments. Specialists in short-term holiday rentals, they also do budget or luxury long-term letting.

Apartments and Homes
154 Main Rd, Sea Point, tel. 439-4126 or 45-3547, fax 439-9621.
Cape Town holiday accommodation and rental specialists. Rates range from R150 per day for two to R3 000 per day for luxury homes or apartments. Hotel accommodation and safaris can also be arranged.

Cape Holiday Homes
5th Floor, 31 Heerengracht, Lower Adderley St, tel. 419-0430, fax 21-7370.
Private self-catering, furnished houses and apartments throughout the Peninsula. A good range of rentals at R260-R1 000 per day. (Reduced rates in winter.)

HOUSE HELP

Personalised Holiday Home Care
12 Saunders Road, Bantry Bay, tel. 439-2172, fax 439-2273.
Maureen Jacobson is a well-connected Capetonian whose business is the care and maintenance of summer homes and cottages. Her company will air out your place, stock the fridge, vacuum carpets, and put towels in the bathroom – everything ready for your arrival. Several of her regular clients also let their homes so it's worth checking with her if you're looking for a short-term rental with a more personal touch.

HOTELS

DE LUXE

Note: Rates for hotels are for high season, and are subject to change.

The Bay
Victoria Rd, Camps Bay, tel. 438-4444, fax 438-4555.
Rates: *(per room and excl. breakfast) mountain-facing double R740, classic R940, sea-facing R1 090, luxury R1 390, suite R1 920, penthouse R3 090.*
Credit: *cards and cheques. No children under 12.*

Accommodation 15

Airy and modern, The Bay Hotel offers slightly larger-than-usual rooms, each with a separate entrance lobby, mini-bar, underfloor heating, heated towel rails, hairdryers and complimentary chocolates. There's a jewellery store and beauty salon, a notable restaurant (*see chapter* **Where to Eat**), as well as less formal dining at the pool and adjacent café. The pool deck attracts the bold and beautiful and provides wonderful views of the mountains and the beachfront. Service is informal, but professional, and includes beach service – drinks and meals delivered and setting up of deck chairs and umbrellas. A courtesy bus service runs to the cableway, city and Waterfront. Wheelchair-accessible.

The Cape Sun
Strand St, Cape Town, tel. 23-8844 or reservations 23-1861, fax 23-8875.
Rates: *(p/p and excl. breakfast) single R650, double R442, suites R1 550, presidential suite R2 500. All rates subject to change.*
Credit: *all cards; cheques by prior arrangement.*
Ritzy and centrally located, the Cape Sun is a smart high-rise hotel with lots of marble floors, mirrors and glass lifts. It's part of the Southern Sun Hotel Group and it has all the facilities of a five-star chain hotel. The rooms have comfortable, smart decor with panoramic city and mountain views. The presidential suites have fax machines, CD players, jacuzzis and fully equipped kitchens. There's a gym, hairdresser and three well-regarded restaurants – Cape Dutch-style Riempies, which specialises in Cape Malay food, the inviting lobby lounge Palm Court for light meals and the elegant and formal Tastevin for classic French food. Wheelchair-accessible.

Cellars-Hohenhort Country House Hotel
15 Hohenhort Ave, Constantia, tel. 794-2137, fax 794-2149.
Rates: *(p/p and incl. English breakfast and morning tea) single R400, double R380, mini-suite R430, suite R490, grand suites R530, garden suite R660. Special corporate rates available May-Sept.*
Credit: *cards and cheques.*
Set in the heart of the Constantia Valley, the Cellars-Hohenhort incorporates the magnificently restored cellars of the 18th century Klaasenbosch wine estate and the splendid Hohenhort manor-house. The hotel is a member of the prestigious *International Relais et Chateaux* group and the 15 spacious suites and 38 en-suite bedrooms have spectacular views and individual decor. The Cellars Restaurant is open daily for breakfast, lunch, tea and dinner. And the hotel is worth staying in for the garden alone – more than 1 500 rose bushes, oaks, camphor trees and rare lotus flowers. Facilities include swimming pools, tennis courts and a helipad. Not wheelchair-accessible.

Ellerman House
180 Kloof Rd, Bantry Bay, tel. 439-9182, fax 434-7257.
Rates: *(per room and incl. airport transfers, breakfast, light lunch, drinks, laundry, ad hoc secretarial services) R1 200-R2 800.*
Credit: *cards and cheques. No children under 18.*
Probably South Africa's most exclusive hotel, Ellerman House has accommodated the likes of Oprah Winfrey, Chris De Burgh and Patrick Lichfield. It's truly magical – an old villa filled with local art and decorated in the style of an English country house. There are magnificent ocean and mountain views, a palm-tree filled garden, large swimming pool and inviting terraces. The rooms are superb – large and beautifully appointed. And the aim in this small establishment is pampering. Meals are tailor-made to guests' requests. Transport is supplied by the hotel's cars, which include a Rolls Royce. And the wine cellar contains some two and a half thousand wines. Elegant, discreet and very luxurious. Not wheelchair-accessible.

The Mount Nelson
76 Orange St, Gardens, tel. 23-1000, fax 24-7472.
Rates: *(per room) single R940, double R1 315, luxury rooms R1 490, large luxury suite R3 150.*
Credit: *cards and cheques.*

The Nellie is one of the city's most beloved institutions – pink-painted, soothing, elegant, and set in renowned gardens. Run by the Orient Express Group, it opened in 1899 and has since been synonymous with gracious living. The Lounge is one of the most inviting places to take tea and the Lord Nelson Bar is a treat (*see chapter* **Where to Eat**). There's a hairdresser, beauty centre, heated swimming pool, tennis courts and a range of restaurants. The 131 rooms and 28 suites are individually furnished and luxurious, and the eight Garden Cottage suites have private patios, kitchenettes, private fax lines and a private swimming pool. Everyone, from heads of state to movie stars, stays here. Most of the hotel is wheelchair-accessible, and assistance is available where it isn't.

The Peninsula

Beach Rd, Sea Point, tel. 439-8888, fax 439-8886, reservations 0800-22-4433 (tollfree).
Rates: *(per room) single/double R1 000, mini-suite R1 055, luxury mini-suite R1 380, super luxury mini-suite R1 715, royal suite R1 915.*
Credit: *cards and cheques.*
All the rooms in this glossy, well-run hotel are suites with kitchen facilities. Book in the new section of the hotel, and bear in mind

Formerly a warehouse, now the very colourful Victoria and Alfred Hotel.

that many of the suites are long and skinny in shape. Prime position in Sea Point, a stroll from shops, eateries and the Promenade, with hotel transport to the Waterfront, make The Peninsula a convenient place to stay. There's a smart bar, Café Bijoux, for inventive light meals and breakfasts (Sunday brunch is particularly good), and the John Jackson, a notable, beautifully designed formal restaurant. Staff are very friendly and helpful and regular returnees vouch for the quality of service at this hotel. Not wheelchair-accessible.

Victoria and Alfred

Pierhead, Waterfront, tel. 419-6677, fax 419-8955.
Rates: *(excl. breakfast) single piazza-facing R440, single mountain-facing R495, double piazza-facing R337,50 p/p sharing, double mountain-facing R377,50 p/p sharing.*
Credit: *cards and cheques.*
Innovative design, superb appointments and location in the heart of the historic 1904 North Quay warehouse at the Waterfront makes the Victoria and Alfred a splendid place to stay. You're virtually on the doorstep of a golf course, gym, tennis and squash facilities, shops, theatre, cinemas, restaurants and bars. The terrace overlooking the Alfred Basin is one of the loveliest places for breakfast or a sundowner, and rooms have beautiful views. Conference facilities are notable and wheelchair access is excellent.

GOOD

See also **Hotel chains** *later in this chapter.*

Ambassador

34 Victoria Rd, Bantry Bay, tel. 439-6170, fax 439-6336.
Rates: *(per room and excl. breakfast) single R300-R375, sea-facing double R540, non sea-facing double R450.*
Credit: *cards but no cheques unless bank-guaranteed and approved by the manager.*
The magnificent setting, literally on the rocks of Bantry Bay above the ocean, makes this a very pleasant place to stay. Waves

Accommodation 17

Restaurant and the popular On The Rocks Bar (*see chapter* **Where to Eat**) offer marvellous views, as does the swimming pool. Besides the standard hotel rooms, there are 29 self-catering, sea-facing apartments across the road at **Ambassador Executive Apartments**. These are fully equipped and cost R500-R1 250. Wheelchair-accessible.

Karos Arthur's Seat
Arthur's Rd, Sea Point, tel. 434-3344, fax 434-9768.
Rates: *(per room and excl. breakfast) standard single R260, superior single R335, double R480.*
Credit: *cards but no cheques.*
A commodious high-rise in the heart of Sea Point, the Arthur's Seat offers very good buffet breakfasts, comfortable rooms, a swimming pool, recreation facilities and easy access to shops, public transport, restaurants and the Waterfront. Wheelchair-accessible.

The Capetonian Protea
Pier Place Heerengracht, City Centre, tel. 21-1150 or reservations 21-5864, fax 25-2215.
Rates: *(per room and excl. breakfast) single R425, family room R480, penthouse R525.*
Credit: *cards.*
On the Foreshore between the harbour and city, this serviceable hotel is well located. Guests have free access to the nearby Health and Racquet Club which offers a pool, squash courts and an ultra-modern gym. The Games Room Bar has pool tables, backgammon and other games. Ask for a room with a mountain view. The hotel restaurant, Fiorino's, is comfortable but not unforgettable. Wheelchair-accessible.

Mijlof Manor
5 Military Rd, Tamboerskloof, tel. 26-1476, fax 22-2046.
Rates: *(per room and excl. breakfast) single economy R200, single luxury R220, double luxury R260. Rates subject to change.*
Credit: *cards and cheques.*
The first farmhouse (1710) in the area now known as Tamboerskloof has been renovated as the Mijlof Manor Hotel & Conference Centre. Homely, comfortable and nicely refurbished, Mijlof Manor is a pleasant alternative to impersonal high-rise hotels. Some of the rooms have self-catering facilities and the food in the hotel restaurant, the Cuckoo's Nest, is very good (*see chapter* **Where to Eat**). The two ladies bars are situated in the old slave quarters of the farmhouse. It's a 10-minute walk from here to the City Centre. Not wheelchair-accessible.

Ritz Inn
Cnr Main and Camberwell roads, Sea Point, tel. 439-6010 or reservations 439-1848, fax 434-0809.
Rates: *(per room) single R270, double R310.*
Credit: *cards and bank-guaranteed cheques.*
Set in the heart of Sea Point, this 21-storey hotel has the Panorama Bar on the top floor and a restaurant with 360 degree views of Table Bay, Robben Island and the coastline from Llandudno to Bloubergstrand. There's a pool, jacuzzi and serviceable rooms. Wheelchair-accessible.

Townhouse
60 Corporation St, City Centre, tel. 45-7050, fax 45-3891.
Rates: *(per room) single R245, double R260.*
Credit: *cards but no cheques.*
Comfortable and within a stroll of the City Centre, the Townhouse frequently accommodates politicians, tour groups and parliamentary correspondents. Most rooms are en suite. The lounge serves light lunches and the popular Townhouse Restaurant opens for breakfast and dinner. Health and Fitness Club next door. Limited wheelchair access.

The Vineyard Hotel
Cnr Colinton and Protea roads, Newlands, tel. 683-3044, fax 683-3365.
Rates: *(per room and excl. breakfast) courtyard-facing single R295, mountain-facing single R420, double courtyard R395, mountain-facing double R520.*
Credit: *cards but no cheques.*
This country-style hotel is convivial and popular, with beautiful gardens, a charming conservatory restaurant and lovely public areas. The recently refurbished rooms have

big bay windows and mountain or courtyard views. Two garden flats are kept for long-term lets and cost R750 per night. Fully wheelchair-accessible.

Winchester Mansions
221 Beach Rd, Sea Point, tel. 434-2351, fax 434-0215.
Rates: (incl. breakfast) single R245, double R390 for two.
Credit: cards but no cheques.
This *grande dame* of Sea Point establishments has the old-fashioned air of a residential hotel and is across the way from the beachfront. There's a pretty courtyard for light meals, the Elephant Walk Bar, the Orangerie, a coffee shop and breakfast room, and the Fountain Restaurant. One-day passes for the nearby Health and Racquet Club are available for R12,50. Partially wheelchair-accessible.

MODERATE

See also **Hotel chains** later in this chapter.

Breakwater Lodge
Portswood Rd, Waterfront, tel. 406-1911, fax 406-1070.
Rates: (excl. breakfast) single sharing shower R129, four-sleeper family room R316.
Credit: cards and cheques.
Once this was the site of the notorious Breakwater Prison (est. 1859) and a labour hostel for dock workers. It's since taken on an infinitely more inviting role, as a Waterfront-area hotel. There's a swimming pool, the airy Stonebreakers Restaurant and the Treadmill Pub. The rooms are small and student-like, not surprising as the lodge also houses many of the full- and part-time MBA students from the Graduate School of Business next door. The rooms do, however, have phones, TVs, a tray of tea/coffee and biscuits and 24-hour security. It's a tiny stroll from the Waterfront. Wheelchair-friendly.

Cape Swiss Hotel
Cnr Kloof and Camp streets, Tamboerskloof, tel. 23-8190, fax 26-1795.
Rates: (per room and excl. breakfast) single or double R198 per night.
Credit: V, Mc, AmEx and bank-guaranteed cheques.
Serviceable and close to the City Centre, the Cape Swiss has 144 rooms, all with phones, air-conditioning, hairdryers, kettles and cable TV. The popular Old Cape Bar is a good place to meet locals and have a pub lunch. The Texas Saloon downstairs has a younger, buzzy vibe. Wheelchair-accessible.

Cape Town Inn
Cnr Strand and Bree streets, City Centre, tel. 23-5116, fax 24-2720.
Rates: (per room and incl. full English breakfast) single R215, double R255, family room (for four) R285, family room (for five) R300.
Credit: cards and cheques by prior arrangement.
Sea and mountain views and location in the city are a big plus here, but rooms can be noisy and this is a good, convenient base rather than a place to be charmed by. All 77 rooms are en suite with phones, air-conditioning and cable TV. There are two bars – La Copa (a cocktail bar) and The Tavern (frequented by locals and regulars). Not wheelchair-accessible.

Carlton Heights
88 Queen Victoria St, City Centre, tel. 23-1260, fax 23-2088.
Rates: (incl. full English breakfast) economy rooms from R130 per night, single R160, double R100 p/p sharing.
Credit: cards and cheques by prior arrangement.
Set in one of the most peaceful corners of the City Centre, opposite the South African Museum and Company Gardens. Rooms have TVs and air-conditioning; self-catering is an option. Not wheelchair-accessible.

Carnaby
Main Rd, Three Anchor Bay, tel. 439-7410, fax 439-1222.
Rates: (excl. breakfast) single R135, double R190 for two.
Credit: cards and bank-guaranteed cheques.

Affordable but basic, the Carnaby offers phones in all rooms, family rooms with three or four beds, a swimming pool with a pretty terrace and some limited glimpses of the sea. Being on a main road, it can be noisy, but proximity to shops, restaurants, the Waterfront, Promenade and public transport are a major plus. Not wheelchair-accessible.

CHAINS

CITY LODGE

Thorough planning, selective services, minimal staff and the elimination of costly frills have made this chain one of the best and most appealing value-for-money deals in the country. Rates are 25-50% lower than full-service hotels, but that doesn't mean no comforts.

Rooms are well-appointed, with air-conditioning, en-suite bathrooms, phones and coffee/tea facilities. Fax and copying facilities on the premises. Breakfast is an extra R20 per person. Wheelchair-accessible.

Special promotions include Spouse-on-the-House, which offers double occupancy at the single room rate over weekends and the Team Scheme, which provides reduced rates if four rooms, with two guests per room, are reserved over weekends.

The Waterfront branch is the best located, an easy walk from the City Centre, and right next to the restaurants, shops and action at the Waterfront. It's nicely designed, with a swimming pool. The Mowbray Golf Park branch is convenient to the airport.

Cnr Dock & Alfred roads, Waterfront, tel. 419-9450, fax 419-0460.
Rates: *single R225, double R133 p/p sharing.*
Credit: *all major cards.*

Mowbray Golf Park (off Raapenberg Rd, at the N2 Pinelands exit), tel. 685-7944, fax 685-7997.
Rates: *single R208, double R104 p/p sharing.*
Credit: *all major cards.*

Cnr Willie van Schoor Ave and Mispel Rd, Bellville, tel. 948-7990, fax 948-8805.
Rates: *single R161, double R92 p/p sharing.*
Credit: *all major cards.*

Formule 1

Stark in concept and design, but cheap and efficient, Formule 1 rooms sleep three in a relatively small space (a single bunk bed above the double). There's air-conditioning, TV, a shower and a budget R6 breakfast. Wheelchair-accessible.

171 Jan Smuts St, Foreshore, tel. 418-4664, fax 418-4661.
Rates: *(excl. breakfast) R104 per room per night.*
Credit: *cards and bank-guaranteed cheques.*

Cnr Arnold Wilhelm and Jean Simonis streets, Parow, tel. 930-5158, fax 930-5338.
Rates: *(excl. breakfast) R104 per room per night.*
Credit: *cards and bank-guaranteed cheques.*

HOLIDAY INN GARDEN COURTS

Greenmarket Square Holiday Inn Garden Court

Greenmarket Square, City Centre, tel. 23-2040, fax 23-3664.
Rates: *(excl. breakfast) single R239, double R134 p/p sharing. Rates subject to change.*
Credit: *all cards; cheques by prior arrangement.*

Overlooking Greenmarket Square's flea market, in the heart of the City Centre, this hotel has access to Long Street's interesting antique and bookshops, shopping centres, museums and eateries. Cycles Restaurant and McGinty's Pub on premises. Wheelchair-accessible.

St George's Mall Holiday Inn Garden Court

St George's Mall, City Centre, tel. 419-0808, fax 419-7010.
Rates: *(excl. breakfast) single R244, double R268 p/p sharing. Rates subject to change.*
Credit: *all cards, cheques by prior arrangement.*

Ideally located in the City Centre and very suitable for business travellers. Comfortable, with La Brasserie restaurant for breakfast and dinner. Wheelchair-accessible.

De Waal Holiday Inn Garden Court
Mill St, Gardens, tel. 45-1311, fax 461-6648.
Rates: *single R244, double R139 p/p sharing. Rates subject to change.*
Credit: *all cards, cheques by prior arrangement.*
A modern hotel situated at the foot of Table Mountain, a stroll from the Gardens Shopping Centre and within walking distance of the City Centre. Comfortable accommodation with restaurants on premises. Wheelchair-accessible.

Eastern Boulevard Holiday Inn Garden Court
Cnr Melbourne and Coronation roads, Woodstock, tel. 448-4123, fax 47-8338.
Rates: *single R215, double R215 p/p sharing. Rates subject to change.*
Credit: *all cards, cheques by prior arrangement.*
Not ideally located if you want easy walking access to shops and restaurants, this hotel does, nevertheless, offer views of Table Bay and the harbour, comfortable rooms and it's a 3-km drive to the City Centre. Wheelchair-accessible.

Newlands Holiday Inn Garden Court
Main Rd, Newlands, tel. 61-1105, fax 64-1241.
Rates: *single R218, double R114 p/p sharing. Rates subject to change.*
Credit: *all cards, cheques by prior arrangement.*
Within walking distance of the Newlands rugby/cricket grounds, shopping centres and public transport, with a breakfast room and steakhouse on premises. Very good value. Wheelchair-accessible.

GUEST-HOUSES

One of your best accommodation bets, many guest-houses offer excellent accommodation, personal service and, with enough advance warning, will arrange good lunches or dinners. All include breakfast.

For reliable guest-house booking and advice, call the **Guest House Hotline (0283) 70-0823**.

Baker House
18 Goldbourne Rd, Kenilworth, tel. 762-4912, fax 797-3769.
Rates: *single R100-R205, double R300 per room.*
Credit: *cards and cheques.*
Designed by renowned architect Sir Herbert Baker, Baker House was built in 1896, and is an appealing blend of sophistication and homely touches. The decor is country style, with lots of antiques and the food is notable. Not wheelchair-accessible.

Brenwin
Cnr Upper Portswood and Thornhill roads, Green Point, tel. 434-0220, fax 439-3465.
Rates: *(per room and incl. breakfast) single R240, double R310.*
Credit: *all cards; cheques by prior arrangement only.*
Close to the city, beaches and Waterfront, this comfortable guest-house provides hearty German breakfasts, a barbecue area and swimming pool. Rooms are en suite with mini-bar, phone, tea/coffee facilities and TV. Not wheelchair-accessible.

Cape Victoria Guest House
13 Torbay Rd, Green Point, telefax 439-7721.
Rates: *R275-R380 per room. All rooms are doubles.*
Credit: *cards and cheques.*
This superbly decorated and antique-filled guest-house is a favourite with international photographic teams and the smart set – for good reason. Each room is individually designed with period furnishings, TV, bar-fridge, phone, en-suite bathroom and mountain or sea views. It's close to the Waterfront and City Centre, although you may not want to budge. And the sundeck, roof terrace and swimming pool are a treat. Really special. Not wheelchair-accessible.

Castle Hill
37 Gatesville Rd, Kalk Bay, tel. 788-2554, fax 788-3843.
Rates: *R100-R125 p/p sharing.*
Credit: *V, Mc and cheques.*

The stylishly decorated Cape Victoria Guest House, favourite of international fashion crews.

Built in 1910, this guest-house has served as a convalescent home for soldiers and as a nursing home. Most of the rooms have sea views, Oregon pine floors and pressed steel ceilings. Not wheelchair-accessible.

Hilltop
30 Forest Rd, Oranjezicht, tel. 461-3093, fax 461-4069.
Rates: *single R300, double R275 p/p sharing.*
Credit: *all cards but no cheques.*
This notable guest-house has wonderful bathrooms, beautiful gardens and hilltop views. Stay for longer than four nights, and a free rental car is provided. Personal service and attention to detail are hallmarks. Not wheelchair-accessible.

Kinneret Guest House
11 Arthur's Rd, Sea Point, tel. 439-9237, fax 434-8998.
Rates: *single R180, double R135 p/p sharing.*
Credit: *cards but no cheques.*
Sandwiched between the beaches and the shops of Sea Point, this charming, pretty guest-house has 10 rooms, each with a bar fridge, phone and TV. Limited wheelchair access.

Its sister establishment, the **Oliver Rd Guest House,** 8 Oliver Rd, tel. 439-9237, is a few blocks away and offers the same homely appeal, but is more modern with better wheelchair access.

Klein Bosheuwel
Klaassens Rd, Constantia, telefax 762-2323.
Rates: *single R200, double R130 p/p sharing.*
Credit: *cards and cheques.*
Bosheuwel (renamed Bishopscourt) was the name of Jan van Riebeeck's farm, and the original boundary runs through the grounds of this guest-house. The garden boasts indigenous trees, a rose garden and a koi pond. Fine views of the Constantia Valley are provided from almost every window. Beautifully decorated in plaids and checks, with en-suite rooms. Not wheelchair-accessible.

Leeuwenvoet House
93 New Church St, Tamboerskloof, tel. 24-1133, fax 24-0495.
Rates: *single R175, double R220 per room.*
Credit: *cards and cheques.*
Leeuwenvoet (Dutch for Lion's Foot) is an apt name for a Victorian house set at the foot of Lion's Head. Built in 1892, the establishment offers six luxury double rooms, all en

suite with Oregon pine doorframes and floors. There's a lovely secluded pool area and the City Centre is a short walk away. Not wheelchair-friendly.

Rodenburg Guest House

8 Myrtle Rd, Rondebosch, tel. 689-4852, fax 689-2065.
Rates: *single R165, double R110 p/p sharing.*
Credit: *V, Mc and cheques.*
With beautiful mountain views, a swimming pool, proximity to public transport, shops and restaurants, this double-storey, airy Victorian house is an interesting place to stay. Decor follows an African theme and rooms are very comfortable. Limited wheelchair access.

Rose House

2 Milner Rd, Rondebosch, tel. 689-9127, fax 689-9126.
Rates: *luxury single R215, en-suite single R189, single R189, double R180 p/p sharing, standard double R120 p/p sharing.*
Credit: *V and Mc but no cheques.*
Eight rooms, each individually decorated and some with balconies and magnificent mountain views. Not wheelchair-accessible.

SELF-CATERING

Flora Bay Resort

Chapman's Peak Drive, Hout Bay, telefax 790-1650.
Rates: *R200 for two people sharing (one-roomed oceanettes) to R450 (bungalows).*
Credit: *cards (except AmEx) and cheques by prior arrangement.*
Situated just below the marvellous Chapman's Peak Drive, Flora Bay Resort has magnificent scenery and views, a private beach, lawns and barbecue area. All bungalows and oceanettes have sea views and are fully equipped – all you have to bring is food. About 20 km from the City Centre. Limited wheelchair access.

Gardens Centre Holiday Apartments

Gardens Centre, Mill St, Gardens, tel. 461-5827, fax 45-1710.
Rates: *R188,10 per flat for two sharing per night, refurbished flats R210,90.*
Credit: *all cards except AmEx; no cheques.*
Located on top of the Gardens Centre shopping complex, these fully equipped, modern apartments are serviced daily Mon-Sat, with phones, TVs and an optional laundry service. With a shopping mall downstairs and the City Centre a reasonable walk away, this is a very convenient, easy base, particularly for families. Wheelchair-accessible.

Inverness Self-catering Apartments

Cnr Camberwell and Grimsby streets, Sea Point, tel. 439-8200, fax 439-8204.
Rates: *R450 per apartment per day.*
Credit: *cards and cheques.*
Catering particularly well to business people, this complex has a boardroom, secretarial and fax service and plenty of parking with 24-hour security. The apartments are comfortable and serviced daily, with TVs and phones. Close to both the City Centre and the Waterfront. Wheelchair access to ground-floor apartments only.

Kutali Holiday Accommodation

Connemara Drive, Tarragona Estate, Hout Bay (near World of Birds), telefax 790-1414.
Rates: *single R75-R150, double R50-R100 p/p sharing.*
Credit: *cheques but no cards.*
Old Cape furniture, washing machines, fireplaces, private gardens and balconies are features in cottages here. Warm and homely, with a swimming pool and magnificent views of the Hout Bay mountains, this holiday accommodation is perfect for families and couples. Not wheelchair-accessible.

Monkey Valley Beach Nature Resort

Monkey Valley, Mountain Rd, Noordhoek, tel. 789-1391, fax 789-1143.
Rates: *R840-R1 100 per night for two- and three-bedroom cottages.*
Credit: *cards and cheques.*
A truly extraordinary experience, Monkey Valley combines spectacular location (below Chapman's Peak Drive and overlooking Noordhoek Beach), easy access to the sea, superb beach views and charming brick and

wooden chalets. Chalets are fully furnished, equipped with linen, crockery, cutlery, phones and TVs and are serviced daily. Limited wheelchair access.

Place On The Bay

Cnr Victoria and Fairway roads, Camps Bay, tel. 438-7060, fax 438-2692.
Rates: *(These are daily, high-season rates.) Open-plan bachelor studio R850-R1 100. Simplex, duplex, front luxury duplex and two-bedroom apartments R1 200-R2 200. Premier suite R950. Prestige suite R1 100. Mini penthouse suite with jacuzzi R2 000. Penthouse (incl. personal chef, chauffeur, vehicle and housekeeper) from R8 000.*
Credit: *cards but no cheques.*
The Place On The Bay overlooks Camps Bay beach and is close to Clifton, upmarket shops and some trendy eateries. It's luxuriously decorated, with fully equipped kitchen, balconies and daily servicing in apartments. Best of all is the dramatic penthouse which comes with a private chef, butler, its own pool and chauffeur. Seriously sybaritic. Wheelchair access to studio apartments only.

Riviera Protea Apartments

273 Beach Rd, Sea Point, tel. 434-1040, fax 439-3265.
Rates: *(per apartment per day) studio (sleeps two) R318, luxury (sleeps four) R350, one-bedroomed R430, two-bedroomed R540, three-bedroomed R640.*
Credit: *cards and bank-guaranteed cheques.*
Riviera has convenience as a major plus – it's across the road from the Sea Point Pavilion and Promenade and a block away from bus stops, shops and restaurants. The apartments are smart and serviceable, with equipped kitchens and 24-hour reception service. The major drawback is the traffic noise from Beach Rd, but this affects the living room and balconies more than the bedrooms. Limited wheelchair access.

Tudor House

43 Simon's Town Rd, Fish Hoek, tel. 782-6238, fax 782-5027.
Rates: *(per apartment per day) one-bedroomed R285, three-bedroomed R530.*
Credit: *cards and cheques.*

Situated on the Catwalk between Sunny Cove and Fish Hoek beach, these lovely apartments with beautiful sea views, separate lounges, and a warm and cosy ambience, are serviced daily. There's a guest pub on the premises, open daily. Wheelchair-accessible.

BUDGET HOSTELS

See chapter **Students & Budget Travellers**.

CAMPING AND CARAVANNING

Many caravan parks, ironically, do not permit camping unless stringent rules are complied with. The biggest bugbear is that campers are frequently compelled to change sites every few days to avoid damaging the grass. However, the settings of many parks and the fact that they're not more than 40 minutes' drive from the city, compensate for the inconvenience. Picture postcard views and walks abound.

Chapman's Peak Caravan Farm

Main Rd, Noordhoek, tel. 789-1225.
Rates: *sites are R12-R15 (incl. electricity) p/p.*
Credit: *cheques but no credit cards.*
Thirty minutes from the City Centre, fairly close to the sensational Silvermine Nature Reserve, and 2 km from Noordhoek Beach, Chapman's Peak Caravan Farm also offers horses for hire and great views.

Oatlands Holiday Village

Froggy Pond, Simon's Town, tel. 786-1410, fax 786-1162.
Rates: *four-person, fully equipped chalets R200-R365. Caravan and camping sites R90 per day, based on four people sharing (incl. electricity).*
Credit: *cards and cheques.*
Close to the warm Indian Ocean, and the exceptionally lovely Boulders beach (a protected home for penguins).

Sandvlei Caravan Park

The Row, Muizenberg, tel. 788-5215.
Rates: *camping and caravan sites R55 for two people, R70 for four. Prices subject to change.*
Credit: *cheques but no credit cards.*

Virtually on Sandvlei Lagoon (a watersports paradise) and close to the beach, there are views of Constantia Mountain from most sites. All sites have electricity.

OUT OF TOWN

ARNISTON

Arniston Hotel
Beach Rd, Arniston, tel. (02847) 5-9000, fax (02847) 5-9633.
Rates: *(incl. English breakfast) single R360, pool-facing double R220-R240 p/p sharing, sea-facing double R260 p/p sharing.*
Credit: *cards and cheques.*
Located almost at the tip of Africa, Arniston was a tiny fishing community until discovered by the artists of the Cape. It still retains much of its original character, though a more affluent holiday section of the village has sprung up recently.

The Arniston Hotel itself is right next to the original fishing village and has used traditional styles and materials in its design and construction. The rooms are pretty, though the bathrooms are small. The public rooms are cosy, with open fireplaces, designed for eating and drinking weekends away from the bustle of Cape Town. The dining room boasts a limited but excellent menu, which changes daily. Breakfasts are an extensive affair.

The coast is rugged and there are lovely walks along the vast stretches of beach. You can also visit Cape Agulhas, where a lone lighthouse guards the southern tip of Africa. Wheelchair-accessible.

FRANSCHHOEK

Le Ballon Rouge Guest House
7 Reservoir East St, Franschhoek, tel. (02212) 2651, fax (02212) 3743.
Rates: *R125 p/p a night for both double and single rooms.*
Credit: *cards and cheques.*
A restored Victorian house decorated charmingly with antiques and four-poster beds. Its restaurant is renowned (*see chapter* **Where to Eat**). Wheelchair access can be arranged.

Auberge Du Quartier Français
Cnr Berg and Wilhelmina streets, Franschhoek, tel. (02212) 2151, fax (02212) 3105.
Rates: *(dinner, bed and breakfast) R595 per room, double R395 p/p sharing.*
Credit: *cards and cheques.*
Wonderfully indulgent with underfloor heating in the luxuriously appointed rooms. Rooms have either a patio or a view of the natural surroundings. Winner of several awards for its restaurant, wine list and accommodation, this is a choice venue in wonderful winelands territory. Wheelchair-accessible.

GREYTON

Greyton Lodge
46 Main St, Greyton, tel. (028) 254-9876, fax (028) 254-9672.
Rates: *(p/p sharing, incl. breakfast) standard rooms R145, de luxe rooms R159, suites R180, royal suites R215, single supplement R80.*
Credit: *cards and cheques.*
A charmingly renovated collection of cottages, typical of the village, Greyton Lodge was originally built as a trading store in 1882 and has served as a police station. It has beautiful rose and vine-filled gardens, mountain views, and log fires during winter. An extensive collection of videos is housed in the library. The royal suites have antique four-poster beds. The Royal Bar Lounge is cosy and stocks more than a dozen different ports. Country cuisine is served. Limited wheelchair access.

HERMANUS

Kenjockity Guest House
15 Church St, Hermanus, telefax (0283) 2-1772.
Rates: *(incl. Continental breakfast) room with semi-private bathroom R85 p/p, en-suite R95 p/p.*
Credit: *all cards except AmEx; no cheques.*
This old Hermanus house is comfortable and serviceable rather than luxurious. But the hominess and personal care give it an edge. Rooms are decorated in country style with

some shared bathrooms and some en suite. Wheelchair access in downstairs area only.

The Marine
Marine Dr, Hermanus, tel. (0283) 701-0000, fax (0283) 70-0160.
Rates: *(per room and incl. breakfast) single R178, double mountain-facing R273, sea-facing bedsits R309, luxury suite R440.*
Credit: *cards and cheques. No children under 12.*
Nicely located, with individually decorated rooms, this seafront hotel is elegantly appointed, with comfortable public rooms, a lovely atmosphere, swimming pool and art gallery. The food can be disappointing, but Hermanus has some fine restaurants if you're not happy to eat in the hotel. Wheelchair-accessible in two rooms.

LANGEBAAN

Club Mykonos Resort
Leentjiesklip St, Langebaan, tel. (02287) 2-2101, fax (02287) 2-2303.
Rates: *R185-R270 per unit.*
Credit: *payment required in advance.*
A Greek island-inspired resort about an hour's drive from Cape Town, Club Mykonos has tavernas, beautiful beaches and fully furnished and serviced kalivas, each with a well-equipped kitchen, private bathroom, TV, sheltered courtyard and shared heated swimming pool. Coffee shops, bars, boutiques, fast foods, watersports, a sports complex, tennis and squash courts and a chapel for christenings and weddings are among the many distractions. Wheelchair access in ground-floor units.

MATJIESFONTEIN

Lord Milner
Matjiesfontein, tel. (02372) 5203, fax (02372) ask for 580.
Rates: *(incl. breakfast) cottages R110 p/p, hotel rooms R125 p/p.*
Credit: *cards and cheques.*
The tiny restored Victorian village of Matjiesfontein in the Karoo is a convenient and delightful day trip and an even better weekend getaway. The Lord Milner Hotel has 14 en-suite rooms, a charming courtyard suite, antique-filled public areas, a delightful country pub and a coffee house. Dinner (R42 p/p) in the gracious dining room is a semi-formal affair, with jacket and ties required for the gents and smart casual gear for the women. A romantic and relaxing sojourn in old world style. Wheelchair-friendly on annexe floor and in the Olive Schreiner cottage.

PAARL

Grande Rôche
Plantasie St, Paarl, tel. (02211) 63-2727, fax (02211) 63-2220.
Rates: *(per room and incl. breakfast) single R790, double R1 280 (duplexes and terraces).*
Credit: *cards and bank-guaranteed cheques.*
One of South Africa's finest hostelries, the award-winning Grande Rôche is an elegant estate hotel, an impeccably restored historic monument splendidly set in its own vineyards. The 29 luxurious suites are set in the wonderfully landscaped grounds. A member of the *Relais & Chateaux Association* and the recipient of the blazon of the *Chaine des Rotisseurs*, the hotel has won several awards, including one for the best wine list in South Africa. This is the place for sheer hedonism – lazy breakfasts on the terrace and marvellous meals in the renowned Bosman's Restaurant (*see chapter* **Where to Eat**). Unabashed luxury. Wheelchair-accessible.

Mooi Kelder
Main Rd, Agter Paarl, tel. (02211) 63-8491, fax (02211) 63-8361.
Rates: *(incl. full English breakfast) single R225, double R195 p/p sharing.*
Credit: *cards and cheques.*
Formerly owned by Cecil John Rhodes, this historic homestead is set on a working farm and is next door to the Boland Wine Cellars. The six rooms are individually decorated in Cape Dutch style, with TV, coffee facilities, phones and fax facilities. Wheelchair-accessible.

Roggeland
Roggeland Rd, Daljosafat Valley, Paarl, tel. (02211) 68-2501, fax (02211) 68-2113.
Rates: *(per room and incl. breakfast and*

dinner) premium R400, superior R440, standard R365.
Credit: *cards and cheques.*
Roggeland was chosen as one of British *Tatler* magazine's 50 best hotels in the world. Housed in a 250-year-old building at the crossroads of four wine routes, Roggeland is an extraordinary blend of simplicity and glamour, more like a private home than a hostelry. The eight individually decorated en-suite rooms have overhead fans and mosquito nets. There's a swimming pool, horses and geese running free, and excellent walks in the area. But best of all is the food (*see chapter* **Where to Eat**). Wheelchair-accessible.

Zomerlust Guest House
193 Main Rd, Paarl, tel. (02211) 2-2117, fax (02211) 2-8312.
Rates: *(incl. breakfast) R430 per room, sleeping two.*
Credit: *cards and cheques. No children under 12.*
Unimposing from the outside, Zomerlust is extraordinary from the minute you walk through the door. The gardens and food in this four-star graded guest-house are first class. The rooms are individually and beautifully decorated, some with antiques, all spacious with luxury touches like heated bathrooms. (There are ten rooms in the manor house and four in Die Stal, the converted stables in the garden, of which two attic rooms are especially cosy.) There's a private swimming pool, a restaurant with indoor and outdoor tables, as well as Die Kraan bar. Altogether, a marvellously romantic setting.

PIKETBERG
Noupoort Farm Conference Centre & Mountain Retreat
PO Box 101, Piketberg, tel. (0261) 5754, fax (0261) 5834.
Rates: *dinner, bed and breakfast R170 p/p, bed and breakfast R130 p/p.*
Credit: *all cards and cheques. No children under 12.*
This very well-priced, private country retreat offers simply but comfortably furnished cottages, superb views of the Sandveld and St Helena Bay, an award-winning wine list and good food – all an easy 90-minute drive from Cape Town. The conference facilities are customised and popular, but the great drawcard (apart from the tranquillity), is the special weekends. Themes include Family weekends (with pantomimes, treasure hunts and children's theatre), Theatre and Cabaret weekends, Wellness and Health, Halloween and Thanksgiving weekends, and Chamber Music getaways. There are also 900 expertly chosen videos (ranging from cult and classic to recent hits) and 350 CDs for guests to select, a jacuzzi, pool, sauna, small gym as well as wonderful walks. Wheelchair-friendly except for small step into cottages.

SOMERSET WEST
Erinvale Estate Hotel and Golf Club
Lourensford Rd, Somerset West, tel. (024) 847-1160, fax (024) 847-1169.
Rates: *(per room) single from R340, double from R430, de luxe R715, honeymoon suite R870. Golf fees additional.*
Credit: *cards and cheques. No children under 12.*
Surrounded by mountains and valleys, Erinvale Estate Hotel adjoins the historic Vergelegen farm and boasts access to the recently opened Gary Player-designed golf course. The restored thatched manor house contains a fine restaurant (*see chapter* **Where to Eat**) and a bar. Grand en-suite bedrooms have been incorporated into the original stables. Upstairs, the rooms are under thatch with skylights. It's decorated in original Cape style, with a swimming pool and easy access to the winelands and historic areas. Limited wheelchair access.

STELLENBOSCH
d'Ouwe Werf
30 Church St, tel. 887-4608, fax 887-4626.
Rates: *(incl. full breakfast) single R225 and R275, double R180 and R195 p/p sharing.*
Credit: *cards and cheques.*
The oldest existing country inn in South Africa has hosted the likes of Prince Alfred and its luxury rooms are furnished with

antiques (some have four-poster beds). There's a swimming pool, a good à la carte restaurant and a lovely bar *(see also chapter* **Where to Eat**). Wheelchair-accessible.

The Lanzerac
Lanzerac Rd, tel. 887-1132, fax 887-2310.
Rates: *(incl. breakfast) classic single R430, premier single R475, classic double R560 for two, premier double R650 for two, luxury double R740 for two, pool suite (with private pool) R1 380.*
Credit: *cards and cheques.*
Set on the renowned Lanzerac wine estate, the hotel is graceful and elegant with comfortable, beautifully furnished rooms. It has a trattoria restaurant, a formal restaurant with an excellent wine list and a good pub *(see also chapter* **Where to Eat**). It's close to Stellenbosch's highly rated 18-hole golf course and on the wine route. Wheelchair-accessible in premier and luxury rooms only.

L'Auberge Rozendal
Omega Rd, Jonkershoek, tel. 883-8737, fax 883-8738.
Rates: *starting at R187 p/p sharing.*
Credit: *all cards and cheques.*
A country inn with a professional winery, L'Auberge Rozendal has Victorian terraced-style rooms, each with an individual patio and great mountain and valley views. L'Auberge has a family-run atmosphere with home-cooked meals, limited in selection, but very tasty *(see chapter* **Where to Eat**). Limited wheelchair access.

L'Avenir
Klapmuts Rd (on the R44 outside Stellenbosch), tel. 889-5001, fax 889-7313.
Rates: *(incl. full breakfast) single R240-R270, double R185-R200 p/p sharing.*
Credit: *cards and cheques.*
A country guest house set on a lovely working wine farm, L'Avenir offers prettily decorated en-suite rooms with well-appointed bathrooms, TVs and phones. There's a swimming pool and it's conveniently close to the local wine route. Not wheelchair-accessible.

SWELLENDAM

Klippe Rivier Homestead
Signposted off the R60, 200 km from Cape Town (call for directions), tel. (0291) 4-3341, fax (0291) 4-3337.
Rates: *(incl. breakfast) single R285, double upstairs R228 p/p sharing, double downstairs R256,50 p/p sharing.*
Credit: *cards and cheques.*
This 1825 homestead, situated just outside Swellendam, is beautifully restored with suites decorated in French fabrics with brass beds, mosquito nets, mountain-view patios or individual herb gardens. Food is homey and stylishly served, and the establishment is family-owned and elegantly run. A grand getaway. Not wheelchair-accessible.

Swellengrebel Hotel
91 Voortrekker St, Swellendam, tel. (0291) 4-1144, fax (0291) 4-2453.
Rates: *R118 p/p sharing double room, R190 per single room.*
Credit: *cards and cheques.*
Pretty gardens, easy access to the 18th century town of Swellendam, wonderful hikes and the nearby Bontebok National Park make this servicable hotel a convenient place to stay. Rooms are either pool or mountain-facing and there's a restaurant, beer garden, jacuzzi and TV in all rooms. There's also a gym and sauna in this 50-room hotel.

WELLINGTON

Onverwacht Resort
Addy St, Wellington, tel. (02211) 64-3096, fax (02211) 3-2237.
Rates: *R240 for two per night, R40 per additional adult, R15 per head for under-12s (units sleep six).*
Credit: *cards and cheques.*
Fifty fully-equipped cottages with fireplaces, barbecue area and good bedding, set on a working wine farm. There are tractor rides into the vineyards, trails in scenic routes and the opportunity to pick your own grapes in season. The downstairs suite is wheelchair-accessible.

CAPE TOWN BY SEASON

When it's hot, cold, blowy – plus all-weather annual events.

WEATHER

Expect a Mediterranean climate with hot, dry summers and cool, wet winters, but weather varies – including by area. Muizenberg may be grim when Clifton's balmy. Newspapers and TV news feature weather forecasts.

Telephonic weather forecast: 4-0881.

WHERE THE WIND BLOWS – AND HOW

The southeaster, known as the **Cape Doctor**, is the city's version of a mistral and it helps create Table Mountain's cloud tablecloth. Fiercest from November to February, its average velocity is 40 km/h (skirt-lifting), but it can hit 150 km/h (roof-lifting). Less famous than its summer sister, winter's northwester comes with rain and occasional floods.

Telephonic wind report for sailing and surfing: Muizenberg 788-8226, Bloubergstrand 56-1723.

EVENTS BY THE SEASON

Cape Town isn't called the Tavern of the Seas in vain. Food and wine frequently feature in seasonal events. But there are also music, cultural and sporting happenings.

Summer is people-watching and party time. Tourists, traders, babes and hardbodies are out in force. With winter, rains and dormouse mentality set in. But there are good events in the city and surrounds all year round.

Events and dates may change. Check with tourist bureaux and newspaper listings.

See also section **Arts & Entertainment**.

WATERFRONT EVENTS

The events calendar at the Waterfront is packed with everything from kids' workshops to free concerts. Seasonal programmes are available at the Waterfront Information Bureau and Waterfront Information Kiosk (tel. 418-2369).

AVERAGE CLIMATES

The Western Cape has a Mediterranean climate with hot, dry summers and cool, wet winters. Average climate conditions are:

Month	Season	Day temperature max °C	min °C	Rain Av mm	Av hours sun daily	Humidity %
JAN	SUM	26	15	7	11	70
APR	AUT	22	11	9	8	76
JUL	WIN	17	7	14	6	81
OCT	SPR	12	10	11	9	74

Cape Town by Season

See also chapters in sections **Sightseeing**, **Special Interest** *and* **Arts & Entertainment**.

SEASONAL EVENTS

JANUARY

The **Coon Carnival**, otherwise known as the **Cape Minstrel Carnival**, is a Cape Town institution, involving hundreds of coloured musical groups wearing bright costumes. It begins on *Tweedenuwejaar* (January 2) with a march from the bottom of Wale St to the Bo-Kaap – well worth a look. There's singing and dancing by competing groups at Green Point and Athlone stadiums. On January 3, there's a Coon Carnival Parade from the City Centre to Green Point Stadium. The next three Saturdays are devoted to competitions at both stadiums. Stadium entry: R15 (adults), R9 (children).

See also chapters in section **Arts & Entertainment**.

The **Five-day Cricket Test Match**, January 2-6, pits touring teams against locals. Newlands Cricket Ground, 161 Campground Rd, Newlands. Info: 64-4146.

The **J&B Met**, possibly the country's premier horse-racing event, begins at 10am on the last Saturday of January at Kenilworth Race Course, Rosmead Ave, Kenilworth. If you don't enjoy horses, go for the upwardly mobile hats and downwardly mobile cleavages. Entrance: R25. Take a picnic or reserve a table at 76-2777.

For the good times fans and die-hard hippies, the **Martell Woodstock Festival** on the banks of the Breede River features live music and a happy vibe. Watch press for details or phone 23-1646 or 23-0093.

Oude Libertas open-air performances. See November.

Appletiser Kirstenbosch Summer Sunset Concerts. See December.

Nedbank Sunday Summer Concerts at the Josephine Mill. See November.

FEBRUARY

Oude Libertas open-air performances. See November.

Appletiser Kirstenbosch Summer Sunset Concerts. See December.

Nedbank Sunday Summer Concerts at the Josephine Mill. See November.

MARCH

University of Cape Town Rag Procession through the City Centre. Third Saturday of the month. Floats, costumes, crowds – and all for charity.

Community Chest Carnival, Maynardville. Four days of music, entertainment and, as a main attraction, food at international stalls. Last weekend of February or first weekend of March.

The 105-km **Argus/Pick 'n Pay Cycle Tour** on the first Sunday of the month combines breathtaking views and breathless excitement and attracts more than 22 500 local and international competitors. Participant's fee: R30-R40. Info and application forms: PO Box 205, Newlands, 7725, tel. 461-2390, fax 461-8781.

EVENT-RELATED NUMBERS

Flower Hotline for where to see the best west coast flowers and accommodation info: 418-3705. **Open:** daily 8am-4.30pm, August to mid-October.

Whale-watching info: (0283) 2-2629 or (0283) 2-1475.

Computicket for theatre, movie and events bookings: 21-4715. *For more on Computicket, see box, Tickets, in section* **Arts & Entertainment**.

Captour Information Office: 418-5202.

The Coon Carnival, otherwise known as the Cape Minstrel Carnival, involves singing, dancing and bright costumes on the streets and in stadiums.

Three days before the Cycle Tour, the **Argus/Pick 'n Pay Life Cycle Expo** at A-Berth Shed, Cape Town Harbour, is the country's largest cycling/health exhibition.

The **Caledon Beer and Bread Festival** on the second weekend of March stars beer, food, a half-marathon and fun run. There's traditional Afrikaans social dancing (*langarm*) in the evening. Entrance: R10 (adults), R5 (children and students with student card). Info: (0281) 2-1256.

Appletiser Kirstenbosch Summer Sunset Concerts. See December.

Oude Libertas open-air performances. See November.

APRIL

The **Cape Town International Film Festival** at the Labia Cinema, Baxter Theatre and UCT Adult Education Campus features local and international movies. Check newspaper listings. Bookings: at venues or Computicket. Info: 23-8257. Also, watch press for details of French, Italian, even Egyptian film festivals throughout the year.

The harvest's first wines are celebrated at Paarl's **Nouveau Wine Festival** with music, wine tasting and food (seafood is the main attraction). Held on the first weekend of April. Entrance: R25. Info: (02211) 2-3605.

Ohlsson's Two Oceans Marathon on Easter weekend attracts more than 8 000 runners. Participation in this 56-km route: R50 (locals), R120 (foreigners). Info: 61-9407.

Rugby season. Tickets for big matches are available at the gate or ticket office, Newlands Stadium, 161 Campground Rd, Newlands. Check newspapers. Info: 689-4921.

MAY

Design for Living Exhibition, Good Hope Centre, City Centre. Clothes, furniture, household equipment for sale or gawking at. Around May 24-June 4. For details, check newspapers.

Rugby season. See April.

JUNE

Worcester Winelands Festival features food, wine tasting, saddle-horse show. First weekend in June. Food, wine and brandy stalls, kids' entertainment and baby-sitting services. Entry: R21 for adults (incl. entrance, glass and wine-tasting coupon book) and R5 for children. Info: (0231) 2-8710.

Restaurants go into creative overdrive, putting perlemoen (abalone) into starters, entrées, but, so far, not pudding, during Hermanus's **Perlemoen Extravaganza**. Info: (0283) 2-2629.

We don't have a white Christmas, but we have a cold one, albeit at the wrong time of year. Some hotels and restaurants now feature mid-year **Christmas menus**. See press for details.

Rugby season. See April.

JULY

Some 350 entrants tackle the **KWV Canoe Marathon** on the Berg River, from Paarl to Port Owen, during the first weekend of July. Info and entry forms: (02211) 7-3104.

Whale-watching season begins now and runs until December along the west coast to Saldanha Bay, the Peninsula Coast on False Bay and further south at Walker Bay (especially Hermanus), and the De Hoop Nature Reserve, as the Southern Right Whales seek somewhere to calf. Captour Tourist Information Bureaux have free whale-watching guides.

Perlemoen Extravaganza. See June.

Rugby season. See April.

It isn't in Cape Town, but one of the world's largest arts festivals – the **Grahamstown National Arts Festival** – is so extraordinary that anyone who enjoys theatre and the performing arts would do well to drive to the Eastern Cape for a culture and adrenalin rush.

The **Martell Woodstock Festival** on the banks of the Breede River features live music and a happy vibe. The festival frequently features good local talent, so it's well worth a visit for anyone interested in checking out the local music scene, besides which it's fun. Watch press for details or phone 23-1646 or 23-0093.

AUGUST

The best month for viewing the Cape's **wild flowers**, especially in renowned Namaqualand. For info on viewing and accommodation, call the Flower Hotline 418-3705.

The **Hantam Meat Festival** in Calvinia, on the last weekend of the month, features meat, meat and (what else?) more meat, and traditional Afrikaans music and dancing (*langarm*). Info: (0273) 41-1794 (mornings only).

Rugby season. See April.

The last week of August stars South Africa's largest fashion happening, the prestigious **Good Hope FM Designer Collection** at Cape Town Civic Centre. With shows at 6pm and 9pm, the event runs for four days and includes a black-tie gala. Info and tickets: 438-2595 or Computicket.

Whale-watching season. See July.

SEPTEMBER

The **Stellenbosch Cultural Festival** features chamber music, art, crafts and food. Entrance: free, except for concerts. Info: 883-3891 or 883-3584.

Fish is the theme for the **Festival of the Sea** at Saldanha Harbour held in the first week of September. Seafood, kids' activities, choirs, craft and a beauty competition feature. Info: (02281) 4-2471.

The **Paarl Sparkling Wine Day** on the first Saturday of the month focuses on local sparkling wine with good food.

The **Whale of a Festival**, Hermanus, is a week-long arts festival with music, cabaret, theatre, kids' events, sports and a fabulous craft market. Info: Hermanus Association for Commerce and Tourism (0283) 2-2629 or Captour 418-5202.

It's **whale-watching peak season** in Hermanus with daily sightings. Info and maps: Hermanus Association for Commerce and Tourism (0283) 2-2629 or Captour 418-5202. See also chapter **Day Trips**.

Rugby season. See April.

The **Cape Independent Winemakers' Guild Annual Auction** at the Lanzerac Hotel near Stellenbosch is a major social and wine event, and one of the country's few rare wine auctions which is open to both the trade and public. For info, contact Barbara Pienaar at 883-8625.

Wild flower shows at their best. See August.

The **Argus/Seeff Gun Run** on the first Sunday of September is the city's largest half marathon. Info and application forms: 438-2595.

OCTOBER

Stellenbosch's Van der Stel Festival is held close to October 14 (Simon van der Stel's birthday). It includes a fancy dress ball, entertainment, craft and food stalls. Entrance: free except for the ball (R110 per couple). Info: 883-3584.

Stellenbosch Food and Wine Festival in the town hall during the last week of October is about eating and wine tasting. Entrance: R8. Info: 886-4867.

Walks of various distances feature in the **Big Walk**, on the second Sunday of October. Profits from more than 8 000 participants go to Rotary charities. Fee: R15. Info: 461-2390.
Rugby season. See April.
Whale-watching peak season in Hermanus. See September.

NOVEMBER

Open-air music and dance performances at the **Oude Libertas Amphitheatre** outside Stellenbosch from the end of November to the end of March. Beautiful gardens and vineyard surroundings are the setting, so bring a picnic. Programmes and bookings: Computicket. Listings in newspapers. Info: 808-7474/3.

Nedbank Sunday Summer Concerts at the Josephine Mill feature musical performances – everything from jazz to classics. Entry: R12. For credit card/phone bookings: 686-4939. *See also chapter* **Music**.

DECEMBER

International Rothmans Week, one of South Africa's largest yachting regattas, begins mid-December in Table Bay. Info: 439-1147 or 21-1354.

Art in the Avenue gives artists a chance to show their work in tree-lined Government Avenue, above the City Centre. If you dislike the art, feed the squirrels. *See also chapters in section* **Sightseeing**.

The Planetarium, 25 Queen Victoria St, shoots for the stars with a season of wonderful lectures, productions and laser shows. Entrance: R5 (adults), R3 (children). Info: 24-3330.

We don't have snow, but we do have **Carols by Candlelight** – at Vergelegen Wine Farm, Somerset West (*see chapter* **Day Trips**), Kirstenbosch Botanical Gardens (*see chapter* **The Sights**) and the Waterfront. Check newspaper listings.

Appletiser Kirstenbosch Summer Sunset Concerts at Kirstenbosch Botanical gardens run every Sunday evening (weather permitting) from December to the end of March. Excellent live music in exquisite surroundings. Entrance: R4 (adults), R1 (children). Donations welcome. Bring blankets, pillows and picnic basket. Info: 762-1166.

The **J&B Rare Designers Award** at Kenilworth Race Course is held during the first fortnight of December. It features a black-tie fashion show in which the creations of some 20 SA designers are judged by an international couturier. Tickets: R150. Info and bookings: 808-6911.

The Gay Pride March in the City Centre on the second Saturday of December attracts hordes of supporters and positive media exposure. It's also fun.

Oude Libertas open-air performances. See November.

Nedbank Sunday Summer Concerts at the Josephine Mill. See November.

Student high jinks and jubilation at the annual Rag Parade.

HISTORY

Cape Town's history is an amalgam of cultures, peoples and influences, all of which come together in a heady blend to provide the city's unique flavour.

Any attempt to tell the story of Cape Town is inevitably confined to what happened after 1652 and finds itself leaving the embrace of the great peninsula, lunging northwards into the African hinterland and then returning home again and again. And that, in a sense, is how Cape Town's tale unfolds. It takes more or less for granted the city's unique position on the planet and largely forgets the millennia before the 17th century. And as it emerges at the end of the 20th century from one of the great crucibles of modern history, it sees itself increasingly as part of a much larger South African, and indeed, African, tale.

Modern Capetonians, like every other being who has dwelt here for any time, are nurtured by the chrysalis of the Table Mountain massif. This beacon at the foot of a continent neatly marked the passsage from one vast ocean to another. But more than this, it represented a connection between two great civilisations that had somehow developed quite independently

A 1746 engraving of the by then almost extinct Khoikhoi.

of one another – a northern world that had plunged itself in and out of war, and an eastern one, no less aggressive, but somehow infinitely more subtle and inventive. This continent in the middle, a mystery to both, had its own corner of Eden with a floral kingdom where the mountain alone is home to over 1 400 unique plant species. What a paradise it must have been!

We still don't know too much about the earliest people who left clues in shellfish middens 100 000 years ago but certainly the local Khoikhoi were described in some detail by the 15th century navigators of Europe. The accidental rounding of the Cape by Portugal's Bartolomeu Dias in 1488 inspired a name that stuck – the Cape of Good Hope. Its other name – the Cape of Storms – might have been a more permanent handle if it had been known at the time that this fortuitous gust would blow the Portuguese, Dutch, English and French into new conflicts of commerce over the centuries that followed.

Less than a decade after Dias, Vasco da Gama also came by, but it wasn't until 1503 that an Iberian actually came ashore in Table Bay. Antonio de Saldanha and his crew helped themselves to fresh water and mutton – ironically close to where a very busy delicatessen is situated today in Buitenkant St – and the locals warned him off with a very nasty wound on his shoplifting arm.

A CLASH OF CULTURES

It was the start of a basic cultural misunderstanding. The Khoikhoi were nomadic pastoralists, wintering in the interior, and their carefully controlled water and pasture rights in the 'empty' peninsula meant nothing to Europeans whose upbringing neatly parcelled all hard-won land and resources into a system of private ownerships. By the time the Dutch East India Company decided in 1652 to establish a revictualling station for its vessels *en route* to Java and the Indonesian spice islands, they realised, but did not understand, that the Khoikhoi had different ideas about personal property, and that helping yourself to a Dutchman's things was not theft, but an honour bestowed on those wealthy enough to share. If you were indigenous and rich, on the other hand, you boasted the fact by smothering yourself in sheep fat – and the Dutch turned up their noses at this early form of sunblock. No wonder it wasn't long after 1652, when Commander Jan van Riebeeck and 80 other employees set up shop here, that he seriously considered cutting off the peninsula from the mainland by digging a canal from Table Bay to False Bay.

The market garden in Table Bay had to contend with more than the southeaster and the assumption that a community that based its wealth on cattle would simply become suppliers. So by 1657 the Company was more or less forced to take a more serious look at how it was going to feed its trade fleet. Nine 'free burghers' became South Africa's first white settlers when they established farms along the Liesbeek River on the other side of Table Mountain, on land the Company graciously granted to them. This led to several skirmishes and a full-scale war that ended in 1677, forcing the Khoikhoi to recognise that the Dutch were not transitory migrants. They were in fact so determined to stay that they called themselves Afrikaners.

The importation of slaves from the Dutch East Indies and Madagascar, to do the work the Khoikhoi spurned, inevitably launched the South African refrain of the universal white boss/black servant story. Like other Europeans in other 'new' lands, by 1720 the Dutch had made the indigenous people totally dependent on them through land dispossession, combat and smallpox decimation. By then the colony had expanded into the more arable hinterland and the larger wheat and wine farms were serviced by a slave workforce that significantly outnumbered both settlers and Khoikhoi. The new pastoralists 'discovered' more 'unoccupied' land until they reached the Fish River in the east and the less docile Xhosa tribes.

Van Riebeeck's original fort, built in 1685.

CORRUPT ADMINISTRATION

The Company ran a tight ship at the Cape. The Governor and Council of Policy kept everyone on his toes (sometimes at the end of a rope) – Company servant, free burgher, slave and Khoikhoi alike. The Castle and Robben Island provided miserable accommodation for those fortunate enough to survive mutilation. The repressive rule and corrupt administration of the Company, in all its territories, made it an easy target for other international traders and it had to be baled out by the Dutch government in 1784. Attempts to clean up its act simply ran out of time when the Batavian Republic became the new power of the Netherlands, but at the invitation of the ousted Prince of Orange the British took the Cape in 1795 after the Battle of Muizenberg. The occupation was never intended as anything more than a stopgap arrangement to safeguard sea routes to the

East and indeed there was some regret that the benign and reforming presence of the British ended in 1803 when they handed the Cape back to the Dutch – but not for long. The growth of French military might under the awesome direction of Napoleon made the British very nervous about the safety of their access to the East and so they returned in 1806, again without intending to stay. The London Convention of 1814 finally brought the Cape-Dutch era to an end.

However unpleasant it must have been to have lived under a greedy and autocratic bureaucracy, the little settlement grew into a simple town with all the traits of Dutch orderliness. The pentagonal Castle, begun in 1666 as the hub of civil and military government, incorporated most of the finer things in life at this God-forsaken distance from the Baroque exuberance of the Motherland. Simple dwellings were embellished and filled by the inventiveness and skill of eastern slave craftsmen as they pillaged the hardwood forests that had waited for hundreds of years to be turned into armoires. The slaves also made two greater contributions to the Cape (and South Africa): Islam and a creole patois that was a genesis in the formation of the Afrikaans language.

FRENCH AND GERMAN SETTLERS

Two hundred French Huguenots, who fled the religious persecution of the Sun King in 1688, began a world-famous wine industry that literaly kept the Cape economy afloat at times. German settlers outnumbered the Dutch but assimilated quickly without leaving quite the same mark on the Cape. The pioneer farms along the Liesbeek became the natural corridor of hamlets and grand estates *en route* to Simon's Town, established as a winter anchorage alternative to the vicious north-westerly gales in Table Bay.

The 20-year administration of Governor Simon van der Stel to 1699 is indelibly linked to images of gables and grapes, but he was succeeded by his son Willem Adriaan who was famed for another sort of whitewash altogether. His six years in office mark him as the first

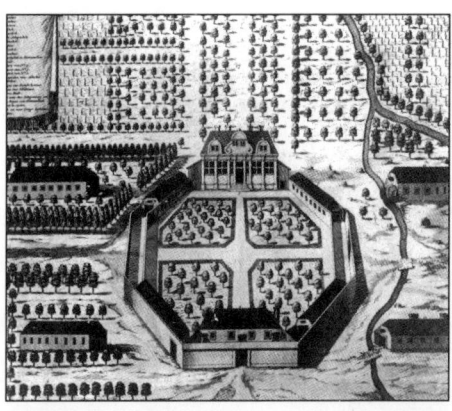

Two views of Willem Adriaan van der Stel's beloved Vergelegen.

South African bureaucrat to get his fingers caught in the till, using Company resources and his own position to secure monopolies. A petition drawn up by the free burghers (who were also his competitors) led the Company to sack him.

The Union Jack was no mere bunting in the Bay. Governor Lord Charles Somerset had an aggressive Anglicisation policy. Free trade and private enterprise were high on the agenda to encourage the Cape to pay its own way. This was a boon to repressed Capetonians but the emancipation of the slaves in 1838 was the final straw for some Cape Afrikaners. Almost ten per cent of them (about 15 000) packed up and left on the Great Trek. It took them northwards, away from the British who gave equal status to all before the law. For others, there was the novelty of a free press, a streamlined civil administration and independent law courts and, eventually, the granting of representative government in 1854. After that the message began to sink in that Westminster was not going to pay all the bills.

Nowhere was this more apparent than in the quest for a decent harbour in Table Bay. A much repaired Van Riebeeck's jetty was still in service in 1818 when the Cape was handling over 30 000 tons of shipping per annum. Even when the *Enterprise* sighted Table Mountain a mere 58 days after leaving Falmouth under the new power of steam in 1825, the Imperial Government was disinclined to spend money on a safe dock.

A SAFE DOCK AT LAST

Several factors helped make the decision, including the refusal of Lloyd's to extend insurance to ships wintering in Table Bay. Also, the establishment of municipal government in Cape Town in 1840 gave a boost to civic pride with an eye on potential prosperity. This was forcibly expressed by the revolt of citizens in 1849 against a proposal that the Cape should become a penal settlement. By then, over 600 vessels were calling each year, linking Britain to India and Australia, replenishing garrisons and stoking commerce. The sponsored emigration to the Cape in the 1820s also began to bear fruit as wheat, wool and timber waited for passage on such leviathans as the 18 000-ton *Great Eastern*. Time now moved faster and 'Home' was closer, even more so in 1860 when no less a personage than Prince Alfred, second son of the Queen herself, inaugurated the breakwater more than two centuries after shipping began to fill the bay.

Thus began a new age of prosperity for Cape Town as it caught up with the Industrial Revolution. In 1864 a suburban railway line linked Cape Town to Wynberg, now a charming Anglo-Indian military furlough village. There was a second wave of German immigration – centred principally on Phillipi – specifically to put fresh fruit and vegetables on the tables of the expanding settlement. The Dutch buildings of the town that had survived being Georgianised, started to give way to Victorian piles that celebrated consumerism. The poor of the city found themselves living in ghettoes like Bo-Kaap and District Six, because municipal franchise was based on property ownership.

GOLD AND DIAMONDS

Now the hinterland of Africa began to take a hand in Cape Town's affairs. The diamond discoveries in Kimberley were quickly followed by the lure of gold on the Witwatersrand, where those travelling Afrikaners had settled, some distance from the British. The news funneled the same cosmopolitan fortune-seeking horde through Cape Town that had swarmed through California and Australia. Picks and shovels, hopes and dreams brought prosperity to farmers and merchants and filled the town with a veritable Babel. The enlargement of the harbour from the Alfred Basin of the 1870s to the Victoria Basin of 1905, and the construction of the Hely Hutchinson Dam on top of the mountain in 1904, brought increasing numbers of Xhosa and Mfengu labourers to a rapidly growing town; more skilled Welshmen, Cornishmen and Irishmen; and luckless Eastern Europeans getting as far as they could from Tsarist pogroms.

Some of the fabulous wealth filtered south and gave Cape Town swish suburban villas, an opera house, grand temples to the steam train,

The very English St George's cathedral dominates the city in this 1845 oil painting.

postage stamp and pound note, and other places for public worship, including a solid City Hall, genteel public library and museum and thrilling pursuits on the track and arena, not to mention an improvement of schools and hospitals. Foremost among the great philanthropists and benefactors in Cape Town was Cecil Rhodes, to whom the city should remain forever grateful for buying up vast tracts of land that survive mainly intact. But in other ways he wrecked a New World city, with the same script as New York, San Francisco or Sydney. His imperial dreams suddenly turned it into a different sort of host: the South African (Boer) War throttled the Empire to the tune of £200 million and a quarter of a million of its men. The determination to control the economic destiny of the region sowed racial sparring that isn't quite spent a century later. It also, inevitably, meant that the British presence at the foot of Africa was no longer confined to the Cape.

SEPARATE DEVELOPMENT

The Union of South Africa, cobbled together in 1910 with imperfect surgery, trade-offs and compromise less than a decade after the conflict, gave Cape Town the status of Parliamentary capital and some solace for a long economic depression. To survive, it became more of an industrial city, serviced by displaced Afrikaners who spawned new municipalities like Bellville and Parow, and sent less fortunate hordes to Langa, Guguletu and Nyanga, racially segregated areas generated by the Ndabeni forerunner to which black Capetonians had been banished during the 1901 plague epidemic. Cape Town's coloured (mixed race) population had the roughest deal as confinement in the characteristic urban slums like District Six left some no option but to seek a better life, miles from employment, in the cheerless new townships of Athlone and Kew Town on the Cape Flats.

April 1994: A watershed year in which, after decades of waiting to vote, millions of South Africans stood patiently in line to participate in the realisation of a long-awaited dream.

CAPE TOWN UNDER APARTHEID

The two World Wars forged a strong Cape Town identity, which was literally torn apart by the policies of the Nationalist Government after 1948. Although it was by no means ever a fully integrated city, Cape Town's people balked at legislated lavatories and restricted recreation. Apartheid law cut into the very heart of a city whose people had shared a love of surroundings. District Six was proclaimed a white group area, coloureds were removed from the voters roll and influx control forced thousands of desperate work seekers, from the Eastern Cape in particular, to erect miserable squatter settlements such as Crossroads at the city's edges.

Discontent with conditions wasn't expressed only after 1948 and masses of Capetonians have always taken to the streets to make their feelings plain. Miraculously, Cape Town was spared the excessive brutalities of a Sharpeville, but has wallowed in teargas and nursed baton thumps too often to forget. When the Mayor and Archbishop gathered 25 000 citizens and marched through the city in 1989, a signal was sent out that never again would they be told they could not gather in their own city. The television screens of the world confirmed it when Nelson Mandela, the planet's best-known political prisoner, newly released, spoke from the balcony of the City Hall before a vortex of change was unleashed throughout the land.

Since then, Cape Town has once again become an international crossroads. More foreign accents and more strange garbs than at any time in its history eddy and swirl with the locals, themselves products of a complicated and heady blend of ingredients, matured over centuries. The embrace of the mountain and the precious remnants of the bountiful natural heritage make it the sort of place that never leaves your soul if you go or stay.

The dawn of a new age. Nelson Mandela on the balcony of City Hall on the day of his release from prison.

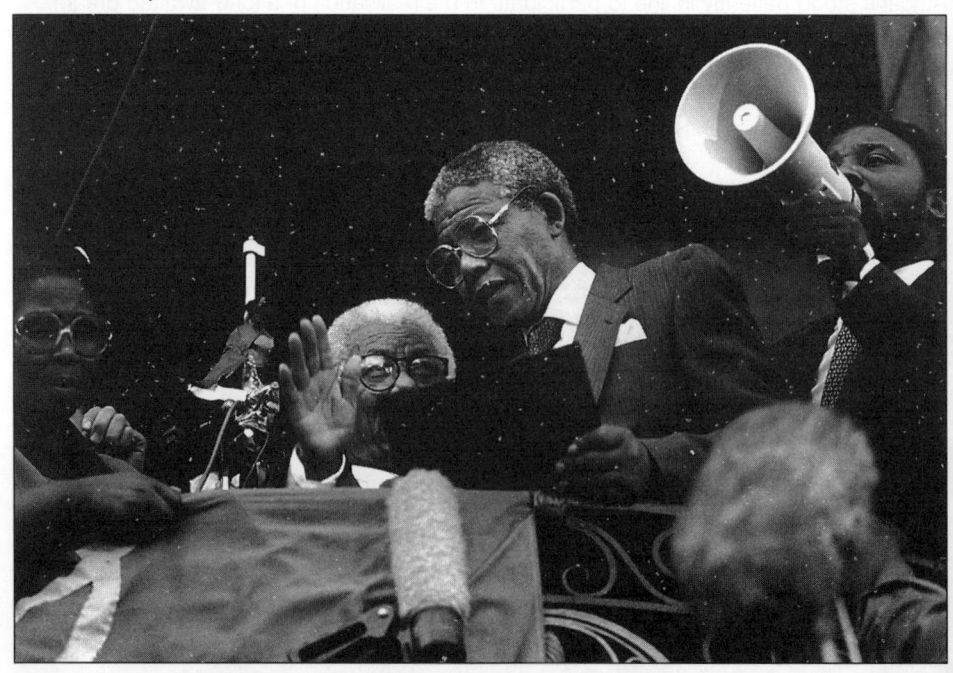

History 39

Clockwise from top left: Bartolomeu Dias, the first European to round the Cape of Good Hope; Jan Van Riebeeck, founder of the Cape Colony for the Dutch East India Company; contemporary and controversial – one of the city's newest statues; statues to commemorate South Africa's fallen soldiers in international conflicts.

SIGHTSEEING

Looking for culture, glitter or just to get away from both? Cape Town's magic is the concentration of choices. Here are the special attractions, the sightseeing highlights, art galleries and museums.

Cape Town's special charm lies in its combination of natural wonders and urban attractions. These can be as little as a 15-minute drive from a mountain or a beach to the Waterfront or the buzzing nightlife in the Waterkant St area. Museums, art galleries, architecture, views and vibes are on offer. And because the city is easily negotiated and difficult to get lost in, most are easy to access, although public transport is limited (*for details, see chapter* **Getting Around**). The major galleries and museums are concentrated within strolling distance of one another in the City Centre, and the Waterfront, which is an enjoyable short walk or a quick bus ride from there, offers a host of shops, restaurants and entertainment options.

Previous page: The neat, colourful interior of this Khayelitsha home belies the jumbled streets outside.

On the Atlantic seaboard side of the City Centre you'll find the splendid beaches, smart villas and high-priced apartments of Clifton, Bantry Bay and Llandudno, Chapman's Peak Drive with its marvellous views, Hout Bay and beach hamlets like Scarborough. To the east of the City Centre, on the N2 to the airport, are the townships and squatter camps of the Cape Flats, Nyanga, Guguletu and Crossroads. And to the north are the residential areas of Goodwood, Parow, Durbanville and Bellville. The southern suburbs, including Newlands, Rondebosch and Wynberg, are leafy, established and staid. Bishopscourt and Constantia, which link the southern suburbs with the False Bay coast, have some grand houses, including ambassadorial residences, rolling hills and gardens with plenty of greenery.

CAPE TOWN'S TOWNSHIPS

Dormitory townships adjoining core cities are a major feature of South Africa. In Cape Town these include Langa, Guguletu, Nyanga, the coloured towns of the Cape Flats, and squatter camps like Crossroads and Khayelitsha. Their existence results from apartheid's policy of racially divided residential areas, and deep heartache, bitter battles and forced removals frequently accompanied their formation. Despite this, these ghettos developed a unique vibrancy and visiting them can provide a chance to sense the afterwash of the wave of 'people's power' that toppled apartheid, as well as an opportunity to enjoy another side of the city.

Townships remain racially divided and underdeveloped. Electricity, water supplies and refuse collection are rudimentary or non-existent and, in many cases, there are few tarred roads and plenty of dumping grounds.

Commonly referred to as 'horse stables' or 'train carriages', these half-roomed 'matchbox' homes were built by the former government, concentrating on quantity rather than quality. Many homes were rented out on a 99-year lease and it was only in 1984 that inhabitants were granted the option of ownership.

Impoverished rural migrants contributed to the massive influx to these areas and this, combined with the authorities' refusal to provide further housing for many years, led to desperate overcrowding and contributed to the sprawl of squatter settlements like Crossroads and KTC. Some 23 000 Capetonians still live in back-yard squats. For now, conditions remain largely bleak, but the new government's Reconstruction and Development Programme aims at redressing imbalances, and these areas are the vital core of the mix from which the new South Africa is forming.

Tourists are still relatively unknown in many townships, and crime is a constant danger. Don't venture in alone; take an organised day or jazz club tour or visit with a resident. *For information on recommended guided township tours, see chapter* **The Sights**.

The oldest of Cape Town's townships, Langa (meaning the sun), was built as a series of two-roomed houses and despite its run-down appearance, its colourful soul shines in areas like the New Flats, with its tuckshops, taverns and shops, some housed in shacks, others in freight containers. You'll find phones, cigarettes, fruit, vegetables and the traditional 'smileys' (sheep's head) here, or you could have a do-it-yourself barbecue at Yeye's, which is adjacent to Tiger's Shebeen, visit Makana Square (named after a chief who was exiled to Robben Island) or drive through the upmarket residential area Settler's Way.

The Old Flats area was the site of a massacre during the 1960 Pass Book March, a landmark event in which 30 000 marchers, mainly Langa residents, converged on Parliament to protest against the system that restricted the movement of black South Africans. Sidney Ndate, tel. 34-8555, or the SANCO offices, tel. 462-3728 or 462-4113 or fax 461-5728, will help with further information on Langa.

The name of Guguletu township, meaning 'our pride', is a poignant paradox considering that its streets are still numbered NY1, NY2, NY3 and so on, the letters standing for 'native yard'. But, once again, vibrancy thrives behind the ageing and decayed façade.

The focus of social and pub life is the shebeens – informal (often illegal) drinking establishments like Busi's, Charlies', Mia's and Miami Tavern. An indoor sports complex was completed in 1994 and has facilities for baseball, basketball and volleyball, and the Guguletu offices of the Food and Allied Workers' Union are a reminder of the unions' vital contribution to resisting apartheid. For further information and practical help in Guguletu, including guides, contact Douglas Mange, tel. 58-7181, or SANCO at tel. 638-5123 ext. 20.

The sprawling squatter camps of Crossroads, near Cape Town Airport, and Khayelitsha are a potent symbol of frenetic urbanisation, forced removals, unemployment and poverty. At the height of the 1985 urbanisation flood, shacks sprang up at an average of one every 26 minutes and the squatter camps are struggling slowly and painfully towards improvement. Khayelitsha has been divided into three 'sites' and elementary services like water supplies and electricity are being provided gradually, but the problem is enormous. Originally designated for 30 000 inhabitants, Khayelitsha has approximately 600 000 residents. Despite this, the emerging entrepreneurial wave manifests in spaza shops (small general-dealer stores), and a number of clinics have been built. Don't visit the squatter camps alone.

On the Cape Flats, neighbourhoods were designed for coloured (mulatto) inhabitants – greater Cape Town is the home of South Africa's coloured population of approximately two million people. Mitchell's Plain, for example, is newer than the black townships and considerably more developed. It's home to more than 100 000 people, many of them descendants or former residents of the vibrant City Centre area known as District Six, which was destroyed in 1966 (*see box on* **District Six** *in chapter* **The Sights**).

Start at the town centre, near AZ Berman Drive, where you'll find a supermarket, boutiques and banks. Nearby, at the undercover Plaza Flea Market, you'll find anything from food to clothes. Westgate Mall offers a cinema complex and eateries, and the Westridge Shopping Centre, cnr Simonsig and Park roads, has a post office, banks and shops. *For details of township and Cape Flats beaches and swimming, see Strandfontein, Mnandi and Monwabisi in chapter* **Wet, Wet, Wet**.

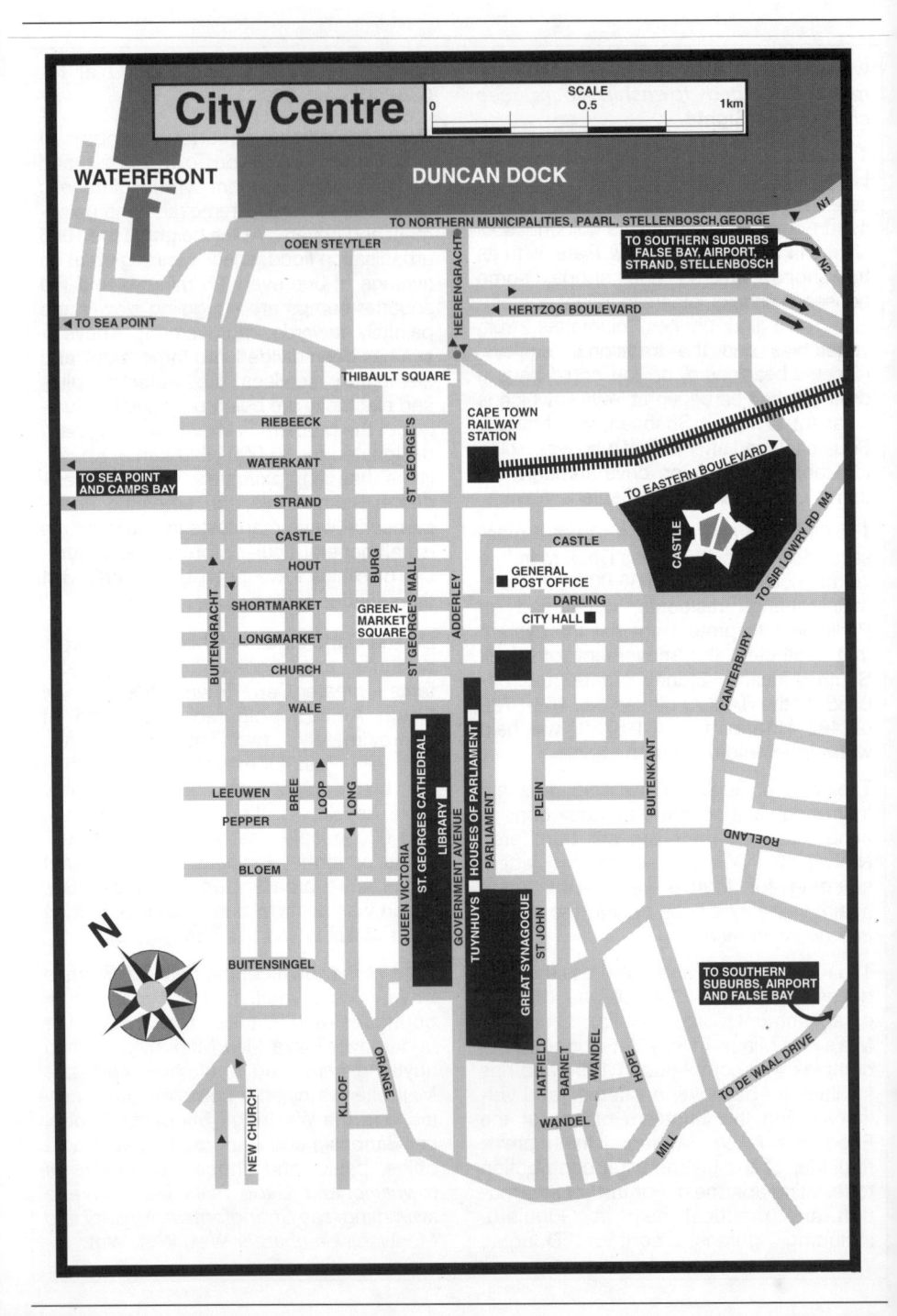

City Centre

THE SIGHTS

Must-see sights, views, tours and drives.

This chapter focuses on major attractions – the ones you may be sorry to miss. Captour Bureaux (*see chapter* **Essential Information**) stock specialist guides to the Wine Route, the Whale Route, the Antique Route, the Fruit Route, the Shipwreck and Lighthouse Route, the Arts and Crafts Route, the Treasure Coast Art Route, the Paarl Language Route, Fynbos Route, the Fireside Guide and the Birdwatchers Guide.

For more attractions and adventures, see chapters **Museums, Art Galleries** *and* **Children's Cape Town**.

Rhodes Memorial, neo-classical monument to Cecil John Rhodes – it's hard to go anywhere in the Cape without bumping into something he built, planned or conquered.

MAJOR ATTRACTIONS

Bo-Kaap Museum
71 Wale St, Cape Town, tel. 24-3846.
Open: *9.30am-4.30pm Tue-Sat. Closed on Good Friday and Christmas Day.*
An 18th century building that recreates a typical 19th century Cape Muslim family home, the intimate Bo-Kaap Museum is the only surviving example of its kind and a reflection of Cape Muslim culture. It includes a bridal chamber, photographs, crafts and a community centre. It was originally owned by Abu Bakr Effendi, a Turkish scholar who came to the Cape to help resolve community disputes. Wheelchair access is difficult – there are steps leading into the house and some doorways are narrow.

Clockwise from right: the UCT Irma Stern Museum; the National Gallery; the Bo-Kaap Museum.

Cultural History Museum
49 Adderley St, City Centre, tel. 461-8280.
Open: *9.30am-4.30pm Mon-Sat. Closed on Good Friday and Christmas Day.*
Originally built as a slave lodge for the Dutch East India Company in 1679 (the traffic island in adjacent Spin St bears a plaque marking the site of the tree under which slaves were auctioned), the building later served as the Cape Supreme Court. Although it's not fully representative, it contains a sampling of some of the cultures of the Cape. Exhibits include early postal stones (under which sailors placed letters for collection by the next caller), the history of South African currency and postage, furniture, glass, ceramics, weapons, toys and archaeology.

One of the city's best-kept secrets is the courtyard café, a tranquil oasis with cheap snacks and the reconstructed tombstones of Jan van Riebeeck and his wife Maria on the walls. Not wheelchair-accessible.

Cape of Good Hope Nature Reserve
Cape Point, tel. 780-1100.
Open: *Daily 7am-6pm (summer) and 7am-5pm (winter).*
Admission: *R5 p/p, minimum R10. Reduced rates to school and college groups.*
Credit: *cheques but no cards.*
Contrary to popular belief, Cape Point is not the southernmost tip of Africa (that honour belongs to Cape Agulhas). It is, however, the place to watch the seas of the Atlantic and False Bay meet. It's also a natural delight – 7 750 ha of indigenous flora and fauna, including baboons and buck, wonderful walks and beaches. Spring, when the wildflowers are in bloom, is particularly lovely, but the variety of hikes and picnic spots make it a delight all year round. Maps are available at the gate. *For more information on hiking trails in the reserve, see chapter* **Sport, Fitness & The Great Outdoors**.

The Flying Dutchman Bus can run you up the hill to the lighthouse (which dates from 1857). A second lighthouse, lower down, dates from 1911. The reserve is not serviced by public transport, but Rikki Taxis can arrange an economical ride for you, particularly if shared (*see chapter* **Getting**

The spectacular view from Chapman's Peak Drive.

Around). The Homestead Restaurant, tel. 780-9040, is open daily 9am-5pm.

If you drive to Cape Point via False Bay, the Historic Mile *en route* contains several museums including the South African Police Museum, the SA Naval Museum, the Simon's Town Museum, Rhodes Cottage, the National Stempastorie and the Natale Labia.

The Castle
Darling St, City Centre (near the Grand Parade), tel. 469-1111.
Open: *9am-4pm daily. Closed on Christmas and New Year's Day, Good Friday, Easter Sunday and Ascension Day.*
Begun in 1666, the Castle of Good Hope is South Africa's prime example of a settler building and it's served a variety of purposes. Under the Dutch, it was headquarters for

the Dutch East India Company, the Governor's residence and a fortress. A new dividing wall with stores, apartments and offices was completed by 1695, and De Kat balcony, with its commanding view, was added. The largest main-floor room accommodated banquets and meetings of the powerful Council of Policy.

Under British rule, the Castle served as government headquarters. The Governor's private residence was located in the Peacock Room and behind the Council Chamber. A series of small rooms was converted, probably in the 1830s, into the upper-floor banqueting hall.

In 1917, the Castle was handed to the South African Defence Force and the British garrison was withdrawn. A two-hour visit could include the *Good Hope Gallery,* the *Military Museum* and the *William Fehr Collection.*

The Good Hope Gallery at the Castle

One of Cape Town's largest, most striking gallery spaces overlooks a beautiful courtyard. The museum also houses an education centre, a music/lecture venue and wonderful function facilities. Not wheelchair-friendly upstairs, but entrance to the ground floor area can be pre-arranged.

The William Fehr Collection
Tel. 469-1160 or 462-3751.

Housed in ancient rooms in the Castle, the superb William Fehr Collection of paintings and decorative arts is one of South Africa's most important public collections, a vivid reflection of the Cape's social, political and linguistic evolution. Acquired from businessman William Fehr (1892-1967), the displays include furniture, ceramics, metalware, art and 17th to 19th century glass.

Begun in 1666, the Castle is South Africa's oldest European building and still a working barracks.

The 17th and 18th century Chinese and Japanese porcelain includes blue-and-white ware, enamelled Imari ware and VOC monogrammed plates. (Look for the Chinese-export porcelain platter with Table Bay motif, c.1750.)

Furniture is 18th century Indonesian and 18th and 19th century Cape-made, with simple, imposing designs suited to unadorned Cape Dutch interiors. The artworks are notable for their scope – topographical views of the Cape settlement and marine paintings by artists like Thomas Baines (1820-1875) and William Huggins (1781-1845).

Contemporary exhibitions are mounted in restored areas – archaeological displays in the Castle's old Grain Cellars (1695), as well as 17th to 19th century glass and porcelain, coins and clay pipes.

City Hall

Darling St, City Centre, tel. 400-2230.
Open: *9am-5.30pm Mon, Wed and Fri, 1pm-6pm Tue, 9am-2pm Thu, 9am-4pm Sat.*

Headquarters of the Cape Town Symphony Orchestra and the City Library, this building was completed in 1905. It overlooks the Grand Parade, the venue for a flea-market on Wednesday and Saturday. It's an appealingly ornate building, faced with Bath stone. Thirty-nine bells are contained in the carillon in the tower, which dates from 1923. The building's interior, particularly the entrance foyer and the Grand Hall, has a special grandeur. Look out for war memorial plaques and marble pillars on the stairs. It was from the City Hall that Nelson Mandela addressed an estimated 100 000 people on the Grand Parade after his release from prison.

Government Avenue and the Company Gardens

Between Adderley and Orange streets, City Centre.

Established in 1652 by Jan van Riebeeck to supply fresh produce to passing ships and later patterned by architect Sir Herbert Baker, the Company Gardens are a tranquil haven in the City Centre. Linking Orange St to Adderley St is the oaktree-lined Government Avenue, which originated from

Checking out the chili bites on the Grand Parade.

the division of the Gardens into 'de laan van der Compagnie' by Governor Simon van der Stel. Notable buildings lie on either side of the Avenue – the Houses of Parliament, the South African Museum and Planetarium, the South African National Gallery, the South African Library, the Great Synagogue, the Jewish Museum, Bertram House (a townhouse museum) and Tuynhuis, offices of the State President. There's an appealing café in the South African National Gallery and the Public Gardens Restaurant, which serves standard light meals and unremarkable but adequate snacks at outdoor as well as indoor tables. In the vicinity of the Public Gardens Restaurant is a statue of Bartolomeu Dias (the Portuguese explorer who rounded the Cape in 1487) and Cecil John Rhodes. The sundial nearby dates from 1787 and the

Bell Tower from 1855. A variety of indigenous and exotic trees and flowers, squirrels, an aviary, fish ponds, chess and backgammon playing and a choice of lovely picnic spots make the Company Gardens a treat for children and adults.

The Grand Parade
This relatively small piece of land has seen the comings and goings of many of the country's political and commercial events. Residents of District Six gathered here to meet and to sell and buy goods. It's also been the scene of many political rallies. On market days (Wed and Sat) it's one of the cheapest places to buy everything from fabric and second-hand books to pots and plants. The Parade is flanked by street sellers and colourful kiosks that sell well-priced, spicy Cape Malay food like samoosas and chili bites (*see chapter* **An Introduction to Cape and South African Cuisine** *in section* **Eating & Drinking**). On non-market days, the Parade is used as a car-park.

Greenmarket Square
The setting for the Old Town House, Greenmarket Square's cobbled streets and outdoor market stalls make for a happy experience in the centre of the city. Wares for sale include clothing, curios, collectables, jewellery and books.

Groot Constantia Manor House and Wine Museum
Groot Constantia Estate, Constantia, tel. 794-5067.
Open: *10am-5pm daily.*
Admission: *R2 adults, R1 children (ages 6-17).*
Surrounded by vineyards and backed by the Constantia Mountains, Groot Constantia is one of the Cape's original wine estates, and one of the most accessible and enjoyable places to buy wine and acquire a sense of the Cape's history. It's part of a larger estate granted to Simon van der Stel in 1685, and is regarded as one of South Africa's foremost wine estates, both historically and aesthetically.

Groot Constantia – one of the first and most famous of the Cape wine estates, and just a short drive from the City Centre.

The manor house portrays life on a farm in the 1800s, with displays of Cape furniture from the mid-1700s and Chinese, Japanese, Rhenish and Delft porcelain. Drinking and storage vessels dating from around 500 BC are also on display. Wheelchair-accessible.

Houses of Parliament
Parliament St, City Centre, tel. 403-2911. (Enter via the Parliament St gate.)
During recess, at 11am and 2pm Mon-Thu, hour-long tours provide an overview of the building's history, chambers and the Constitutional Assembly. During session, visitors may watch parliamentary debates, 2.15pm Mon, Tue and Thu, 10am Fri and 3pm Wed. Monday and Friday are devoted to Constitutional affairs and members of the public are welcome to attend.

Jewish Museum
See chapter **Museums**.

Kirstenbosch Botanical Gardens
Rhodes Drive, Newlands, tel. 762-1166.
Open: *daily 8am-7pm (Sep-Mar), 8am-6pm (Apr-Aug).*
Admission: *R4 adults, R1 children. Free entry for pensioners on Tue. Free entry for members of the Botanical Society.*
Credit: *cheques but no cards.*
South Africa's oldest and largest botanical garden and home to the National Botanical Institute provides glorious walks and views in 528 ha that are almost entirely covered with indigenous species, including proteas and ericas.

The gardens originated in 1895, when Cecil John Rhodes purchased the farm Kirstenbosch to preserve Table Mountain. Fig and camphor trees, still growing today, were planted under his direction. The gardens also house a nursery, library, curio shop and the University of Cape Town Botany Department. Reasonably priced food is served at the Kirstenbosch Tea House, tel. 797-7614 (*see chapter* **Where to Eat**). The Appletiser Summer Sunset Concerts (Dec-Mar) are a wonderful experience, well worth attending and free of charge apart from the usual entry fee (*for details, see chapter* **Music**). There are also occasional concerts throughout the year. (Watch press for details.)

A club-car service takes visitors through the gardens at R10 p/p. Maps and information are available from the Information Office (open daily 8am-4pm) and guided tours are available. There's a Braille Trail and the gardens are wheelchair-accessible. (Wheelchairs are also available at the information kiosk.) Buses to Kirstenbosch depart from Mowbray Station (on the Simon's Town line).

Koopmans De Wet House
35 Strand St, City Centre, tel. 24-2473.
Open: *10am-4.30pm Tue-Sat.*
Behind the polite exterior of the 1701 Koopmans De Wet is an elegant home that belonged to Marie Koopmans de Wet, a free-spirited woman who entertained lavishly here. It was later used as a clothing depot for Boer POWs during the Boer War. A typical 18th century patrician townhouse, it features flagstone floors, murals, an attic storeroom, cobbled courtyard and Cape and European furniture, Cape silver, European glass, blue-and-white VOC porcelain and Dutch Delftware. Not wheelchair-friendly.

Long Street
The 300-year-old Long Street is one of Cape Town's most picturesque streets. It runs from the financial sector at the north-west end of the city, where many major corporations have modern headquarters, towards Table Mountain in the south-east. The section between Strand and Orange streets is lined with antique and collectables shops, second-hand bookstores and boutiques. The architecture is a charming blend of Georgian, Victorian, Art Nouveau, Cape Malay and modern. And its history is as colourful as its appearance.

In the 17th century, Cape Malays were the first inhabitants of this street and it was a town boundary known as the Lion's Rump Boundary of the Vlek. It's also been known as the third Mountain Cross Street, probably because it runs into Kloof Nek, the pass that winds from the city to the Atlantic seaboard past Table Mountain. (It was renamed Long

Street in 1790.) One of the city's first general merchants was established in Long St in 1808 by JC Hertz. The University of Cape Town, then called the South African College or Athenaeum, was established in this street in 1829 in the front room of Orphan House. For decades it was a thoroughfare running all the way down to Roggebaai beach and its 19th century inhabitants included fishermen, shoemakers, masons and artists.

In 1885, trams were introduced here, and the Afrikaner Bond met at the White House Hotel, which was on the corner of Long and Strand St. During the Boer War it was the setting for soldiers, tramcars, fruit barrows and buskers. In the 1960s and 1970s it was a favourite with pub-crawlers and hookers. It's also provided inspiration to some notable local writers including Athol Fugard and Pieter-Dirk Uys, who set one of his plays *Karnaval* in Long St's *Carnival Court*.

Walk along the street, from the smartest end near the harbour to the Long Street Baths just below Orange St. (*For information on the Long St Baths, see chapter* **Wet, Wet, Wet**.) Alongside the Palm Bottle Store (established in 1925 to cater for 'the high-class family trade'), you'll encounter the Palm Tree Mosque at Number 185 (a Georgian building converted into a mosque in 1807 by freed slave Jan van Boughies), a wide range of stores, appealing delis and some reminders of its former reputation as the city's red-light district.

Don't miss Second Time Around for well-priced vintage clothes, Clarke's Bookshop for books and Africana and Morris's Butchery for meat and biltong, if you've acquired a taste for it (*see chapter* **Shopping**).

Mariner's Wharf Complex
Hout Bay, tel. 790-1100.
Open: *8.30am-5.30pm Mon-Fri, 8.30am-6pm Sat-Sun.*
South Africa's first harbour-front emporium, this nautical theme complex boasts a liquor store selling wine-in-a-fish bottles, a shell shop and two restaurants (one of which is a bistro). Main courses at the bistro are around R15. At the restaurant, they're around R45. The Fish Market is a strong drawcard. By-products of fish and related items are also sold here. Wheelchair-accessible.

Mayibuye Centre for History and Culture in South Africa
Library Level One, University of the Western Cape, Bellville, tel. 959-2954.
Open: *9am-4.30pm Mon-Fri.*
Mayibuye, an Nguni word meaning 'let it return', is an appropriate name for a project designed to simultaneously conserve and express the anti-apartheid struggle and to provide a platform for creative expression. The return of exiles and free political expression meant that films, photographs, tapes and writing needed a centre, and that, among other things, is what Mayibuye is about. A great deal of assistance in establishing and running the centre has come via the formerly London-based International Defence and Aid Fund, which raised funds for the anti-apartheid struggle and documented its progress.

As an extraordinary collection of videos, artworks, posters, oral history tapes and rare 'struggle' documents, Mayibuye provides a unique introduction to South African history. Film festivals, debates and publishing are also included in its programmes. Be warned: the centre is difficult to get to unless you have private transport or a large taxi budget, and despite the wealth of material, it's not easy to negotiate the exhibits, which are basically displayed in a storeroom environment.

Natale Labia Museum
192 Main Rd, Muizenberg, tel. 788-4106.
Open: *10am-5pm Tue-Sun.*
An elegant villa, former home to Prince Natale and Princess Ida Labia, the Natale Labia Museum is a graceful series of gilded-ceilinged ballrooms, reception rooms and exhibition spaces filled with European paintings and ornate furniture. Known as *The Fort*, the house was built in 1929 on a site that may date to the fortification of the False Bay coast by Dutch colonists. Its architect, Fred Glennie, was also instrumental in designing the remodelled façade of the Old Supreme Court Building (now the South African Cultural History Museum) and the

A stroll down Government Avenue, a cool haven in the heart of the city.

outstanding Art Deco-style Old Mutual Building (14-18 Darling St). The Fort was converted into a satellite museum of the South African National Gallery in 1988, and contemporary exhibitions, concerts, lectures, poetry-reading and workshops also feature. The charming ground-floor Café Labia serves home-made cakes, sandwiches and good breakfasts. The Café is open 9.30am-4.30pm. Wheelchair access is via the back of the building – ring the bell for elevator access. Also in the area: Rhodes' Cottage Museum, tel. 788-1816, the South African Naval Museum, tel. 787-4635, Simon's Town Museum, tel. 786-3046, the South African Police Museum and the Stempastorie Museum for National Emblems, tel. 786-3226.

Rhodes Memorial
Off Rhodes Drive (on the Freeway), Rondebosch, tel. 689-9151.
Set on the mountain slopes, this tribute to Cecil John Rhodes (Prime Minister of the Cape from 1890-1896) was built from Table Mountain granite. It provides panoramic views of the suburbs, Cape Flats, False Bay and the Hottentots-Holland Mountains. It's also a good place to spot the protected fallow deer that frolic on the slopes. The popular Rhodes Memorial Tea Room (behind the monument) serves meals and teas in a cosy stone and thatch restaurant (*see chapter* **Where to Eat**).

South African Museum
25 Queen Victoria St, City Centre, tel. 24-3330.
Open: *10am-5pm daily. Closed on Christmas Day and Good Friday.*
Fascinating permanent exhibitions of natural history, archaeology, a printing museum, an education garden and a resource centre including African art, rock painting and Stone Age tools. Don't miss the Whale Well, a four-storey exhibition area designed by artist John Kramer – three suspended whale skeletons and recordings of whale songs. The Planetarium, housed here, offers new

shows every three months and runs an outstanding holiday season of lectures, productions and laser shows. Limited wheelchair access, but assistance is available.

South African National Gallery
Government Ave, Company Gardens, City Centre, tel. 45-1628.
Open: *1pm-5pm Mon, 10am-5pm Tue-Sun. Closed Christmas Day, Good Friday and Workers' Day (May 1).*
The SA National Gallery is South Africa's premier art museum, and is the venue for impressive temporary and permanent exhibitions of southern African and international art and craft, including long-overdue attention to indigenous African art and craft.

Temporary exhibitions are notable for their diversity and imaginative display – Ndebele beadwork, paintings by 17th century Italian masters, photography, architecture. The contemporary art is comprehensive, current and incisive, making this flowing, light-filled space an immediate avenue into understanding South African culture. Lectures, workshops, concerts, a reference library and movies also feature.

The Gallery's newsletter *Bonani* (R1 in the Gallery Shop or R20 for a year's subscription) carries information on exhibitions, lectures, workshops, movies and guided tours. The bright Gallery Café, tel. 461-4647, serves sandwiches, pastas, soups, teas, coffees, cakes, and the Gallery Shop carries good art books, cards, jewellery, fabrics, baskets, beadwork and assorted craft. Free parking at the adjoining Annexe. Wheelchair-friendly.

St George's Cathedral
Wale St, City Centre, tel. 24-7360.
Open: *7am-6pm Mon-Fri, 7am-noon Sat, 7.15am-11.30am Sun.*
Designed by renowned architect Sir Herbert Baker, St George's Cathedral is a Gothic-style building, the foundation stone of which was laid in 1901 by the later King George V of England. It contains some of the finest stained glass in Africa, particularly the 26-ft-high Great North window, which depicts the saints and pioneers of the Anglican church. In the Treasury is a book containing 27 500 names of the British and Allied Forces who lost their lives in the boer War, as well as a Coptic cross that was picked up at the Magdala battlefield in Abyssinia in 1868.

St George's Cathedral has been a sanctuary in the true sense of the word. During the apartheid years, particularly the 1970s, protesters under attack from the police took shelter here. It is also the seat of Cape Town's liberal archbishops and the scene of many protest activities. Performances of liturgical masses are held on the last Sunday of every month at 11am. Limited wheelchair-access.

Table Mountain
Probably the best-known landmark in South Africa, Table Mountain is 900 million years old and encompasses Lion's Head and Signal Hill on the north-western side, the central plateau and Devil's Peak to the east – in total 6 000 hectares rising to a height of 1 082 m.

The upper plateau, which gives the impression of being bisected by Platteklip Gorge, extends down in a southerly direction to form the back table. Orangekloof, a broad valley, lies in the southern part flanked by Constantia Corner and the Twelve Apostles.

Known by the Cape's early Khoi inhabitants as Sea Mountain and named Table Mountain by Antonio de Saldanha, the first European to reach its summit, this huge block of shale, sandstone and granite is criss-crossed with paths and a walk or drive along Signal Hill, known as the Lion's Rump, passes four karamats, believed by Muslims to provide protection for the city. There's no charge for public entry to the karamats, but they're religious buildings and you're advised to dress modestly and remove your shoes before entering.

You can reach the top of the Mountain by cable car, walking or climbing – or combine a trip up by cable car with a walk down. Book for the cable car at Captour, 3 Adderley St, City Centre, or the Waterfront Information Office. The cable car doesn't run in bad weather and high wind. The restaurant at the top cable station serves lunch, supper and a substantial climber's breakfast.

Two Oceans Aquarium
Dock Rd, Waterfront, tel. 418-3823.
Open: *10am-7pm daily.* **Credit:** *cards.*
Admission: *R16 adults, R8 children. Group and pensioner discounts.*
The 4 000 square metre Aquarium represents the theme of 'two oceans around the Cape coast', and some 5 000 fish of 300 species are on display here, including large species like snoek (which has never been held in an aquarium before), yellowtail and shark. A kelp forest, some of the plants six metres high, grows in the watery wilderness of the two huge tanks. The touch pools house some tame fish species. Computer touch screens and interactive exhibits add to the excitement. A gift shop and the family oriented restaurant, Sharkey's, are also on the premises. Extensive facilities for the disabled. Tours are also offered.

UCT Irma Stern Museum
Cecil Rd, Rosebank, tel. 685-5686.
Open: *10am-5pm Tue-Sat.*
If you're interested in art, interiors, exotica or the creative process, don't miss the Irma Stern Museum, a permanent exhibition of artist Irma Stern's work, held in *The Firs,* her home from 1928 to 1966. Stern, one of South Africa's greatest pioneering artists, was a discriminating collector, gathering art and artefacts from all over the world. The house is filled with outstanding furniture, including the Buli Stool (one of only 20 known works by master Zaïrean carver Buli), carved Zanzibar doors, fine 17th century Spanish furniture, Egyptian and early Greek artefacts, Buddhist art, Chinese ceramics, pre-Colombian masks and Coptic weavings. The studio, with the artist's paint brushes, palettes and paint box, untouched since her death, is a focal point. Excellent temporary exhibitions are also held here.

There's no museum shop, but postcards, catalogues, prints and posters are for sale. Wheelchair-friendly on ground floor only.

The Victoria & Alfred Waterfront
Victoria and Alfred Basins, Table Bay Harbour.
With a massive range of eateries, stores and entertainment venues, splendid views, tight security, sympathetic architecture and well-conceived design, the Waterfront has succeeded in eclipsing every local attraction bar Table Mountain. And there's no better proof of its success than the fact that this combination of working harbour and recreation centre is in a continual state of expansion, with a million visitors annually.

In 1860, Prince Alfred, second son of Queen Victoria, tipped the rock for the construction of the breakwater for Cape Town's harbour, and the Alfred Basin (completed in 1870) provided shelter for shipping. A second basin, the Victoria Basin (completed in 1905), the Duncan Dock (opened in 1944) and a new dock on the seaward side of Duncan Dock accommodated further trade. The historic Victoria and Alfred basins became the centre for the fishing industry and small-scale ship repairs, but it took years of lobbying and negotiation before proposals to develop the area as a tourist/leisure and residential centre were accepted. The redevelopment of the area began early in 1990 and included the conversion of old buildings into a hotel, quayside taverns, restaurants, a small theatre and maritime museum. It was a smash hit, followed by major expansion.

As a tourist attraction, the Waterfront manages to combine charm and convenience – children's activities, edibles ranging from take-out pancakes to formal dining, regular free music events, and plenty of shopping. The Information Centre provides excellent information on events and attractions, as well as a brochure for those interested in doing an historical walk of the area. Entertainment options include movies, theatre and live music. *For information on public transport to the Waterfront, see chapter* **Getting Around***.*

World of Birds
Valley Rd, Hout Bay, tel. 790-2730.
Open: *9am-5pm daily.*
Admission: *R14 adults, R7 children and pensioners.*
Credit: *cards and cheques.*
Over 100 walk-through aviaries containing 3 000 birds and other animals can be seen at this exciting bird park. Kept in natural sur-

roundings for closer contact, animals here include meerkat and monkeys. The associated Imhoff Gift Farm in Kommetjie breeds the endangered South African blue crane. Large pens house bigger birds such as emus, ostriches and cassowaries.

DISTRICT SIX

One of the most haunting symbols of apartheid, District Six, which once ran east of the Castle to the foot of Devil's Peak, was a predominantly working-class residential area inhabited from the late 19th century by a populace of mixed ethnic groups. A vibrantly cosmopolitan neighbourhood, District Six was home to gangsters, intelligentsia, poets, musicians, gamblers, hookers, political groups and cultural societies.

Then, in a 1966 proclamation in terms of apartheid's notorious Group Areas Act, District Six was condemned as a slum and reserved for white ownership and occupation. A Cape Town City Council resolution passed by 34 votes to one, calling for the repeal of the proclamation, was rejected by the government of the day. Demolition and the resettlement of thousands of District Six residents began. Except for a sprinkling of holy buildings – churches and mosques – nothing was spared. Former District Six residents were relocated in the Cape Flats townships. But the memory of District Six has never died. 'District Six lives on beyond the confines of its geography – hauntingly', wrote poet Adam Small. And the scarred hillside remained underbuilt, save for the Cape Technikon campus and dormitories and a few housing developments. Even its name was changed to 'Zonnebloem', which means 'sunflower'.

In April 1995 the name District Six was revived in a ceremony attended by hundreds of former residents. Redevelopment is planned.

OTHER ATTRACTIONS

Dibano Craft Village
Firlands Farmstall (on N2 between Somerset West and Sir Lowry's Pass), Somerset West, tel. (024) 58-1135.
Open: *9am-5pm daily (closes at 6pm in summer).*
Admission: *R5 adults, R2 children.*

Forty unemployed people from the surrounding area built this village, using traditional materials of mud and cowdung. Typical of many of South African tribal kraals, it's a skills-training facility that displays the architectural styles of the Ndebele, Xhosa, San (Bushmen), Zulu and Sotho. From here, craftspeople sell their wares. The entrance fee goes to the unemployed.

Cape Town Harbour
In contrast to the glossy design of the Victoria & Alfred Waterfront, Cape Town Harbour has the atmosphere of the working quayside, complete with hookers. For a dose of salt air and views of ships, it's fun to stroll around. Panama Jacks, an interesting restaurant, is situated in the harbour (*see chapter* **Where to Eat**).

Kalk Bay (Lime Bay)
Named after the kilns where shells were burned to produce lime, Kalk Bay (Capetonians say 'Cork Bay') is a cheerful mix of antique and bric-à-brac shops, eateries and good swimming. There's a tidal pool, the popular Brass Bell restaurant (*see chapter* **Where to Eat**) and the harbour where you can buy fresh fish and calamari. Behind the village are the Kalk Bay Caves and some lovely hikes.

Koeberg Power Station Visitors Centre
Off West Coast Rd, Melkbosstrand, tel. 553-2133.
Open: *8.30am-4.30pm Mon-Fri and 2pm-4.30pm on the second and last Sun of the month.*

This may seem like an unusual destination, but the country's only commercial nuclear power station, a 30-km drive from Cape Town, provides education on nuclear power and electricity, including a video and fun

The anything but pedestrian inhabitants of Cape Town's main pedestrian walkway, the St George's Mall.

with a Van De Graaff generator. Nearby walking trails include the Grysbok trail (one hour) and the Dikkop trail (four hours), which starts 8 km down the road in the nature reserve. Craggy cliffs, stretches of white beach, saltpans and indigenous flora can be seen on the Dikkop trail. Limited wheelchair access.

Montebello Design Centre
31 Newlands Ave, Newlands, tel. 686-7115.
Open: *9am-5pm Mon-Fri, 10am-3pm Sat, 10am-3pm Sun.*
A sprawling art and craft centre set in lush gardens and historic farm buildings in the leafy suburb of Newlands, Montebello promotes local design and employs craft for job creation as well as providing outreach programmes in township and rural areas, adult and child education programmes and on-site design studios, exhibition spaces, a shop and The Gardener's Cottage restaurant (*see chapter* **Where to Eat**). Ceramics, blacksmithing, pottery and jewellery are among the excellent craftware available and a herb-cum-health stand offers massages on the premises. Wheelchair-friendly.

SCENIC DRIVES

ATLANTIC COAST & INTERIOR
City to Camps Bay over Kloof Nek
This drive takes you up from the city with Signal Hill on the right and down over the Nek, on a winding and shady route with several look-out points, entrances to trails and picnic spots.

City to Signal Hill
The road begins directly opposite the turn-off to Table Mountain at the top of the Nek. Turn on the right-hand side and you'll be rewarded with spectacular views of the city and harbour. From the car-park at the top, 350 m above sea level, there are breathtaking vistas of the Atlantic seaboard. Just behind the car-park is a Muslim shrine (*see box on* **Karamats** *overleaf*).

Table Mountain beyond the Cableway
A few kilometres after the entrance of the lower cable station at the top of Kloof Nek Rd, continue driving to reach a reservoir *en route* for a quick dip and tranquil views.

Camps Bay to Noordhoek along the Atlantic Coast

From Camps Bay's Victoria Rd, follow the ocean drive for a truly spectacular tour that takes you to a 600-m-high summit with picture-postcard views, craggy cliff faces and Cape baboons. You'll pass Llandudno and then Hout Bay (*see chapter* **Wet, Wet, Wet**).

Constantia Nek to Rhodes Drive

Take De Waal Drive out of the city, past the University of Cape Town and on to the Constantia turn-off. Take the Constantia turn-off for a lush and leafy route past the millionaires' mansions of Southern Cross Drive, along a cool and shady road with lovely picnic spots and forest trails.

INDIAN OCEAN COAST

Muizenberg to Cape Point

Follow the Main Road from Muizenberg past the hamlet of St James, the quaint fishing village of Kalk Bay, Fish Hoek and Simon's Town and its naval base. From here, the road with its dramatic sea views winds to Cape Point.

WEST COAST

Milnerton to Melkbosstrand

Pass Milnerton Lagoon with its upmarket Woodbridge Island housing complex and then drive on to the suburban resort of Bloubergstrand with its picture-postcard views of the city, Table Mountain, the bay and its sandy, but often windy, beach. Continuing further up the beach road, there are a number of parking areas and picnic spots among the bushes. Drive further to reach the popular holiday resort of Melkbosstrand.

KARAMATS

During the 17th century, Muslim spiritual leaders (Imams) in the former Dutch East Indies were exiled to the Cape and incarcerated on Robben Island. On their release, a number of Imams joined the community of Indonesian, Javanese and Malayan slaves and artisans who had settled on the slopes of Signal Hill in the Bo-Kaap.

Twenty-five tombs of the Imams, the Karamats, are laid around Cape Town, from Robben Island to the Cape Flats, Muizenberg, Constantia, Oudekraal Peak (above Llandudno) and on Signal Hill. It is believed that this circle of Karamats creates a protective spiritual boundary around the city, shielding it from natural disasters.

The best-known karamat is that of Tuan Guru, the first Imam in the Cape, and the founder of the earliest mosque. Tuan Guru's shrine is still visited by men and women in search of spiritual direction, professional, romantic and personal advancement and help.

Karamats are open to all and there's no entrance fee. Dress modestly – no shorts, miniskirts or revealing clothes.

Karamat Tours
Sulayman Habib, a registered tour guide steeped in knowledge of local history and culture, arranges custom-designed minibus tours of karamats. Cost depends on individual tour. For info, tel. 24-0719 or 23-5579.

COACH TOURS

Tours and operators, offering everything from half-day to week-long excursions, abound in the Peninsula. Rates range from R80 upwards. Established operators, many of whom can arrange foreign language-speaking guides, include the following.
Hylton Ross Tours, *tel.* 51-11784.
Mother City Tours, *tel.* 56-2580 *or* 418-2580 *or* 56-2580 *(a/h).*
Springbok Atlas Tours, *tel.* 25-1271 *or* 448-6545.
Welcome Tours, *tel.* 26-2134 *(tours conducted in English and German).*
Topless Tours
Tel. 448-2888.
Tours in a topless bus include a two-hour City-Signal Hill/ Atlantic Coast tour (R25 p/p)

and a day trip to Cape Point (R60 adults, R30 children). Tours depart from the Captour Bureau, 3 Adderley St, City Centre. Call in advance to check availability and dates.

SPECIAL FEATURE TOURS

Adventure Safaris
Tel. 438-5201, fax 438-4807.
Credit: cards and cheques.
Operating in an air-conditioned microbus, Adventure Safaris offer fishing day trips, tours to popular sights, winelands and wildlife walkabouts, and a range of four-day mini-safaris, including a Seafood Safari. The Garden Route Cycle Tour includes a ride on the Outeniqua steam train.

Beau Séjour Tours
Telefax 788-2710.
Credit: cheques but no cards.
Tailor-made, expert and unusual tours focusing on areas like the winelands, historic architecture, cradle culture (exploring Malay, Dutch and German influences in the city), women's contributions (including art, cuisine and wine), Cape crafters (including visits to potters, silversmiths, jewellers, lacemakers and glass-blowers). Prices of local, full-day tours start at R160, including collection and drop off, refreshments and guide.

Cape Malay Music Experience
Contact Hassiem Salie, tel. 697-3042, or Shereen Habib, tel. 24-0719.
Cape Malay singers, Kawali bands (Muslim choirs), traditional dancing and 17th century slave songs feature in these custom-designed performances held in the Bo-Kaap.

Green Cape Tours
Tel. 797-0166 or 082-891-5266.
Expert tours focusing on the birdlife, flora and geology of the Western Cape, including Rondevlei, the Berg River estuary, Saldanha, Langebaan, Cape of Good Hope Nature Reserve, Strandfontein, Kirstenbosch Botanical Gardens and whale-watching (Jun-Nov). Overnight trips are also available. A maximum of seven passengers are accommodated in a microbus. Tours are conducted in English and Afrikaans only.

Jochen Beckert Tours
Tel. 22-1849, fax 23-0515.
Credit: cards and cheques.
Tailor-made golfing tours and sightseeing on trips ranging from one day to two weeks.

One City Tours
Tel. 387-5351 or 387-5165.
Fascinating scheduled minibus tours into the townships and squatter camp areas like Langa, Crossroads, KTC and Khayelitsha. R75 p/p, half price for under 12s. Also available are tours to the Waterfront and Kirstenbosch Botanical Gardens.

Otherside Tours
Tel. 591-7225 or 531-8528, pager 21-5420 code 64384.
Established guide Ali Khan's The Route of Many Cultures Tour provides an impressive introduction to South African politics, history and sociology via a five-hour journey that follows the route taken by the thousands of people subjected to forced removals under apartheid's Group Areas Act. It includes the site of District Six, squatter camps and the townships of Rylands, (the first declared Indian area), Guguletu, Crossroads, Khayelitsha and Mitchell's Plain.

Personal Shopper and Shopping Tours
Tel. 439-1254.
Internationally experienced fashion stylist and shopping consultant René Reay provides personalised shopping trips, from craft stores to antiques, collectables, designer and bargain shops. R100 per day includes collection and drop off at your hotel/home.

Quagga Tours
Tel. 685-7203 or 082-455-4247.
Credit: cheques but no cards.
Tours include the Mother City, Cape Peninsula, winelands, the scenic Four Passes Tour, West Coast, Cape hinterland, Cape Town by Night, Table Mountain, Kirstenbosch and Groot Constantia.

Tana Buru Tours
Tel. 24-0719 or 24-0529.
Shereen Habib is widely regarded as one of

the specialists on the Bo-Kaap area and she's shown people around for 16 years. Her family has a long history in the Bo-Kaap – her father's uncle, Dr Abduraghman, started the Bo-Kaap's first school and her grandfather bartered with Chinese sailors at the turn of the century. Shereen's two-hour walking tour includes expert overviews of the Bo-Kaap's history, culture and social life, and includes entry into the Auwal Mosque – a great deal at R45 p/p. The lazy alternative is a half-hour pony cart ride through the area. Also available are traditional Cape Malay lunches or dinners in private homes.

ROBBEN ISLAND

The 3-km-long 'Alcatraz of South Africa' was most infamous when its maximum-security prison housed prisoners of consequence, including Nelson Mandela and fellow ANC members like Walter Sisulu.

It was originally named by the Dutch after its large seal (rob) population, and it was a well-known resting place for seafarers. In 1575 a Portuguese settlement was established using convict labour and Jan Van Riebeeck later used the island first for keeping sheep and cattle, and later as a prison – lunatics and even a former king of Madura were incarcerated here. It also served as a leper colony.

The island's isolation has ensured that it is a pristine habitat for flora and fauna; endangered species, which include jackass penguins, buck and arum lilies abound. The fate of the island is controversial – suggestions include monument, nature reserve, hotel and casino. Visitors are allowed on the island, but tours are booked way in advance. For information, contact the Department of Correctional Services, tel. 411-1006 ext 208. *See also chapter* **Wet, Wet, Wet** *for cruises to the island.*

Which Way Adventures
Tel. (024) 852-2364.
Credit: *cards and cheques.*
Day tours are offered in and around Cape Town including Table Mountain and Cape Point. Longer trips include a four-day excursion to the winelands, Houw Hoek Valley, Kagga Kamma, Lamberts Bay and Bird Island, the Garden Route Tour, incorporating the Cango Caves and ostrich farms near Oudtshoorn, and river-rafting trips. German and Dutch-speaking guides available by prior arrangement.

BICYCLE/MOTORBIKE TOURS

Bikeabout Cycle Tours
Tel. 531-3274.
Credit: *no cards or cheques.*
Excellent picnic lunches are included in cycle tours of Tokai forest, Grabouw forest, the winelands and Table Mountain. Longer tours, from two days to two weeks, also offered. Bike rental available.

Le Cap Motorcycle Tours
Tel. 23-0823, fax 23-5566.
Credit: *cards but no cheques.*
Short-term motorbike hire and two- to ten-day motorbike tours to destinations like the western and southern Cape (which take in the Klein Karoo and the Garden Route) are offered here.

YACHT CRUISES

See also chapter **Wet, Wet, Wet**.

Maharani Cruises
Tel. 21-5420 code 90219 or 082-412-2222 or (011) 728-4450.
This 66-foot yacht provides cruises for up to eight passengers along the Cape coast, around Cape Point, along the west coast to Saldanha Bay and Langebaan, and to Hout Bay, Dassen Island and Robben Island. Day trips include leisurely Sunday cruises to Simon's Town.

DO-IT-YOURSELF WALKING TOURS

Deco Architecture Walk

For Art Deco fans, the City Centre is a treasure trove and a fascinating mix of commercial styles and local blends. Just look upwards (many of the Art Deco buildings have shops on ground floor level).

Begin at the landmark General Post Office in Darling Street (1938-1940), a solid mixture of Transvaal and Cape granite and reconstructed stonework. Across the road stands the splendid SA Mutual Life Assurance Society Building, now known as the Old Mutual Building. Once South Africa's tallest building, it reflects a solidity and longevity amid the 1930s poverty and gloom, and is strongly reminiscent of New York's Chrysler Building. The Old Mutual Building was designed by WH Louw, noted for his 'invention' of the modern style of Afrikaans church buildings prevalent nowadays, possibly in association with Fred Glennie. Sculptor Ivan Mitford-Barberton executed the bas-relief decorations that adorn the exterior. A sumptuous combination of proportion, function and decoration, its Deco sculptures, frescos and friezes illustrate the history, flora, fauna and peoples of South Africa. Public access is on the ground floor only – but that alone is a fabulous experience.

The old OK Bazaars building with its canopy, buff marble and plaster decoration, on the corner of Darling and Plein streets, and the Ackermans and Cuthberts buildings in Plein St, form an interesting group of understated Deco variants. But there's also much evidence that the fate of commercial buildings is to have their façades ruined in the march of modernisation – as Ottawa House further up the road testifies. Nevertheless, the chrome, terrazzo, marble and typically Deco features are still in evidence.

After turning right along Spin St, enter Church Square, where Geneva House in Parliament St stands as a wonderfully intact example of the period. A major highlight of the walk, probably the *pièce de résistance* of the city's Deco architecture, is the remodelled Victorian building now J Muller & Sons Optometrists whose chrome and vitrolite features are superb evocations of the genre. (Diagonally opposite, Diamond House is a marvellous example of the Bauhaus influence.)

As you proceed up Longmarket St towards Adderley St, note the few remaining unspoiled shop frontages from the 1930s on your left. Argus Chambers (across Adderley St, up Church St, on the right beyond St George's Mall) features evocative terrazzo facings and precast decorative panels that go largely unnoticed by passers-by.

Turn right into Burg St, towards bustling Greenmarket Square and you'll find the greatest concentration of commercial Deco in the Cape. The imposing Shell House (now a Holiday Inn Garden Court hotel), which was built in two stages (1929-1941), features subdued classical elements and was designed by WH Grant. The beautiful and sympathetically restored corner building, Namaqua House, has green and marble street-level facings, plaster and precast ornamentation, and an attic with a strong cornice. Kimberley House with its sandstone base and black tile accent stands alongside the Commercial Union Building, designed around 1932 by WH Grant and boasting a black marble plinth and brush-hammered pink Transvaal granite. Finally, there's the Sun Assurance Block (circa 1933), featuring both Deco and classical elements in plaster and concrete complemented by a wonderfully sympathetic 1990s extension by architect Louis Karol.

The **Cape Town Art Deco Society** runs on an informal and hospitable basis. You can join and receive the newsletter, or pay a nominal fee and catch up with events that range from lectures on decorative and fine art to walking tours. For information, contact Peggy Lipinski or Brent Meersman at Noupoort Guest Farm and Conference Centre, PO Box 101, Piketberg, 7320, tel. (0261) 5754, fax (0261) 5834.

Bo-Kaap or Cape Malay Quarter

The contribution of the Cape Muslims to Cape Town's history, culture and commerce is inestimable. The Afrikaans language, the development of the city's artisan skills, even

Details of some of the city's outstanding Art Deco buildings.

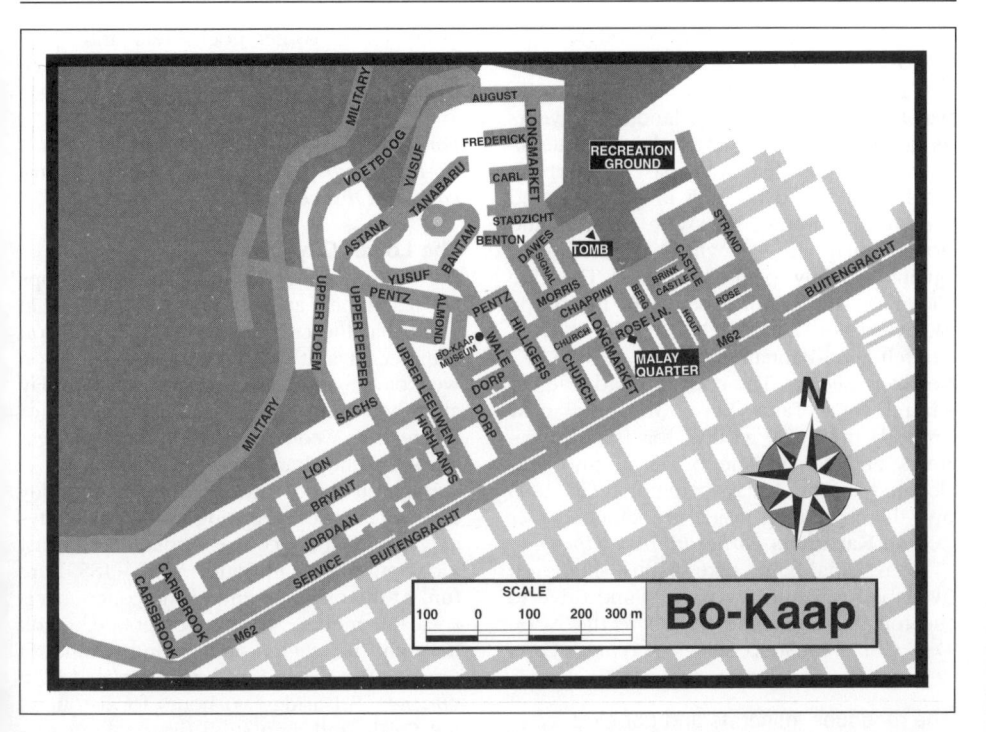

foods which are considered typically South African – sosaties, bredies, samoosas – owe a huge debt to this community. Cape Muslim master builders, tailors, masons, dressmakers and labourers helped provide the city's practical infrastructure, and Muslim intelligentsia, politicians, artists and craftspeople contributed to its flavour and political progress.

The Bo-Kaap district (set between Buitengracht St and Signal Hill) is ancestral home to many of the city's Muslims and is one of Cape Town's oldest residential areas. A series of cobbled streets, mosques, minarets, historic buildings and bustling life, the Bo-Kaap houses one of Cape Town's oldest cemeteries and the burial ground of pioneers and holy saints, political exiles who were imprisoned on Robben Island in the 17th century.

Occupation of the Bo-Kaap began in 1780, and the first house was bought by a church sexton in 1760. Otherwise known as the Cape Malay Quarter, the Bo-Kaap escaped apartheid's bulldozers and proclamations that ravaged communities like District Six, although land was lost under the Slums Act of 1934. A slow yuppification is occurring, but it's a long way from losing its character – if, indeed, it ever will.

If you want to take your own walking tour of the Bo-Kaap, don't wear revealing clothes (this is home to a deeply religious community), leave valuables at home, and stick to main streets. Despite attempts to upgrade security, there is a crime and gang problem in the area, and unless you're really skint, it's preferable to take guided walking tours, some of which are the only way to get into notable buildings like the Auwal Mosque.

Begin at 71 Wale St by visiting the Bo-Kaap Museum (*see chapter* **Museums**) to get a sense of the domestic life of a typical 19th century Cape Muslim family. Turn right when you exit the Museum, into the small, unnamed lane to get to Dorp St and South Africa's first mosque, the Auwal Mosque. The first book in Afrikaans was written here and it is believed that Afrikaans and Arabic were first taught here. The Auwal Mosque was established in 1793 by the Bo-Kaap's first Imam (Muslim leader) Tuan Guru, who was banished to Robben Island for 13 years as punishment for staging political protests.

From the Mosque, walk past 79 Dorp St, the first house to be built in the area, and then walk through the Wale St arch and down Chiappini St., which is lined with quaint, brightly painted houses. The fine Victorian architecture between the Cape Malay section and the Military Base (from Church St to Bantam St) is one of the city's best kept secrets. The cobbled road leads to Church St's Tana Baru (meaning new ground), a burial ground for Islamic pioneers and saints. The burial ground was donated to the Malay community in 1805 and there's seating inside the karamats (*see box on* **Karamats** *earlier in this chapter*).

From Tana Baru, take a bus shuttle (if available) or return to Wale St and drive to the top of Longmarket St where the Noon Day Gun Tea Shop serves a typical Cape Malay tea of sweet koeksisters and spicy chili bites and samoosas (*see chapter* **Where to Eat**).

For information on recommended guided Bo-Kaap tours, see **Special Feature Tours** *earlier in this chapter.*

The Lower City Centre

Set aside a day for this walk, including stops for tea, lunch and shopping, and bear in mind that the city can be steaming hot on summer days. It's also advisable to do it on weekdays – the city empties on Saturday afternoons and Sundays. The best day for this walk is Wednesday, when there's a flea-market at the Grand Parade.

Begin at Cape Town Station on Adderley St – its mosaics depicting early Cape days and the main concourse display of the first locomotive used in South Africa (1859) are fun. At the opposite end of the concourse is a scale model steam locomotive. Walk through the station and along Strand St towards the Castle (*see listing earlier in this chapter*). Set aside two hours for a tour of the Castle and then stroll diagonally across the Grand Parade to the delightfully ornate City Hall (*see listing earlier in this chapter*).

Grab a spicy samoosa or some chili bites at the small cafés around the Parade, or try the take-out fish from Texies. (Watch out for pickpockets on the Parade.) From here, walk around the Post Office, through Trafalgar Place, a narrow street reserved for flower-sellers, and you'll find yourself on Adderley St, a main road lined with shops and shopping malls. Cross Adderley St on Longmarket or Shortmarket St to reach Greenmarket Square with its open-air stalls and eateries. From here, walk up a block to Long St, one of the city's most picturesque streets, with its antique and collectables shops, second-hand bookstores and delis. You can either head up Long St (*see listing earlier in this chapter*) towards the Long Street Baths, a Victorian building that houses a public swimming pool, or down in the direction of the Foreshore and back to the Station via Strand St and the pedestrian walkway of St George's Mall.

The mosques, minarets and cobbled streets of the Bo-Kaap.

FRUIT HAWKERS, FLOWER SELLERS & FRUIT-PICKING

Street fruit and vegetable hawkers are an integral part of the Cape Town landscape, and despite numerous restrictive bylaws, they've flourished – to the benefit of consumers too. Their wares (R1-R4 a bag) are often cheaper than supermarkets and can be found near all major shopping areas. Rough charm and friendliness are usually part of the deal, and this may be your opportunity to overhear the kind of colourful street lingo you wouldn't repeat to your mother.

Flower-sellers also ply their wares near shopping areas, but the best-known and most concentrated sales area is Trafalgar Place, sandwiched between OK Bazaars and the Standard Bank in Adderley St.

Competition is fierce and bargaining is the order of the day.

Spring and summer bring an opportunity to pick your own fruit and flowers at farms outside the city. Picking times are mid-November to mid-December for apricots, mid-December to end of March for peaches and November to March for grapes. Strawberries can be picked on Mooiberg Farm, tel. (881) 3222, from October to December. Rose-picking at 75c per stem, peaches at R2,50 per kg (Oct-Jan) and grapes at R2,50 per kg (Jan-Mar) can be done at the Chart Farm in Wynberg, tel. 761-0434. Klondyke Farm, tel. (0233) 2-2085, offers cherry-picking (Nov-Jan) at R8-R11 per kg.

Flower-seller in the Adderley St flower market.

MUSEUMS

Johannesburg may have money, glitz and pace, but, as Capetonians are keen to note, money can't buy a rich cultural heritage ...

Cape Town and the Peninsula contain more than 30 museums, with additions every year as the city gears itself to international tourism and communities discover a pride that needs to be exhibited alongside the mainstream. The subcontinent's oldest museum is the South African Museum in the Company Gardens, established by proclamation of Governor Lord Charles Somerset in 1825 'for the reception and classification of various objects of the animal, vegetable and mineral kingdoms which are found in South Africa'. It first shared quarters with the South African Library and the South African Cultural History Museum, which now has five satellites of its own.

The SA National Art Gallery can be traced to Cape Town's first public art collection in 1761. On view in the Dutch Reformed sexton's house (in modern Adderley St), for three hours on Wednesday afternoons, were 32 paintings.

Most of the city's museums are cross-historical and Western, and there are some excellent house museums. Both colonial attitudes and apartheid largely sidelined the huge cultural resources of indigenous southern Africans and darker-hued immigrants, celebrating rather Dutch, English, French and German newcomers and their South African-born descendants. But some excellent collections relate to pre-colonial and African cultures, and there's a genuine movement to address past imbalances and to be inviting and inclusive.

Surprisingly, no museums reflect the city's passion for sport, international reputation for New World wine and three centuries of performing arts. Many museums are housed in historic buildings, and are not always wheelchair-friendly. They do, however, have the advantage of being concentrated largely in the City Centre. The majority are free or charge such minute fees that international travellers are frequently astounded. Donations are definitely welcome.

The Whale Well at the South African Museum.

MAJOR ATTRACTIONS

The Castle
See chapter **The Sights**.

Mayibuye Centre for History and Culture in South Africa
See chapter **The Sights**.

ART, ARCHITECTURE AND CRAFT

Durbanville Cultural Society
Durbanville Cultural Centre, Wellington Rd, Durbanville, tel. 96-4691 or 96-8706. This incorporates the Clay Museum of Rust en Vrede.
Open: *9am-6pm Mon-Fri.*
Housed in an 1850 complex and set in a beautiful landscaped garden, the Clay

Museum of Rust en Vrede has served as a prison, magistrate's court, school and private residence. On exhibition is the Oude Meester Collection, which includes pieces from shipwrecks, African pottery and ceramics by outstanding contemporary ceramists. The building also houses a vibrant arts centre (see **The Arts Association of Bellville** in chapter **Art Galleries**).

Michaelis Collection

Old Town House, Greenmarket Square, City Centre, tel. 24-6367.
Open: *10am-5pm daily. Closed on Good Friday, Christmas Day and New Year's Day.*
Cape Town's former city hall, a charming Rococo-style building dating from 1755, houses a renowned collection of 17th century Dutch and Flemish masters. It often holds temporary exhibitions and special events.

Rust en Vreugd

78 Buitenkant St, City Centre, tel. 45-3628.
Open: *9am-4pm Mon-Sat.*
Part of the William Fehr Collection (which is housed in The Castle), Rust en Vreugd, a late 18th century townhouse, focuses on 17th to late 19th century artwork on paper, with superb records of Cape Town's history. The renowned herb and rose-crammed garden is a recreation of a historical Dutch garden. Upstairs is a gallery for commercial exhibitions of contemporary art and an exceptional conference facility/small function venue (catering available). A garden gazebo is used for parties and music recitals, and there's off-street parking. Wheelchair-friendly on ground floor only – make prior arrangements.

South African National Gallery
See chapter **The Sights**.

UCT Irma Stern Museum
See chapter **The Sights**.

CULTURAL HISTORY

Cultural History Museum
See chapter **The Sights**.

Cape Education Museum

9 Aliwal Rd, Wynberg, tel. 762-1622.
Open: *8.30am-3pm Mon-Fri.*
The Education Museum is a largely undiscovered gem, a comprehensive collection of teaching materials from the end of the last century onwards. Contrary to what you might expect, there's nothing dull about this nostalgia trip. It includes a replica of a Victorian schoolroom complete with blackboards and dipping pens, Victorian school uniforms in which visiting children get to dress up, school bells from dormant village schools and everything from epidiascopes and Gestetner machines (remember those?) to faxes and telescopes. Not wheelchair-accessible.

Jewish Museum

84 Hatfield St, Gardens, City Centre, tel. 45-1546 or 434-6605.
Open: *2pm-5pm Tue and Thu (open 10am-5pm Tue and Thu during Dec-Mar), 10am-12.30pm Sun.*
Towards the end of the 19th century eastern European and Russian pogroms drove Jews to South Africa, and the Jewish Museum, part of South Africa's oldest synagogue, contains significant historical and ceremonial items, providing fascinating insight into a community that has had a huge impact on the country's cultural, commercial and social life.

Josephine Mill

Boundary Road, Newlands, tel. 686-4939.
Open: *9am-4pm Mon-Fri, 10am-4pm Sat-Sun (Nov-Feb). Tea garden open throughout the week.*
Cape Town's only surviving and operational water mill (established in 1840) also houses conference facilities and the tranquil Threshers Tea Garden (*see chapter* **Where to Eat**) and it produces Josephine stoneground flour. The Nedbank Sunday Summer Concert Season (Nov-Feb) features outdoor classical, jazz, folk, swing and choral music on the banks of the tree-fringed Liesbeek River (*see chapter* **Music**). Disabled access is extremely limited.

Natale Labia Museum
See chapter **The Sights**.

HOUSE MUSEUMS

Bertram House
Cnr Government Ave and Orange St, City Centre, tel. 24-9381.
Open: *9.30am-4.30pm Tue-Sat.*
This elegant, late Georgian red brick house typifies early 19th century Cape British patrician architecture. It's the last extant example of its kind in the city and probably the best of the house museums. The nucleus is the Anna Lidderdale Collection, superbly displayed furniture, ceramics, silver and *objets d'art*. Notable exhibits include four-poster beds, needlepoint samplers and tapestry. Concerts are also held here.

Rust en Vreugd, a typical 18th century burgher's house with a renowned herb and rose garden in historical Cape Dutch style.

The best, and most enjoyable way to get to Bertram House is via Government Avenue – either from below the Mount Nelson Hotel towards Adderley St, or up from Adderley St. Not wheelchair-friendly.

Bo-Kaap Museum
See chapter **The Sights**.

Groot Constantia Manor House and Wine Museum
Groot Constantia Estate, Constantia, tel. 794-5067.
Open: *10am-5pm daily. Closed on Good Friday and Christmas Day.*
Groot Constantia is a prime example of Cape Dutch architecture and wines from this estate graced the tables of European royalty during the 1700s. Part of the larger estate granted to Governor Simon van der Stel in 1685, Groot Constantia is regarded as the country's most historically important wine estate.

The house portrays life on a farm in the 1800s. The collection comprises Cape furniture from the mid-1700s and Chinese, Japanese, Rhenish and Delft porcelain. The Wine Museum has wine-drinking and storage vessels in glass, silver, copper and stoneware dating from 50 BC to the 19th century. You can buy wine from 10am-5pm daily (shipping available), and daily cellar tours are on the hour from 10am-4pm during season. Out of season tours are at 11am and 3pm only, except for large groups. For more info, tel. 794-5128. There are two steps up to the house and from there it's wheelchair-friendly.

Koopmans De Wet House
See chapter **The Sights**.

NATURAL HISTORY

South African Museum
See chapter **The Sights**.

ART GALLERIES

Here's where to look, buy and get expert advice, framing and aesthetic enjoyment.

Cape Town's art world is moving out of repression and isolation into a revitalised political, social and creative landscape. The city is home to some of South Africa's finest artists and art consultants, and some outstanding artists teach at or emerge from local art schools – Michaelis, Ruth Prowse, Frank Joubert, CAP (Community Arts Project) and The Artists Co-operative.

Local art has a definite flavour. Southern Africa's quality of light – clear yellow in contrast to the colder blue European light – frequently results in brighter work and primary colours. Eurocentric influences are found alongside township art, rural art and reflections of unique Cape culture.

As happens anywhere, galleries must balance the saleable – for example, accessible, decorative landscapes – with more progressive work, and it's to the credit of determined gallery owners, passionate curators and loyal fans that Cape Town boasts a number of long-standing, quality galleries.

The list of notable local artists is a long one, but outstanding names include Tyrone Apollis, Beezy Bailey, Willie Bester, Rochelle Bomberg, Gail Catlin, Paul Emslie, John Kramer, Eric Laubscher, Zwelethu Mtwetwa, Catherine Paynter, Michael Pettit, David Saal, Francine Scialom Greenblatt, Larry Scully, Eris Silke, Cecil Skotnes, Pippa Skotnes, Robert Slingsby, Helmut Starcke, Jeanette Unite, Louis Jansen van Vuuren, Jan Vermeiren and Judy Woodborne. For sculpture, don't miss the work of Jane Alexander, Kevin Brand, David Brown, Lorraine Edelstein, Flying Cow (a conglomerate that produces anything from major works to one-of-a-kind mobiles), Maureen Langley, Brett Murray and Gavin Younge.

The Castle Brewery Building, formerly the Woodstock Brewery, houses the studios and headquarters of some 45 artists, sculptors and designers. Captour, galleries and selected stores stock the free *Arts and Crafts Map* and for an upbeat, innovative journal on contemporary culture, try *ADA Magazine* (from upmarket bookshops and art/craft-oriented stores).

Alfred Mall Gallery
Shop 9a, Alfred Mall, Waterfront, tel. 419-9507.
Open: *9am-7pm Mon-Tue and Thu, 9am-9pm Wed, Fri-Sat, 10am-7pm Sun.*
The Alfred Mall Gallery, superbly situated in the Waterfront complex, shows paintings, ceramics, sculpture and jewellery. Limited

Artist Jane Solomon, designer of funky silkscreened fabric at Icon Print.

edition prints, one-offs, artists' postcards and brightly painted cotton wall hangings. Wheelchair-friendly.

The Arts Association of Bellville Gallery & Art Centre

The Library Centre, Carel van Aswegen St, Bellville, tel. 918-2301 (gallery) or 918-2293 (art centre).
Open: *9am-8pm Mon-Fri, 9am-5pm Sat.*
The Arts Association of Bellville, a branch of the well-regarded South African Association of Arts, is a vibrant, inviting space. The well-lit, white-finished gallery upstairs features 12 rotating annual exhibitions, including a Ceramist of the Month (beginning on the 20th of every month). The ground floor arts centre offers art and craft classes (for details, call 96-4691). There's also a coffee shop, art reference books in the Bellville Library, lunchtime videos, lectures, meet-the-artist sessions, demonstrations, workshops and community projects. Wheelchair-friendly.

Atlantic Gallery

Scotts Bldg, 41 Church St (cnr Long St), City Centre, tel. 23-5775.
Open: *10am-4.30pm Mon-Fri, 10am-1pm Sat.*
Proprietor Riva Cohen has been in the art game since 1968. A warm, informal series of art-crammed rooms, the gallery combines professionalism, a genuine love of art and unofficious service – nothing pushy or glitzy about this one. For a/h consultations, call 439-3968.

The Chelsea Gallery

51 Waterloo Rd, Wynberg, tel. 761-6805.
Open: *9.30am-5.30pm Mon-Fri, 9.30am-1pm Sat.*
The decade-old Chelsea Gallery, in the heart of Old Wynberg Village (also known as Wynberg Chelsea), is located in a beautifully restored historical building, *Die Ou Pastorie*. Owner Lieschen Heinz has been in the gallery game for more than 20 years, and she's blended informal atmosphere with careful aesthetic choices. The Chelsea comprises two halls, the larger, main hall for monthly exhibitions and the Old Church Hall for permanent showings. Paintings, bronzes, ceramics and sculptures feature, but the Chelsea is particularly known for its original graphics. There's one small step, but otherwise it's wheelchair-accessible.

The Kunskamer

14 Burg St, City Centre, tel. 24-4238.
Open: *9am-5pm Mon-Fri, 9am-1pm Sat.*
A Madison Avenue-like gallery that specialises in blue-chip and collectable artists like Irma Stern, Pierneef and Maggie Laubser. Well established and for serious collectors.

The New Cape Gallery

60 Church St, City Centre, tel. 23-5309.
Open: *9.30am-5pm Mon-Fri, 9.30am-1pm Sat.*
Set in a pedestrian walkway, between antique and collectables stalls and shops, the New Cape Gallery is an inviting, comfortable space, a series of airy rooms featuring accessible, popular art. Exhibitions are thematic – Cape scenery (beginning in Sep), wildlife (beginning in Feb/Mar) and eclectic subjects like miniatures, maps and myths in winter (Jun/Jul). Wheelchair-friendly, except for one small step.

Primart Gallery

Warwick Square, Warwick St, Claremont, tel. 64-4440.
Open: *9am-5pm Mon-Sat.*
Exhibitions by a variety of well-regarded artists, some local and some international, show at Primart on a three-weekly basis. Some 200 artists are represented by this large, spacious gallery. Packing and shipping service available. Wheelchair-friendly.

Rose Korber Upstairs at Martin Melck House

96 Strand St, City Centre (above A Table at Colin's restaurant), tel. 419-6533 or 438-9152.
Open: *9.30am-11pm Mon-Fri, 5pm-11pm Sat, or by appointment.*
A magnificent 18th century townhouse, with a stylish restaurant downstairs, this is a fascinating environment for vibrant, changing exhibitions of works by leading contempo-

Art Galleries

Sculptor Thami Kiti with his works at the UCT Irma Stern Gallery.

rary South African, African and British artists, selected by the keen eye of noted art consultant Rose Korber. Packing and shipping service available. Not wheelchair-accessible.

Seeff Gallery
Seeff House, 42 Hans Strydom Ave, Foreshore.
Open: *9am-9pm daily. (The gallery curators can be contacted at the adjacent framing shop, The Framing Company, tel. 25-2266, which is open 9am-6pm Mon-Fri and 9.30am-1.30pm Sat.)*
Housed on three floors of the Seeff Organisation's corporate headquarters, the Seeff Gallery specialises in interesting contemporary art, frequently showing group work around a central theme. Apart from the art, there's the attraction of being in a lovingly restored historic building that boasts Cape Town's oldest working lift and a colourful history as a former fruit and fish storehouse and one-time brothel. Wheelchair-friendly.

The Sembach Gallery
17 The Passageway, Main Rd, Hout Bay, tel. 790-7324.
Open: *9.30am-5.30pm Mon-Fri, 9.30am-1pm Sat. After hours by appointment.*
Housed in one of Hout Bay's oldest fishermen's cottages, the Sembach Gallery specialises in original contemporary South African art, ceramics, free-blown glass, jewellery and sculpture. Owners Karl and Rea Sembach represent some 60 artists and make four annual countrywide trips to acquire new works. Shipping arrangements available. Wheelchair-friendly.

South African Association of Arts/Metropolitan Gallery
35 Church St, City Centre, tel. 24-7436.
Open: *10am-5pm Mon-Fri, 10pm-1pm Sat. Closed on public holidays.*
Established, prestigious gallery comprising three viewing areas, all designed for easy visibility. The speciality is contemporary Western Cape artists, but other South African

and international works also show. The wide range of exhibitions includes paintings, photographs, sculptures, ceramics, jewellery, textiles and installations. Located along a pedestrian walkway lined with antique and collectables shops and coffee bars, the gallery is an inviting, professionally run space. Wheelchair-friendly, but use the kitchen entrance (next to adjacent Café Mozart), or let the gallery curator know when you're arriving.

OUT OF TOWN GALLERIES

Onrus Gallery
19 Van Blommenstein St, Onrusrivier, tel. (0283) 6-2525.
Open: *9am-5.30 Mon-Fri, 9am-5pm Sat, 10am-1pm Sun. (Extended hours in holiday season.)*
The Onrus Gallery is a treat for both experienced art lovers and the uninitiated. It's a relaxed environment in which browsing and conversation, over some good filter coffee and home-made cakes, are encouraged. Fine art, ceramics, art framing and handmade jewellery feature and notable artists shown include Gregoire Boonzaier, Marjorie Wallace and Solly Malope. Onrus village is home to an impressive group of artists and craftspeople, many of whom are represented here. Partially wheelchair-accessible, help provided.

Daljosafat Arts Foundation
Non Pareille Farm, Daljosafat, tel. (02211) 68-2924.
Situated on two farms in the beautiful Daljosafat Valley, 65 km from Cape Town, the Daljosafat Arts Foundation is an independent project that provides artists and writers with homes and studios. The gallery is an airy series of rooms dedicated to contemporary fine art, craft and *objets d'art*. Phone for details.

Metal sculpture exhibition at the National Gallery.

Art Galleries 73

Dorp Street Gallery
176 Dorp St, Stellenbosch, tel. 887-2256.
Open: *10am-5pm Mon-Fri, 10am-1pm Sat.*
Dorp Street Gallery is housed in the 1694 Colony House building, (the site of Stellenbosch's oldest dwelling) and it features cheerful, sociable openings with good food and wine, a fire in winter and a fine collection of South African art, sculptures, jewellery, ceramics and craft, including Stellenbosch artists and outstanding works by Zulu ceramists from KwaZulu-Natal's renowned Ardmore Studios. The annual eight to ten exhibitions are good for spotting fresh talent. Wheelchair-friendly – use side entrance.

FRAMING & ART CONSULTANTS

Art Route Studio Tours
Tel. 438-1131.
Easy, expert access to a wide range of Western Cape art, this is the aesthetic equivalent of smelling the greasepaint backstage at the theatre. Arlene Traub, who provides this unique facility, collects and ferries art lovers to the homes and studios of some 150 artists, ranging from established to up-and-coming.

The Framing Company
Seeff House, Shop No 3, 42 Hans Strydom Ave, City Centre, tel. 25-2266/7.
Open: *9am-6pm Mon-Fri, 9.30am-1.30pm Sat.*
The number of Cape Town artists who use The Framing Company vouches for the quality of its creative and functional framing. Competitively priced, with around 600 mouldings, friendly, switched-on service, private parking, art consultancy plus craft, gifts, original and repro art and good filter coffee. Wheelchair-friendly.

Galeria João
301 Namaqua House, 36 Burg St, City Centre, tel. 23-5403.
A highly regarded consultant, João Ferreira imports top international art and exports contemporary South African art. His presentation room is in a beautiful Art Deco building in the City Centre, but João also sources individual pieces on request and consults to collectors in their homes and corporate environments. By appointment only. Wheelchair-friendly, except for outside step where help is available.

In-Fin-Art
60 New Church St, City Centre. 23-2090/1/2.
Open: *9am-5pm Mon-Fri, 9am-1pm Sat.*
Renowned for creative, specialised framing and gilding, the three-storey In-Fin-Art also offers consultancy services, original and repro art, limited-edition prints and custom-designed mirrors. Framing is done in the massive on-site factory and the showrooms are elegant, uncluttered and easy for browsing. Private parking. Wheelchair-friendly, but park at the door – the parking area is gravel.

Primart Framing
Upper Mall, Cavendish Square, Claremont, tel. 64-2839.
Open: *9am-5pm Mon-Sat.*
Extensive range of art supplies, prints and lovely mirrors. Restoration and preservation service available. Creative custom-framing including hand-coloured gilded frames. Wheelchair-friendly.

Rose Korber Art Consultant
48 Sedgemoor Rd, Camps Bay, tel. 438-9152 or 438-9998.
Open: *9am-5pm Mon-Fri, weekends by appointment.*
Extraordinary selection of paintings, graphics, sculpture, ceramics, tapestries, tableware and beadwork by some 150 top contemporary South African, African and international artists. Also expert advice to private and corporate buyers and interior designers from one of South Africa's most highly regarded art consultants.

Maxwoods Framers
27 Hope St, Gardens, tel. 45-4345.
Open: *8.30am-5pm Mon-Thu, 8.30am-4.30pm Fri, 9am-noon Sat.*
Extensive range of imported, custom-made and local mouldings. Maxwoods is renowned for conservation framing, providing loving

framing and careful treatment of antique and vintage art – museums like the South African National Gallery are customers. Gilding of everything from frames to furniture is also available. And it's housed in an historic Cape Dutch house. On-premises parking. Wheelchair-friendly.

CRAFTED ART

Galleries and specialised markets frequently feature indigenous collectables – ceramics, jewellery, glass and handblown glass. Look out for extraordinary cutlery by Carrol Boyes and glass by David Reade and Morgenster Studio. Outstanding ceramists include André Bonthuys, Katherine Glenday, Angelique Kirk, Clementina van der Walt and Cilla Williams. Stellenbosch University boasts an exceptional jewellery design department and you'll find fine contemporary work in Cape Town and Stellenbosch, notably the designs of Dieter Dill and Amulet Jewellers.

Montebello Craft Centre
31 Newlands Ave, Newlands, tel. 686-7115.
Open: *9am-5pm Mon-Fri, 10am-3pm Sat-Sun.*
A sprawling art and craft centre set in lush gardens and historic farm buildings, Montebello promotes good local design and uses craft for job creation as well as providing outreach programes in township and rural areas, adult and child education programmes and on-site design studios, exhibition spaces, a shop and restaurant. Ceramics, blacksmithing, pottery and jewellery are among the craftware available. Wheelchair-friendly.

PRIVATE CRAFT STUDIOS

Amulet Jewellery
602 Geneva House, 28 Parliament St, City Centre, tel. 45-2612.
Open: *9am-5pm Mon-Fri, Sat by appointment.*

Outstanding custom-made designs in silver, semi-precious and precious stones. Wheelchair-friendly.

Lisa Abrahams Ceramics
1 Lower Trill Rd, Observatory, tel. 47-2514.
Open: *9am-4pm Mon-Fri. Call for appointment.*
Tin-glazed earthenware, decorated with oxides and stains. Wheelchair-friendly except for two steps to the porch, but help is available.

Tania Babb Ceramic Sculptures
Dawidskraal, 38 Whittler's Way, Hout Bay, tel. 790-4103.
Brightly glazed earthenware usually featuring women. By appointment. Limited wheelchair access (there are three steps up and steps inside).

The Barn Art Gallery
170 Church St, Worcester, tel. (0231) 2-8136.
Open: *9am-5pm Mon-Fri, 9am-2pm Sat, 10am-5pm Sun.*
Veteran master glass-blower for functional and sculptural free-blown glass. The coffee shop serves light lunches. Wheelchair-friendly except for three small steps at the entrance.

Icon Print
6 Venken Lane, Long St, City Centre, tel. 22-2572.
Open: *9.30am-5pm Mon-Fri. It's advisable to call in advance.*
Hand-painted and printed T-shirts, clothing and fabric in a wide variety of designs based on ancient to everyday symbols. Inventive, inviting and highly desirable. Not wheelchair-friendly, but help is available.

Barbara Jackson
33 Sunset Ave, Llandudno, tel. 790-2922.
Accessible, contemporary ceramics. By appointment only. Wheelchair-friendly.

The Jewellery & Gemstone Design Studio
1 Rouxville Rd, Kalk Bay, tel. 788-8159.
Open: *10am-4pm Tue-Thu, 10am-1pm Fri-Sat.*

Original hand-crafted jewellery in 9ct, 14ct and 18ct gold, silver and South African gemstones. Hand-crafted gold chains, remodelling of jewellery and repairs.

Jacqueline Lloyd Jeweller
Old Castle Breweries, 6 Beach Rd, Woodstock, tel. 448-5014.
Open: *9am-5pm Mon-Thu. Phone ahead for appointment.*
Personalised designs in precious materials. Not wheelchair-accessible.

Morgenster Studio
Morgenster Farm, off Lourensford Rd, Somerset West, tel. (024) 51-6526.
Glass panels and decorative acrylic pieces. By appointment only. Wheelchair-friendly, except for lawn area.

Mustardseed and Moonshine
61 Trill Rd, Observatory, tel. 448-5062.
Open: *9am-5pm Mon-Fri, 9am-1pm Sat. Call in advance.*
Brightly pretty, fine ceramic and mostly functional earthenware based on floral forms.

The Potter's Shop and Studio
6 Rouxville Rd, Kalk Bay, tel. 788-7030.
Open: *9.30am-1pm and 2pm-4.30pm Mon-Thu, 9.30am-1pm Fri-Sat.*
This village gallery in the bohemian, antique and collectables store-lined Kalk Bay offers informed service, ceramic *objets* and supplies. Expert tuition and firing service also available. Partially wheelchair-accessible – there are two small steps, but help is on hand.

The old Castle Brewery Building, a home for artists, designers and photographers.

CAPE TOWN ARCHITECTURE

The Cape's fascinating, chequered history is characterised by shifting economies, cultural diversity and the styles of successive colonial administrators – a complex past reflected in both historic and contemporary buildings. You'll see Cape Dutch, Georgian, Victorian, Edwardian and Art Deco influences and a considerable dash of post-modern California-meets-the-Med around Clifton, Bantry Bay and Camps Bay.

Cape Town began as a larder for malnourished sailors making the treacherous passage around the Cape of Storms, but towards the end of the 17th century the strategic importance of this lucrative trade station became clear, and plans were hastily made to cast the tiny settlement's identity in stone. Van Riebeeck's mud and grass-sod fort, built soon after his arrival in 1652, was replaced with the moat-surrounded, pentagonal Castle. **The Castle** is South Africa's oldest surviving building and it has served as a fortress, jail, government headquarters and governor's residence. Recently restored, its notable architectural features include the De Kat Balcony, the Dolphin Pool and impressive banqueting halls (*see chapter* **The Sights**).

CAPE DUTCH

From the end of the 17th century until around 1750, the Cape colony grew steadily. Simply gabled, thatch-roofed homes in the Cape Dutch style gradually sprang up in a widening circle around the safe haven of the Castle. Cape Dutch architecture remains one of the Peninsula's most popular building styles, much in evidence in Cape Town and neighbouring towns like Stellenbosch and Franschhoek. It's derived from Holland's baroque architecture, but adapted to hot Cape summers and wet winters, and is characterised by white, plastered gables and thatched roofs. It's best represented by the stately **Rust en Vreugd House** in Buitenkant St. Look for the unusual, obliquely clipped façade end portico, magnificently carved front door, and detailed transom and fanlights. Also worth looking at is the city's first civic building, **The Burgher Watch House**, erected on Greenmarket Square in 1755. This fine example of Cape Dutch architecture has been renamed the **Old Town House** and it's home to the Michaelis Art Collection (*see chapter* **Museums**). Although the interior's been changed, the façade is still more-or-less intact and the arcaded loggia and balcony, the fanlights and fine plaster work are worth noting.

European demand for fresh produce and more diverse traffic strengthened the Cape's ties with the cosmopolitan world. One of the significant consequences of this development was a new religious tolerance. **The Dutch Reformed Groote Kerk** in Adderley St, dates from 1699, but it was only in 1780 that Lutherans were allowed formalised services. Their church, which began as a wine store to which a façade was added, has been embellished and rebuilt over the years, resulting in a Cape Gothic-style building, notable for beautiful wood carvings by architect-craftsman Anton Anreith. This central city building in Strand St forms part of a complex that contains the **The Sexton's House** (1787) presently occupied by the Dutch embassy and **Martin Melck House** (1781) at 96 Strand St. Martin Melck House contains the restaurant A Table at Colin's and the Rose Korber Gallery, thus providing an ideal combination of good eating, art and typical architecture of the period – airy, large rooms, wooden floors and high ceilings. The roof room and gable are worth noting – they were uncommon features on double-storey buildings at the time.

THE EMPIRE ARRIVES

At the behest of the Dutch, the British acquired the colony between 1795 and 1803 and they obviously enjoyed their stay – by 1806 they were back. The Cape continued to thrive under English rule and the Industrial Revolution's technological advances precipitated a building boom. The majority of houses were now single-storey and flat roofed. Precincts of these terraced cottages still exist in the **Bo-Kaap** area (*see chapter* **The Sights**). Originally, the parapets and pediments of the Bo-Kaap's dignified townhouses were adorned with neo-classical urns and pots, but most of this has disappeared. Nevertheless, this historic home to Cape Town's Muslim community contains noteworthy Georgian and Victorian architecture and a high concentration of mosques.

With the Empire came empire builders, the most influential of whom was Cecil John Rhodes. Under his patronage, architect Herbert Baker (later Sir Herbert Baker), rose to prominence. During the 20 years he spent in South Africa (1892-1912), Baker designed impressive homes and public buildings. You can see his elegant approach in the **Mount Nelson Hotel**, but his great regard for local style is best observed in the stately **Genadendal** (formerly Groote Schuur), a fine example of Cape Dutch architecture, and home to South Africa's State President.

Under British rule, the Company Gardens acquired a distinctly botanical flavour, and became a grand thoroughfare terminating at the Northern Gate (now Adderley St). This, in turn, led to a promenade and jetty that tied the city's green heart to the sea. Important buildings situated in and around the Company Gardens are the **South African Library** (1818), **St George's Cathedral** (1830), the **Houses of Parliament** (1885), the **Great Synagogue** (1905) and the **National Gallery** (1928) – most are copies of grand European civic structures, but together, they're a graceful collection of buildings, well worth visiting. (*See chapters* **Museums, Art Galleries** *and* **The Sights** *for details.*)

Thanks to mass production and prefabrication, Victorian architecture, that elaborate, pattern-book style, set its seal on Cape Town's older suburbs – Green Point, Sea Point,

Before and after: Victorian and modern side by side.

Woodstock, Observatory, Mowbray, Rondebosch, Claremont and around Long St in the City Centre.

The railway and motor car changed the face and nature of the city most substantially. Graceful *grachts*, with canals and trees (much like those still seen in Stellenbosch) were widened for traffic. As the central city became a thriving business district, remaining residents joined the exodus to suburbs that were springing up along the railway line. Office blocks rose and the city, as we see it today, began to take shape.

ART DECO

For Art Deco fans, Cape Town is a treasure trove. (*See chapter* **The Sights** *for a suggested walking tour of the Art Deco buildings in the City Centre.*)

A BIRD'S EYE VIEW

Head for the summit of Table Mountain for a fine view of Cape Town. Below lies the city bowl. The oldest part of the Bo-Kaap nestles on the slopes of Signal Hill on the fringes of the CBD, and the railway snakes eastward to the newer southern suburbs. Northwards is a formless urban sprawl. From here, you can see the vacant lot that is the scar of District Six, a thriving neighbourhood demolished under apartheid (*see chapter* **The Sights**).

The impact of foreshore land reclamation, which cut the city off from the sea and created a vast, unfriendly no-man's-land beneath a spaghetti of megalithic flyovers is also evident. In a spectacular capitulation of man to motor, this urban decay has been compounded by the burial of much of the shopping precinct below ground, but happily, efforts are being made to address problems.

FUTURE PLANS

The pedestrian walkways in St George's Mall and around Greenmarket Square have created an appealingly human and thriving core. And the Waterfront, an outstanding commercial success, is a striking conversion of the historic Cape Town harbour. The nucleus of renewal proposals is a transport canal connecting the harbour to the City Centre and the extension of this development eastwards to the disused railway yards and District Six. These steps will repopulate and energise the City Centre, embracing the optimism embodied in the name Cape of Good Hope.

EATING & DRINKING

Food, glorious food – and lots to drink – are the focus here. As with the rest of this book, this section doesn't claim to be an encyclopedia of every option, but rather a good range of suggestions. As with the rest of this book, probably even more so, there's no accounting for tastes and no guarantee of quality. Restaurants have good days and bad days, just like human beings. Many restaurants have extended hours during summer. And you're strongly advised to book. That said, *bon appetit.*

AN INTRODUCTION TO CAPE AND SOUTH AFRICAN CUISINE

Snoek and salomies, malva pudding, melktert and moerkoffie ... Cape cuisine is literally a melting pot of flavours and it ranges from foods you may not be able to pronounce (but will love to eat) to imports from America, Europe and the East.

Freshness and variety are the keys to cuisine in an area that has long been associated with excellent fruit, wine and fish, as well as a melange of culinary influences.

When the Dutch arrived in 1652, Jan van Riebeeck headed up a way-station designed to provide fresh supplies to Dutch East India Company ships on their way to and from the East. **The Company Gardens** (now a tranquil, tree and museum-filled park between Orange and Adderley streets), were originally the fruit gardens planted to provide sailors with protection from scurvy.

At the time of Van Riebeeck's arrival, the Cape was inhabited by the Khoikhoi people, nomadic farmers with huge herds of fat-tailed sheep, the San, who hunted game, and the Strandlopers, who enjoyed seafood and game.

Subsequent food influences came from all over the globe. Slaves from Indonesia (then known as Batavia), Madagascar and India became the Cape Malay people and brought

Set in a beautifully restored Franschhoek farmhouse, Polfyntjies offers excellent local cuisine. *For details, see chapter* **Where to Eat.**

EATING ETIQUETTE AND USEFUL INFORMATION

Most restaurants take bookings and booking is advisable. VAT of 14% is added to bills, but service isn't, unless indicated. The form is a 10-15% tip. And you can bring your own wine to most eateries, but expect to pay a corkage fee. Liquor isn't served in Cape Malay (Muslim) restaurants.

As for dress codes, dining is generally an informal affair, although you may feel out of place in shorts and sandals at smarter venues. The general rule is the ubiquitous 'smart casual', meaning decent. Sexy, eye-catching gear rules in trendy eateries, but in traditional Cape Malay restaurants, for example those in the Bo-Kaap area, revealing clothing is not a good idea.

with them the rich, spicy-sweet dishes which are so much part of local cuisine today.

The French Huguenots, who fled to the Cape to escape religious persecution, established superb vineyards and fruit farms in **Franschhoek** (literally French Corner) and provided French recipes. The culinary legacy of having once been a British colony remains in the preponderance of English breakfasts, roasts, high tea and a widespread devotion to traditional Christmas Day lunch, even though a summery Cape Christmas is ill-suited to steaming turkey and hot pudding.

Capetonians also owe a debt of gratitude to the Italian prisoners of war whose presence in the country around the time of World War II taught locals a thing or two about good cooking. Immigrants from Portugal and Greece have also played a major role in contributing to South African food.

Indigenous dishes include traditional African recipes, frequently based on *pap* (a maize porridge) and Afrikaner cooking, which is big on meat, sweet puddings and stews. You'll also find Cantonese, Indian, Chinese, Thai, French, Italian and Bulgarian restaurants. And, of course, Capetonians are a trendy bunch, hot for whatever's the rage in LA or New York. The last few years have seen a burgeoning of Tex-Mex and Oriental eateries, and no deli worth its hip clientele would run short of sun-dried tomatoes and pesto.

For café society fans, the city offers superb summers and some gorgeous inhabitants, both of which create lovely window-front and outdoor eating. Historic **Waterkant** and **Long** streets and the walkways surrounding **Greenmarket Square** and **St George's Mall** boast cafés and bistros where people-watching is the primary activity.

What can you eat that's typical of the Cape and South Africa? Plenty – starting with ...

Biltong is dried beef or game, salty, filling and an acquired taste.

Boerewors is a spicy, coriander-flavoured sausage.

The ***braai*** or BBQ is the cooking equivalent of a religious experience in South Africa, very popular with blacks and Afrikaners who like nothing so much as cooking in the great outdoors. Ideally, *braaiing* is done by the menfolk who stand around the coals, drinking beers and telling jokes, while the women cluster in the kitchen whipping up rice salads. Whatever advances feminism has made in South Africa, the braai remains one of the last macho bastions. And predictably, Capetonians are big on fish braais. Favourite fishy ingredients: snoek or yellowtail.

Bredies (say Breedees) are tasty stews, the best Cape version being *waterblommetjiebredie* in which green water hyacinth predominates.

Chili bites are round, deep-fried savoury snacks available in two versions – the strongly flavoured, potato based Indian chili bite and the pea-flour based, spiced Cape Malay version. The best in the city are to be found at the Noon Gun Tea Shop, Bo-Kaap (*see chapter* **Where to Eat**).

Curries prepared in the spicy style of traditional Cape Malay cooking or in various Indian recipes, often appear on restaurant menus – a reminder of the slaves and immigrants who have contributed to Cape culture and cuisine.

Kingklip, a firm, white fish, frequently appears on restaurant menus and is delicious grilled or fried.

Koeksisters, a much-loved Afrikaner treat, are sweet and sticky. The Cape koeksister is oval and juicy, flavored with cumin and coated with coconut, unlike its upcountry cousin which is plaited and syrup-dipped.

Malva pudding is a sweet, calorific blend of milk, sugar, cream and apricot jam.

Melktert or milk tart is a staple Cape Malay pudding/tart, dating to early Dutch recipes. It consists of cinnamon-dusted baked custard in a pastry base.

Moerkoffie is a sludgy coffee simmered from early morning and generally found in traditional farm homesteads.

Pap is the staple African food, thick maize-meal porridge served with stew or syrup and milk.

Potjiekos, a slowly simmered meat/vegetable stew, is made in a *potjie* (three-legged iron pot) over an open fire.

Pumpkin fritters dusted with cinnamon sugar are second only to malva pudding as a comfort food.

Salomies, a brilliant fast food, are flour pancakes (rotis) wrapped around curried beans, meat or vegetables. Some of the best salomies can be found at Zorina's (Loop St) and Medina (at the Grand Parade).

Rooibos, a rich tea from the Clanwilliam district is rumoured to cure everything from arthritis to ailing hearts. Most of the claims are dubious, but it is tasty and tannin-free.

Samoosas, fried, crispy pastry triangles filled with curried mince or spicy vegetables, are served everywhere from society bashes to corner cafés. In Cape Malay homes and restaurants they're usually a starter served with coriander-dusted lemon. Good samoosas are available at Zorina's (Loop St), Medina (at the Grand Parade), Rose Café (cnr Rose and Wale streets, Bo-Kaap) and the Noon Gun Tea Room (Bo-Kaap).

Seafood is notable, if pricey. The choice includes crayfish (rock lobster), *perlemoen* (abalone), oysters (notably Knysna oysters), mussels and calamari (either deep-fried or as a grilled steak).

Skop is sheep's head, popular in township and rural communities.

Snoek, a bony, fatty fish, is smoked, used in paté or in *smoorsnoek*, which combines snoek, potatoes, onions and tomatoes. In line with the sweet-sour tradition, it's served with a sweet chutney. Traditional Afrikaner recipes include snoek barbecued with apricot jam (a surprisingly good combination) or served with side orders of *korrelkonfyt* (grape jam) and *mielie* (corn) bread. Cape Malay snoek recipes include masala snoek (deep-fried with lemon and green coriander) and snoek breyani (with basmati rice and spices).

Sosaties, like Thai/Indonesian satay, are marinated, skewered beef, lamb or chicken.

Vetkoek, a deep-fried doughy bun, is eaten with jam or minced meat.

Read Myrna Robins' *The Cape Cookbook* and Cass Abrahams' *Cuisine of the Cape Malays* for definitive insights. *See chapter* **Cape Town by Season** *for wine and food-related events*.

CAPE WINES

How will you eat, drink and be merry if you don't know what to drink? Dip into this general guide to local reds and whites, that's how. Then go out and give your palate a good time.

Cape wines are just beginning to achieve international recognition again. While they may lag slightly behind their New World cousins, a 'beaker of the warm south' is still easily affordable in the Cape. And nature is on the Cape's side when it comes to wine production. Regular, sunny summers and winter rainfall ensure quality for virtually every vintage. In the coastal region, (which includes Constantia, Durbanville, Stellenbosch, Paarl, Overberg and the Swartland), the best wines are produced with plenty of help from cool breezes, which ameliorate temperatures at harvest time (between January and March). Inland are the wine-producing areas of Robertson, Worcester, Tulbagh, Swellendam and the Klein Karoo. And bulk wines of average quality are produced in the Orange River and Olifants River regions.

With all these natural advantages, it's not surprising that the first vineyard was planted in 1655, three years after the Dutch settlement. In 1679, Simon van der Stel arrived in the Cape Colony as Governor, and it was during his administration that knowledgeable French Huguenots came to the Cape, and by his order that the renowned winelands of Stellenbosch and Constantia (named after Van der Stel's wife Constance) were established.

Within a century, Cape winemakers were producing worthy rivals to Europe's fortified wines and madeiras, and fans included Louis XVI, Bismarck, Louis Phillipe and later Queen Victoria. Napoleon requested Constantia wines to help console him during his exile on St Helena.

CAPE WINE RENAISSANCE

During the last 25 years, a welcome renaissance has occurred in the Cape wine industry and the finest local wines are among the best, if not the best of the so-called New World wines, particularly where value is concerned.

As a rule with Cape wines, you get what you pay for ... but the price difference between ordinary and special is often small and well worth the extra few rands.

The best **Cape reds** are made from Cabernet Sauvignon, some pure and others blended with 25% Merlot, which is the classic Bordeaux blend. These must not be compared with the great Chateaux of Medoc, Graves or St Emilion. Nor can the popular, but pricey pure Merlots match Petrus of the Pomerol. However, Pinotage – a hybrid of Pinot Noir and Hermitage – is unique to the Cape, and is soft, smooth, rarely bad, often wonderful and usually modestly priced. Spend a few rand on a couple of years of ageing on a Cabernet, Pinotage or a Cabernet blend.

Restaurant wine prices vary and fancy establishments generally load the prices of fashionable labels so the cost doesn't always justify the premium. The quality of middle-priced wines is almost as good as very expensive. At the other end of the scale, avoid wine by the glass or carafe except in good wine bars.

When it comes to **white wines**, it will probably always be difficult for the Cape to match the great white Burgundies, but progress has been made in the last few years and some notable Sauvignon Blancs, and lovely Sauvignon Blanc-Chardonnay blends have appeared. Remarkable Chardonnays are also available, although not for the budget-conscious.

In unpretentious restaurants, where food is the main event, more modest Chardonnays are usually available for an extra five to ten rands, but this isn't to say that the ordinary whites are not adequate or even pretty good.

Among the best of these are Blanc de Blancs, Blanc Fumés (wooded Sauvignon

Blancs), Rieslings, Rhine Rieslings, Chenin Blancs and some Traminers. Fortunately, the oddly named Premier Grand Crus have all but vanished.

Cheap, low-alcohol Fernão Pires (really a sort of grapeonade) is good for washing down with or after peri-peri and curries, for those who pass up the beer.

The Cape's superb **dessert wines** hold their own with any – this is the great Cape tradition of which Napoleon was a fan. An inexpensive luxury is a glass of iced Constantia Red Muscatel or Robertson Hanepoot or any of the sweet fortified wines, a category in which Cape winemakers excel. Try the naturally sweet late harvest dessert wines but even a small bottle of the 'big names' can be costly. Port labels to look out for: Allesverloren and Boplaas. In place of cognac, try KWV five-, ten- and twenty-year-old brandies.

The Cape's **sparkling wines** range from Cap Classiques, fermented in the bottle in the traditional champagne method, to inexpensive fizzes. Villeira's Tradition is made from classic Pinot Noir and Chardonnay. Pongrâcz won the trophy for best Method Champenoise at Britain's International Wine and Spirit Competition. Tank-fermented types include Nederburg Kap Sekt, made to German regulations. On the sweeter, Spumante-style side, try Cinzano and JC le Roux Le Domaine.

TOURING THE WINELANDS

Although Cape Town has reliable wine bars, liquor stores and wine shops, a trip to the winelands is practically obligatory, thoroughly enjoyable and one of the best and most economical ways to taste and buy local wines.

If your time's limited, do a morning tour of the three historical oldest Constantia wineries – Groot Constantia (the Cape's oldest), Klein Constantia and Buitenverwachting. A full-day trip should include Stellenbosch (visit Simonsig, Delheim, Rust en Vrede and/or Kanonkop) and Franschhoek (don't miss Boschendal, L'Ormarins and Clos Cabriere).

And if time permits, call at the Paarl wineries of Nederburg, Backsberg, KWV, Fairview and Landskroon. The Robertson and Tulbagh districts are further afield, but well worth visiting.

If you're buying by the label, look out for the great houses – Nederburg for everything, and the Bergkelder family. For whites try Klein Constantia, Buitenverwachting, Thelema, Hamilton Russel. For reds try Meerlust, Rust en Vrede, Overgaauw, Neethlingshof, the Pinotages of Kanonkop, Zonnebloem and Meerendal. And of course, there are others, including, if you know the right people, the exclusive KWV bottlings, particularly the older reds.

For more on the winelands see chapter **Day Trips**.

Rust en Vrede, one of the highly recommended estates on the Stellenbosch wine route.

WHERE TO EAT

From fish and chips to crayfish thermidor, curries to cheesecake, here are some of the nicest excuses for abandoning your diet. Reservations advisable.

HAUTE CUISINE

Buitenverwachting
Klein Constantia Rd, Constantia, tel. 794-3522.
Open: *noon-3pm Tue-Fri, 7pm-9pm Tue-Sat.*
Credit: *all cards and cheques.*
This must be one of South Africa's finest restaurants, living up to its name which means 'beyond expectation'. Set among sheltered vineyards on one of Constantia's original estates, the old homestead building contrasts with the spare, slightly exotic decor. The menu offers *prix fixe* or limited, but very fine, entrées. European chefs, personal service. Expensive by local standards, Buitenverwachting never fails to delight. It's fully licensed and the wines from the estate are also great.

Constantia Uitsig
Spaanschemat River Rd, Constantia, tel. 794-4480.
Open: *noon-2.30pm and 7pm-late daily.*
Credit: *all cards and cheques.*
Remarkable French, Provençal and Mediterranean food and splendid decor in elegant manor house overlooking the Constantia Valley. Casseroles, duck, excellent pasta – everything's of a high standard. Convivial, warm, inviting. Licensed.

Floris Smit Huijs
55 Church St, City Centre, tel. 23-3414.
Open: *noon-2.30pm and 7.30pm-10.30pm Mon-Sat.*
Credit: *all cards and cheques.*
Set in an exotically restored Cape Town house, Floris Smit is a visual and taste treat. The chandeliers are made from ostrich eggs and the walls of the two small, elegant dining rooms are covered with local art. The service is of high standard and starters like the pretty and delicious Collage (three seasonal soups separate but in the same bowl) set the tone for the rest of the evening's fare. Licensed.

Leinster Hall
7 Weltevreden St, Gardens, tel. 24-1836.
Open: *noon-3pm Mon-Fri, 7pm-10.30pm Mon-Sat.*
Credit: *major cards and cheques.*
An appealing setting (a national monument with lovely gardens and fountain), a terrace for summer dining, a lounge with a fire in winter, and interleading dining rooms make Leinster Hall a pretty smart place to dine. The decor's cheery, rather than appropriately grand, but even if it were a hole in the wall, it would be worth visiting for the duck in fig sauce, prawns in coconut milk, wonderful soups, veal ginger scaloppini and fried icecream. Menu changes seasonally. Licensed.

Mount Nelson Grill Room
Mount Nelson Hotel, 76 Orange St, Gardens, tel. 23-1000.
Open: *7pm-midnight daily.*
Credit: *all cards and cheques.*
Cape Town's premier dine-and-dance venue features a pianist Sun-Tue and a band Wed-Sat. A romantic, classy venue in lush red tones, it's dressy, romantic and intimate – just the place for a seduction, anniversary or celebration. The specialty is châteaubriand, but there's lots else, including Beluga caviar, giant tiger prawns, duck, springbok and rack of lamb. If you're determined to skip the luscious crêpes suzette, try the Cape malva pudding or the strawberries charlotte. Indulgence is mandatory. Impressive wine list. Round the evening off or begin it at the hotel's clubby, intimate Lord Nelson Bar.

Old Colonial
39 Barnet St, Gardens, tel. 45-4909.
Open: *noon-2pm Mon-Fri, 7pm-10pm Mon-Sat.*
Credit: *cards and cheques.*
The Old Colonial isn't madly trendy, but that's probably why it never goes out of fashion. It's housed in an historic cottage, with warm atmosphere, professional service and almost infallibly good, traditional food, some Swiss and Austrian, some South African – curries, bredies, duck, venison and seafood. Very established, and popular with business people and politicos. Booking advisable. Licensed.

The Restaurant at the Bay
The Bay Hotel, Victoria Rd, Camps Bay, tel. 438-4444.
Open: *7am-10.30am and 7pm-10.30pm Mon-Sat, 7am-11am Sun.*
Credit: *major cards and cheques.*
Not really frequented by locals, the Restaurant at the Bay is a good place for an expensive evening out. The room has a lovely view over Camps Bay, so make sure you sit by the window – the upper level is a bit of a visual Siberia. The food's elaborate, lots of strange but tasty combinations. Very attractive and attentive serving staff. Also superb for breakfast. Awarded a blazon by the *Chaines des Rotisseurs*. Licensed.

Rozenhof
18 Kloof St, Gardens, tel. 24-1968.
Open: *12.30pm-3.30pm Mon-Fri, 7pm-11pm Mon-Sat.*
Credit: *all cards and cheques.*
An 1852 Georgian house with separate dining rooms and classical music is the setting for this elegant and consistently fine restaurant. Regulars include politicians, top media brass and business people. Innovative, but unselfconscious cuisine based on fresh seasonal ingredients. Fully licensed.

1703 Room
Alphen Hotel, Alphen Drive, Constantia, tel. 794-5011.
Open: *7am-10am, 12.30pm-2.30pm and 7pm-10pm daily.*
Credit: *all cards; cheques by prior arrangement.*

An elegantly hushed manor house surrounded by oak trees and featuring typical Cape Dutch architecture, provides happy surprises with its modern, inventive dishes. Dishes featured include game, beef and polenta, crayfish half-smoked and half-roasted, and salmon *mille-feulle*. Sweet temptations include Stilton pie with poached cabernet pears and spiced honey parfait. Licensed.

MODERATE

Cuckoo's Nest
Mijlof Manor, 5 Military Rd, Tamboerskloof, tel. 26-1476.
Open: *7am-11.30pm daily.*
Credit: *all cards and bank-guaranteed cheques.*
Large, open and unpretentiously decorated, Cuckoo's Nest has Table Mountain views, friendly service and tasty, homey food. Everything's served in hearty helpings and you can't really go wrong with anything on the menu, but it's worth abandoning your diet for the oxtail and lamb pie. Licensed.

The Gardener's Cottage
Montebello Centre, 31 Newlands Ave, Newlands, tel. 689-3158.
Open: *7.30am-4.30pm Tue-Fri, 8.30am-4.30pm Sat-Sun.*
Credit: *all cards and cheques.*
Originally the gatekeeper's lodge, this tranquil, pretty eatery also has garden tables under camphor trees and squirrels running around. Natural, wholesome food with a fresh twist predominates – try the spinach and ricotta panzerroti, garlicky roasts on Sunday and chicken salad with apricots, almonds and creamy curry dressing. Fresh herbs, mainly grown on the premises, provide a wonderful edge. Brunch on public holidays includes heart- and body-warming dishes like haddock kedgeree, liver and bacon. Unlicensed.

On the Rocks
45 Stadler Rd, Bloubergstrand, tel. 56-1988.
Open: *noon-2pm Tue-Fri and Sun, 7pm-10pm Tue-Sun.*
Credit: *all cards and cheques.*

As the name suggests, On the Rocks is on the rocks. A bit of an oasis in Blouberg-strand's culinary wasteland, it offers good old-fashioned South African dining and beautiful Table Mountain, Table Bay and Robben Island views. Sunday's family day, but mid-week and week nights the climate's a bit more cosmopolitan. Licensed.

Peddlars On The Bend
Spaanschemat River Rd, Constantia, tel. 794-7747.
Open: noon-11pm daily.
Credit: all cards; cheques by prior arrangement.
Wholesome, hearty meals and fresh ingredients are the cornerstones of this warm, informal Cape Town institution. Try the fresh linefish, casseroles and Cape brandy pudding. Bar/tavern and dining area. Good value for money. Fully licensed.

Simply Delicious
105 Regent Rd, Sea Point, tel. 439-8504.
Open: noon-11pm daily, except Tue.
Credit: all cards; cheques with ID.
Tucked away in a narrow space is a great little eatery and Sea Point institution. The kitchen produces marvels, especially considering its size. The service can be very patchy, but the angels' hair pasta balsamico, Greek lamb and grilled chicken are excellent. The clientele's fairly arty. Though licensed for wine and beer, the management has a very liberal attitude towards bringing your own liquor. Booking advisable.

TRENDY & INTERESTING

Bistro
BMW Pavilion, Granger Bay Boulevard, Waterfront, tel. 418-4210/5.
Open: 10am-11pm daily.
Credit: major cards and cheques.
Post-modern decor with lots of metal and picture windows are the setting for a line-up of dishes like rare roast beef fillet with wild mushroom risotto, trio of linefish, seafood and steak tartare. Light meals, filled baguettes and scrumptious puddings like chocolate tower, bread and butter pudding and poppyseed cheesecake also star. The trendy sister to the City Centre's Chez Simone.

Blues
9 The Promenade, Victoria Rd, Camps Bay, tel. 438-2040.
Open: noon-midnight daily.
Credit: all cards and cheques.
Pretty is the word that springs to mind here – pretty clientele, pretty waiters, sparklingly pretty sea views. The decor in this airy, large restaurant is unobtrusive but appealing, with an open kitchen area, and Blues has remained one of South Africa's most fashionable eateries for years – this is trendy people and visiting celeb turf. The Californian menu ranges from seafood to pasta, but the food is very patchy and quality can vary wildly. The wine and cocktail list is good, and as long as you're not set on finding the ultimate meal and your budget is fairly hefty, it's a most seductive environment.

Cafe Erté
265 Main Rd, Sea Point, tel. 434-6624.
Open: 7pm-late daily.
Credit: all cards and cheques.
With board games, light meals, music videos, cocktails and slightly tacky OTT decor, this coffee bar and eatery is a terrific place to tête-à-tête. Grab a corner couch.

Café Paradiso
110 Kloof St, Gardens, tel. 23-8653 or 23-5556.
Open: 9am-11pm daily.
Credit: cards and cheques.
Café Paradiso has a wine bar, patio, delicatessen, indoor restaurant and small gift/groceries shop. The food's consistently good, with daily specials, and excellent salads, casseroles and delicious puddings and cakes. Unpretentious, informal and definitely the prettiest place to buy late night milk. Licensed.

Chariots
104 Main Rd, Green Point, tel. 434-5427.
Open: 9.30am-11pm Mon-Thu, 9.30am-midnight Fri-Sun.
Credit: cards and cheques.

Beautiful people and a buzz at Chariots.

Looking around Chariots, you'd be forgiven for believing that only rich, gorgeous and trendy people are allowed in. Drop-dead fashionable, with good salads, light meals, cakes and a bar area, but you can go for cappuccino and rubbernecking. It's decorated with *faux* marble pillars and model types.

Col'Cacchio
Seeff House, 42 Hans Strydom Ave, Foreshore, tel. 419-4848.
Open: *noon-2.30pm Mon-Fri, 6.30pm-11pm daily.*
Credit: *cards; cheques with ID.*
How can one not love a place which serves cream and caviar pizza? Col'Cacchio's star turn is pizzas – light-crust designer ones, with toppings like peri-peri prawns, spiced chicken, clams, mussels and calamari. Don't miss the cassata. Pretty, with paint-finished walls and candelabra. Unlicensed.

Dunes
Beach Crescent, Hout Bay Beach (Chapman's Peak side), Hout Bay, tel. 790-1876.
Open: *noon-5pm and 7pm-10.30pm daily.* *(Sometimes closed for lunch and Mon in winter.)*
Credit: *all cards and bank-guaranteed cheques.*
Very pretty, yellow-toned beach cottage with spectacular views, practically a hop from the sea. The inventive Californian menu includes seafood, pasta and positively dangerous puddings like tiramisú, hazelnut crêpes and port litchis stuffed with roquefort. Begin with a drink at the upstairs bar, and watch out for Romeo the parrot. Licensed.

Emily's
77 Roodebloem St, Woodstock, tel. 448-2366.
Open: *noon-2pm Tue-Fri, 7pm-10.30pm Tue-Sat.*
Credit: *major cards and cheques.*
Casual, convivial, nicely offbeat atmosphere and very good value for money, with great bistro food – terrines, linefish, bredie, and chicken with jerepigo and moskonfyt (jam). Emily's has been a winner since it began, and it continues to deliver delicious treats. Not licensed.

Fiddlewoods
40 Trill Rd, Observatory, tel. 448-6687.
Open: *8am-5pm Mon-Fri, 7pm-late Fri, 8.30am-2pm Sat-Sun.*
Credit: *all cards (except AmEx) and cheques.*
One of those happy, relaxed eateries that invite a carefree lazy time, especially over breakfast, Fiddlewoods is a pretty, brightly painted restaurant with a small outdoor patio. It's often packed at lunchtime and features excellent value for money – generous portions and well-flavoured breakfasts (including vegetarian), light meals, pastas and main dishes like fillet stirfry and spanakopita. The specials are inventive – vegetable couscous and spinach and feta soup – and the puddings and daily cakes are diet-breaking delights. Friday nights feature live, but unobtrusive music and a bistro menu. Licensed.

i-Café
273 Long St, City Centre, tel. 24-6576.
Open: *10am-2am Mon-Sat, 6pm-2am Sun.*
Credit: *cards and cheques.*
i-Café is just the ticket for Internet surfers and computer nuts. For R10 an hour you get access to Internet, computers, printing and scanning facilities and you can open an e-mail address here. And that's not all. The atmosphere is relaxed and inviting. Plus the food's good – soup, baquettes, patés, dish of the day, a full license and teriffic cocktails – not that the hardcore Internet junkies notice what they're eating ...

Jaws
41 Victoria Rd, Camps Bay, tel. 438-1213.
Open: *5pm-late Mon-Sat.*
Credit: *all cards and cheques.*
This modern, elegant restaurant delivers the Cape's most renowned offerings – views, wines and seafood. It's one of the few sources of giant wild Knysna oysters, and other indigenous specialties include good game and unusual biltong-based meals (biltong, like beef jerky, is dried, salted meat). Vegetarian dishes are innovative and starters are beautifully presented and recommended. The sister restaurant at the Waterfront Aquarium is more moderately priced.

La Med
Glen Country Club, below Victoria Rd, Clifton, tel. 438-5600.
Open: *11am-2am Tue-Sun.*
Credit: *cards and cheques.*
Favourite watering hole for ageing hippies and surfing yuppies, La Med gets full marks for location (on the bluffs, overlooking the sea), and there are few places better to be than at one of the stone tables at sunset. It's fully licensed and serves food – sort of (mussels, salads, seafood). Fish braais in summer.

Parks
114 Constantia Rd, Wynberg, tel. 797-8202.
Open: *noon-1.45pm Tue-Fri, 7.30pm-8.45pm Mon-Sat.*
Credit: *cards and cheques.*
When well-known restaurateur Michael Olivier quit Hermanus to return to Cape Town, there was much excitement among the locals. His previous restaurant, The Burgundy, had been one of the best-loved establishments outside the city. For his Cape Town restaurant, Olivier chose a big Victorian house in Wynberg, which he lavishly restored, creating a series of cosy and invitingly warm rooms. The service is excellent and the wine list is extensive and modestly priced. The food is standard fare lifted beyond the ordinary, not too glamorous to be intimidating. No flash in the pan, Parks has retained its popularity since its opening crush and patrons often have to book several weeks in advance. Licensed.

Quay Four
Pierhead, Waterfront, tel. 21-2088 or 419-2009.
Open: *restaurant: noon-3pm and 6.30pm-midnight daily, pub: 9am-midnight daily.*
Credit: *major cards and cheques.*
Quay Four has truly splendid views, and is cleverly divided into a very popular, casual terrace eatery, a tavern, and an à la carte upstairs restaurant. The extensive restaurant menu ranges from Thai-style calamari or roast duckling to rump steak or seafood platter. There's a broad wine list and a very tempting dessert trolley – try the mango

mousse if it's in season, and the langoustine or crayfish if you're in the money.

Roxy Coffee
14 Wandel St, Gardens, tel. 461-4092.
Open: *7pm-2am Mon-Fri, 7pm-2am daily (extended hours in season).*
Credit: *Mc, V, Diners and cheques.*
Bohemian eatery with witty decor of B-grade movie posters, crowded tables and a Dinky car-decorated ceiling for the amusement of strenuously partied-out diners. Try the salads, hot meals, boozy coffees and cakes.

Rustica
70 New Church St, City Centre (the entrance is on Buitengracht St, next to In-Fin Art), tel. 23-5474.
Open: *noon-3pm Mon-Fri, 6pm-11pm daily.*
Credit: *cards and cheques.*
Rustica hit the ground running when fashionable and beautiful people immediately turned it into their mecca. It's crowded and convivial, with lots of table hopping and a roof garden and bar. Begin with homebaked bread and olive oil. From then on, the large choice of well-priced Californian-style Mediterranean food includes butternut gnocchi, steamed mussels, garlic roast chicken and damn-the-calories desserts, including tiramisú, which is to the 90s what power breakfasts were to the 80s. Reservations advisable.

Scoozi
Lower Mall, Cavendish Square, Claremont, tel. 683-5458/9.
Open: *9am-11pm Mon-Sat.*
Credit: *all cards and cheques.*
Large, chic and buzzy, Scoozi offers a wine bar (where you can also order a meal or coffee), breakfast, lunch and dinners. It's right next to the cinema and it's perfect for shoppers who are about to drop. Champagne/liqueurs by the glass, imported beers and good wine. The eclectic menu ranges from bagels to pasta, (sort of) Thai and fish. There are daily specials and an irresistible cake display. Happy vibe and attractive, smart decor. Licensed and moderately priced.

The elegant interior of A Table at Colin's, a restaurant set in an historic Cape Dutch building.

A Table at Colin's
Martin Melck House, 96 Strand St, City Centre, tel. 419-6533.
Open: *12.30pm-2.15pm Mon-Fri, 7.30pm-10pm Mon-Sat.*
Credit: *cards and cheques.*
Though it provides good, not exceptional food, it's hard to beat the experience of an evening here. Set in Martin Melck House (he was a wealthy 18th century burgher) it exudes Cape charm. The back rooms overlook a pretty walled garden with a lily pond. The food is Cape modern – meat, game, poultry and fish with contemporary flair. Agreeable staff. Licensed.

CHEAP & CHEERFUL

The Crypt
St George's Cathedral, 1 Wale St, City Centre, tel. 23-1936.
Open: *7.30am-4pm Mon-Fri.*
Credit: *cards and cheques.*
Housed in the crypt of St George's Cathedral (1834), it has stone walls embedded with historic tablets and drapes. There's an outdoor tea garden in summer, and leaded bay windows provide glimpses of the Company Gardens. Reserve the cushioned window seats. Simple, home cooking with daily specials, all-day breakfasts, light meals, bottomless coffee – and all under R15.

Don Pedro's
113 Roodebloem Rd, Woodstock, tel. 47-4493.
Open: *7pm-2am daily.*
Credit: *Mc, V and cheques.*
Once a favourite ANC intelligentsia haunt, Don Pedro's still attracts an equally politically correct but younger crowd, creative folk and bohemians. The food and drink is inexpensive, the clientele expansive. Fresh fish and good pizzas, plus daily specials – always extremely good fare at fair prices. Fully licensed.

Duck's
12 Kloof Nek Rd, Tamboerskloof, tel. 23-4246.
Open: *9am-late Tue-Sat, 9am-5pm Sun-Mon.*
Credit: *Mc, V and cheques.*
Breakfasts average R12, lunches go for R13 and specials, including vegetarian, are around R15 at this cottagey restaurant set in an old house. The crowd ranges from grannies to the rowdier crowd who hang out at the bar. Drinks at half-price 5pm-7pm Fri. The soups are filling and good value for money.

Kuzma's
91 Main Rd, Rondebosch, tel. 689-3762.
Open: *8.30am-4.45am Mon-Sat, 8.30am-4pm and 6pm-3.45am Sun.*
Credit: *all cards but no cheques.*
More filling than snacks, but less than a full meal is the order of the day here – burgers, stuffed pitas, shwarmas and energy-replenishing puddings. Local fans have frequented this haunt for a decade and it's a very flexible social vibe. Early evening attracts an older crowd and later into the night, clubbers hit the place. Comfortable and relaxed.

Mr Pickwick's
158 Long St, City Centre, tel. 24-2696.
Open: *8am-2am Mon-Tue, 8am-4am Wed-Sat.*
Credit: *cards and cheques.*
Terrific value-for-money oversized sandwiches, soups, cakes, pastas and hefty, homey meals served on tin plates. It's fully licensed with friendly staff and a great vibe.

The Planet
3 Station Rd, Observatory, tel. 47-3589.
Open: *7pm-1.30am daily.*
Credit: *cards and cheques.*
A true raver's den with an upstairs bar and live music on weekends (when there's a R2 cover charge). The Greek-oriented menu has some unexpected items like curry and two burgers for the price of one (on Tue). Happy hour, with half-price drinks, is 7pm-8.30pm. Hearty, plain meals average R15 and the crowd is laid-back, arty and bohemian.

The Ploughman's Pub & Bar
3 Church Square, Parliament St, City Centre, tel. 45-4597.
Open: *7am-7pm Mon-Fri, 7am-2pm Sat.*
Credit: *all cards and cheques.*
The hokey decor, worn upholstery and plastic table mats haven't deterred everyone from parliamentarians and cabinet ministers to meter maids from making the Ploughman's their regular haunt. And for good reason. This is the place for a square, homestyle meal – sandwiches, pastas, breakfasts and jolly good steak and kidney pie.

Spanish Gardens Bistro
Tex Arcade, Main Rd, Claremont, tel. 61-0441.
Open: *7pm-2.30am daily.*
Credit: *cards and cheques.*
The only concession to Spain in the Spanish Gardens is bullfighting posters, and you get to it via a little alley. This is kitchen chairs and paraffin lamps territory. But the vibe is warm, and the food is excellent value for money – a huge range of liqueurs, boozy hot chocolates and coffees, and generous portions for under R20. Olé!

Theresa's Restaurant
11 Palmer Rd, Muizenberg, tel. 788-8051.
Open: *8.30am-4pm Tue-Fri and Sun, 8.30am-2pm Sat, 7pm-10.30pm Wed-Sat.*
Credit: *cards and cheques.*
Bohemian-budget with odd metal and wooden chairs, sackcloth ceiling and yellow walls. The menu – hearty, big servings – includes enormous English breakfast (R10,95), daily specials and excellent

casseroles, lamb curry and salads. A sociable hangout for local writers, artists, surfers and professionals. Licensed, but you're welcome to bring your own drinks.

BREAKFASTS & LIGHT MEALS

Atlantic Express Cake & Coffee Train
1b Regent Rd, Sea Point, tel. 439-3038.
Open: *8am-1.30am daily.*
Credit: *cards but no cheques.*
There's something irresistible about sitting in a train carriage in the middle of a main road. Fun for tête-à-têtes, full English breakfasts, light meals, stuffed pancakes and late-night cake and Irish coffee. Licensed.

Café Bodega
Picbel Parkade, Strand St, City Centre, tel. 419-1708.
Open: *7am-5.30pm Mon-Fri, 7am-1pm Sat.*
Credit: *cards; cheques by prior arrangement.*
This charming little luncheon place has been a favourite with middle-aged movers and shakers and city folk for years. The food's German – sausage, bratwurst and great goulash. The daily special's tasty, filling and good value and the adjacent patisserie, also owned by Café Bodega, sells delicious home-made chocolates.

Café Matisse
76 Main Rd, Kalk Bay, tel. 788-1123.
Open: *9.30am-11pm daily. Closed on Tue in winter.*
Credit: *all cards and cheques (at a push).*
Pretty café with adjacent shop, Matisse-inspired friezes and relaxed atmosphere. All-day breakfast, pizza, cakes, light meals. It's one of the nicest places to laze away an afternoon – there's beer/wine by the glass and chess, scrabble, backgammon and cards.

Café Mozart
37 Church St, City Centre, tel. 24-3774.
Open: *7am-3.30pm Mon-Fri, 8am-1pm Sat.*
Credit: *Mc, V, AmEx and cheques.*
Set between street stalls, antique shops, and art galleries, Café Mozart is great people-watching territory, with outside and inside tables and reliable, plain fare like soups, sandwiches and cakes. Not licensed.

Charly's Waterfront Café
Shop 152, Ground Floor, Victoria Wharf, Waterfront, tel. 418-5522/3.
Open: *9am-6pm Mon-Tue, 9am-midnight Wed-Sun.*
Credit: *cards and cheques.*
Breakfasts, light meals, cakes and a daily buffet with a selection of quiches, pies and delicious salads are Charly's stock in trade. Its outside seating area, with great views of the passing parade, is a very popular hangout, one of *the* Waterfront social spots. The decor's bright and casual.

Chicco Coffee & Confection
Shop 5b, Adelphi Centre, Main Rd, Sea Point, tel. 434-7987.
Open: *8am-5pm Mon-Fri, 8.30am-1.30pm Sat.*
Credit: *Mc, V and cheques.*
Very pleasant, informal coffee bar with counters and some outside tables in the shopping centre. Good, fresh rolls and salads, a nice selection of coffees to consume on premises or to make at home, as well as cookies, make this a popular meeting place.

EmGees
49 Cologne House, St George's Mall, City Centre, tel. 24-5507.
Open: *7am-7pm Mon-Fri, 8am-3pm Sat.*
Credit: *cards but no cheques.*

Shop 6, Corwen Rd, Claremont, tel. 61-7351.
Open: *7am-8pm Mon-Fri (kitchen closes at 4pm), 8am-2pm Sat.*
Credit: *cards but no cheques.*
Coffees, cakes, sandwiches, lunch specials and light meals in convivial surroundings. The City Centre branch has indoor and outdoor seating – brilliant for people-watching. Licensed.

Foti's
375 Main Rd, Observatory, tel. 448-6938.
Open: *8am-7pm Mon-Fri and Sun, 8am-3pm Sat.*

Credit: *no cards or cheques for bakery; for restaurant, major cards accepted.*
Bakery with notable Greek biscuits, chocolate cake and croissants. The restaurant is extremely basic – not decor so much as furniture (in this case, corner café tables and slasto floors). But that, along with light snacks and Sunday roast lunch, is part of the charm. Lots of regulars, including the odd Sartre-reading beatnik. Not licensed.

Giovanni's Deliworld
103 Main Rd, Green Point, tel. 434-6893.
Open: *8.30am-9pm daily.*
Credit: *cards and cheques.*
With its buzzy vibe, small, crowded coffee-counter and tempting Italian foods, breads, take-outs and cappuccinos, Giovanni's is simply one of *the* places to be.

Hartlief Gourmet
Shop 32 Gardens Centre, Mill St, Gardens, tel. 45-2729.
Open: *8.30am-6pm Mon-Thu, 8am-6pm Fri, 8am-1pm Sat.*
Credit: *cards and cheques.*
Cape Town's answer to those marvellous Hamburg delis – dauntingly efficient and hyper-organised, with superb meat, breads, steak tartare rolls and German specialties.

The Italian Coffee Shop
34 Parliament St, City Centre, tel. 461-5195.
Open: *7am-4pm Mon-Fri, 8.30am-1pm Sat.*
Credit: *cards and cheques.*
Quaint and charming for breakfast, lunch and coffee. Popular with everyone from parliamentarians to pretty people.

The Jolly Roger
Alfred Mall, Waterfront, tel. 419-6485.
Open: *9am-7pm daily (extended weekend hours if it's busy).*
Credit: *major cards and cheques.*
Light meals, breakfasts and cakes in comfortable café, with views of the harbour, seagulls and mountain.

Kirstenbosch Gardens Tea House
Kirstenbosch, Rhodes Drive, Newlands, tel. 797-7614.

The crowded espresso bar at Giovanni's Deliworld.

Open: *9am-5pm Mon-Sat, 8.30am-5pm Sun.*
Credit: *major cards; cheques by prior arrangement.*
Simple, basic food – English breakfasts, roasts, snacks and renowned apple tart – in a family-oriented eatery with outdoor and indoor tables. The food and decor's plain, but the botanical garden setting is dazzling.

La Playa
Shop 224, Victoria Wharf, Waterfront, tel. 418-2800.
Open: *9am-1am Mon-Sun.*
Credit: *major cards and cheques.*
Popular, swish-ish hang-out with outside and inside seating, light meals, good cakes and coffees. Cheery, airy vibe and social buzz.

Le Petit Paris
36 Burg St, City Centre, tel. 237-648.
Open: *7am-6pm Mon-Sat.*
Credit: *all cards (except AmEx) and cheques.*
Splendid people-watching turf overlooking Greenmarket Square, Le Petit Paris is beloved by beautiful people, models and trendies. Small, often crowded and fun, with baguettes, toasted sandwiches, croissants and bistro-style lunch specials.

Mark's Coffee Bar
105 St George's Mall, City Centre, tel. 24-8516.
Open: *6.30am-4.30pm Mon-Thu, 6.30am-4pm Fri, 7am-noon Sat.*
Credit: *cards and cheques.*

The colonial splendour of high tea at the Mount Nelson.

Mark's bills itself as Cape Town's oldest coffee shop. It's certainly well-established, popular and practically headquarters for newspaper folk. Cosy, old-fashioned booths indoors, and outside tables in summer. No fireworks, but basic, homey breakfast, daily specials, cakes, good coffee and wonderful service from waitresses who've worked there for years.

High tea at the Mount Nelson Hotel
Mount Nelson Hotel, Orange St, Gardens, tel. 23-1000.
Open: *high tea is served 2.30pm-5.30pm daily.*
Credit: *cards and cheques.*
Ditch the diet and treat yourself to the Nellie's irresistible temptation. An antique table (a relic of a Union Castle Liner which once sailed between Britain and Cape Town), is laden with gateaux, patisserie, cucumber and smoked salmon sandwiches, cream scones and local delicacies like Cape brandy tart. The setting is divine – English country house decor with plush conversation corners. In winter there's a fire, in summer take tea in the conservatory or on the terrace. One of those experiences which serves as a useful reminder that life is grand. R32,50 per person.

New York Bagel Deli
51 Regent Rd, Sea Point, tel. 439-7523.
Open: *8am-8pm daily.*
Credit: *major cards and cheques.*
Easy-going, well-priced deli with a good range of pickles, meats, pastries, breads, take-out and chopped liver as good as bobba's. Which is not to overlook the bagels – cinnamon and raisin, onion, wholewheat, pumpernickel and the Everything Bagel for those who can't decide. Well-priced hamburgers and hot beef on rye available for consumption at frequently crowded counters.

The Quarterdeck
Jubilee Square, Simon's Town, tel. 786-3825.
Open: *9am-4.30pm Mon-Sat, 9.30am-4.30 Sun.*

Credit: all cards and cheques.
The Quarterdeck serves solid, if not madly inspiring, breakfasts, light meals and teas. With marvellous harbour views and a terrace, it's also a relaxed environment for families and kids. Unpretentious, easy-going and conveniently *en route* to Cape Point.

Rhodes Memorial Tea Garden
Rhodes Estate, Rondebosch, tel. 689-9151.
Open: 9.30am-5pm Tue-Fri, 9.30am-5.30pm Sat, 1pm-5.30pm Sun.
Credit: Mc and V; cheques by prior arrangement.
Set on the slopes of Devil's Peak, above Rhodes Memorial, the Tea Garden offers gorgeous views of the suburbs and Hottentots-Holland from the outside patio and a cosy cottage. Sandwiches, cakes, Sunday lunch roast, daily specials.

Rieses Delicatessen
367 Main Rd, Sea Point, tel. 434-1938 or 434-3465.
Open: 8.30-7pm daily, and in summer till around 8.30pm.
Credit: major cards and cheques.
Smart and well established, Rieses has deli meats, cheeses, fish and breads, a coffee bar and popular outdoor tables. Emergency supplies of exotic imported and pre-cooked foods – providing you're happy to pay the price for delicious convenience.

San Marco
128 Victoria Wharf, Waterfront, tel. 418-5434.
Open: 8am-midnight Sun-Thu, 8am-1am Fri-Sat.
Credit: cards but no cheques.
This is *the* place to shmooze at the Waterfront. The outdoor views are particularly good, by which we don't mean only the water and seagulls, but the people-parade as well. Cappuccino, good salads, sandwiches, pastas and great ice-creams. Lovely for a light lunch or dinner. Licensed.

Sugar Loaf Café
261a Main Rd, Sea Point, tel. 434-4421 or 434-4106.
Open: 9am-5pm Mon-Sat.
Credit: Mc, V and cheques.
Unpretentious, friendly café with some outdoor tables and a straightforward menu of coffees and light meals.

Threshers Tea Garden
Josephine Mill, Boundary Road, Newlands, tel. 685-6233.
Open: 8.30am-4.30pm Mon-Fri, 8.30am-2pm Sat, 8.30am-5.30pm Sun.
Credit: Mc, V and cheques.
Housed in Cape Town's only surviving and operational water mill (established in 1840), Threshers Tea Garden is a terrific breakfast place. Snacks, lunches, specialty salads, soups in winter, quiches, pies and ploughman's platters too. The bread, baked on the premises, is beautifully fresh.

The Yellow Pepper Deli
138 Long St, City Centre, tel. 24-9250.
Open: 8.30am-5pm Mon-Sat and 7.30pm-11pm Fri-Sat.
Credit: cards and cheques.
Located a stroll away from Greenmarket Square, between Long St's bohemian collectables stores and bookshops, The Yellow Pepper has location on its side. It's also pretty, convivial and popular, with tasty, reasonably priced hot and cold buffets like grilled peppers (natch), lamb pie, vegetarian lasagna, moussaka, mezze, design-your-own salads, cold platters and baguettes so large that they're a logistical challenge.

Zerban's and H&H Cake and Coffee
The Promenade, Victoria Rd, Camps Bay, tel. 438-2322.
Open: 8am-6pm daily.
Credit: major cards and cheques.

Zerban's, Gardens Centre, Mill St, Gardens, tel. 461-4060.
Open: 7am-6pm Mon, Tue and Thu, 7am-10pm Wed and Fri, 7am-2pm Sat, 9am-2pm Sun.
Credit: major cards and cheques.
Established café chain with cachet, coffee and cakes. Zerban's also does German dishes and light meals. The cakes look marvel-

Long Street's Yellow Pepper Deli.

lous, but sometimes taste rather factory line, however, the pastries, all-day breakfast and breads are excellent. The Camps Bay branch has great beach views. The Gardens branch is a well-run institution and does a fuller, twice-weekly dinner – chicken schnitzel, oriental chicken curry, duck ...

FISH & SEAFOOD

Black Marlin
Main Rd, Millers Point, Simon's Town, tel. 786-1621.
Open: *noon-3pm daily, 7pm-10pm Fri-Sat (winter) and Mon-Sat (summer).*
Credit: *all cards and bank-guaranteed cheques.*
Loads of tour buses hit the Black Marlin en route from Cape Point, and it's known for fresh fish and seafood and marvellous sea views from the patio tables. Kids', vegetarian and non-fish menu available. There's also a bar and marquee. A relaxing venue with an impressive wine list.

Brass Bell
Kalk Bay Station, Main Rd, Kalk Bay, tel. 788-5455/6.
Open: *12.30pm-3pm and 6.30pm-10.30pm daily.*
Credit: *all cards; cheques by prior arrangement.*
A favourite watering hole next to the sea, across the railway tracks, the Brass Bell is a veritable institution, commanding magnificent views across the bay. The smartish, à la carte restaurant specialises in fish and seafood. The next-door pub is cheerful, open all day and relaxed. And downstairs is an open-air patio for fish barbecues and light meals. There's a convivial vibe, wide range of ages and classes, and swimming literally a stone's throw away. Licensed.

Chapman's Peak Hotel
Main Rd, Hout Bay, tel. 790-1036.
Open: *noon-3pm and 6pm-9.30pm daily.*
Credit: *all cards and bank-guaranteed cheques.*
You may have to fight for a good terrace table or wait ages for your food, but fans would do more than that for the pan-fried calamari. There's also linefish, crayfish, prawns, seafood platters, steaks and chicken peri-peri. Friendly and informal. Licensed.

Delmitchies
78 Main Rd, Sea Point, tel. 434-0726.
Open: *7.30pm-late Mon-Thu, 7pm-late Fri-Sat. Open for lunch in season or occasions like Mother's Day.*
Credit: *major credit cards; cheques by prior arrangement.*
Delmitchies is heaven for seafood lovers who can't make up their minds. For around R60, you get starters, home-baked bread, mussel chowder soup, then as much as you can eat and select from the buffet – veggies, salads, pastas, casseroles and an assortment of calamari, linefish, prawns and more. Nice puddings and coffee included. All food is halaal. Licensed.

Europa
78 Regent Rd, Sea Point, tel. 439-2820 or 439-3369.
Open: *noon-2.30pm daily, 6pm-10pm Tue-Fri, 6pm-11pm Sat-Sun.*
Credit: *all cards and cheques.*
Set in an old house, Europa is a local fixture. It's best at lunch if you have time and can sit outside and get slightly tipsy on chilled Cape wine. The fish is good, though not exceptional, but the overall ambience is pleasant and relaxed and the paella renowned. There are also special 'early' low-price menus. Licensed.

Fisherman's Cottage
3 Gray Rd, Plumstead, tel. 797-6341.
Open: *12.30pm-2pm Tue-Fri, 7pm-10pm Tue-Sat.*
Credit: *all cards and cheques.*
Housed in one of the area's oldest buildings, this enormously popular cottage restaurant concentrates on fresh ingredients and gimmick-free food. The focused menu includes trout tartare, prawns in olive oil and garlic, grilled fish and seafood. There's also good steak and veal. Not licensed.

Harbour Tavern
49 Beach Rd, Mouille Point, tel. 439-1470.
Open: *noon-10.30pm Mon-Sat.*
Credit: *major cards and bank-guaranteed cheques.*
Longstanding seaview restaurant with no frills, but lots of seafood to choose from a large tank. Live crayfish, oysters and black mussels as well as Portuguese dishes. Licensed.

The Mussel Cracker
222 Victoria Wharf, Waterfront, tel. 419-4300/1.
Open: *12.30pm-2.30pm and 6.30pm-10.30pm daily.*
Credit: *major cards and cheques.*
Great buffet beginning with homemade bread, anchovy butter, fish paté and seafood soup. Hot and cold dishes include roast tuna, herring, gravadlax, seafood casserole, fish bobotie, casseroles and tons of vegetables. Puddings include lemon meringue and pecan nut pies. Fully licensed.

Panama Jack's Tavern
Quay 500 (off Goliath Rd), Cape Town Docks, tel. 47-3992.
Open: *noon-3.30pm Mon-Fri and Sun, 7pm-late daily.*
Credit: *major cards and cheques.*
There's something charming about a warm, inviting eatery set in the docks, and Panama Jack's boasts appealing simplicity and informality. The menu is limited and, anyway, most people go for the crayfish which are priced according to weight. It's convivial fun, but despite the simplicity of the setting, it's not exactly cheap. Friendly service. Licensed.

WEST COAST FISH BARBECUES

You may drive for up to two hours, but there's nothing like eating freshly barbecued fish, seafood, traditional stews, and bread baked in an open fire, right next to the beach. The appeal of these venues is the informality and authenticity – at some, mussel shells substitute for cutlery and plates are paper. Go hungry, and take sunscreen and a sweater. Booking advisable.

Die Strandloper, *Langebaan, tel. (02281) 5-1611.*

Muisbosskerm, *Lamberts Bay, tel. (027) 432-1017.*

Pampoenkraal, *Durbanville, tel. 689-9642.*

ETHNIC

Africa Café   AFRICAN
213-Lower Main Rd, Observatory, tel. 47-9553.
Open: *noon-3pm Mon-Fri, 6.30pm-midnight Mon-Sat.*
Credit: *major cards and cheques.*
One of the first mainstream restaurants to bring the exciting tastes of the Dark Continent to light, Africa Café has an earnest student quality about it. Chickpea and chicken dishes abound, and the menu covers most areas of Africa, from the Côte d'Ivoire and Nigeria to closer to home. Waiters will guide you through uncharted waters. If you want a taste of African cuisine and not just South African food, this is a good place to start. Licensed.

Mama Africa Restaurant and Bar
178 Long St, City Centre, tel. 24-8634.
Open: *12am-3pm and 7pm-11pm Mon-Sat. The bar stays open much later, and can close as late as 4am.*
Credit: *cards and cheques.*
Mainly South African dishes like ostrich steak, stews, Cape Malay roast lamb, oxtail as well as poultry and fish feature on the menus here, but the food isn't the main attraction (in fact it can be rather standard). The best thing about Mama Africa is the decor – a cavernous space, it features a python-shaped bar, bamboo-covered walls and Zulu shields. The mood is relaxed and it's extremely popular. Booking is advisable for Friday and Saturday.

The Balkan   BULGARIAN
30 Shortmarket St, City Centre, tel. 24-9337.
Open: *noon-3pm and 7pm-late Mon-Sat.*
Credit: *major cards but no cheques.*
Bulgaria may not be famous for haute cuisine, but they sure know how to have a good time at The Balkan. This basement restaurant was established by emigrants, and hearty servings of spicy, homestyle cooking (like kebab, peppers, meatballs and casseroles) and fruit brandies are just some of the ways in which they're enlivening Cape Town. Warm atmosphere and lavish hospitality. Bulgarian wines are served and there's an international wine shop next door. Licensed.

Morton's on the Wharf   CAJUN/CREOLE
Shop 221, Victoria Wharf, Waterfront, tel. 418-3633/4.
Open: *noon-3pm and 6.30pm-11pm daily.*
Credit: *major cards and bank-guaranteed cheques.*
Noisy, fantastically popular New Orleans-style bistro with outdoor and indoor seating. Cajun dishes like blackened linefish, barbecue shrimp, seafood gumbo and puddings like chocolate mousse cake and chocolate brownies feature. Booking essential. Licensed.

Kaapse Tafel   CAPE DUTCH
Montreux Bldg, 90 Queen Victoria St, City Centre, tel. 23-1651.
Open: *noon-3pm and 6pm-10.30pm Mon-Sat.*

Credit: *all cards and cheques.*
An unlikely looking building for such a restaurant, but inside it's warm and cosy, as is the food which tends toward hearty Cape cooking. If you want authentic Cape traditional, this is the place – from waterblommetjiebredie (a stew with waterlilies – actually delicious) to bobotie (a spicy Cape curry). Save room for malva tart or Cape brandy pudding. No dieters allowed.

Andy's Bistro   FRENCH
5 Clarens Rd, Sea Point, tel. 439-2470.
Open: *7pm-11pm daily (lunches by prior arrangement).*
Credit: *all cards; cheques by prior arrangement.*
A typical bistro – glowing yellow light, candles in wine bottles, wintertime fire and buzzy, close-set tables. Although not as cheap as you might imagine, the blackboard menu features dishes like onion soup, fillet and the specialties of the house – braised oxtail and duck. Homey, comfortable food with no fireworks and a friendly, longstanding and very convivial vibe. Licensed.

Au Jardin   FRENCH
Vineyard Hotel, Colinton Rd, Newlands, tel. 683-1520.
Open: *noon-2pm Tue-Fri, 7.15pm-9pm Mon-Sat.*
Credit: *all cards and cheques.*
Au Jardin was an instant success, and its high standards, inventive touches and inviting atmosphere make it one of the city's most outstanding restaurants. Stroll through the surrounding gardens with their wonderful mountain views and then prepare to relinquish your diet for the sake of culinary delight. Fully licensed.

Bistrôt La Boheme   FRENCH
52 Barnet St, Gardens, tel. 45-2550.
Open: *noon-3pm and 6pm-11pm Mon-Sat.*
Credit: *all cards; cheques with ID.*
A crowd-pleaser with a sexy, warm vibe and closely set tables, La Boheme is a favourite with politicos and business people, and provided you don't mind the proximity of fel-

low diners, it's a wonderful place for a seduction. French Mediterranean fare starting with a tray of antipasto or onion soup, and following with choices like bouillabaisse, good oxtail casserole and Moroccan lamb couscous. Well-priced. Licensed.

Chêz Simone   FRENCH
Thibault Square, City Centre, tel. 21-7736.
Open: noon-2.30pm Mon-Fri. (Dinner served in summer.)
Credit: major cards and cheques.
Chêz Simone is one of Cape Town's most renowned and established restaurants. The food is consistently good, the decor crisp and smart, and the service professional. Not surprisingly, this is media-Mafia and power-broker turf. Inventive, but unpretentious dishes include roast rack of lamb, notable linefish and chicken breast stuffed with feta and spinach. Booking essential. Licensed.

Maria's   GREEK
31 Barnet St, Gardens, tel. 45-2096.
Open: 12.30pm-11pm Mon-Fri, 6pm-11pm Sat-Sun.
Credit: all cards and cheques.
Set in sociable, buzzy Dunkley Square, Maria's has a downstairs and upstairs section, and an outside piazza in summer. Taverna decor and food – lamb, spanakopita, aubergine and starters like dolmades and hummus. There's no culinary drama and the service can be slow, but this is a local institution with a good buzz and it's a fine place for a party. Not licensed.

Bi-Bi's Kitchen   INDIAN
Broad Rd, Medicentre, Wynberg, tel. 797-1054.
Open: noon-2.30pm Mon-Thu and 7pm-10.30pm Mon-Sat.
Credit: all cards and bank-guaranteed cheques.
Strictly halaal restaurant, with fabric-draped ceilings and split-level seating. Specialties include breyani and chicken tandoori.

Elaine's Curry Bistro   INDIAN
105 Lower Main Rd, Observatory, tel. 47-2616.
Open: noon-2.30pm Mon-Fri, 6.30pm-midnight Mon-Sat, 6.30pm-11pm Sun.
Credit: all cards and cheques.
Indian murals, draped ceilings and mismatched furniture are the setting for lamb, beef, vegetable, chicken and seafood curries in varying degrees of fieriness. There's a non-curry menu, but why miss the specially blended spices? Upstairs is a fabulous dinner-cabaret venue (*see chapter* **Theatre**). Licensed.

Gaylords   INDIAN
65 Main Rd, Muizenberg, tel. 788-5470.
Open: 12.30pm-2.30pm Wed-Sun, 6.30pm-10.30pm Wed-Mon.
Credit: all cards and cheques.
Gaylords has a long-established reputation as one of the city's best curry venues. Good starters (try the mini samoosas and the lentil cake) and a wide choice of curries, from seafood with tamarind, garlic and coriander to lamb. Good vegetarian options and Indian sweetmeats. Licensed.

Aldo's   ITALIAN
Shop 153, Victoria Wharf, Waterfront, tel. 21-7876.
Open: noon-2.30pm and 6pm-10.30pm daily.
Credit: major cards; cash cheques by prior arrangement.
Some of the city's better Italian food, including saltimbocca Romana, osso bucco, calamari steak and pastas. Convivial, warm, inviting and frequently crowded, Aldo's has facebrick walls inside and outdoor patio seating in summer. Booking advisable. Fully licensed.

Enrica Rocca   ITALIAN
19 Wolfe St, Wynberg, tel. 762-3855.
Open: noon-2.30pm Tue-Fri, 7.30pm-9.30pm Tue-Sat (kitchen closes at 9.30pm).
Credit: all cards (except AmEx) and cheques.
Known to regulars, of whom there are many, as Enrica's, this small eatery was an immediate hit. Make a meal of the antipasto, a massive array, including mushrooms, kidneys, leeks with olive oil, aubergine, salads,

calamari. If, however, you can still eat after that, main courses include roast lamb and pasta. Not licensed.

Fellini's Trattoria ITALIAN
79 Durban Rd, Little Mowbray, tel. 686-8847/8.
Open: *noon-2pm Tue-Fri, 7pm-10.30pm Tue-Sun.*
Credit: *cards; bank-guaranteed cheques.*
Notable linguine pescatore, taglioline Napoli pesto and gnocchi with gorgonzola. Blackboard menu and inviting, casual atmosphere. Booking essential. Fully licensed.

Hildebrand ITALIAN
1st Floor, Old Mutual Centre, cnr Strand and St George's streets, City Centre, tel. 25-3385.
Open: *noon-2.30pm and 6pm-10pm Mon-Sat.*
Credit: *major cards and cash cheques.*
Italian and seafood are specialties at this cosmopolitan, highly regarded restaurant. Hildebrand is one of South Africa's oldest restaurants, and it's still going strong. The decor is dated or old-fashioned, depending on your wine consumption. Main attractions include piccata limone and pasta. Park in nearby Picbel Parkade. Fully licensed.

La Mafia ITALIAN
39 Main Rd, Green Point, tel. 434-1090.
Open: *10am-11pm Mon-Fri, 6.30pm-11pm Sat.*
Credit: *all cards and cheques.*
Good Italian fare in simple surroundings. Star turns include gnocchi, seafood pasta, osso bucco, oxtail and rabbit. Good wine list with notable selection of Italian wines. Reliable, consistent and nicely noisy when it's full, which is frequently. Fully licensed.

La Perla ITALIAN
Beach Rd, Sea Point, tel. 434-2471.
Open: *9am-midnight daily.*
Credit: *major cards and cheques.*
One of Cape Town's most established and successful restaurants, La Perla has warm, old-fashioned decor (red velvet and large chairs), polished service and a comprehensive wine list. It overlooks the Sea Point promenade. The menu concentrates on pastas and seafoods and the management concentrates on pampering the rich, the pretty, the famous and the almost famous. Altogether this is a very happy arrangement. Although it's not cheap, La Perla is hardly ever disappointing and it's one of those environments which encourages romance, or at least good conversation. Fully licensed.

Mario's ITALIAN
89 Main Rd, Green Point, tel. 439-6644.
Open: *12.30pm-2.30pm Tue-Fri and Sun, 6.30pm-late Tue-Sun.*
Credit: *major cards and cheques.*
This family-run restaurant is more than a trattoria. The food is basic Italian, but with a real home-cooked quality – very much an extension of the family kitchen. The roast veal with roast potatoes can be outstanding, the stuffed chicken is a treat, the antipasto is a meal in itself. Fully licensed.

Nino ITALIAN
52 Shortmarket St, Greenmarket Square, City Centre, tel. 24-7466.
Open: *8am-6pm Mon-Tue, 8am-midnight Wed-Fri, 8am-6pm Sat.*
Credit: *cards; cheques by prior arrangement.*
Everyone from business people and journalists to fleamarket traders wanders into Nino, a very large, casual eatery with liberal dashings of music and conversation to create a buzz. Pastas (with a large choice of sauces), veal and pizzas are the main menu billings – it's also good for breakfast. And, of course, if you have a window table, it's ideal for people-watching. Booking now essential. Fully licensed.

Pizzeria Napoletana ITALIAN
178 Main Rd, Sea Point, tel. 434-5386.
Open: *6pm-11.30pm Tue-Sun.*
Credit: *all cards and cheques.*
The Pizzeria's been around for more than three decades, and it remains an appealing, consistently satisfying old faithful. Good seafood and veal, pasta and meat dishes. It's smallish, often crowded, and unassuming.

San Marco — ITALIAN
92 Main Rd, Sea Point, tel. 439-2758.
Open: *6pm-11pm Mon and Wed-Sat, noon-11pm Sun.*
Credit: *all cards and cheques.*
Classy, informal, fantastically popular restaurant which also attracts lines of ice-cream addicts in summer. Excellent homemade pasta, great veal, seafood, poultry and steak. Try the grilled calamari with garlic and chili. Interesting wine list. Fully licensed.

Fujiyama — JAPANESE
The Courtyard, 100 Main Rd, Sea Point, tel. 434-6885.
Open: *7pm-midnight daily.*
Credit: *major cards and cheques.*
Dramatic decor with modern Italian furniture and massive drapes make Fujiyama a stand-out environment. A trio of Japanese chefs make the sushi, sashimi, tepanyaki, tempura and other typical dishes. Relatively pricey. Fully licensed.

Kotobuki — JAPANESE
Avalon, Mill St, Gardens, tel. 462-3675/6.
Open: *noon-2pm Tue-Fri and Sun, 7pm-10.30pm Tue-Sun.*
Credit: *cards and cheques.*
Housed in an Art Deco building, Kotobuki has lovely, simple decor and a small bar. Its à la carte and set menus provide the best Japanese food in town – vouched for by the number of Japanese regulars. It's not cheap, but everything from the sushi to the tempura is so good that your taste-buds will regard it as a bargain. If you're feeling flush, ask the chef to design your menu. Fully licensed.

Tokyo — JAPANESE
31a Long St, City Centre, tel. 23-6055.
Open: *noon-2pm Mon-Fri, 7pm-10.30pm Mon-Sat.*
Credit: *cards; cheques by prior arrangement.*
Tokyo began as a one-room sushi bar, but thanks to its immediate popularity, it expanded. The expansion hasn't really helped the atmosphere, but the food hasn't suffered as a result. Tokyo carries the full complement of Japanese food, and given the high cost of Japanese food worldwide, the prices are reasonable. If you're a sushi/sashimi fan, there's a huge 'boat' of stuff that is enough to satisfy even the most determined appetite. The full-course dinner (miso soup, salad, sushi, sashimi, tempura, fruit, dessert, tea) also represents great value for money for the really hungry. Relaxed, friendly atmosphere.

Cantina Tequila — MEXICAN
Quay 5, Waterfront, tel. 419-8313.
Open: *11am-11pm daily (kitchen closes at 11pm; the bar is open till late).*
Credit: *cards and cheques.*
Mexican staples like tacos, fajitas, enchiladas and quesiladas as well as more unusual dishes like tostados de ceviche (tortilla with avocado and lime juice-marinated linefish) and – wait for it – tequila mousse. There's a big, buzzy bar, and a very sociable vibe in this frequently crowded and much-loved eatery. Fully licensed.

Mexican Kitchen — MEXICAN
13 Bloem St, City Centre, tel. 23-1541.
Open: *11am-midnight Mon-Sat.*
Credit: *all cards and cheques.*
Brilliantly painted, cheerful cantina-style eatery, popular with fashion folk. Enchiladas, burritos, fajitas and the like. Prices are smallish, and so are the servings, but the food's tasty and service friendly.

Nando's Tasca — PORTUGUESE
Shop 154 Victoria Wharf, Waterfront, tel. 21-5820.
Open: *noon-3pm and 6pm-12pm Mon-Fri, noon-late Sat-Sun.*
Credit: *major cards and cheques.*
Big, buzzy and incredibly popular, Tasca is a favourite with those with a yen for tasty, well-priced Mediterranean food – from great grilled calamari and the specialty, flame-grilled peri-peri chicken, to casseroles, seafood and chicken livers. There's also wonderful lamb curry, oxtail, osso buco, salads and puddings like homemade cheesecake and pasteis d'nata. Comfortable, casual and noisy. Booking advisable.

Pablo's SPANISH
20 Station Rd, Rondebosch, tel. 689-2666.
Open: *noon-2pm Wed-Fri, 6.30pm-late daily.*
Credit: *cards and cheques.*
A peasant-style eatery, complete with rickety tables and lopsided paintings, Pablo's does a good garlic and olive oil laden dip, salad with cottage cheese, almonds and green olives and tasty vegetarian dishes like aubergine and diced vegetables. Puddings feature some exotic combinations and notable sauces. Proximity to the train station (visible from the window) is an advantage. Unlicensed.

Biesmiellah Restaurant and Take Out
TRADITIONAL CAPE MALAY
Cnr Wale and Pentz streets, Bo-Kaap, tel. 23-0850 or 24-2972.
Open: *restaurant: 12pm-3pm and 6pm-11pm Mon-Sat, take-away: 7am-11pm Mon-Sat.*
Credit: *all cards and cheques.*
Cape Malay and Indian food like mutton and chicken curries, breyani and chili bites to eat in or take out. No alcohol served and don't bring your own.

Cosy Corner TRADITIONAL CAPE MALAY
119 Ottery Rd, Wynberg, tel. 797-2498.
Open: *9am-1am Mon-Thu, 1.30pm-4am Fri-Sat, 10am-1am Sun.*
Credit: *all cards and cheques.*
Cape Malay curries (including good vegetable curry), linefish, crayfish, peri-peri grills and breyani with yoghurt have made Cosy Corner a popular, well-established eatery. Try the Bombay Crush (nut-flavoured milkshake). Fully licensed.

Noon Gun Tea Room TRADITIONAL CAPE MALAY
273 Longmarket St, Bo-Kaap, tel. 24-0529.
Open: *9am-11pm daily for teas. Check opening times for meals and pre-book menus a day in advance.*
Credit: *cheques only.*
No decor fireworks, but wonderful views from this house at the top of the Bo-Kaap, and it's one of few, if not the only, specialised source of authentic Cape Malay food in the city. Dishes are traditional local and Indonesian – penang curries, denning meat (soft, sweet-and-sour stew), breyani and curries. Discuss the menu with the proprietor Miriam Misbach in advance and she'll prepare a very reasonably priced feast. Don't miss the koeksisters – the genuine Cape article – round, lightly spiced and sweet. No alcohol served, and don't bring your own.

Happy Wok THAI/CHINESE
62a Kloof St, Gardens, tel. 24-2423.
Open: *noon-2pm Mon-Fri, 5.30pm-10.30pm Mon-Sun.*
Credit: *Mc, V and cheques.*
Truly a happy place, this casual, buzzy Thai/Chinese café is justifiably popular with delicious food and excellent prices. There's sit-down and take-out dim sum, green curry, chicken, duck, seafood, beef and vegetable dishes. Vegetarians should try the tofu with ginger and spring onions, and the Tom Yum Khung prawn soup, chili fish and aromatic crispy duck with pancakes are stand-outs. Arrive early – it's very popular. Licensed.

Mr Chan THAI/CHINESE
178 Main Rd, Sea Point, tel. 439-2239.
Open: *noon-2pm and 6pm-10pm daily.*
Credit: *all cards and cheques.*
Modern, elegantly decorated and upmarket restaurant specialising in Cantonese, Beijing and Szechwan dishes like outstandingly good duck, braised abalone, prawns and spare ribs. Expensive, but consistently good. Fully licensed.

Pagoda Inn THAI/CHINESE
29 Bree St, City Centre, tel. 25-2033 or 25-4935.
Open: *noon-2pm Mon-Fri, 6pm-10pm Mon-Sat.*
Credit: *all cards and cheques.*
Longstanding, traditional Chinese restaurant with nice spring rolls, chop suey and seafood. Even better is the take-out next door – you wait in the bustling kitchen area. Cure nocturnal hunger attacks with the sticky Hong Kong chicken. Licensed.

Sukhothai   THAI/CHINESE
16 Hof St, Gardens, tel. 23-4725.
Open: *noon-3pm Mon-Fri, 7pm-11pm daily.*
Credit: *all cards and local cheques.*
Cape Town's first original Thai restaurant does fine starters and a welcome alternative to the usual limp excuses for oriental cuisine. Herbs and spices are imported from Thailand and dishes tend to be hot and spicy, although you can request toned-down versions. Order several dishes together and dip in. Booking advisable. Fully licensed.

Wangthai   THAI/CHINESE
31 Heerengracht, Adderley St, Foreshore, tel. 418-1858.
Open: *noon-3pm Mon-Fri, 6.30pm-late Mon-Sun.*
Credit: *all cards and bank-guaranteed cheques.*
Regarded by many as Cape Town's most authentic Thai eatery, Wangthai is large and simply decorated, with charming service. This is a great way to discover the delights of chili, lemon grass, coriander and coconut milk. Try the steamed chili fish and spring rolls. The satay sauces and spicy prawns in lemon grass soup are stand-outs, but you can't go wrong with any of the dishes. Just be warned – when these people say spicy, they mean it. Order medium curry if you don't like it hot. Fully licensed.

Anatoli   TURKISH
24 Napier St, De Waterkant, tel. 419-2501.
Open: *7.30pm-11pm Tue-Sun.*
Credit: *cards but no cheques.*
Anatoli's unforgettable – and not only because most of the food is loaded with garlic. Wonderfully creative decor in a 1904 warehouse and interesting clientele. The best way to eat here is to make a meal of the large pita breads and mezze – tzatziki, chicken and walnut purée, olives, peppers, etc. – all carried to your table on an enormous tray. Sweets include baklava, crème caramel and rice pudding, but perhaps the best treat is stuffed apricots.

STEAKS

Barristers
Cnr Main St and Kildare Rd, Newlands Village, tel. 64-1792 or 61-5991.
Open: *noon-midnight Mon-Fri, 6.30pm-midnight Sat.*
Credit: *all cards and cheques.*
Dark, warm and rustic, Barristers is a favourite with carnivores, locals and business people. Its Tudor-style decor, dishes like chicken-liver peri-peri, calamari and prawns, and pub lunches account for some of its appeal, but the main features are the steaks and spare ribs – served with a variety of sauces and excellently grilled. Nicely priced wine list. Fully licensed.

Bayside Café
51 Victoria Rd, Camps Bay, tel. 438-2650.
Open: *noon-2.30pm Sun, 6pm-late Mon-Sun.*
Credit: *all cards and cheques.*
Swish but easy-going, this favourite with the smart Atlantic Seaboard set has good sea views and a relaxed atmosphere. The menu is consistently good – dishes like lamb, fish, ice-cream and chocolate sauce, but the steaks are best of all. Fully licensed.

Buz Bey Grill
14 Three Anchor Bay Rd, Three Anchor Bay, tel. 439-5900.
Open: *6pm-midnight Tue-Thu and Sun, 6pm-1am Fri-Sat.*
Credit: *major cards; cheques with ID.*
Long-established steak and seafood eatery with open-plan grill and comfortable atmosphere. The menu features dishes like baby prawn cocktail, calamari, linefish, ribs and lambs, but the steaks are the big draw. Hamburger fans also swear by it. Fully licensed.

Theo's Steaks
Cnr Park and Beach roads, Mouille Point, tel. 439-3494.
Open: *noon-2.30pm Mon-Fri, 6pm-10.30pm Mon-Thu, 6pm-11pm Fri-Sat.*
Credit: *all cards; cheques by prior arrangement.*
You don't go to Theo's for the decor (unless

you fancy a sort of beachfront, Greek-ish refectory). Nor do you go there for trendy socialites or madly inventive salads. But you do go for the steaks, which are a little pricey but worth every cent. Ask which is the best one – you won't be sorry. Greek and seafood dishes also available. Licensed.

Watney's
55 Nu Metro Centre, Main Rd, Sea Point, tel. 434-4424.
Open: *noon-2pm and 7pm-late Mon-Sat.*
Credit: *all cards and cheques.*
Watney's is a long-time institution with consistently good steakhouse food and friendly service. A vibey pub area and comfortable atmosphere account for lots of regulars. You can get seafood, light meals and burgers, but the steaks are the real ticket. Fully licensed.

VEGETARIAN

Despite the demand for vegetarian food, few no-meat restaurants have survived in Cape Town. But that doesn't mean vegetarians are in for a rough ride. Most conventional eateries offer vegetable-based dishes and salads. Delis and Mediterranean eateries are also good bets. Ironically, some of the most reliable and varied salad bars and the best baked potatoes are to be found at steak ranch chains like Spur and Steers.

Here are some of your best options ...

Fruits and Roots
84 Kloof St, Tamboerskloof, tel. 23-9587.
Open: *9am-6pm Mon-Fri, 9am-1pm Sat.*
Credit: *cards and cheques.*
Simply wonderful health store and restaurant with a good range of local cheeses and vegetarian food. Check with venue for dinner hours.

Little Bombay
245 Main Rd, Three Anchor Bay, tel. 439-9041.
Open: *noon-11pm daily.*
Credit: *cards and cheques.*
Cape Town's only exclusively vegetarian Indian restaurant offers excellent value curries and main dishes. Sunday buffets include two curries, savoury dishes, dahl and rice for R19,99. De-luxe thalie (two curries, rice, starter, pudding and tea) is R30. There are also paranita pizzas with salad toppings and à la carte and set menus.

The Macrobiotic Centre
48 Cheviot Place, Green Point, tel. 434-4298.
Not a restaurant *per se*, but a service venue where macrobiotic expert Erica Weiner cooks for people with ailments or those wanting to maintain balance in their lives and bodies. Breakfasts include miso soup and a grain, three-course lunch (around R35) and dinner (R45). Sit-down or take-out, but advance notice is essential.

Marigolds Coffee Shop
5 Grove Bldg, Grove Ave, Claremont, tel. 64-4670.
Open: *8.30am-4.30pm Mon-Fri, 9am-2pm Sat.*
Credit: *Mc, V and cheques.*
Imaginative range of vegetarian meals in a non-smoking eatery. The crêpes are good and there's a daily quiche (around R19), an interesting red lentil and tomato paté, and salads at around R15. Nutritious winter food too. Not licensed.

Sunflower Health Café
161 Longmarket St, City Centre, tel. 24-6560.
Open: *8.45am-5.30pm Mon-Fri, 9am-2pm Sat.*
Credit: *cards (except AmEx); no cheques.*
Nutritious vegetarian meals for sit-down or take-out. The two hot daily dishes are along the lines of vegetable curry and lentil lasagne (around R11). There's also a large range of salads and hearty meals available for less than R15. Fresh fruit and veggie drinks, eggless cakes and muffins. Health shop on premises.

FAST FOOD & TAKE-OUT

Aris Souvlakia
150 Main Rd, Sea Point, tel. 439-6683.
Kings Warehouse, Waterfront, tel. 418-5544.
Blouberg Shopping Mall, Bloubergstrand, tel. 557-255.
Greek specialties like shwarma, souvlaki, baklava.

Call-a-Pizza
Sea Point, tel. 434-0818/9/.
Wynberg, tel. 762-1212.
Observatory, tel. 448-6147/8.
Bellville, tel. 948-9005/6.
Pizzas, pastas, side orders delivered.

Dodge City Diner
Victoria Wharf, Waterfront, tel. 418-1445.
American fast food like hamburgers and giant milkshakes in fun diner decor.

Fallafel King
Galleria Centre, Main Rd, Sea Point, tel. 439-8506.
Tasty Mediterranean fast food.

Nando's Chickenland
Bellville: Edward St, Oakdale, tel. 99-9935.
City Centre: Cnr Long and Waterkant streets, tel. 419-6191.
Kenilworth: 67 Rosmead Ave, tel. 683-2716.
Mitchell's Plain: 3 Metro Centre, tel. 32-9136.
Retreat: Cnr Main and Tokai roads, tel. 75-0445.
Sea Point: 128 Main Rd, tel. 439-7999.
Portuguese with good peri-peri chicken.

Spur Steak Ranches
City Centre: Strand Towers, Strand St, tel. 25-3868.
Bellville: Tyger Valley Centre, Willie van Schoor Ave, tel. 948-0507.
Claremont: Main Rd, tel. 683-3860.
Fish Hoek, tel. 782-2631.
Gardens: Gardens Centre, Mill St, tel. 461-5060
Newlands: Maindean Shopping Centre, tel. 685-1764.
Rondebosch: Main Rd, tel. 689-1370.
Sea Point: Main Rd, tel. 434-1732.
Waterfront: tel. 418-3620/1/2.
Steakhouse fare.

St Elmo's
Camps Bay: Broadway Bldg, Victoria Rd, tel. 438-2690.
Claremont: Cavendish Close, Warwick St, tel. 61-0365.
Gardens: Kloof St, tel. 22-2261.
Hout Bay: 3 Village Square, Main Rd, tel. 797-2102 or 790-4909.
Sea Point: 118 Main Rd, tel. 434-0771.
Table View: Beach Boulevard, tel. 557-8634/5/6.
Three Anchor Bay: 64 Main Rd, tel. 434-7390.
Waterfront: Victoria Wharf, tel. 21-7005.
Pizzas, pastas and good minestrone.

Wimpy
Bellville: Tyger Valley Centre, Willie van Schoor Ave, tel. 948-0425.
City Centre: Strand Concourse, Golden Acre, Adderley St, tel. 419-1220.
Sea Point: Carousel, Beach Rd, tel. 439-2938.
Reasonably priced light meals, breakfasts, family fare.

OUT OF TOWNERS

Some of South Africa's finest restaurants are in magnificent natural and architectural settings, within an hour or so's drive from Cape Town. It's well worth making an indulgent aesthetic and sensory day of it, especially since nearby or on-premise wine estates and tastings almost always come with the territory. The majority of wine estates serve at least light lunches and standards are generally high, although they can get mighty crowded in season. Here are some stand-outs. Booking is highly recommended.

FRANSCHHOEK

The heritage of the French settlers who first developed Franschhoek is very much in evidence in local restaurants, and you'll rarely go wrong with any of them. Here, however, are some blazing culinary stars.

La Maison de Chamonix
Uitkyk St, tel. (02212) 2393.
Open: 12.30pm-3pm and 7pm-11pm Tue-Sat, 12.30pm-3.30pm Sun.
Credit: all cards; cheques by prior arrangement.
The beautifully appointed Chamonix serves an inspired and imaginative menu, ranging from basics with a wonderfully creative twist

to unexpected and delicious surprises. The wine list includes wines from the estate, and accommodation is available. Fully licensed.

La Petite Fêrme
Pass Rd, tel. (02212) 3016.
Open: noon-4.30pm daily.
Credit: all cards and cheques.
Situated on a fruit farm, with magnificent valley views and an open fire in winter, La Petite Fêrme serves classy country cuisine and specialises in trout dishes. The wine list includes local bottlings. Fully licensed.

Le Ballon Rouge
12 Reservoir St, tel. (02212) 2651.
Open: 8am-9.30am, noon-3pm and 7pm-9pm daily.
Credit: all cards and cheques.
Housed in a charming restored homestead with its own guest-house, Le Ballon Rouge is relaxed and inviting with an award-winning wine list. Food is French country cooking style – home-grown vegetables and herbs, garlic fillet, duck and fresh fish. Fully licensed.

Du Quartier Français
16 Huguenot Rd, tel. (02212) 2151.
Open: 12.30pm-1.45pm daily, 7.30pm-8.45pm Mon-Sat.
Credit: all cards and cheques.
An award-winning wine list, crisp linen and fabulous pastries have contributed to the enormous popularity of Du Quartier Français. Food is a blend of Cape Malay and Provençal (a logical combination considering the culinary and cultural impact these two cultures have had on the Cape). Fully licensed. Next door is the deli-bistro, Brinjals, which is open noon-9pm daily for stylish, light take-out or sit-down meals.

Polfyntjies
Main Rd, tel. (02212) 3217.
Open: 10.30am-4.30pm Tue-Sun.
Credit: all cards and cheques.
Situated in an 1860s farmhouse, this charming Cape country restaurant has tiled floors, beamed ceilings, a fireplace and superb garden and mountain views. There's a verandah for teas and specialties include fresh soups, trout and casseroles. Fully licensed.

HERMANUS
Bientang's Cave
Marine Drive (next to old harbour), tel. (0283) 2-3454.
Open: 11am-4pm Mon-Tue and Thu, 7.30pm (for 8pm sitting) Fri-Sat, Sun buffet 12.30pm (for 1pm sitting). Open evenings for private functions.
Credit: all cards (except AmEx) and cash cheques.
Marvellous cave with sea views, seasonal whale sightings, wooden benches, long tables, the Moby Dick's Deck and meals cooked on open fires. Food is served buffet-style and the focus is on local dishes, including good salads, fresh fish, lamb stews and homey puddings. There are lots of steps to the place. Bookings essential. Fully licensed. Open weather permitting.

The Burgundy
Old Market Square, tel. (0283) 2-2800.
Open: 10am-4.30pm daily, 7pm-late Mon-Sat. Closed Mon from May-Aug.
Credit: credit cards; cheques by prior arrangement.
Rustic cottage with outdoor and indoor seating and consistently good food. Brandied duck, delicacy of the day, fresh fish and ice-cream crêpes are typical fare. Well-priced wine list and inviting atmosphere. Fully licensed.

Ouzeri
60 St Peter's Lane, tel. (0283) 70-0532.
Open: 6.30pm-11pm Tue-Sun. Open noon-2pm Tue-Sun in season.
Credit: all cards (except AmEx) and cheques.
A Greek taverna with bright decor and buzzy vibe for a relaxed, fun meal of inventive and extensive mezze, main, vegetarian and specialty dishes. The crowd ranges from beach fans to the established older set and the place is very popular in high season. Save space for pudding. Fully licensed.

Al fresco — Le Pique Nique at Boschendal.

KUILS RIVER

Zevenwacht Pride
Zevenwacht Wine Estate, Langverwacht Rd, tel. 903-5123.
Open: *noon-2pm Tue-Fri, 7pm-9.30pm Tue-Sat, Sun buffet noon-2.30pm.*
Credit: *all cards and cheques.*
Complete with a helipad for guests who don't like driving, Zevenwacht boasts outstanding pastries, expert entrées and excellent wines. For Tue-Sun lunch, there's also a garden menu, picnic basket or BBQ satay basket (skewers of lamb, chicken and prawns for your own garden barbecue). Fully licensed.

PAARL

Boschendal
Pniel Rd, tel. (02211) 4-1252.
Open: *restaurant: 12.30pm-1.30pm daily, picnic: 12.15pm-1.30pm daily (Nov-Apr).*
Credit: *all cards and cheques.*
Grand Cape estate with generous hot and cold buffets including casseroles, meat, fish, innovative vegetarian dishes and renowned malva pudding. The nearby manor house was once home to Cecil John Rhodes. You can get light meals and cakes at Le Café, also on the premises. And a local institution and great treat is Le Pique Nique (Nov-Apr), French-style picnic baskets served under the pine trees. Booking essential. Good wines available.

Bosman's
Grande Roche Hotel, Plantasie St, tel. 0800-210-257 (tollfree reservations) or (02211) 63-2727.
Open: *7am-10.30am, noon-2pm and 7pm-9pm daily.*
Credit: *all cards and cheques.*
Housed in a renowned hotel and located in the heart of the winelands, this opulent, award-winning restaurant and terrace are gourmet heaven. The wine list is remarkable, the views marvellous and the food so stunning that it's drawn accolades from the likes of Robert Carrier and raves in *Gourmet* magazine. Crystal chandeliers and elegant mirrors are the aesthetic highlights, and seasonal dishes based on fresh ingredients are the culinary ones. The menu is changed frequently and features fish, meat and outstanding vegetarian dishes. Sumptuous dining in a gourmet establishment named after Hermanus Bosman who was granted the original piece of land in 1707. Fully licensed.

Laborie Wine House
Taillefer St, Southern Paarl, tel. (02211) 7-3095.
Open: *12.30pm-2pm daily, 7pm-9.30pm Sat-Sun.*
Credit: *cards and cheques.*
Historic building on the KWV wine estate, known for good value traditional dishes, like dish of the day, steaks, lamb, duck, calamari schnitzel and great array of local wines. Wine tasting 9am-5pm weekdays.

Roggeland Country House
Roggeland Rd, Daljosafat Valley, Northern Paarl, tel. (02211) 68-2501.
Open: *daily from 12.30pm, dinner from 8pm.*
Credit: *all cards but no cheques.*
Rated by UK *Tatler* magazine's 1994 guide to international hostelries as one of the world's 50 most perfect places to stay, this hostelry and restaurant are so inviting that guests have been known to remain for more than a month at a time. The food is both informal and glamorous, based on local and home-grown ingredients. The menu's very seasonal, but typical dishes might include a combination of quail, pigeon, duck, turkey, goose and ostrich or yellow pepper and yellow tomato salad with courgette flowers in coriander dressing. Booking is essential. Not licensed, but wine is served with meals.

SOMERSET WEST

Die Ou Pastorie
41 Lourens Rd, tel. (024) 852-2120.
Open: *12.30pm-2pm and 7pm-9.30pm Tue-Fri, 7pm-9.30pm Sat, noon-late Sun lunch.*
Credit: *major cards; cheques by prior arrangement.*
Set in the first of the area's country inns, Die Ou Pastorie offers good quality South African cooking with a resourceful twist. There's also a classy ladies bar and interleading rooms with fires in winter and a verandah for lovely summer meals. Fully licensed.

Die Voorkamer
Erinvale Estate Hotel, Louresnford Rd, Somerset West, tel. (024) 847-1160.
Open: *7am-10am, noon-2.30pm and 7.30pm-10pm daily.*

Credit: *all cards; cheques by prior arrangement.*
The Hottentots Holland Mountains are the backdrop to this lavish recreation of a Cape Dutch manor house. The food mirrors the surroundings – well-presented and tastefully prepared, it has a sophistication lacking in many premium restaurants. Desserts see many old favourites lifted to new heights. Booking advised. Fully licensed.

Lady Phillips Tea Garden
Vergelegen Estate, tel. (024) 852-6666.
Open: *9.30am-4pm daily.*
Credit: *all cards and cheques.*
Teas, light meals and lovely well-priced salads, pastas, fish and pies feature at the charming garden tables and the restaurant of this historic estate. In winter, there are hearty dishes like rib of beef and oxtail. Also on the menu are weekly specials and quiche of the day. Not surprising the wine list concentrates on Vergelegen and wines from nearby Boschendal. The nearby sandwich deli features choose-your-own fillings and outside tables. Be warned – it's busy and you may have to stand in line. The estate's homestead and gardens are lovely.

L'Auberge Du Paysan
Zandberg Farm (off Winery Rd), Firgrove, tel. (024) 842-2008.
Open: *12.30pm-2pm Tue-Sun, 7.30pm-late Tue-Sat.*
Credit: *all cards and cheques.*
Rated as one of the Cape's top restaurants, this wine estate-surrounded restaurant has a crisp French elegance and three relaxed dining rooms. Home-grown vegetables and expert preparation turn even standards like chicken liver paté into marvels. Excellent wine list. Fully licensed.

STELLENBOSCH

Cortina
Cnr Bird and Merriman streets, Bergzicht, tel. 886-6474.
Open: *noon-2.30pm Tue-Sun, 6.30pm-9.30pm Tue-Sat.*
Credit: *cards and cheques.*

Notable Northern Italian cuisine, with good game, tripe, homemade pastas and excellent gnocchi. There's a bar for espresso and drinks and a lively, warm atmosphere. Fully licensed.

De Volkskombuis
Old Strand Rd, tel. 887-2121.
Open: noon-2pm daily, 7pm-10pm Mon-Sat.
Credit: all cards and cheques.
An award-winning restaurant in which the focus is on local dishes and the atmosphere is convivial. Outstanding dishes include springbok, rib, pies, and tongue with mustard. There are also steaks, salads, fish and a set menu for Sundays. Varied wine list. Fully licensed.

d'Ouwe Werf
30 Church St, tel. 887-4608.
Open: 7am-9pm Mon-Sat, 8am-9pm Sun.
Credit: all cards and cheques.
A warm, agreeable atmosphere and the setting of an antique-filled hostelry, this restaurant is built on the foundations of a church dating to 1687. The food tends to wholesome traditional dishes – oxtail, seafood, pastries and the like. Fully licensed.

Lord Neethling
Neethlingshof Estate, Polkadraai Rd, tel. 883-8966.
Open: noon-2.30pm and 7pm-10.30pm Tue-Sun.
Credit: all cards but no personal cheques.
Housed in a classic, beautifully restored 1814 homestead, Lord Neethling has separate dining rooms, each with its own decor. The menu features dishes like smoked crocodile, Hungarian goulash soup, chicken and beef Vienna-style, surf and turf, lamb and châteaubriand. The Palm Terrace, also on the estate, serves light meals like quiches and soups. Prize-winning wines. Fully licensed.

Ralph's
4 Het Laantjie, 13 Andringa St, tel. 883-3532.
Open: 11am-3pm and 6pm-late Mon-Fri, 5pm-late Sat. Open on Sun for special occasions like Mother's Day only.
Credit: all cards and cheques.

Dramatic food, a dramatic proprietor and generous servings of favourite country foods make Ralph's a well-established favourite. Try the fillet, the inventive pasta, game or tongue, and it's difficult to believe that something so simple as bread and butter pudding could be taken to such heights. Fully licensed.

Ralph's at The Guinea Fowl
Saxenburg Wine Estate, Polkadraai Rd, tel. 903-6569 or 903-4308.
Open: noon-11pm Tue-Sat, noon-3pm Sun-Mon.
Credit: cards and cheques.
A seasonal menu with daily specials features classic international dishes with a distinct and inventive twist. A good wine list, including those from the estate. Fully licensed.

Vinkel en Koljander
Lanzerac Hotel, Jonkershoek Rd, tel. 887-1132.
Open: 10am-5pm daily.
Credit: all cards and cheques.
In an historic hotel setting, Vinkel en Koljander offers a traditional country menu for lunch, tea and drinks. The decor is charming and the food includes fish, lamb, the Country Table for cheese, breads and preserves, and open sandwiches.

The adjoining **Lanzerac Restaurant** is more formal with an excellent wine list. Fully licensed, it's open 7pm-9.30pm for dinner daily. The à la carte menu features international dishes and changes monthly.

WELLINGTON

Blake's
Onverwacht Wine Estate, Adderley St, tel. (02211) 64-1377.
Open: 10am-2.30pm Tue-Sun, 6pm-late Tue-Sat.
Credit: all cards; cheques by prior arrangement.
Flair, freshness and a creative modernity are the keys at this farmhouse restaurant with contemporary decor and riverside picnic spots. Local produce and fresh seafood, and a blend of Cape and classic cuisine are the

bases of a menu which includes casseroles and wonderful puddings. Interesting, well-priced wine list.

BARS & PUBS

Cape Town has a good, solid bar and pub culture – from the suburban hangouts to the concentration of action bars and happening venues at the Waterkant-Loop St junction. You'll find a nice spread of places to hang out at the Waterfront, which has the advantages of being buzzy, fun and very safe. Here are some notables.

Ambassador On the Rocks
Victoria Rd, Bantry Bay, tel. 439-6170.
Open: *10am-midnight Mon-Sun.*
Credit: *cards and bank-guaranteed cheques.*
Commanding an impressive view over the ocean in wind-free Bantry Bay, the bar's been refurbished. The crowd is early thirties, and, of course, hotel patrons. On weekends and in season it still rocks after happy hour. Great place to watch the sun go down.

Brass Bell
Kalk Bay Station, Main Rd, Kalk Bay, tel. 788-5456.
Open: *11am-late Mon-Sun.*
Credit: *cards but no cheques.*
Cosy upstairs bar, part of a water's edge complex which is a Cape Town insitution. It's convivial, frequented by a wide range of ages and types, and anything but formal. Real fun. The best way to do it is to take the train out, walk across the tracks and there you are.

Crowbar
42 Waterkant St, City Centre, tel. 419-3660.
Open: *11am-late Mon-Sat.*
Credit: *cards and cheques.*
A decades-old landmark that has been popular with differing clientele over the years, Crowbar attracts a mixed social bag. There's an action bar downstairs and a club upstairs. Specials on drinks 8pm-10pm Mon-Thu. Pub lunches are very good and this is the place to find Mediterranean macrobiotic food.

Dirty Dick's
Harbour Rd, Hout Bay, tel. 790-5609.
Open: *11am-2am daily.*
Credit: *all cards and bank-guaranteed cheques.*
Dance floor, live entertainment, bands and good Sunday sundowners make this a very 'happening' venue. Spectacular views of the harbour and Chapman's Peak and a small pub menu. Upstairs is a more sophisticated (but not amazing) menu and resident pianist.

Duck the Fox
166 Main Rd, Sea Point, tel. 434-4424.
Open: *10am-2am Mon-Sat, 7pm-2am Sun.*
Credit: *all cards but no cheques.*
Housed alongside a good steakhouse, this English-style pub attracts lots of regulars and has a laid-back vibe and good pub lunches.

Dunes
Beach Crescent, Hout Bay Beach (Chapman's Peak side), Hout Bay, tel. 790-1876.
Open: *noon-late daily. (Sometimes closed for lunch and Mon in winter.)*
Credit: *all cards and bank-guaranteed cheques.*
Very pretty, yellow-toned beach cottage with spectacular views, practically a hop from the sea. Verandah and indoor bar with a snack menu and hot chocolate and boozy coffees in addition to the usual bar line-up. Fires in winter and buzzy vibe on weekends.

Ferryman's Tavern
East Pier Rd, Waterfront, tel. 419-7748.
Open: *11am-11pm Mon-Sat, noon-10.30pm Sun.*
Credit: *all cards; cheques with ID.*
Famous for its drunken beef stews and curry, this old-style pub serves good food, at around R20 for hot dishes. There are food specials daily and a sociable crowd of regulars. It's situated alongside Mitchell's Brewery and it supplies fresh draught beer on tap, including the pub's own brew, Ferryman's ale. Upstairs and downstairs seating, outdoor tables in summer.

The Firkin Brewpub
22 Kloof St, Gardens, tel. 24-4222.
Open: *noon-midnight Mon-Sat. Open Sun in summer only.*
Credit: *all cards and cheques.*
The novelty of a bar set in a mini-brewery contributed to the instant success of Firkin Brewpub, and it attracts a trendy, interesting bunch of regulars. The downstairs area, with its fireplace and communal noticeboard, can get crowded, but there's a quieter section upstairs. Wide range of imported beers and home brews produced on premises.

Forester's Arms
Newlands Ave, Newlands, tel. 689-5949.
Open: *10am-11.30pm Mon-Sat.*
Credit: *cards but no cheques.*
One of Cape Town's most famous watering holes, Forrie's is a favourite with university students. The food is mainly pub lunch style – lots of pies and chips and the beer flows freely. Students here are more likely to talk rugby or surfing than the meaning of life, and it would be difficult to find a more carefree crowd in the Cape. In the warm weather there's an outside beer garden.

The George
32 Waterkant St, City Centre, tel. 25-3636.
Open: *11am-late daily.*
Credit: *all cards and cheques.*
This is one of Cape Town's oldest pubs and its lunch-time clientele ranges from business people to hip ravers. There's a buzzing dance area downstairs and the dark, easygoing Harley Davidson Bar upstairs. Unpretentious, established, and the food's good too.

Havana Bar
45 Waterkant St, City Centre, tel. 419-7041.
Open: *8pm-late Tue-Sat.*
Credit: *all cards and bank-guaranteed cheques.*
Smart, nicely decorated late-night eatery and bar in the heart of the nightlife area. Upstairs and downstairs areas and a balcony with great views of the street. Full dinners as well as a snack menu are available. Happening and hip.

The Inn Place
Shop 30, Westgate Mall, cnr Vanguard Dr and Morgenster Rd, Mitchell's Plain, tel. 31-5086.
Open: *6.30pm-midnight Thu, 2.30pm-3.30am Fri, 11.30pm-2.30am Sat.*
Credit: *cards but no cheques.*
An energetic jazz-oriented pub usually with live bands and pub food like seafood pizzas and steaks. Set in a shopping centre in the Cape Flats suburb of Mitchell's Plain, this is a venue for people who know how to have a good time.

The Keg and Grouse
Shop 40, Riverside Centre, Main Rd, Rondebosch, tel. 689-3000.
Open: *noon-midnight daily.*
Credit: *all cards and cheques.*
Smartly but not overwhelmingly decorated and popular with the 25-45 set, including lots of business people, The Keg and Grouse has a broad cocktail list, pub menu with lunch specials and 40 imported beers to choose from (consume 20 different ones and your achievement is preserved for posterity in brass above the bar). Braille menu. Minimum entry age: 23.

Lord Nelson Bar
Mount Nelson Hotel, Orange St, Gardens, tel. 23-1000.
Open: *5pm-1am Mon-Sat, 5pm-midnight Sun.*
Credit: *all cards and cheques.*
Cape Town's most elegant watering hole is intimate, classy and cosy, with studded-leather conversation-corners and a log fire in winter. Cocktails from Orient Express hotel menus around the world, and a fine selection of cognacs and cigars available.

Nauty's Pub
23 Main Rd, Rondebosch, tel. 689-4442.
Open: *10.30am-1.30am Mon-Sat, 6pm-1.30am Sun.*
Credit: *cards but no cheques.*
A popular student hangout, with specials on beers and draughts, live music and a rowdy, convivial atmosphere.

The Noon Gun Bar
Cape Sun Hotel, Strand St, City Centre, tel. 23-8844.
Open: *11.30am-1am Mon-Sat.*
Credit: *all cards but no cheques.*
At double, sometimes triple the average drinks prices, The Noon Gun attracts tourists and occasional expense account locals. It's beautifully decorated in a nautical theme and suitably subdued.

Perseverance Tavern
83 Buitenkant St, City Centre, tel. 461-1981 or 461-2440.
Open: *noon-midnight Mon-Thu and Sat, noon-1am Fri.*
Credit: *all cards and cheques.*
Cape Town's oldest pub (1808) has a fantastically convivial atmosphere, two dining rooms, a beer garden and a verandah. In addition to the usual alcoholic offerings, there's excellent, homestyle pub food.

Prosit
Cnr Alexander and Atlantic roads, Muizenberg, tel. 788-6633.
Open: *4pm-late Sat-Thu, 2pm-late Fri.*
Credit: *Mc, V and cheques.*
A motley assortment of ravers haunt this local pub – everyone from geriatrics and down-and-outs to bohemians and rising professionals. Slightly seedy – but that's the appeal. The food sounds better than it tastes, but this is a good place to meet locals. Live entertainment on Wed and Sat. Disco on Fri.

The Pumphouse
Dock Road Complex, Dock Rd, Waterfront, tel. 419-7722.
Open: *noon-late daily.*
Credit: *all cards; cheques with ID.*
This authentic harbour pumphouse contains the original pipes, iron walkways and multi-level seating and people-watching areas. There's frequently live music, ranging from original to rock and jazz. At lunchtime, you can eat here along with dock employees, and an average simple meal costs R12-R15. At night there are gourmet pizzas in addition to offerings from the bar.

Rick's Cafe Americain
196-198 Loop St, City Centre, tel. 22-2378.
Open: *7pm-2.30am Mon-Fri, 7pm-4am Sat (extended hours in season).*
Credit: *cards; cheques by prior arrangement.*
You've seen the movie now visit the bar/restaurant ... Rick's attracts pretty people and offers everything from coffees to full meals. The dress code is that peculiarly South African anomaly, 'smart casual'. This means no shorts or sneakers. Very popular.

Seagulls Pub and Bistro
Fritz Sonnenberg Rd, Green Point, tel. 419-0295.
Open: *10am-midnight Mon-Sat, 10am-7pm Sun.*
Credit: *all cards and cheques.*
This pub-cum-bistro is well-located, close to the Waterfront and the Sunday Green Point flea market. There's plenty of parking and basic, but cosy decor. The fairly extensive menu includes pizzas (R14-R18), pastas and main dishes. Frequented by local business people at lunchtime. The pleasant outside beer garden is set under vines, and there's also a tea garden and bistro on the premises.

The Sports Café
Shop 259, Waterfront, tel. 419-5558/9.
Open: *noon-2am Mon-Sat, noon-1am Sun.*
Credit: *all cards and bank-guaranteed cheques.*
Popular macho, multi-level hangout, with 60 screens showing local and international sports events. It's buzzy and crowded, with a dance bar and patio. Filling food like grilled linefish, steaks, burgers and chicken wings. You can't book for dinner, but you're advised to do so for lunch.

Stag's Head
71 Hope St, City Centre, tel. 45-4918.
Open: *10am-late Mon-Sat, 2pm-late Sun.*
Credit: *all cards; cheques at management's discretion.*
Pool tables, upstairs and downstairs sections and a very mixed crowd – from prostitutes to business people – make this one of Cape Town's favourite hangouts. The downstairs

area is quieter and frequented by (mainly) older regulars. Upstairs are the 13 pool tables, loud music, pinball machines and games. Pub lunches served. No trendy frills, just good times.

The Woodstock
9 Essex Rd, Woodstock, tel. 47-7726.
Open: 11am-late Mon-Fri, 5pm-late Sat.
Credit: all cards; cheques by prior arrangement.

If you want to get warm, this is the place. There are four fireplaces in winter, good prices, a nice range of schnapps and interleading rooms furnished with rough wooden chairs and tables. Happy hour is 5pm-7pm.

For more restaurants see listings in chapters **Late Night/Early Morning, Children's Cape Town, Gay Cape Town** *and* **Women's Cape Town.**

SHEBEENS AND TOWNSHIP TAVERNS

Shebeens (also known as taverns) originated when it was illegal for black South Africans to buy 'white' liquor. A thriving trade in traditional African brew began, but laws dictated that taverns had to be a certain size, offer extensive ablution facilities and comply with complicated red-tape requirements. Illegal shebeens began in private homes and became known by word of mouth. A shebeen owner was entertaining 'guests' and this tradition of hospitality continues. Shebeens are an integral part of township life – meeting places that are often set up in backyards or garages. With few exceptions, the decor is rudimentary – corrugated iron roofs and concrete floors. But the atmosphere, based on the humanistic African philosophy of *ubuntu*, is sociable and unpretentious. Booze isn't sold in tots, but in miniature bottles and measures of nips, half-jacks and quarts.

Opening hours may be irregular and the best (and often the only) way to find them is to go there. It's advisable to go into the townships with a resident or at least in a group, and this isn't the place to flaunt your emeralds.

Some of the good shebeens in Guguletu include Busi's Tavern (on NY1), Nobantu's Tavern (on NY108), Charley's Tavern (on NY119), Mia's Tavern (on NY123) and Miami Tavern (on NY123). Miami is the most upmarket, with tight security.

In Langa, directly opposite the Langa High School is the typically rough-and-ready Tiger's Shebeen. Buy meat at the adjacent Yeye's butchery where barbecue facilities are also provided.

Binta's in Khayamandi (just outside Stellenbosch) is very welcoming and very vibey.

In Oceanview (near Kommetjie) Grace's Place in Site 5 is a non-stop party with dancing and music and The Fisherman's Tavern has pool and darts.

For guided tours of Clubs, Pubs and Township Jazz, try **Heart Stoppers**, *tel. 797-4128 or 683-3227 (a/h).* **Daytrippers Tours**, *tel. 531-3274, offers a combination of a Winelands trip with a Tavern and Township tour.*

SHOPPING & SERVICES

Useful, fun and fabulous shops and services, from fashion and flowers to bodyguards and emergency domestic help. Here's where to buy it, find it, source it and spend it.

SHOPPING

Some people are born to shop. Some have shopping thrust upon them. Either way, here's where to buy it ...

Capetonians are pretty proud of their dress and decorating style, and can be downright snobby about their upcountry cousins, the Johannesburgers, who are widely regarded as way too glitzy. When it comes to food, collectables or furniture, those with an eye on image drive miles for a secret source of decor, sun-dried tomatoes or shoes. This is also a city of flea-markets, antique stores and good second-hand bookshops. If you love bargains, you'll find everything from sheets to swimwear at numerous discount stores. There are enough factory shops to fill a book – Pam Black's indispensable *A-Z of Factory Shops* (available at leading bookstores).

Because of the exchange rate (and some greedy retailers), imports are horrendously expensive; local fashions tend to copy European designs. Fun flea-market finds, art and interesting craft may be your best buys. Post-Christmas and mid-year sales feature 20%-50% markdowns. There's 14% VAT on goods and services with the exception of some foods. Shopping hours outside high season are 8.30/9am-5pm weekdays and until 1pm on Saturday, but some centres, notably at the Waterfront, have extended hours and are open on Sundays.

The immensely popular Victoria Wharf shopping mall at the Waterfront.

SHOPPING MALL HEAD OFFICES

Adelphi, tel. 434-2931.
Cavendish Square, tel. 64-3050.
Constantia Village, tel. 794-5065.
Golden Acre, tel. 419-4190.
Sun Gallery, tel. 21-1144.
Tyger Valley, tel. 948-5905.
Victoria Wharf (Waterfront), tel. 419-2885.
N1 City, tel. 595-1170.

SERIOUS SHOPPING ZONES

ACCESS PARK

Access Park is South Africa's largest factory shop complex and it's a source of everything from discount baby goods, furniture and groceries to cut-price housewares, linen, clothes and shoes. Don't expect glamour and be prepared to rummage in some cases. While you're at it, check out nearby Glosderry and Warrington roads for bargain clothes (men's, women's and kids'), accessories and shoes. Access Park is in Myhof St (off Lansdowne Rd), Kenilworth.

Shopping 117

ATLANTIC SEABOARD TO HOUT BAY

Sea Point's Main Rd offers a sometimes patchy range of shops, including some nice collectables stores and boutiques, a high concentration of restaurants and two small shopping malls (Galleria and the Adelphi Centre).

A 10-15 minute drive from here, past Clifton, takes you to The Promenade in Camps Bay, a tiny, exclusive little centre opposite the beach. From here, a 10-15 minute drive gets you to Hout Bay, where all things quaint and cottagey reign supreme. Hout Bay Harbour's Mariner's Wharf is a good source of fish and souvenirs.

CITY CENTRE

Street markets in Greenmarket Square and Church St offer clothes, gifts, collectables and antiques, and nearby St George's Mall has eateries, buskers, street stalls and shops. From here, walk a block up to Long St, which is great for antiques, second-hand books, vintage collectables and eateries (*see also chapter* **The Sights**).

A block down from Greenmarket Square and St George's Mall is Adderley St with more conventional stores, a flower market (*see chapter* **The Sights**) and the Golden Acre shopping centre, which is linked underground to the Sun Gallery shopping mall.

The best way to shop in the City Centre is on foot – to avoid parking hassles and gain maximum enjoyment of the pedestrian malls and street markets.

A five-minute drive from the City Centre gets you to Tamboerskloof, a largely residential area with lots of Victorian homes. It does, however, have a handful of shops (florists, boutiques, decor and antique stores), and almost all of them are notable.

CLAREMONT & NEWLANDS

If department stores, malls, ladies-who-lunch and smart (if largely conventional) shopping are what you're after, Claremont is your goal. Three shopping malls – Cavendish Square, The Link and The Atrium are within a stone's throw of one another and there are two movie complexes and plenty of eateries. It's easily accessed from the City Centre by train.

Newlands's Dean St, less than five minutes' drive from Claremont, has a small, but smart shopping area.

CONSTANTIA

A mix of shopping mall, stores and good farm stalls, eateries and antiques in an upmarket, leafy residential area.

FALSE BAY COAST

Known as the Treasure Coast, the False Bay coastline is trendy, relaxed and popular. The best shopping is in Kalk Bay, which has a small but interesting range of antique shops, cafés and collectables stores. Prices have kept pace with the trendiness, but this remains a good source of vintage crockery, furniture and curiosities. And all of it is practically on the water's edge.

MAIN RD, OBSERVATORY

Observatory's shopping area is not exactly a monument to conspicuous consumerism – you can walk up and down Main Rd in ten minutes – but there are some funky little shops and eateries, and the area's a cheerful mix of bohemia, die-hard hippie and up-and-coming professionals.

TYGER VALLEY

The mother of all shopping malls – for Cape Town at any rate – Tyger Valley has around 200 shops, tons of parking, cinemas, scores of eateries, a take-out court and some outstanding stores. Big, popular and well designed.

THE WATERFRONT

Safe, secure, open seven days a week with a terrific range of stores, craft stalls, masses of eateries, activities, music and theatre venues and superb sea and harbour views, the Waterfront is a fine answer to most shoppers' prayers. It's crowded on weekends, public holidays and during high season, but there's plenty of parking (free outside and charged indoors), a bus service (*see chapter* **Getting Around**), good kids' activities, regular free concerts and a great range of boat trips (*see chapter* **Wet, Wet, Wet**).

GOING, GOING, GONE

Ashbey's
43 Church St, City Centre, tel. 23-8060.
Open: *8.30am-4.45pm Mon-Fri, 8.30am-11.45pm Sat.*
Viewing: *8.30am-4.45pm Mon-Tue, 8.30am-3.45pm Wed, 8.30am-11.45am Sat. Auctions are on Thu starting at 9.30am and ending around 1.30pm.*
Credit: *cheques but no cards.*
Reputable and popular, Ashbey's began in 1891, and it's still one of the best sources of anything from almost-new Alessi kettles to carpets. Antiques, second-hand goods and assorted chattels are auctioned weekly. The buyer's premium (incl. VAT) is 11,4% on antiques and household goods. The seller's premium (incl. VAT) is 11,7% for antiques and 14,55% on household goods.

JJ Hofmeyr & Son
13 Piers Rd, Wynberg, tel. 761-3419 or 761-1803/4.
Open: *8.30am-1pm and 2pm-5pm Tue and Fri. Auctions are on Sat and Wed starting at 9.30am.*
Credit: *cheques but no cards.*
JJ Hofmeyr dates to 1857, when goods up for grabs included cattle and farms. Nowadays, it's mostly second-hand furniture and some antiques, silver and jewellery. There's no buyer's commission, but 18,5% commission plus VAT is charged to the seller.

DEPARTMENT & CHAIN STORES

The city's smartest department store is **Stuttafords** (Cavendish Square and Tyger Valley). For cosmetics, men's, women's and kids' clothes, shoes, linen and the like, there's also **Garlicks** (Parow) and **Edgars** (which has several stores city-wide). **Truworths** features off-the-peg men's and women's clothes (there are stores city-wide, but the best are in Adderley St, Tyger Valley Centre and Claremont). LTD, a division of Truworths in the Victoria Wharf at the Waterfront, stocks well-designed men's, women's and kids' clothes along the lines of The Gap and Banana Republic. **Foschini** (city-wide) has chain-store women's fashions. And for outstanding quality men's, women's and kids' clothes, fabulous food and linen, try **Woolworths**. There are branches city-wide – the best are Sea Point Main Rd, Adderley St (City Centre), Tyger Valley Centre and Claremont.

PERSONALISED SHOPPING

Shop Hound
Tel. 439-1254.
Internationally experienced fashion stylist and shopping consultant René Reay provides personalised shopping trips, from craft to antiques shops, collectables stores, designer boutiques and bargain shoes. R100 per day includes collection and drop off at your hotel/home.

BEAUTY & BATH PRODUCTS

The big department stores are your best bet for big-name beauty products.

The Bubble Shop
Ground floor, Victoria Wharf, Waterfront, tel. 25-2141.
Open: *9am-7pm Mon, Tue and Thu, 9am-9pm Wed-Sat, 10am-6pm Sun.*
Lower Mall, Cavendish Square, Claremont, tel. 683-2580.
Open: *9am-5pm Mon-Sat.*
Shop 518, Tyger Valley Centre, Tyger Valley, tel. 948-8897.
Open: *9am-5.30pm Mon-Thu, 9am-7pm Fri, 9am-5pm Sat. Also, in summer 10am-2pm Sun.*
Credit: *all branches take cards and cheques.*
Towels, gowns, bubble baths and soaps as well as good giftpacks and monogramming make this a good stop-off for scented soap, presents and pampering paraphernalia.

Ecoco
Shop 6, Gardens Centre, Mill St, Gardens, tel. 461-0877.
Open: *9am-5.30pm Mon-Fri, 8.30am-2pm Sat.*
Credit: *cards and cheques.*
Shop 145, Victoria Wharf, Waterfront, tel. 419-2606.
Open: *9am-7pm Mon-Tue, 9am-9pm Wed-Sun.*
Credit: *Cards and cheques.*
Similar in concept to the Body Shop chain, Ecoco is a delicious route into all things nice and natural – aromatherapy oils and soaps, essential oils and herb extracts, which promise to heal everything from PMT to stress. There are also skin care products, beechwood bathroom accessories and giftpacks. Tranquil and green.

Perfums De France
Shop 22, Constantia Village, Constantia, tel. 794-3327/8.
Open: *9am-7pm Mon-Fri, 9am-6pm Sat, 9.30am-1.30pm Sun.*
Credit: *cards and cheques.*
French perfumes, major treatment houses like Clarins and Decleor and the services of two beauty therapists make this a good place to head for if you want to indulge and get gorgeous.

BOOKS

Caxton's Booksellers
278 Main Rd, Kenilworth, tel. 762-1613.
Open: *8.30am-5pm Mon-Fri, 8.30am-1pm Sat.*
Credit: *cards and cheques.*
Adults and children's books, audio tapes and fancy stationery are on offer at this long-established store.

Clarke's Antiquarian
211 Long St, City Centre, tel. 23-5739.
Open: *8.45am-5pm Mon-Fri, 8.45pm-1pm Sat.*
Credit: *cards and cheques.*
Rumour has it that if you sit in Clarke's for long enough (and it's a thoroughly inviting place to hang out), you'll bump into everyone of note passing through Cape Town. So far that roll-call has included Graham Greene, the CIA's William Casey, Wilbur Smith, Nadine Gordimer and a host of ambassadors. Clarke's is a fantasy of what an antiquarian book shop should be like – not an ounce of glitz, just shelves and tables piled with new, second-hand and antiquarian books. Collectable maps and prints also for sale.

Central New Agency (CNA)
See **Stationery** *later in this chapter.*

Exclusive Books
Constantia Village Shopping Centre, Spaanschemat River Rd, Constantia, tel. 794-7800.
Open: *8.30am-9pm Mon-Fri, 9am-9pm Sat, 9am-5pm Sun.*
Credit: *cards and cheques.*
Victoria Wharf, tel. 419-0905.
Open: *9am-10.30pm Mon-Fri, 9am-11pm Sat, 10am-9pm Sun.*
Credit: *cards and cheques.*
Lower Mall, Cavendish Square, Claremont, tel. 64-3030.
Open: *8.30am-9pm Mon-Thu, 8.30am-10pm Fri-Sat, 10am-5.30pm Sun.*
Credit: *cards and cheques.*
South Africa's best-stocked and most browsable bookshops. Exclusive's stores fill a major literary gap and provide book-lovers with a place to buy, hang out and dream. Most books not in stock can be ordered, although this can take time. Good for international magazines and new local writers too.

ID Booksellers
122 Longmarket St, City Centre, tel. 23-9104.
Open: *8.30am-5pm Mon-Fri, 8.30am-12.45pm Sat.*
Credit: *cards and cheques.*
Fiction, non-fiction books, local magazines and French and German books and magazines.

Jeffrey Sharpe
Shop 1, Alfred Mall, Waterfront, tel. 25-4641.
Open: *9.30am-6.30pm Mon-Fri, 9.30am-5pm Sat-Sun.*

Credit: cards and cheques.
Original Africana books, outstanding antiquarian maps and prints are the starring features at this elegant shop in the Waterfront.

Juta's Bookshop
1 Bree St, City Centre, tel. 418-3260.
Open: 8.30am-5pm Mon-Fri, 8.30am-1pm Sat.
Credit: cards and cheques.
Louvville Place, Church Square, Bellville, tel. 948-7700.
Open: 8.30am-5pm Mon-Fri, 8.30am-1pm Sat.
Credit: cards and cheques.
Medical, academic reference and a large general book department, as well as specialists in school books, from junior to high, and general academia.

Leisure Books Book Club
Shop 544, Tyger Valley Centre, Tyger Valley, tel. 945-4128
Open: 9am-9pm Mon-Sat, 9am-5pm Sun.
Credit: cards and cheques.
This large bookshop is the centre of a mail order book club and besides books it stocks educational games, tapes, CDs and videos at discounts.

BARGAIN BOOKS

If the number of good second-hand and discount bookshops is anything to go by, Capetonians either read more than other South Africans or they're meaner. For a nice range of second-hand books (and a good charitable cause) try the **CAFDA** shops, *44 Main Rd, Sea Point, tel. 44-6149* and *Werdmuller Centre, Claremont, tel. 64-2230.* The **Book Warehouse**, *Main Rd, Rondebosch, tel. 686-4795,* is unmissable for its expertly chosen range of unmissable reads. The far end of Long St (towards Orange St) in the City Centre has a terrific selection of good second-hand book and comic stores. Hours are generally 9am-5pm Mon-Fri and 9am-1pm Sat.

CAMERAS & ELECTRONICS

Audiolens
144 Victoria Wharf, Waterfront, tel. 25-2804.
Open: 9am-7pm Mon-Fri, 9am-5pm Sat, 10am-5pm Sun.
Credit: cards and cheques.
Photographic supplies, dictaphones, cordless phones, binoculars, accessories for video cameras, audio/video cassettes and a wide range of batteries are among the gadgets, gizmos and useful tools on sale here.

CHILDREN

See chapter **Children's Cape Town**.

COLLECTABLES & ANTIQUES

Cape Town boasts a host of collectables and antiques shops, and your best bet is to head for the City Centre, up Church St and along Long St to browse and buy. Kalk Bay also offers some good finds along a stretch of Main Rd, which is almost edge to edge vintage and antiques shop. The Church St Market has stalls with period jewellery, knick-knacks, crockery and cutlery.

China Town
70 Main Rd, Kalk Bay, tel. 788-1823.
Open: 9.30am-5pm daily.
Credit: cards and cheques.
'We buy and sell any old thing' is the motto at this crammed, specialist shop in which the china for sale includes shelves of plates and glasses, miniature booze bottles, some Wedgwood, Royal Doulton, Royal Albert, Shelley, Royal Minton and the occasional piece by Clarice Cliff. There's a bargain corner with items from R1 upwards.

Collector's Corner
73 Burg St, City Centre, tel. 23-3820.
Open: 9am-5pm Mon-Fri, 9am-1pm Sat.
Credit: cards and cheques.
Collector's Corner is crammed with crockery, glassware, cutlery, jewellery, light fit-

tings, much of it well-priced and plenty of it irresistible. Good for gifts and curiosities, as well as chandeliers.

Cries of London
82 Main Rd, Kalk Bay, tel. 788-3256.
Open: *10am-6pm daily (open until 7pm in summer).*
Credit: *cards and cheques.*
Antique furniture, fine jewellery (mainly Victorian), old linen, glassware and fun finds star in this pretty Kalk Bay store.

David Porter
24 Dreyer St, Claremont, tel. 64-1070.
Open: *9.15am-5pm Mon-Fri, 9.15am-1pm Sat.*
Credit: *cards and cheques.*
Fine antiques, porcelain, silver, paintings, objets d'art.

Düycker Gallery
7 Corporation St, City Centre, tel. 61-9359.
Open: *10am-6pm Tue-Fri.*
Credit: *cards and cheques.*
Housed in a building that resembles a gorgeous slice of wedding cake, this shop stocks intriguing and beautiful antiques and art.

Gilles de Moyencourt
54 Church St, City Centre, tel. 24-0344.
Open: *10am-4.30pm Mon-Fri, 10am-1pm Sat.*
Credit: *cards and cheques.*
The rakishly charming Gilles de Moyencourt sells only what he considers beautiful, curious or rare and *that* ranges from outrageous junk like teddy bear eyes, fifties chairs and stuffed fish to beautiful crystal and antiques. He's also the creator of a range of much-imitated ostrich-egg lights – more magical than they sound. If the weird or the wonderful is your thing, don't miss this one.

Hans Niehaus
37 Upper Vineyard Rd, Claremont, tel. 64-3901 or 64-3796.
Open: *9am-5pm Mon-Fri, 9am-1pm Sat.*
Credit: *cards and cheques.*
Antiques, china, jewellery and collectors' items.

Jinty's Junk
84 Long St, City Centre, tel. 24-2883.
Open: *9.15am-5pm Mon-Fri, 9am-1pm Sat.*
Credit: *cards and cheques.*
Lights from Victorian to modern are the specialty here, but there's also bric-à-brac, furniture and medical and nautical instruments.

John's Collectables
60 St George's St, Simon's Town, tel. 786-3121.
Open: *9am-4pm Mon-Fri, 9am-1pm Sat. Open Sun in season in the afternoons.*
Credit: *cheques but no cards.*
Packed with collectors and collectables, this specialist in military, postal and railways memorabilia also stocks postcards, antique pocket watches, coins and vintage Dinky toys. Wooden ship's crests can be made to order.

The Junk Shop
206 Long St, Blue Lodge, City Centre, tel. 24-0760.
Open: *9am-5pm Mon-Fri, 9am-2pm Sat.*
Credit: *cards and cheques.*
The Junk Shop is, indeed, filled with much of what was once regarded as junk – vintage toys, juke boxes, glass, mirrors, lights and more. Much of that junk has now become collectable, and this is a fun place to browse – it's difficult not to fall for something in this crowded, well-priced store.

Klooftique
87 Kloof St, Gardens, tel. 24-9458.
Open: *8.30am-5.30pm Mon-Thu, 8.30am-4.30pm Fri, 9am-1pm Sat. (Extended hours by appointment.)*
Credit: *cards and cheques.*
Klooftique has one of the best selections of Art Deco furniture in the city, 40s and 50s lounge furniture, Victorian pieces as well as excellent Deco reproductions. Shipping can be arranged, and plenty of furniture from this unpretentious and rakishly eccentric shop has landed up in grand homes in Europe and America. Interesting fabrics are also in stock.

Peter Visser Antiques
Cnr Long and Church streets, City Centre, tel. 23-7870.
Open: *9.30am-4.30pm Mon-Fri, 10am-1pm Sat, 7pm-11pm Sun.*
Credit: *cards and cheques.*
Highly regarded and long established, this shop stocks some outstanding antiques and specialises in Africana maps and prints, period furniture and modern ceramic works.

Warsaw Antiques
309 Long St, City Centre, tel. 23-0777.
Open: *9.30am-3.30pm Mon-Sat.*
Credit: *cards and cheques.*
This inviting treasure chest, at the top of Long Street's speciality shops, specialises in 18th to 20th century furniture, silver, pictures and icons. There's a coffee shop on the premises for traditional Polish food.

Wembley Philatelic
12 Cavendish St, Claremont, tel. 64-1540.
Open: *8.45am-5pm Mon-Fri, 8.45am-5pm Sat, 8.45am-1pm Sun.*
Credit: *cards and cheques.*
Collectable and investment stamps, postcards, albums, philatelic accessories as well as a history section make this a rewarding destination for stamp-lovers.

Ye Olde Artifact Cove and Shipwreck Shop
Mariner's Wharf, Hout Bay Harbour, Hout Bay, tel. 790-2870.
Open: *9am-5.30pm Mon-Fri, 9am-6pm Sat-Sun.*
Credit: *cards and cheques.*
This curiosity shop specialises in maritime memorabilia, nautical antiques, scrimshaw and shipwreck relics – all appropriate things to buy in the setting of Mariner's Wharf in Hout Bay harbour.

COMPUTERS

See also chapter **Business***.*

Cape Software Library
92 High Level Rd, Green Point, tel. 434-6759.
Open: *9am-5pm Mon-Fri, 9am-noon Sat.*
Credit: *cards and cheques.*
Choose from a catalogue of more than 5 000 subjects, including games, accounting, engineering, maths, business packages, databases, graphics, word processing and language programs. It's fabulous for kids and graphic designers. Prices are extremely competitive and service is very clued-up.

CRAFT & CURIOS

African Image
52 Burg St, City Centre, tel. 23-8385.
Open: *9am-4.30pm Mon-Fri, 9am-1.30pm Sat.*
Credit: *cards and cheques.*
You'll find everything from papier mâché tigers to superb Kente cloth and collectable beadwork in this airy, well-run store. Emphasis is on distinctive tribal art and craft – not a kitsch curio in sight. A brilliant source of gifts, investments and souvenirs of the real Africa.

Cape Heritage Shop
Cape Heritage House, Cnr Church and Burg streets, City Centre, tel. 24-9590.
Open: *9am-5pm Mon-Fri, 9am-1pm Sat.*
Credit: *cheques but no cards.*
Friendly, knowledgeable service and a smallish but carefully selected range of gifts and household accessories make this a standout. The theme is Cape craft and emphasis is on the cheerful, bright and handmade. Ceramics, fabric, toys, books, linen, jewellery and more. Shipping facilities available.

The Collector
59 Church St, tel. 23-1483.
Open: *9am-4.30pm Mon-Fri, 9am-1pm Sat.*
Credit: *cards and cheques.*
Superb quality is the bottom line at this extraordinary shop. Stock includes local and West African art, interesting and unusual craft and outstanding beadwork. Be prepared to pay for the distinctive standard – it's well worth it.

Indaba
1 Harbour Café Annexe, Waterfront, tel. 25-3639.
Open: *9am-9pm Mon-Sat, 10am-7pm Sun.*
Credit: *cards and cheques.*
Choice is a major advantage at this well-stocked, popular African craft and curio shop. The goods range from inexpensive knick-knacks, beads and gifts to huge wooden giraffes, baskets and contemporary craft. It's an excellent source of gifts, well-priced souvenirs and craft. There are branches citywide, but this branch has longer shopping hours.

Out of Africa
Shop 125, Victoria Wharf, Waterfront, tel. 418-5505.
Open: *9am-9pm Mon-Sat, 10am-6pm Sun.*
Credit: *cards and cheques.*
Rare African art pieces and antiques, Kenyan carvings, beadwork, traditional clothing, musical instruments, glassware and local and imported fabrics are among the ethnic goods for sale here.

Montebello Design Centre
31 Newlands Avenue, Newlands, tel. 685-6445.
Open: *9am-5pm Mon-Fri, 10am-3pm Sat-Sun.*
Credit: *cards and cheques.*
Housed in an historic farmstead, Montebello promotes local design and uses craft for job creation. You'll find metalworkers, ceramists, potters and jewellers in workshops converted from stables. It's a marvellously soothing environment, with an on-site restaurant, The Gardener's Cottage (*see chapter* **Where to Eat**), a gift shop and a herb/massage stand.

Third World Spectator
Shop 8, Protea Assurance Bldg, St George's Mall, City Centre, tel. 24-2957.
Open: *9am-5pm Mon-Fri, 9am-1pm Sat.*
Credit: *major cards and cheques.*
High-quality African artifacts, ceramics, furniture, fine art, toys, basketware, textiles and jewellery, acquired from field trips far and wide are on offer here. And if you do fall in love with a massive carving, there's a shipping service.

Errol Arendz, designer to the likes of Joan Collins and South Africa's smart set, with Gloria Arendz, his sister and the director of the Arendz salon.

FASHION

WOMEN'S CLOTHING
Labels, labels, labels, sweetie-darling ... Here are some of the best – from couture to hip and inexpensive.

Errol Arendz Couture
66 Hout St, City Centre, tel. 23-7973.
Open: *8am-5pm Mon-Fri.*
Credit: *cards and cheques.*
Darling of the smart set, award-winning Arendz's trademark is high-octane glamour. Clientele includes local social stars and business women as well as Joan Collins and Priscilla Presley.

Jenni Button
Upper Level, Victoria Wharf, Waterfront, tel. 21-1344.
Open: *9am-7pm Mon, Tue, Thu and Sat-Sun, 9am-9pm Wed and Fri.*
Credit: *cards and cheques.*
The Place, Dreyer St, Claremont, tel. 683-1015.
Open: *9am-5pm Mon-Sat.*
Credit: *cards and cheques.*
Separates, suits and evening gear, heavily influenced by Armani and Donna Karan, as well as classic handbags and shoes, most of which are local copies of European designs. The blonde Jenni Button – and her clothes – are eminently photographable.

Callaghan Collezioni
6 The Place at Cavendish Square, Claremont, tel. 683-1716.
Open: *9am-5pm Mon-Sat.*
Credit: *cards and cheques.*
Glossy and smart, Callaghan carries labels like Ghost, Patrick Gerard, Et Vous and Lolita Lempicka. Investment dressing with a classy edge.

Habits
64 Vineyard Rd, Claremont, tel. 61-7330.
Open: *9am-5pm Mon-Fri, 9am-1pm Sat.*
Credit: *cards and cheques.*
Switched-on and effortlessly stylish, Jenny Le Roux spent 15 years as a fashion editor before opening the fantastically successful and aptly named Habits. The clothes, accessories and shoes are so addictive that commuters have been known to drive past the shop and order items in the window via their car telephones.

Dickie Longhurst Couture
153 Loop St, City Centre, tel. 23-5233.
Open: *by appointment.*
Credit: *cards and cheques*
Dickie Longhurst's career began in the theatre, and it shows in his award-winning dramatic couture. The stylish, sexy and less expensive ready-to-wear range is sold at:
6 Cavendish St, Claremont, tel. 64-3439.
Open: *9am-5pm Mon-Fri, 9am-1pm Sat.*
Credit: *cards and cheques.*

Renaissance
210 Dunkley House, 32 Barnet St, Gardens, tel. 434-4429.
Open: *8.30am-5pm Mon-Fri, 9am-1pm Sat.*
Credit: *Visa and cheques.*
Versatile, minimum-fuss style at good prices. Clothes for day and night.

Elzbieta Rosenwerth
Shop G41 Cavendish Square, Claremont, tel. 64-2910.
Open: *9am-5pm Mon-Sat.*
Credit: *cards and cheques.*
Elegant classics and private orders by special appointment, from a doyenne of South African fashion and her designer daughters.

10 to 4 Boutique
1st Floor, Regent Place, Regent Rd, Sea Point, tel. 434-5810.
Open: *10am-4pm Mon-Fri. Closed Sat.*
Credit: *cards and cheques.*
Imported clothes from houses like Tehen and Hexagone, all chosen with an impeccable eye. Seriously stylish and much loved by Cape Town's best-dressed set – for good reason.

Underworld
Shop 273, Victoria Wharf, Waterfront, tel. 21-1618.
Open: *9am-7pm Mon-Tue and Thu, 9am-9pm Wed and Fri-Sat, 10am-7pm Sun.*
Shop GB11, Cavendish Square, Claremont, tel. 683-4855.
Open: *9am-5pm Mon-Thu, 9am-7pm Fri, 9am-5pm Sat.*
Tyger Valley Centre, Tyger Valley, tel. 948-8969.
Open: *9am-5pm Mon-Thu, 9am-7pm Fri, 9am-5pm Sat.*
Credit: *all branches take credit cards and cheques.*
Partners Cheryl Arthur and Kathy Pagewood produce wonderfully cheeky dresses, drop-dead evening gear and clever contemporary clothes – all excellently priced, unpretentiously sold and designed for women who have a party on their diary or in their heads.

Gert van de Merwe
12 Gardens Business Village, Incholm Place, Gardens, tel. 461-0538.

Open: by appointment only between 8am-5pm.
Credit: cards and cheques.
Made-to-order day and evening gear and sumptuous wedding dresses.

HIP & CASUAL

ACA Joe
Upper Level, Victoria Wharf, Waterfront, tel. 21-5600.
Open: 9am-7pm Mon-Tue and Thu, 9am-9pm Wed, 9am-10pm Fri-Sat, 9am-5pm Sun.
Credit: cards and cheques.
Stylish, comfortable men's and women's wear mainly in cotton, linen and denim. A small range of shoes and a few items for kids are also on offer.

Colours
59 Burg St, City Centre, tel. 23-7474.
Open: 9am-5pm Mon-Fri, 9am-2pm Sat.
Credit: cards and cheques.
Trendy men's and women's shoes, leather accessories, jackets, bags, scarves and ties, sold in the heart of the City Centre, overlooking Greenmarket Square.

Concrete Clothing
Shop 27, Upper Level, Victoria Wharf, Waterfront, tel. 21-4119.
Open: 9am-7pm Mon-Fri, 10am-5pm Sat-Sun.
Credit: cards and cheques.
Nicely designed separates and suits mainly in linen.

Crazy 'Bout Cape Town
Shop 3, Victoria Wharf, Waterfront, tel. 21-6460.
Open: 9am-9pm Mon-Sun.
Credit: cards and cheques.
Terrific T-shirts and casual gear in assorted styles, all decorated with fun cartoon faces.

Diesel
36a Burg St, City Centre, tel. 24-2297.
Open: 9am-5pm Mon-Fri, 9am-3pm Sat.
Credit: cards and bank-guaranteed cheques.
Diesel stocks designer and utility jeans, Spanish boots, T-shirts, denim jackets, shirts, belts, leather and trendy accessories.

Hilton Weiner Basics
Shop 229, Victoria Wharf, Waterfront, tel. 418-5508.
Open: 9am-9pm Mon-Thu, 9am-10pm Fri-Sat, 10am-9pm Sun.
Credit: cards and cheques.
Understated men's and women's clothes in natural fibres and neutral colours. If you're looking for cerise skintight frocks and latex waistcoats, you're at the wrong shop. If, however, linen and cotton are to your wardrobe what ceilings were to Michelangelo, then you'll find that Hilton Weiner is just the ticket.

JB Inc
Upper Level, Victoria Wharf, Waterfront, tel. 41-9838.
Open: 9am-7pm Mon-Tue and Sat-Sun, 9am-9pm Wed and Fri.
Credit: cards and cheques.
The Place, Dreyer St, Claremont, tel. 683-1015.
Open: 9am-5pm Mon-Sat.
Credit: cards and cheques.
Casual unisex utility wear, including well-cut denim and hip club gear.

Skinz Leather
86 Long St, City Centre, tel. 24-3978.
Open: 8.30am-5pm Mon-Fri, 9am-2pm Sat.
Credit: cards and cheques.
Specialists in leather clothing, including jackets, skirts, bikinis and accessories. They'll also custom-make clothes and provide a great fit in made-to-measure leather pants.

Truworths Ltd
Shop 108 Victoria Wharf, Waterfront, tel. 418-5520.
Open: 9am-7pm Mon-Tue and Thu, 9am-10pm Wed, 9am-10pm Fri, 9am-10.30pm Sat, 10am-8pm Sun.
Credit: cards and cheques.
Well-designed, comfortable leisurewear along the lines of Banana Republic and The Gap for women, men and kids, as well as fashionable shoes and accessories. Fun and well priced.

RECYCLED & VINTAGE CLOTHES

Vintage and second-hand clothes are a good deal in Cape Town, compared to what you'd pay in major European and American cities. Shoes from the 50s, dresses from the 20s and plenty of clothes from the 60s are still available and it's worth investigating if, like Bianca Jagger and Nicole Kidman, you like that sort of thing.

For a fun and almost always successful expedition into the world of nostalgia, begin at **Second Time Around**, *196 Long St, City Centre, tel. 23-1674.* A tiny shop, started in 1972, it's so filled with clothes, curiosities and accessories that the dresses literally hang from the ceiling. The prices are excellent and the owner provides great advice.

Second-Hand Rose, *28 Main Rd, Claremont, tel. 64-4270*, offers some beautiful vintage beaded handbags, hats, clothes and accessories like gloves, although you may have to dig for your treasures among the second-hand gear.

For outstanding quality second-hand clothing, try **Stock Exchange**, *116 Kloof St, Gardens, tel. 24-5971*. The clothes for sale here are either imported or local designer, and there's a very good range of shoes and bags.

Deja Vu, *278 Main Rd, Kenilworth, tel. 797-7373*, also stocks second-hand clothes and accessories.

Although not all these shops are as upmarket as Stock Exchange, they're cheaper and you stand a good chance of finding something you'll be delighted to own. All of the above shops take clothes on consignment, if you're wanting to sell.

Vertigo
Shop 20, Gardens Centre, Mill St, Gardens, tel. 461-1483 or 461-4391.
Open: *8.45am-6pm Mon-Fri, 8.30am-3pm Sat.*
Credit: *cards and cheques.*
Riverside Shopping Centre, Main Rd, Rondebosch, tel. 689-4043.
Open: *8.45am-6pm Mon-Fri, 8.30am-3pm Sat.*
Credit: *cards and cheques.*

Understated, laid-back men's and women's clothes with the emphasis on wearability. There are around ten styles of T-shirts, some three styles of jeans, dresses, men's suits, Doc Martens shoes. The Gardens store is worth visiting for the beautifully painted floor alone. The Rondebosch branch has a small discount section.

MEN'S CLOTHING

Fabiani
Shop G20a Cavendish Square, Claremont, tel. 64-4625.
Open: *8.30am-5pm Mon-Fri, 8.30am-1pm Sat.*
6 St George's Mall, City Centre, tel. 25-2500.
Open: *8.30am-5pm Mon-Fri, 8.30am-1pm Sat.*
Shop 272, Victoria Wharf, Waterfront, tel. 25-1810.
Open: *9am-7pm Mon-Tue and Thu-Fri, 9am-9pm Wed, 9am-5pm Sat, 10am-5pm Sun.*
Credit: *all branches accept cards and cheques.*

Upmarket menswear, shoes and accessories from one of Cape Town's best clothing shops. Labels include Hugo Boss, Stone River and Mario Delfino.

Michael R
Victoria Wharf, Waterfront, tel. 21-6339.
Open: *9am-7pm Mon-Fri, 9am-5pm Sat, 10am-5pm Sun.*
Credit: *cards and cheques.*
4 Upper Level, Gardens Centre, Gardens, tel. 461-9583.
Open: *9am-5.30pm Mon-Fri, 9am-1pm Sat.*
Credit: *cards and cheques.*

Upmarket, mainly locally made casual clothes and suits in imported fabrics, as well as shoes and accessories. Service is friendly and there's a tailoring service available.

Porcelli and Levy Tailors
9th Floor, Thibault House, Thibault Square, City Centre tel. 419-8166.
Open: *8.30am-4.30pm Mon-Fri, 9am-noon Sat.*
Credit: *cheques but no cards.*
This business began around a half century ago and it continues the tradition of fine Italian craftsmanship and impeccable tailoring. A bit old fashioned, this is, nevertheless, the place to find someone who understands the nuances of the art of bespoke apparel.

Uzzi Clothing
Shop 136, Lower Level, Victoria Wharf, Waterfront, tel. 25-1617.
Open: *9am-11pm daily.*
Credit: *cards and cheques.*
Semi-casual wear including suits, shirts and jackets, mainly in natural fabrics, as well as accessories.

FURNITURE & INTERIORS

Block and Chisel
35-43 Durban Rd, Wynberg, tel. 797-8658.
Open: *8.30am-5pm Mon-Fri, 9am-1pm Sat.*
Credit: *cards and cheques.*
Visiting Block and Chisel is like wandering into a beautifully decorated house and being able to buy anything that takes your fancy. Set in a period building in the heart of Wynberg's Chelsea Village, it's a superb source of Provençale, contemporary and antique furniture, *objets d'art*, imported and local fabrics and decorative household items, all brilliantly selected. It is one of the city's most accessible and outstanding interior-decorating resources.

Boardmans
Shop 561 Tyger Valley Centre, Willie Van Schoor Ave, Tyger Valley, tel. 948-4023.
Open: *8.30am-5.30pm Mon-Thu, 8.30am-7pm Fri, 8.30am-5pm Sat, 9.30am-1pm Sun.*
Cnr Warwick and Cavendish streets, Claremont.
Open: *8.30am-5.30pm Mon-Thu, 8.30am-6.45pm Fri, 8.30am-5pm Sat, 10am-2pm Sun.*
30 Burg St, City Centre, tel. 23-5040.
Open: *8am-5pm Mon-Fri (opens 8.30am on Mon), 8am-1pm Sat.*
Credit: *cards and cheques are accepted at all branches.*
Contemporary household items, from furniture and bathroom accessories to teapots and glasses, all excellently displayed so you can see how it works together, are the backbone of Boardmans' success. Not quite Conrans, it does, nevertheless, have its own modern, workable and consistent style. It's also a good bet for pots, pans and kitchen utensils.

Clarewood Antiques
Cnr Vineyard and Cavendish streets, Claremont, tel. 683-4839.
Open: *8.30am-5pm Mon-Fri, 8.30am-2pm Sat.*
Credit: *cards and cheques.*
It's difficult to classify this large, inviting store – the choice includes gifts, antiques, vintage jewellery, local craft, fabrics, glass and contemporary furniture, all attractively displayed. You could walk in looking for a cushion and walk out with a cupboard. You won't be sorry though.

Colonial Cotton Company
309a Main Rd, Kenilworth, tel. 762-1481.
Open: *9am-5pm Mon-Fri, 9am-1pm Sat.*
Credit: *cards and cheques.*
Cotton upholstery fabrics, linen, rag rugs, ceramics and glassware are among the items available at this very well-stocked and tempting shop.

Innovations
179 Loop St, City Centre, tel. 23-9036.
Open: *8.30am-5.30pm, 9am-1pm Sat, 10am-2pm on the 1st Sun of every month.*
Credit: *cards and cheques.*
Domestic furniture predominantly imported from Italy, lots of chrome and black leather,

classic and unusual designs, Dauphin office chairs and locally made desks are some of the items that have made Innovations one of the city's most prestigious furniture stores.

Martha's Vineyard
Lower Mall, Cavendish Square, Claremont, tel. 61-4226.
Open: *9am-5.30pm Mon-Thu, 9am-8.30pm Fri, 9am-5pm Sat, 10.30am-3.30pm Sun.*
Credit: *cards and cheques.*
Homey, warm and quaint in that way that only a really sophisticated style can be, Martha's Vineyard stocks gifts, plates, bookends, glassware, crockery, a few antiques, artificial flowers, candles and beautiful cards. Everything is carefully chosen and it rarely disappoints.

Peter Visser Interiors
63 Loop St, City Centre, tel. 22-2660.
Open: *9am-5pm Mon-Fri, 9.30am-1pm Sat.*
Credit: *V, Mc and cheques.*
If you're looking for a creative, offbeat route into local craft, this is one of the best places to find it. The goods include linen, lovely fabric, furniture, mirrors and glassware as well as assorted *objets*. A favourite among decor editors, and a terrific alternative to run-of-the-mill craft shops and curio stores.

The Red House
Heighton House, 30 Kloof St, Gardens, tel. 26-2515.
Open: *8am-5pm Mon-Fri, 10am-1pm Sat.*
Credit: *cards and cheques.*
An interior design consultancy housed in a Victorian building, The Red House offers design to corporate and domestic clients, as well as a beautifully chosen range of traditional and modern interior design pieces.

Shades of Provençe
90 Kloof St, Gardens, tel. 24-5621.
Open: *9am-5pm Mon-Fri, 9.30am-1pm Sat.*
Credit: *cards and cheques.*
This warmly inviting shop, set in a period building, sells fabrics, soft furnishings and decorative objects as well as glassware and art. The painted tablecloths are particularly nice.

Spilhaus
Cavendish Square, Claremont, tel. 64-3350.
Open: *9am-5pm Mon-Fri, 9am-4pm Sat.*
Credit: *cards and cheques.*
Lalique crystal, sterling silver cutlery, Caithness paperweights and similar decorative objects are sold at this prestigious shop. The place where most brides would probably like to leave their wedding gift lists, Spilhaus is quality at a price, but it *is* quality, and the sales are well worth looking out for.

FARM STALLS

Elgin Farm Stall
61 Rosmead Ave, Kenilworth, tel. 61-3996.
Open: *8.30am-6pm Mon-Sat, 9am-2pm Sun.*
Credit: *cards and cheques.*
Good quality fresh vegetables, cakes, pies, breads, flowers and plants.

Oakhurst Farm Stall
Concorde House, Summerly Rd, Kenilworth, tel. 762-1827.
Open: *8.30am-5.30pm Mon-Fri, 8.30am-1pm Sat.*
Credit: *cards and cheques.*
Fresh produce, preserves, spices, sprouts, nuts, organic yoghurt, free-range eggs and freshly baked cakes and breads are the stock in trade of this popular farm stall.

Old Cape Farm Stall
High Constantia Rd, Constantia, tel. 794-7062.
Open: *8.30am-6pm daily.*
Credit: *cards and cheques.*
The Old Cape Farm Stall has been going for more than 20 years, and it's a local institution. It's a great source of fruit, specialised items like fresh asparagus, figs, okra, imported meats and cheeses, rabbit, guinea fowl, free-range eggs and fresh herbs. There are also excellent cakes, tarts and homemade pies.

Olieboom Farm Stall
226 Main Rd, Diep River, tel. 72-8563.
Open: *7.30am-7pm Mon-Fri, 8am-5pm Sat, 8am-3pm Sun.*
Credit: *no cards or cheques.*

A wide range of fruits and vegetables, free-range eggs, honey, jams and cakes make this a popular stop-off.

FLORISTS & NURSERIES

See also chapter **Services** *and box on* **Fruit Hawkers, Flower Sellers and Fruit Picking** *in chapter* **The Sights**.

Bishopsford Bonsai and Art Centre
Cnr Main and Victoria roads, Hout Bay, tel. 790-3478.
Open: *9am-5pm daily.*
Credit: *cards and cheques.*
A farm containing some 2 000 bonsai trees, with 6,5 acres landscaped in Japanese style, birds and squirrels is the setting for this unusual nursery. For sale are tools, fertilisers, books on bonsai and trees, jewellery, ceramics, sculpture and art. There are also regular bonsai classes.

The Greenhouse and Effects and Barbara's Flowers
143 Kloof St, Gardens, tel. 23-8441.
Open: *8am-5pm Mon-Fri, 8am-1pm Sat.*
Credit: *cards and cheques.*
Fabulously pretty plant shop and florist in an old house. This isn't triangular arrangements territory – the designs are contemporary and creative, and the nursery specialises in landscaping and potscaping for small gardens and terraces, patios and jacuzzis. The alley at the back is filled with herbs and plants.

Poppets Garden Nursery and Landscaping
56a Regent Rd, Sea Point, tel. 439-3344.
Open: *9am-5pm Mon-Fri, 9am-3pm Sat-Sun.*
Credit: *all cards and cheques.*
Horticulturist Rod Mackenzie specialises in indigenous and coastal gardens and his nursery is an oasis in the middle of Sea Point's shops and apartments. Everyone from jewel-bedecked ladies-who-lunch to grannies pop into Poppets. Specimen plants and medicinal herbs are among the greenery for sale. Unflashy and relaxed with expert advice.

Proprietor Vaughan Johnson in the Waterfront's unsnobby and superbly stocked Vaughan Johnson's Wine Shop.

FOOD & DRINK

ALCOHOL

Harley's Cape Wine Cellar
53 Wale St, City Centre, tel. 24-1128.
Open: *9am-8pm Mon-Fri, 9am-5pm Sat.*
Credit: *cards and cheques.*
Specialists in Cape wines, Harley's provides a convenient alternative to doing the wine route. Rustic decor and professional advice make it a happy way to explore the local vintages.

The Oaks Wine Club
140 Loop St, City Centre, tel. 22-2170.
Open: *8am-5pm Mon-Fri.*
Credit: *cards and cheques.*

After an intitial payment of around R70, annual membership of this wine club costs some R170 and entitles you to discounts on new and big-name wines. There's also a cellar and wine centre downstairs for one-off purchases.

Palm Bottle Store
191 Long St, City Centre, tel. 23-1212.
Open: *9am-6pm Mon-Fri, 9am-1pm Sat.*
Credit: *cards but no cheques.*
This venerable institution, neighbour to a mosque, was established in 1925 to cater for 'the high class family trade'. It's still going strong and it has the advantage of being set in one of the city's most interesting streets.

Picardi
Shop 5, Seeff House, Hans Strydom Ave, City Centre, tel. 25-1639.
Open: *9am-6.30pm Mon-Fri, 9am-2pm Sat.*
Credit: *cards and cheques.*
4 Parliament St, City Centre, tel. 461-5187.
Open: *8.30am-6pm Mon-Fri, 8.30am-1.30pm Sat.*
Credit: *cards but no cheques.*
16 Hans Strydom Ave, City Centre, tel. 25-1930.
Open: *8.30am-6pm Mon-Thu, 8.30am-1pm Sat.*
Credit: *cards and cheques.*
A large range of wines, spirits, beers and liqueurs, some at discount prices, are on offer here.

Rebel Bottle Stores
11 Buitensingel, City Centre, tel. 24-6116.
Open: *8.30am-6.30pm Mon-Fri, 8.30am-2pm Sat.*
Cnr Loch and Lansdowne roads, Claremont, tel. 683-1634.
Open: *8.30am-6.30pm Mon-Fri, 8.30am-2pm Sat.*
Blue Route Centre, Tokai, tel. 72-5082.
Open: *9am-6.30pm Mon-Thu, 8.30am-7pm Fri, 8.30am-5pm Sat.*
Credit: *cards and cheques are accepted at all branches.*
You'll find some good discounts and a wide range of wine, beer and spirits at these city-wide stores.

Solly Kramer's Liquor Stores
Cnr Varney and Amin roads, Green Point, tel. 434-4302.
Open: *9am-6pm Mon-Thu, 9am-6.30pm Fri, 8.30am-5pm Sat.*
Shop 131, Gardens Shopping Centre, Mill Street, Gardens, tel. 45-4269.
Open: *9am-6pm Mon-Thu, 9am-6.30pm Fri, 9am-4pm Sat.*
Shop 1, Shoprite Centre, Cnr Main and Atlantic roads, Muizenberg, tel. 788-1157.
Open: *9am-6pm Mon-Thu, 9am-6.30pm Fri, 9am-4pm Sat.*
Credit: *cards and cheques are accepted at all branches.*
Solly Kramer has been established for half a century and it's an excellent all-purpose bottle store offering regular discounts. There are nine branches throughout Cape Town, but the ones above are chosen for their convenient location.

Stephen Rom
Shop 12-13, Galleria Centre, 76 Regent Rd, Sea Point, tel. 439-6043.
Open: *8.30am-6.30pm Mon-Fri, 8.30am-5pm Sat.*
Credit: *cards and cheques.*
Shop 3 Stanley Place, Bay Point, Three Anchor Bay, tel. 439-1112.
Open: *9am-6.30pm Mon-Fri, 9am-5pm Sat.*
Credit: *cards and cheques.*
A wide range of vintage wines, French and local liqueurs, brandies and spirits make this a popular choice. The Three Anchor Bay branch is the smaller of the two, and both export wines for estates in the Western Cape.

Vaughan Johnson's Wine Shop
Dock Rd, Waterfront, tel. 419-2121.
Open: *9am-6pm Mon-Fri, 10am-5pm Sat, 10am-5pm Sun.*
Credit: *cards and cheques.*
A large, user-friendly shop, Vaughan Johnson's carries a massive, well-priced range of wines and drinks, sold in an unpretentious, helpful way. The shop's own range, with appealing labels like Very Good Plonk and Good Everyday Red, are not only excellent, but are a fine indication of the lack of snobbery combined with expertise.

VAUGHAN JOHNSON'S
WINE SHOP

SOUTH AFRICA'S ONLY TRADITIONAL WINE MERCHANT

- ❖ *Stockists of hundreds of* EXCITING WINES *from house wines for everyday enjoyment to the rarest vintage wines*
- ❖ *Daily* TASTINGS
- ❖ *Expert* ADVICE *on investment wines and cellar valuations*
- ❖ *Wine orders gladly* EXPORTED *to all corners of the globe at special rates*
- ❖ *Wine* GIFTS *and Accessories*
- ❖ *Guidance on* VISITS *to vineyards*
- ❖ PARKING *available behind the shop*

Dock Road, Waterfront, Cape Town
Tel: (27) (21) 419-2121 Fax: 419-0040

PO Box 50012,
Waterfront 8002, S.A.

'I saw this estate with exceptional pleasure, since everything there was laid out wonderfully finely"

This quote by the Reverend Francois Valentijn is as relevant today as it was in 1705 when he first visited Vergelegen.

The historic Estate is now open to the public seven days a week from 09h00 to 16h00 and has much to offer the visitor:

- The Interpretive Centre and Gift Shop
- Homestead surrounded by Gardens and Grounds
- Lady Phillips Tea Garden - (024) 852-6666
- Library: 11h00 to 15h00 (Closed Sundays)
- Wine Tasting Centre (Closed Sundays)
- Winery Tours: 3 tours daily by appointment (024) 852-6668 (Closed Sundays)

Entry fee:	Adults	R6.00
	Children Aged 4-12	R4.00
	Pensioners	R4.00

Directions to the Estate from Cape Town:
- N2 to Somerset West and take Exit 43
- Turn left at top of ramp to Somerset West (R44)
- Turn right at first traffic light (into Main Road)
- Turn left at third traffic light (into Louresnford Road)
- Proceed up Lourensford Road for 3,5km • Turn right to Vergelegen

**Vergelegen,
Lourensford Road,
Somerset West
Tel (024) 517060
Fax (024) 515608**

VERGELEGEN
ANNO 1700

Woodstock World Of Wines
222 Albert Rd, Woodstock, tel. 47-0645.
Open: *8.30am-6pm Mon-Fri, 8.30am-1pm Sat.*
Credit: *cards and cheques.*
If you don't want to drive to the winelands, Woodstock World of Wines, a maze of rooms crammed with wines from some 48 estates (with emphasis on smaller and lesser known ones), is a good alternative. There are regular tastings, sound advice and very good prices.

DELICATESSENS

See listings under **Breakfasts & Light Meals** *in chapter* **Where to Eat**.

FISH & MEAT

One of the nicest ways to buy fresh fish is at Kalk Bay harbour, where you can get it from the fishermen. (If squid are part of the day's run, ask for the ink to be removed.) You'll also find excellent fresh and fried takeout fish at the unprepossessing looking Texies on the Grand Parade in the City Centre. Mariner's Wharf in Hout Bay is great for everything from oysters to snoek, and you'll also find a wine shop with local wines, curio stores and antiques.

The Biltong Bar
53 Regent Rd, Sea Point, tel. 434-9337.
Open: *8am-5pm Mon-Fri, 8am-1pm Sat.*
Credit: *cards and cheques.*
Excellent quality biltong, including beef, kudu and springbok is on sale at this well-run specialist butchery.

Captain Bartholomeu
Shop 159, King's Warehouse, Victoria Wharf, Waterfront, tel. 25-1246.
Open: *9am-11.30pm daily.*
Credit: *cards and cheques.*
This excellently stocked store carries a large and inventive range of fish and seafood, from abalone sausages to oysters. You're bound to find something fresh and inviting to be skinned and weighed at the large counter at the back. The freezer's stacked with convenience fish dishes and ingredients and the relishes are excellent. There's also a restaurant and sushi bar on the premises.

Morris's Boerewors
265 Long St, City Centre, tel. 23-1766.
Open: *8am-6pm Mon-Fri, 8am-1pm Sat.*
Credit: *cards and cheques.*
The boerewors (peasant/farm sausage) and biltong (dried meat) here are renowned and have been the source of endless nostalgia and intercontinental requests from many South African emigrants. The butchery was established in 1959, the original recipes are still being used and it still has the appealing look and atmosphere of an old-fashioned butcher shop.

SPECIALTY STORES

Atlas Trading
94 Upper Wale St, City Centre, tel. 23-4361.
Open: *8am-5.15pm Mon-Fri, 8.30am-1pm Sat.*
Credit: *no cards or cheques.*
Established in 1944, Atlas is a landmark in the Bo-Kaap area – quaint, well stocked and well priced. It's a picturesque and budget-minded place to buy rice, exotic spices, herbs, legumes and seeds.

Honey Warehouse
King's Warehouse, Waterfront, tel. 25-1700.
Open: *9am-7pm Mon-Tue and Thu-Sat, 9am-9pm Wed, 10am-6pm Sun.*
Credit: *cards and cheques.*
Bring a container or buy one here to be filled with one of the honeys on offer. There are also honey-related products like beeswax candles and furniture polish, honeybush tea, honeycomb, honey hair-conditioner, royal jelly and B Pollen capsules. The honey crêpes are one of the best bargains in town, not to mention one of the most delectable snacks.

San Marco Ice Cream
92 Main Rd, Sea Point, tel. 439-2758.
Open: *10am-11.30pm Mon and Wed-Sun.*
Credit: *no cards or cheques.*
San Marco started supplying Capetonians with real Italian ice-cream in 1955, and

Capetonians have been grateful ever since. The queues in summer are ample testimony to the power of the litchi and chocolate flavours, but there's a minimum of 18 choices to agonise over.

Say Cheese
King's Warehouse, Waterfront, tel. 419-1718.
Open: *9am-7pm Mon-Tue and Thu-Sat, 9am-9pm Wed, 10am-6pm Sun.*
Credit: *V, Mc, D and cheques.*
Imported and local cheeses and meats, spices, olive oil and pastas make this small, inviting shop a good place to stock up, spoil yourself or your guests or simply enjoy yourself.

Tea and Coffee Importers
King's Warehouse, Waterfront, tel. 25-1457.
Open: *8am-midnight daily.*
Constantia Village, Constantia, tel. 794-5544.
Open: *9am-6pm Mon-Fri, 9am-4pm Sat, 9am-1pm Sun.*
Gardens Centre, Mill St, Gardens, tel. 461-4300.
Open: *9am-6pm Mon-Fri, 9am-4pm Sat, 9am-1pm Sun.*
The Link, Claremont, tel. 64-1600.
Open: *9am-6pm Mon-Fri, 9am-4pm Sat, 9am-1pm Sun.*
Credit: *cards and cheques are accepted at all branches.*
A wide range of imported and local specialty coffees and teas has made this long-established chain a local institution, and one of the most inviting places to get your caffeine and tannin fix. Good advice on blends.

Waterfront Farmstall
Shop 66, King's Warehouse, Victoria Wharf, Waterfront, tel. 419-4895.
Open: *9am-7pm Mon-Tue and Thu-Sat, 9am-9pm Wed, 10am-6pm Sun.*
Credit: *cards and cheques.*
This outstanding fruit and vegetable shop could convert almost anyone to vegetarianism – the quality is superb, the service is knowledgeable and you can order exotic items if you hanker for them. Food from here is frequently used in adverts, but it's not about looks so much as tastes that haven't been subjected to all manner of chemicals and treatments. The service is old-fashioned and friendly and the free-range eggs, including double-yolk, duck and quail eggs, are terrific.

SUPERMARKETS

Woolworths produces something like home-made food – except that most homes don't produce food this good – a range that includes delicious snacks, excellent fruit and vegetables, convenience food and meat. There are branches city-wide – try Claremont, Adderley St (City Centre) and Tyger Valley Centre (Tyger Valley). For less expensive supermarket food and groceries, try Pick 'n Pay which has city-wide branches, the best being in the Victoria Wharf at the Waterfront and on Main Rd, Camps Bay. Other supermarket chains include Spar and Shoprite/Checkers. The 7/11 stores in Sea Point's Main Rd are open late for basic foods and emergency supplies.

GIFTS

Above All Discount Gifts
11 Regent Rd, Sea Point, tel. 434-2829 or 434-5786.
Open: *9am-5pm Mon-Fri (until 5.30pm in summer), 9am-1pm Sat.*
Dean Street Arcade, Dean St, Newlands, tel. 685-5826.
Open: *9am-5pm Mon-Fri, 9am-1pm Sat.*
Tyger Valley Centre, Tyger Valley, tel. 949-1876.
Open: *9am-5.30pm Mon-Thu, 9am-7pm Fri, 9am-5pm Sat, 9.30am-1.30pm on public holidays.*
Credit: *cards, cheques and Buy-aid are accepted.*
You won't get bargain-basement prices, but you won't get bargain-basement products either at these well-stocked shops. Discounted goods on offer include terrific wedding gifts, kitchenware, crockery, glassware and frames.

Zun
Victoria Wharf Shopping Centre, Waterfront, tel. 21-5381.
Open: *9am-9pm Mon-Thu, 9am-10pm Fri, 9am-10pm Sat, 10am-7pm Sun. (Shorter hours in winter.)*
Credit: *cards and cheques.*
This little kiosk is a wonderful source of gifts and small indulgences – hair and travel accessories, Fossil watches, great hats and prettily presented soaps. Packaging themes include angels, cherubs and Egyptian.

GLASSES

Eyelights
Shop 31, Strand St, City Centre, tel. 24-2519.
Open: *9am-5pm Mon-Fri, 9am-1pm Sat.*
Victoria Wharf Shopping Centre, Waterfront, tel. 419-9222.
Open: *9am-7pm Mon-Thu, 9am-10pm Fri-Sun.*
The Link, Claremont, tel. 61-4889.
Open: *9am-2pm and 3pm-5pm Mon-Fri, 9am-3pm Sat.*
Tyger Valley Centre, Tyger Valley, tel. 948-9222.
Open: *9am-5.30pm Mon-Thu, 9am-6.30pm Fri, 9am-4.30pm Sat.*
Credit: *cards and cheques are accepted at all branches.*
An excellent range of sunglasses in classic and high-fashion styles.

Frames Unlimited
Cnr Waterkant St and St George's Mall, City Centre, tel. 25-3430.
Open: *9am-5pm Mon-Fri, 9am-1pm Sat.*
Credit: *cards and cheques.*
Shop 59, N1 City, Goodwood, tel. 595-1310.
Open: *9am-5.30pm Mon-Fri, 9am-3pm Sat.*
Credit: *cards and cheques.*
Shop G31, The Atrium, Claremont, tel. 61-2954.
Open: *9am-5.30pm Mon-Fri, 9am-3pm Sat.*
Credit: *cards and cheques.*
Tyger Valley Centre, Tyger Valley, 949-1936.
Open: *9am-5.30pm Mon-Fri, 9am-3pm Sat.*
Credit: *cards and cheques.*
Somerset Mall, Somerset West, tel. (02485) 2-2241.
Open: *9am-5.30pm Mon-Fri, 9am-3pm Sat.*
Credit: *cards and cheques.*
Discounts on a huge range of frames and sunglasses. Take your prescription along.

Sunoptika
Shop GB25, Lower Level, Cavendish Square, Claremont, tel. 61-8011.
Open: *9am-5pm Mon-Sat.*
Credit: *cards and bank-guaranteed cheques.*
All the sunglasses here are imported, and include Ray Ban, Sting, Police and Gianni Versace. There are also accessories like chains, cords and cases.

NATURAL FOOD & REMEDIES

Fruits and Roots Natural Food Market
84 Kloof St, Gardens, tel. 23-9587.
Open: *9am-6pm Mon-Fri, 9am-1pm Sat.*
Credit: *cards and cheques.*
This is the place to find freshly baked health food like sugarless muffins, and organic vegetables. There's a good range of macrobiotic and vegan products, sun-dried fruits, nuts and legumes. There's also a restaurant on the premises in case the thought of cooking with all that bran makes you want to sit down (*see also chapter* **Where to Eat**).

Nature's Best
66 Main Rd, Sea Point, tel. 439-1484.
Open: *9am-6pm Mon-Fri, 9am-2.30pm Sat.*
Credit: *cards and cheques.*
This well-stocked shop carries a wide range of nuts and dried fruits, vitamins, minerals, macrobiotic and health foods, aromatherapy oils and fresh items like tofu.

Natural Remedies Centre
Pearce Rd, Claremont, tel. 64-1692.
Open: *8.30am-5.15pm Mon-Fri (except Tue when it opens at 9am), 8.30am-1pm Sat.*
Credit: *cards and cheques.*
An extensive range of homeopathic and herbal remedies, from Bach Flower remedies to aromatherapy oils, powders, herb teas and crystals are for sale here. Good advice is usually at hand too.

Neal's Yard
Shop 1d, The Link, Claremont, tel. 683-3663.
Open: *9am-5pm Mon-Sat.*
Credit: *cards and cheques.*
Healthy snacks like carob-coated rice cakes, dried fruit and nuts, as well as muesli, brans and flours, pickles, sauces, legumes and grains are on sale in this clean, appropriately wholesome-looking shop.

Vitamin Express
King's Warehouse, Waterfront, tel. 25-2819.
Open: *9am-7pm Mon-Fri, 9am-11pm Sat, 9am-9pm Sun.*
Credit: *cards and cheques.*
A smallish but concentrated range of natural remedies, herbs, oils, herb teas, fruit drinks and vitamins are for sale here. There's also a takeout counter for salads, muffins and light meals.

The Kite Shop – for flying fun.

The Wholefood Store
73 Lower Main Rd, Observatory, tel. 477-7375.
Open: *9.30am-5.45pm Mon-Fri, 9.30am-1.30pm Sat.*
Credit: *cards and cheques.*
With its impressive range of health foods, natural cosmetics, aromatherapy oils, health shoes, juice bar and environmentally friendly clothing, the Wholefood Store could turn most hamburger junkies into tofu fans. But then what else can one expect from an area in which sandalistas still reign supreme and the local gynaecologist burns aromatherapy essences in her waiting rooms?

INTERESTING & UNUSUAL

Flag World
Shop 131, Victoria Wharf, Waterfront, tel. 418-5545.
Open: *9am-11pm daily.*
Credit: *cards and cheques.*
Flags from more than 100 countries in a range of sizes, as well as rugby and soccer jerseys, wall charts, souvenirs, patches, caps and T-shirts are sold here.

The Jensen Japan Futon
54 Church St, City Centre, tel. 24-0406.
Open: *9am-5pm Mon-Fri, 9am-2pm Sat.*
Credit: *cards and cheques.*
This is your best source of pure cotton futons, thicker and fluffier than traditional Japanese sleeping mats, in sizes ranging from cot- to king-size.

The Kite Shop
Shop 110, Waterfront, tel. 21-6231.
Open: *9am-9pm Mon-Fri, 9am-5pm Sat, 10am-5pm Sun.*
Credit: *cards and cheques.*
Specialists in stunt kites and power flying. Largest range of custom-designed and imported kites in the country.

Le Papier Du Port
Shop 266, Victoria Wharf, Waterfront, tel. 21-2305.
Open: *9am-7pm Mon-Tue and Thu-Fri, 9am-9pm Wed, 9am-5pm Sat-Sun.*

Credit: cards and bank-guaranteed cheques.
Calligraphy tools, handmade paper, paints, and a service for providing hand-made invitations, birthday cards and personalised stationery. Creative and inspiring.

Nocturnal Affair
Shop 3a, Gardens Centre, Mill St, Gardens, tel. 461-1746 or 461-1780.
Open: 9am-5.30pm Mon-Fri, 9am-1.30pm Sat, 10am-1pm Sun.
Credit: cards and cheques.
Bedrooms are the focus here and the inviting linen, perfumed drawer-liners, soufflé cotton face-cloths, light-fittings and men's and women's sleepwear make one want to get into bed immediately. All sheets and fabric items are locally made in cotton, and the colours are neutral, with some embroidery and appliqué. A lovely baby range is also available.

JEWELLERY

Jewel Tree
Protea Assurance Bldg, Greenmarket Square, City Centre, tel. 23-0747.
Open: 9am-5pm Mon-Fri, 9am-1pm Sat.
Credit: cards and cheques.
The Jewel Tree is appropriately set in a stretch of notable art deco buildings, for it's a notable shop. The antique jewellery pieces for sale are chosen with an impeccable eye and real treasures at prices which are serious but not exorbitant are the norm. Service is friendly and expert and the atmosphere is relaxed.

Kay's Antiques
Ground Level, Cavendish Square, Claremont, tel. 61-8998.
Open: 9am-5pm Mon-Sat.
Credit: cards and cheques.
This tiny shop has a well-deserved reputation for stocking beautiful antique jewellery, plus a smattering of glass, porcelain and silver. Knowledgeable advice and some real temptations are on offer.

Köhler Master Goldsmiths & Jewellers
64 St George's Mall, City Centre, tel. 24-6968.
Open: 9am-5pm Mon-Fri, 9am-1pm Sat.
Credit: cards and cheques.
Exclusive handmade jewellery with top-quality diamonds and gemstones. The workmanship is quite unlike anything else you'll find in Cape Town.

Myra's Antiques
78 Church St, City Centre, tel. 23-6561.
Open: 9.30am-4.30pm Mon-Fri. Closed Sat.
Credit: cards (except AmEx) and cheques.
Established and small, Myra's stocks a range of jewellery from Georgian and Victorian to art nouveau and art deco, although you may find the odd piece from later periods.

Peach
2 Marine House, Main Rd, Sea Point, tel. 439-7420.
Open: 9am-5pm Mon-Fri, 9am-1pm Sat.
Credit: cards and cheques.
Accessories like scarves, handbags and belts, and some imported lingerie are for sale here, but the main attraction is the costume jewellery – big, bold, or small and playful and generally scene-stealing. The combination of appealing designs and the elegant decor have made Peach a standing favourite, even among women who can afford the real thing.

Penny Murdoch
50 Victoria Rd, Camps Bay, tel. 438-1600.
Open: 10am-5pm Mon-Fri except Tue, 10am-1pm Sat.
Shop 28, The Link, Claremont, tel. 64-3860.
Open: 9am-5pm Mon-Fri, 9am-5pm Sat.
Credit: cards and cheques are accepted at both stores.
Jewellery designs here are modern classics with an understated, unflashy but individualistic edge.

Pinn's the Jewellers
30 St George's Mall, City Centre, tel. 418-2530.
Open: 8am-5pm Mon-Fri, 8am-1pm Sat.
Credit: cards and cheques.
The Bay Hotel, Victoria Rd, Camps Bay, tel. 438-4444.

Shopping

Open: 8am-8pm daily.
Credit: cards and cheques.
Individually designed, handcrafted fine jewellery is the simple description of what Pinn's does. But that's an understatement according to many who know about such things and regard them as one of the best jewellers in Cape Town.

Renée's Antique Jewellery
Victoria Wharf, Waterfront, tel. 419-0302.
Open: 9am-7pm Mon-Tue and Thu-Fri, 9am-9pm Wed, 9am-noon Sat, 10am-5pm Sun. (Extended hours Dec-Feb.)
Credit: cards and cheques.
A beautifully designed shop with high-quality antique jewellery, silver and *objets de virtu*, this is the place to invest, indulge and forget about the price.

Schwartz Jewellers
Shop 12, Alfred Mall, tel. 418-2094.
Open: 9.30am-8pm Mon-Sat, 10.30am-8pm Sun.
Credit: cards but no cheques.
The well-established and reputable Schwartz Jewellers combines a sense of African style and international polish in many of the designs, and the quality of stones is excellent. Custom-designed pieces can be provided, but there's also a good range of stock available.

Trigg Jewellers
Shop G5, Cavendish Square, Claremont, tel. 61-5050/1.
Open: 9am-5pm Mon-Thu, 9am-5.30pm Fri-Sat.
Credit: cards and cheques.
Established and reputable, Trigg specialises in upmarket pieces, including coloured gemstones, the manufacture and redesign of jewellery, and watches and accessories by Cartier, Ebel, Baume & Mercier and Omega.

Uwe Koetter Jewellers
12th Floor, St George's Mall, City Centre, tel. 24-5335.
Open: 9.30am-5pm Mon-Fri, 9am-1pm Sat.
Shop 14, Victoria and Alfred Arcade, Waterfront, tel. 21-1039.

Open: 9.45am-6pm daily.
Credit: cards and cheques are accepted at both stores.
Established more than 20 years ago, Uwe Koetter Jewellers has won awards from De Beers, Intergold and the Jewellery Council for innovative design and outstanding craftsmanship. The style combines classic and organic shapes, and high-quality gemstones are used. A tour of the design and setting workshops can be arranged.

PHARMACIES

See chapter **Services**.

SHOES

Capricho
Shop 243, Victoria Wharf, Waterfront, tel. 418-1635.
Open: 9am-7pm Mon-Fri, 9am-5pm Sat, 10am-5pm Sun.
Credit: cards and cheques.
Good quality shoes and boots from Spain.

Carmen Ruiz Shoes
Shop 534, Tyger Valley Centre, Tyger Valley, tel. 949-9604.
Open: 9am-5pm Mon-Thu, 9am-7pm Fri, 9am-5pm Sat.
Credit: cards and cheques.
Wonderful women's shoes are to be found here – all Spanish and frequently in designs that are difficult to get elsewhere.

Collection Privé
101 Garfield Rd, Claremont, tel. 61-9772.
Open: 8am-4.30pm Mon-Fri, 9am-12.30pm Sat.
Credit: cards and cheques.
Collection Privé is for the woman who regards shoe buying as a tortuous series of compromises between style, colour and wishing the things had, or didn't have, bows on them. An elegantly decorated store in the heart of discount and factory shop turf, it provides sample shoes that can be made up in a variety of colours and materials.

Enrico Designer Shoes
70 Wale St, City Centre, tel. 24-9294.
Open: *9am-4.30pm Mon-Thu, 9am-3pm Fri. Closed Sat.*
Credit: *cards and cheques.*
Uruguayan Enrico Irla is one of South Africa's few bespoke shoemakers, producing women's shoes that are regarded as so special that they're signed, dated and guaranteed for life. Heaven for rich shoe fetishists and fashion lovers.

Marcellos
38G Cavendish Square, Claremont, tel. 64-1581 or 61-8944.
Open: *9am-5pm Mon-Sat.*
Credit: *cards and cheques.*
Imported and local shoe specialists for men's and women's shoes. The designs tend towards classic rather than instant fashion.

Nina Roche
Shop 8, The Place, Cavendish Square, Claremont, tel. 61-3533.
Open: *9am-5pm Mon-Fri, 9am-3.30pm Sat.*
Credit: *cards and cheques.*
Established in 1990 by former music teacher Linda Janse van Rensburg, this is *the* shoe shop for women who can afford imports starting at the R500 mark. Serious shoe labels like Stephane Kèlian are sold with lots of charm by people who know about heels and vamps.

WC Clift & Sons
Trust Bank Centre, Adderley St, City Centre, tel. 418-2702.
Open: *8am-5.30pm Mon-Fri, 8.30am-1.30pm Sat.*
Credit: *cards and cheques.*
High fashion and medium-to-low prices for men's and women's shoes, is a formula that has made WC Clift a favourite among models, teenagers and professionals for years. Quick to latch onto international trends, this is a relatively inexpensive way to find the latest fashions for your feet. Apart from the City Centre shop above, there are several branches of WC Clift city-wide, including Claremont (tel. 683-5900), Mowbray (tel. 689-1029) and Tyger Valley (tel. 948-3606).

Xtra
120 Buitengracht, Cape Town, tel. 23-0318.
Open: *8.30am-5.30pm Mon-Fri, 8am-1pm Sat.*
2 Fir St, Claremont, tel. 64-2845.
Open: *8.30am-5.30pm Mon-Fri, 8am-1pm Sat.*
Pick 'n Pay Centre, Main Rd, Retreat, tel. 72-9684.
Open: *8.30am-5.30pm Mon-Fri, 8am-5pm Sat.*
Credit: *cards and cheques are accepted at all branches.*
Huge range of local and imported shoes. Xtra stocks men's, women's and kids' shoes, all at excellent prices. It's a terrific source of bargains and you'll find high fashion items among the wide selection.

SPORTS GEAR SHOPS

See chapter **Sport, Fitness & The Great Outdoors**.

STATIONERY

See also chapter **Business**.

CNA (Central News Agencies)
You'll find this chain of shops city-wide and it's useful for stationery, magazines, CDs and books – mainly the practical and the best-seller variety. You'll find Mills & Boon or the latest Jackie Collins and *Hello!* magazine, but don't hold out hope for anything by Edith Wharton or Toni Morrison. Cards and cheques are accepted at all CNAs. The following are convenient, well-stocked branches:
Golden Acre, City Centre, tel. 21-7760/1.
Open: *9am-5pm Mon-Fri, 9am-2pm Sat.*
146a Victoria Wharf, Waterfront, tel. 418-3510.
Open: *9am-9pm Mon-Fri, 9am-10pm Sat-Sun.*
Atlantic Rd, Muizenberg, tel. 788-2778.
Open: *9am-5pm Mon-Fri, 9am-2pm Sat.*
Medical Centre, Main Rd, Sea Point, tel. 434-2767.
Open: *9am-8pm daily.*
38 Tyger Valley Centre, Willie van Schoor Ave, Tyger Valley, tel. 54-1261.
Open: *9am-9pm daily.*

MARKETS

Informal traders, street stalls and outdoor markets have increasingly become a feature of Cape Town life. Don't forget to bargain – Cape Town isn't Cairo, but some discounts are usually achievable. These are just some of the options.

The Grand Parade
Darling St, City Centre.
One of the City's historic squares and a military parade area during the 18th and 19th centuries, the Grand Parade (opposite City Hall) is a parking lot most of the week, but it turns into a flea-market on Wednesday and Saturday from 8am-2pm. You'll find everything from fruit and flowers to fabric, plants, bric-à-brac, second-hand books and kitsch.

Patriotic member of the informal retail sector.

Church Street Market
Between Burg and Long streets, City Centre.
Quaint, established and cosy, the Church St Market is set between cafés, antique shops and art galleries. For sale: small antiques, crockery, collectables and fun vintage junk. It's open Monday to Saturday 8am-4pm, but it's best for a Friday or Saturday browse.

Cape Town Station
Cape Town Station, Adderley St, City Centre.
On Monday to Friday between 8am-5pm and Saturday between 8am-2pm stalls at the front of the station and on the station deck sell clothing, shoes, jewellery, old books, music and assorted new and second-hand items.

Constantia Craft Market
Alphen Centre, Main Rd, Constantia.
Craft stars at this country fair-style market, and there's a good diversity and some quality pieces. Look out for the goods from elsewhere in Africa – ebony walking sticks and sculptures, beads and Kente cloths. Worth a visit even if it's only to soak up the picturesque surroundings. It operates between 9am-2pm on the first and last Saturdays of every month on the corner of Spaanschemat River and Ladies Mile roads.

Craft In The Park
Rondebosch Park, cnr Campground and Sandown roads, Rondebosch.
Held on the second Saturday of every month from 9am-4pm, this large market offers good craft ranging from genteel housewifely items like patchwork and pottery to hand-printed T-shirts, painted silk and wooden toys.

Greenmarket Square
Burg St, between Long and Shortmarket streets, City Centre.
Open from 8am-5pm on Monday to Friday

and 8am-2pm on Saturday, the Greenmarket Square market is a city institution. Once the area served as a fruit and vegetable market and the cobbled stones and interesting architecture in the surrounding square – art deco, Georgian and modern – as well as the range of people who buy and sell here, make it a fun experience. You'll find lots of T-shirts, clothing, some antique and crockery stalls, but less craft than commercial factory outlet goods.

Green Point Market
Alongside Green Point Stadium, Green Point.
If markets are among your favourite things, you could make a Sunday of it, by starting at the nearby Waterfront markets, then strolling to the Green Point Market and ending at the adjacent Seagulls Bar or Chariots and Giovanni's on Main Rd, Green Point. The market runs 8am-5pm every Sunday and on public holidays and it's large, crowded and a source of some surprisingly good finds and bargains. Stalls include everything from clothes, underwear and electrical appliances to African craft, curios, antiques and miscellaneous junk. There's plenty of busking.

Groot Constantia Antiques and Collectables Market
Groot Constantia Estate, Constantia.
Held on Saturday, Sunday and public holidays on the historic Groot Constantia estate, this market provides an enjoyable way to combine lunch at the estate, wine-sampling and buying and hunting for treasures. The stalls specialise in antiques and period items and you can find some good deals and great gifts. The same venue is also used for the Medieval Craft Fair, which is held six times a year – on the second weekend of October, early December, the second week of February, Easter weekend, the beginning of May and the second week of July. For enquiries about this, watch press or call Lorraine Bester, tel. 511-4632.

The Red Shed
King's Warehouse, Victoria Wharf Complex, Waterfront.
Watch crafters in action and buy goods ranging from glass and silk paintings to carvings and candles. It's open Monday to Saturday 9am-6pm and Sunday 10am-6pm.

Waterfront Victoria & Alfred Art and Craft Market
The Red Shed, Waterfront.
Traditional crafts, creative design, good fast food and home cooking are the main attractions at this charming craft market. It's a good source of decoupage, household items and gifts, and the standard of products is consistently high.

Muslim children play in the cobbled streets of the Bo-Kaap.

Fishermen prepare to set sail from Hout Bay harbour.

SERVICES

Looking for a tattoo, nail extensions, a bodyguard, acupunture or more mundane services like shoe repairs and babysitters? Help is at hand.

ALTERNATIVE HEALTH

Cape Town is big on alternative treatments for mind, body and soul. The top astrologers are booked up months in advance and there are workshops for everything from acupuncture to yoga. The bi-monthly, free networking publication, *Link-Up*, available at health food stores and specialty shops, lists events, tuition and treatments. And *Odyssey* magazine, 'an adventure in more conscious living', is available at selected newsagents and bookstores for R6,80. It covers subjects like personal and spiritual growth, holistic health and metaphysics, along with classifieds. No self-respecting local New Ager would do without either publication. *See chapter* **Sport, Fitness & The Great Outdoors** *for yoga, tai chi and aikido classes.*

ACUPUNCTURE

The Acupuncture Association of the Western Province is the official registering body for practitioners. For info, tel. 761-7742.

ALEXANDER TECHNIQUE CLASSES

For information contact Barry Kantor, tel. 439-3440.

AROMATHERAPY

The Aromatherapy Association of Southern Africa can recommend an aromatherapist in your area, tel. 531-2979.

HERBALIST

Barbara Lewis, tel. 797-8145, offers treatment with medicinal herbs.

HOMEOPATHY

The Homeopathic Association of South Africa, Western Cape branch, will help you locate a good practitioner in your area. For info, tel. 689-5061.

MEDITATION

Natalia Baker, tel. 788-2900, offers basic, intermediate and advanced courses in four weekly sessions (R200).

REFLEXOLOGY

The International School of Reflexology and Meridian Therapy (37 Talana Rd, Claremont, tel. 61-9671) offers classes and consultations. R45 for a treatment of around 45 minutes.

The South African Reflexology Society represents some 150 local reflexologists. For info, tel. 782-1558 or 61-6514.

RESOURCE CENTRE

The Wellstead
1 Wellington Ave, Wynberg, tel. 797-8982.
Weekly meditations, videos, lectures, reference and like-minded souls, all under one roof.

SPIRITUAL HEALERS

The Confederation of Complementary Health Associations of South Africa (COCHASA) is an umbrella body for a wide range of complementary healing therapists, including spiritual healers. For info, tel. 58-8709.

Centre of Spiritual Philosophy
242 High Level Rd, Sea Point, tel. 434-1879.
Free of charge spiritual healing in a peaceful atmosphere on Monday at 7pm. Also weekly programme of lectures on esoteric topics at a nominal fee.

BARTENDERS

Ronnie Gallant
Tel. 638-2073.
Bartending for a variety of functions.

Frank Smith
Tel. 686-4874 or 637-4653.
Established bartending for events ranging from silver-service celebrations to informal functions.

BODYGUARDS

Protection
Tel. 418-4616 ext. 8437.
Feeling threatened? Wearing the family fortune in emeralds around your neck? Or could you be a rock star? Alan Forsyth directs a team of six internationally trained operatives for chaperoning assignments lasting anything from an hour to months. Fees are around R65 per hour.

BABYSITTERS & DOMESTIC HELP

Large hotels and established guest houses provide babysitting services. *See chapter* **Children's Cape Town** *for listings of well-established babysitting companies.* Book well in advance during the holiday season.

Dynamic Domestics
Office 1, 45c Second Ave, Harfield Village, tel. 683-3430.
Supervised drop-and-collect char services (R55 per day), upholstery and carpet cleaning and spring cleaning specials including cleaning equipment (price varies according to the job).

Rent-a-Student
7 Murray House, 25 Hout St, City Centre, tel. 24-6666.
Reliable male and female students (18-22 years old) for babysitting or au pair work at R12 per hour or R60 per day (excl. travelling costs). The agency is open 10am-4pm Mon-Fri.

BEAUTY

The Chelsea Health and Beauty Clinic
17 Wolfe St, Wynberg, tel. 797-7066 or 797-6754.
Open: *8am-7.30pm Mon-Fri, 8am-5.30pm Sat.*
Credit: *cards and cheques.*
Exclusive, soothing salon with high-tech services including biolift facials, toning machines, aromatherapy treatments for men and women.

Clinique Colleen
Shop 11, Corwen St, Claremont, tel. 683-2199.
Open: *8am-5.30pm Mon, Wed and Fri, 8am-9pm Tue and Thu.*
Credit: *cards and cheques.*
Calm, well-located salon with a good range of treatments and a loyal clientele.

Dawn's Skincare Clinic
Medical Square, Main Rd, Sea Point, tel. 434-5580.
Open: *8am-5pm Mon-Fri, 8am-1pm Sat.*
Credit: *cards and cheques.*
Dawn's is practically an institution, with a clientele who wouldn't go a month without their treatments here. Soothing, professional service.

The Face Place
Regent Place, Regent Rd, Sea Point, tel. 434-5486.
Open: *8am-1pm Mon, 8am-5.30pm Tue-Fri, 8am-3pm Sat.*
Credit: *cards and cheques.*
Upmarket, madly fashionable salon with an extensive range of pampering and beauty services.

Linda van Niekerk
Victoria Wharf, Waterfront, tel. 419-2606.
Open: *9am-7pm Mon-Tue, 9am-9pm Wed-Sun.*
Credit: *cards and cheques.*
Elegantly decorated, well-situated and very popular salon.

Regis
This chain of beauty parlours, located in hair salons, offers pleasant service and a full range of beauty services including massage. **Regis** branches are found at:
Hair & Beauty Express, Burg St, City Centre, tel. 234-548.
Hair & Beauty, Picbel Parkade, tel. 419-1936.
Hair & Beauty, Cavendish Square, Claremont, tel. 683-5625.
Hair & Beauty, Adelphi Centre, Sea Point, tel. 434-9070.

Sharon's Skin Care Clinic
Hopeville St, Gardens, tel. 461-1417.
Open: *8am-7pm Mon-Fri, 8.30am-4.30pm Sat.*
Credit: *cards and cheques.*
A highly regarded clinic for a range of professional treatments, including renowned facials.

Taylor House of Health and Beauty
2 Teldol Court, Rosmead Ave, Kenilworth, tel. 61-6224.
Open: *8.30am-5.30pm Mon-Fri, 8.30am-12.30pm Sat.*
Credit: *cards and cheques.*
Expert beauty treatments, including one of the best facials in town and superb aromatherapy, in a wonderfully calming environment.

CELLPHONE HIRE

See chapter **Business**.

COSTUME HIRE

Stage Creations RSA
90 Longmarket St, City Centre, tel. 461-6960 or 45-2510.
Open: *9.30am-4.30pm Mon-Fri, 8.30am-12.30pm Sat.*
Credit: *cheques but no cards.*
Some kids' costumes, but mainly dress-up for adults, as well as hats, wigs, masks, stage make-up and special effects like fake blood. Bring ID or passport.

COURIER SERVICES

See chapter **Business**.

DRYCLEANING

Nannucci
One of the country's largest drycleaning operations, Nannucci has 50 branches throughout the Peninsula. For information on the one nearest to you, call head office, *tel. 761-1120.*

Personal Cleaners
72 Regent Rd, Sea Point, tel. 434-5935.
Excellent service with 25 branches and agents city-wide.

EXCESS BAGGAGE

Dateline
Tel. 934-3656.
For the acquisitive and the packing-challenged – sea and air freight to international destinations, packaging, storage and insurance. Charge per kilogram, documentation and collection. Now that you know, get out and buy things.

FOOD DELIVERY

For couch potatoes, convalescents and sybarites ...

Call-A-Pizza
Sea Point area, tel. 434-0818/9.
Wynberg area, tel. 762-1212.
Observatory area, tel. 448-6147/8.
Bellville area, tel. 948-9005/6.
Open: *5pm-10.30pm Mon-Fri, noon-11pm Sat, noon-10.30pm Sun.*
Credit: *cards and cheques.*
Pizzas, pastas, side orders delivered city-wide. Average delivery fee is R2,30-R6,60.

Mr Delivery
Tel. 439-9916.
Open: *6pm-11pm daily.*
Credit: *cards and cheques.*

Mediterranean, Italian, Oriental, steakhouse and bistro food from a good variety of eateries. Delivery fees R2,70-R6.

FLORAL DELIVERY

Most Cape Town florists are linked to Interflora or Teleflorist, both of which arrange floral delivery nationwide and internationally. And, of course, you can save a bundle and have fun doing so by buying from the flower sellers on Adderley St (next to the Golden Acre) or the Grand Parade (opposite City Hall). Both are Cape Town institutions and you can haggle. The following offer either good prices or truly outstanding arrangements.

Barbara's Flowers (at The Greenhouse and Effects)
143 Kloof St, Gardens, tel. 23-8441.
Open: *8am-5pm Mon-Fri, 9am-1pm Sat.*
Credit: *cards and cheques.*

Barbara's Flowers at The Greenhouse and Effects, 143 Kloof St.

Located in a wooden-floored Victorian building, alongside a marvellously creative nursery/artistic plant shop, Barbara's Flowers is not the place for stiff triangular arrangements. Exquisite continental bouquets and free-style arrangements in recycled paper and moss-covered pots are more the shape of things.

The Flower Warehouse
Shop 3, Palace House, Malta Rd, Salt River, tel. 448-5472/3.
Open: *8.30am-5pm Mon-Thu, 8am-4.30pm Fri, 8am-11.45pm Sat.*
Credit: *cards and cheques.*
Excellent prices and deliveries from R35 upwards, as well as seasonal fruit baskets and arrangements (kosher can be arranged).

Petals
Pier House, Heerengracht, Foreshore, tel. 25-2420.
Open: *8am-5pm Mon-Fri, 7pm-3pm Sat.*
Credit: *cards and cheques.*
The aptly named Flower Walker's distinctive arrangements have adorned some of the city's most fashionable homes and decorated some seriously upmarket establishments. The classy designs and creative approach could turn Morticia Adams into a flower fan.

GIFT DELIVERY

Brittan's Sweets
140 Victoria Wharf, Waterfront, tel. 418-5503.
Open: *8am-10.30pm Mon-Thu and Sun, 8am-11.30pm Fri, 8am-1am Sat.*
Credit: *cards and cheques.*
Irresistible edibles – chocolates (local and imported), dried fruit and nuts in arrangements starting at around R50. Delivery is a minimum R10 charge.

Cape Fruit Supply
56 Newmarket St, Lower Main Rd, Woodstock, tel. 45-1038.
Open: *8am-5pm Mon-Fri, 8am-1pm Sat.*
Credit: *cards and cheques.*
Specialists in fruit and chocolate baskets,

starting at around R25 for a fruit basket, although you can spend R160 on amazing chocolates. Same-day service if you put your order in early.

Hello Baby
1st Floor, Clarensville, 60 Regent Rd, Sea Point, tel. 439-5329.
Open: *9am-1pm Mon-Fri. Closed Sat.*
Credit: *cards and cheques.*
Dried fruit, chocolates (kosher available), champagne, wine and, natch, baby gifts. Fruit baskets are R40 upwards, wine/chocolates start at R55.

GLASSES

See chapter **Shopping**.

A cut above — Yazo 4 Sebastian Designs

HAIRDRESSERS

The following are among the city's most fashionable and highest quality salons, but wherever you go, it's advisable to book in advance during high season. Tipping the shampooist is good form, and you can tip the hairdresser unless you loathe the result.

Aura
Shop 201, Victoria Wharf, Waterfront, tel. 21-4131.
Open: *8.30am-5pm Mon-Fri, 8am-4pm Sat, 10am-4pm Sun.*
Credit: *cards and cheques.*
Excellently situated in the heart of the Waterfront, with free or paid parking areas, and excellent wheelchair access and security, Aura is a seriously hot salon.

Bartholomews Hair
37 Burg St, City Centre, tel. 24-5948.
Open: *8.30am-5pm Mon-Fri, 8.30am-2pm Sat.*
Credit: *cards and cheques.*
Loyal clientele includes models and fashion folk and the quality of cutting, particularly, is notable.

Carlton Hair
Shop 5, The Place, Cavendish Square, Claremont, tel. 61-6882.
Open: *8.30am-5pm Mon-Sat, 10am-2pm Sun.*
Credit: *cards and cheques.*
One of a nationwide chain of salons, so if you can't get an appointment here, get the number of another Carlton hair branch from this one.

D&D Designers for Hair
Tyger Valley Centre, Tyger Valley, tel. 948-4707.
Open: *8am-5pm Mon, 8am-6pm Tue-Thu, 8am-7pm Fri, 8am-5pm Sat.*
Credit: *cards and cheques.*
The sprawling Tyger Valley Centre has enough stores to satisfy even the most avaricious shopper, ample parking and children's activities – all of which means you can *really* concentrate on getting the ultimate hairdo.

Raoul Hair Design
The Courtyard, Main Rd, Sea Point, tel. 439-1885 or 439-1898.
Open: *8am-5pm Mon and Wed-Sat.*
Credit: *cards and cheques.*
Nicely laid-out salon with some slick, expert hairdressers – and within easy walking distance of good delis and renowned San Marco ice-cream.

Yazo 4 Sebastian Designs
Shop 4-5, Victoria and Alfred Hotel Bldg, Pierhead, Waterfront, tel. 21-7745/6.
Open: *9am-5pm Mon-Sat, 10am-5pm Sun.*
Credit: *cards and cheques.*
It's worth going to Yazo for the decor alone – great paint effects and views of the harbour. But the colouring and treatments are particularly good and the clientele is drop-dead trendy.

LAUNDRY

You'll find laundries in most suburbs and generally services include drop-and-collect and coin-operated washing machines. DIY is R2,50-R18 per load and drying is extra, around 50c for five minutes of hot air. You'll find laundries dotted around the city but here are some good and conveniently placed ones:

Bright Wash Laundrette
10 Main Rd, Mowbray, tel. 689-5675.
Open: *7.30am-7pm Mon-Fri, 8am-7pm Sat, 8.30am-4pm Sun.*

Bubbles
48 Regent Rd, Sea Point, tel. 439-7419.
Open: *8am-7pm Mon-Sat.*

Econowash
Adelphi Centre, Main Rd, Sea Point, tel. 434-9728.
Open: *7.30am-8pm Mon-Fri, 8am-5pm Sat, 9am-5pm Sun.*

Lou Mill Laundrette
37 Atlantic Rd, Muizenberg, tel. 788-5389.
Open: *7.30am-7pm Mon-Sat.*

LIBRARIES

Foreigners can become paying members of the City Library and other computerised libraries on a Holiday Visitor Card, valid for three months. Around R12 a card allows you to take out one book, another R12 a second book, etc.

City Library
City Hall, Darling St, City Centre, tel. 462-4400.
Open: *9am-5.30pm Mon, Wed and Fri, 1pm-6pm Tue, 9am-2pm Thu, 9am-4pm Sat.*
In addition to books, the City Library has local, national and international newspapers and magazines in the reading room on the non-fiction floor.

LOST PROPERTY

Items lost on trains or stations, tel. 405-4045. Losses in the city: South African Police, Caledon Square Station, Buitenkant St, tel. 461-7282 ext. 265.

MASSAGE

The Holistic Massage Practitioners Association is an umbrella body that can put you in touch with a a reliable masseuse in your area. For information contact Briony Esterhuizen, tel. 782-5909, or Gayle Friedman, tel. 47-0042.

NAILS

For manicures, see also sections **Beauty** *and* **Hairdressers**.

The Face Place
Regent Place, Regent Rd, Sea Point, tel. 434-5486.
Open: *8am-1pm Mon, 8am-5.30pm Tue-Fri, 8am-3pm Sat.*
Credit: *cards and cheques.*
For the Edwina Scissorhands in you ... fibreglass and gel nails only. By appointment.

PETS

Super Sitters
Tel. 439-4985.
Rates: per visit R16,50, overnight R50,16, 24-hour service (excl. food) R94.
Pet-minding, and visiting and feeding pets for up to 1 hour.

PHARMACIES

See chapter **Survival** for late-night pharmacies. The following offer a good selection of vitamins and homeopathic remedies.

Hypermed Pharmacy
Cnr York and Main roads, Green Point, tel. 434-1414.
Open: 8.30am-9pm daily.
Credit: cards and cheques.
An excellent range of alternative products in addition to conventional medicines plus great service.

A White's Pharmacy
77 Plein St, City Centre, tel. 45-3382.
Open: 8am-5pm Mon-Fri, 8.30am-1pm Sat.
Credit: cards and cheques.
Half of this well-stocked pharmacy is devoted to natural remedies by Weleda, Bioforce and Natura, as well as tablets, tinctures and ointments made on the premises.

REPAIRS: SHOES & HANDBAGS

The following do fine quality repairs, dyeing and shoe covering:

Premier Shoes
155 Kloof St, Tamboerskloof, tel. 24-4904.
Open: 8.30am-1pm and 2pm-5pm Mon-Fri, 8.30am-1pm Sat.
Credit: cards and cheques.

Rocksole
61 Wale St, Bo-Kaap, tel. 24-3858.
Open: 7.30am-5.30pm Mon-Fri, 7.45am-12.30pm Sat.
Credit: cards and cheques.

Modern shopping centres like Cavendish Square abound outside the City Centre.

Shoe Inn
79 Regent Rd, Sea Point, tel. 434-9262.
Open: 9am-5.30pm Mon-Fri, 9am-2pm Sat.
Credit: cards and cheques.

RELIGIOUS SERVICES

CHRISTIAN
The Anglican Church Diocese of Cape Town provides details of 50 Cape Town churches. For information, tel. 23-1253 (weekdays).

JEWISH
The Union of Orthodox Synagogues carries details of the city's eleven synagogues. For information, tel. 461-6310.

MUSLIM
Cape Town boasts a massive number of mosques and the Muslim Judicial Council carries details. For information, tel. 696-5151 or 696-5150 (9am-2pm). Worth noting is the Auwal Mosque (founded in 1798), Dorp St, Bo-Kaap (*see box on the* **Bo-Kaap** *in chapter* **The Sights**).

TATTOOS & BODY PIERCING

Metal Machine
Room 31, 3rd Floor, Sturk's Bldg, Long St, City Centre, tel. 24-0877.
Open: 10am-6pm Mon-Sat.
Credit: cheques but no cards.
Thousands of designs, sterilised needles and body piercing with stainless steel jewellery by a qualified member of the European Professional Piercers Association.

VIDEO HIRE

Movie Magic
Gardens Centre, Mill St, Gardens, tel. 45-6435.
Open: 9am-8.30pm daily.
Nedbank Centre, Kloof Road, Sea Point, tel. 439-2601.
Open: 9am-10pm Mon-Fri, 9am-midnight Sat-Sun.
Cnr Main Rd and Dean St, Newlands, tel. 686-3863.
Open: 9am-8.30pm daily.
Rates: R9 for new videos and R5 for older ones. Contracts start at R26 for four new videos or eight older ones.

Showtime Video
85 Piccadilly Court, Regent Rd, Sea Point, tel. 434-8666.
Open: 9am-midnight daily.
Rates: R9 for new releases and R6,50 for older ones. Contracts start at R25 for eight units.

Paradise Pictures
Cnr St John's and Main roads, Sea Point, tel. 434-3903.
Open: 24 hours daily.
Rates: R9 for one video, R16 for two videos, R21 for three videos, R24 for four videos, R25 for five videos. Video players are R25 a night (R200 deposit).

Pyramid Video Hire
233 Main Rd, Three Anchor Bay, tel. 439-5392.
Open: 9am-midnight daily.
Rates: casual hire R7 per video; contracts start from R50 for 11 videos.

Wild at heart. Cape Town's utterly singular version of the customised bike.

THE ARTS AND ENTERTAINMENT SECTION IS SPONSORED BY

94·5 K-FM

ADDICTIVE RADIO

ARTS & ENTERTAINMENT

Fun, fun, fun – from late-night clubbing and opera to reading all about it – is what this section is all about. We've got the lowdown on the media, upfront news on the clubbing and late-night scene, plus film, theatre, music and dance.

Previous page: David Kramer, singer, composer, local theatre impresario.

TICKETS

Computicket ticket agencies city-wide handle theatre, cinema, film festival and special events bookings. Credit cards are accepted.

Computicket enquiries: 21-4715. Computicket branches are open 9am-5pm Mon-Fri and 9am-4pm Sat, except where indicated below:

City Centre:
Sun Gallery, Cape Sun Hotel *(closes at 1pm on Sat).*
Ground Floor, Gardens Centre, Mill St, Gardens.
Heroes, Piazza Level, Golden Acre, Adderley St *(closes at 1pm on Sat).*
Boardmans, Burg St *(closes at 1pm on Sat).*
Victoria Wharf, Waterfront.
Nico Theatre Complex, Foreshore *(closes at 1pm on Sat).*

Southern Suburbs:
Baxter Theatre Complex, Main Rd, Rondebosch.
Shop 3, Hyperama, Blue Route Centre, Tokai.
AP Jones, Main Rd, Fish Hoek *(closes at 1pm on Sat).*
Howard Centre, Pinelands *(closes at 1pm on Sat).*
Exclusive Books, Constantia Village, Constantia.
Maynard Mall, Wynberg *(closes at 1pm on Sat).*

Northern Suburbs:
Garden & Home, Tyger Valley Centre, Tyger Valley.
Centre Point, Milnerton *(closes at 1pm on Sat).*
Shop 8, Hyperama, N1 City, Goodwood.
First Floor, Sanlam Centre, Parow.

Atlantic Seaboard:
Satbel Centre, Somerset Rd, Green Point *(closes at 1pm on Sat).*
First Floor, Adelphi Centre, Sea Point *(closes at 1pm on Sat).*
Theatre on the Bay, Camps Bay.

Computicket Teletex Service, tel. 21-4715, takes phone bookings with a credit card number.

MEDIA

The food, wine and scenery may make you forget about the rest of the world, but in case you need reminding, here's the dope on newspapers, magazines, radio and TV.

It may be the summertime and easy living, it may be the city's liberal reputation, but creative folk have traditionally been attracted to Cape Town. With tourism and electronic communication booming, and life in a gentler environment becoming increasingly alluring, upcountry media people are heading here in droves. So are international photographers, movie- and commercials makers who've spotted the potential of the good light, great weather and budget-busting (for them) foreign exchange rate.

Cost-cutting proximity to the harbour and the moderate climate meant that major local publishing houses were established here even though the majority of consumers are concentrated around Johannesburg.

NEWSPAPERS

LOCAL PAPERS

The *Cape Times* is the city's morning paper, upgraded by Independent Media owner Tony O'Reilly. Events listings are good and there are reviews in the arts-oriented *Focus* section. The fatter Friday edition contains the entertainment-geared *Top of the Times* supplement. The *Cape Times* also runs good motoring, property and business supplements.

The *Argus* is the daily afternoon paper. Weekday editions contain the entertainment-oriented *Tonight!* supplement. And the *Weekend Argus*, with Saturday and Sunday editions, contains entertainment and news supplements.

Cape Ads, a classifieds-only publication, is the place to look or advertise for everything from flat rentals to cars. Ads are placed free and it's available at R3 from news-stands and stores.

NATIONAL PAPERS

A number of national English-language newspapers are available in Cape Town. *Business Day*, produced in Johannesburg by Times Media, focuses largely on national and international business news. Available Mon-Fri.

The Citizen, also headquartered in Johannesburg, is available Mon-Fri in Cape Town. Notorious for its spelling errors and history – it was first set up by the apartheid government as a propaganda vehicle – it runs plenty of international wire-service copy.

The Sunday Times, the country's highest-circulating publication, is a mélange of international and national news with a magazine and arts section. The Cape Town edition contains a *Metro* section for Cape news and listings.

Newspaper vendors plying their trade in the City Centre.

The Sowetan, a Johannesburg paper edited by the outspoken Aggrey Klaaste, is available Mon-Fri and contains some national and international news, but emphasises the Johannesburg area.

New Nation, a weekly that comes out on Friday, has a long anti-apartheid history and a strong political slant, generally focused on the Johannesburg region.

The Weekly Mail & Guardian, an independent weekly, appears on Fridays and contains excellent news and features produced by local writers, foreign correspondents and sections culled from the British Guardian.

City Press, a Sunday paper, is big on political and grassroots issues with a high black readership.

INTERNATIONAL PUBLICATIONS

Major British, American and European glossy magazines are available at most news agents and bookstores but they're generally two months out of date and expensive.

AFTER-HOURS BOOKSHOPS

Paperbacks at:

Picbel Parkade Building, Strand St, tel. 419-1784.

Gardens Centre, Mill St, Gardens, tel. 45-7654.

204 Main Rd, Sea Point, tel. 439-4624.

Exclusive Books at:

Constantia Village, Constantia, tel. 794-7800.

Lower Level Cavendish Square, Claremont, tel. 64-3030.

225 Victoria Wharf, Waterfront, tel. 419-0905.

For more on bookshops, see chapter **Shopping**.

International newspapers available include The London Financial Times, London Sunday Times, Sunday Telegraph, Observer, Independent, Weekly Express, Telegraph and International Herald Tribune. You may have to order them in advance, and they're pricey.

Selected foreign-language publications are available at **ID Booksellers**, 26 Parliament St, City Centre, tel. 23-9104 and **Deutsche Buch und Kunsthandlung**, 17 Burg St, tel. 23-7832.

MAGAZINES

There's a fairly wide selection of local magazines, although the choice isn't a patch on Europe's or America's. Freebies include What's on in the Cape (available at tourist information bureaux). For listings and travel information, try the monthly Going out in the Cape (entertainment listings) and the monthly Getaway (travel between the Cape and Kenya).

In a league of its own in terms of quality and style is ADA, an idiosyncratic, independent and beautifully produced publication edited by architect Jennifer Sorrell. Its focus is South African culture and you'll find it at stores like Exclusive Books.

For general interest served with a heavy dollop of tabloid stories, there's weekly mega-seller You, and weekly Personality.

For gloss, glitz and glamour, try Style (Cape edition) and Tribute, a glossy with a predominantly black, upmarket readership and focus.

The top English women's glossies are Fair Lady (fortnightly), Femina (monthly) and Cosmopolitan (monthly). All contain features, fashion, food, beauty and decor.

The financial publications are the weekly Financial Mail and Finance Week and Black Enterprise, a publication devoted to black business.

SPECIALIST MAGAZINES

For health and fitness, try Longevity. For gun news there's Magnum, and Sports Illustrated Monthly is precisely what its title implies. Jive is young and music-geared, and Leadership is a high-gloss, socio-politically-oriented publication out approximately every two months. The wonderfully titled *Noseweek* is the closest South Africa gets to *Private Eye*, with gossip, investigative pieces and humour. It's approximately quarterly. And if all the reading gets you down, buy the monthly *Wine* magazine for news on the most palatable way to drown your sorrows.

THE BOX

The South African Broadcasting Corporation (SABC) TV stations, TV1, CCV and NNTV, offer news, talk shows, game shows, sport, kiddies' programmes, education and movies. These aren't always arranged according to language, so don't be suprised to see programmes and presenters switch from English to Xhosa to Zulu to Afrikaans.

Quality varies. Ever since *Dallas* hit the country in the 70s, soap opera plots and stars have been national preoccupations. *The Bold and the Beautiful* and *Neighbours* have ardent, frequently obsessive fans. Even Winnie Mandela is rumoured to love *Loving*. And South Africa has its own soap, *Egoli*.

The independent pay-channel, M-Net, features entertainment, sports and movies, and satellite channels provide a large variety of couch potato options.

LET'S TALK ABOUT SEX ...

Since the censorship-battling launch of *Penthouse* in 1991, sexy adult magazines have mushroomed in South Africa. Once the land of printers' stars and the moral minority, the country now even boasts a Johannesburg-based swingers magazine. The pin-up/adult magazines also includes *Playboy*, *Hustler* and *Scope*.

RADIO

Cape stations like **KFM** (94,5 fm band) and **Radio Good Hope FM** (94-97 fm band) are music-geared. KFM offers a diet of adult contemporary; Good Hope's selection is younger and boppier. FMR (Fine Music Radio) is devoted to classical, jazz, screen and world music.

English-language national stations available in Cape Town include **SAfm** (104-107 fm), which features news, talk shows, classical music, sports and radio plays. **5FM** (88,2-89,9 fm) and **Radio Metro** are music-oriented. **Radio Lotus** (97,8 fm band) is aimed at Indian listeners and features news, music and talk shows. There's also **Afrikaans Stereo** (100-104 fm band), **Radio Xhosa** and several other indigenous African-language stations.

Offices of Radio KFM, the Cape's fastest growing radio station.

THEATRE

Although it will never beat cricket in the popularity stakes, Cape Town's theatre scene aims at quality, whether the fare is Fugard or Feydeau.

The debate over whether Cape Town or Johannesburg is South Africa's cultural capital is a long and ongoing one, and the answer you'll get will probably depend on whether you're talking to a Capetonian or a Jo'burger. Certainly, what the Mother City provides in terms of creative stimulation and sheer beauty is equalled by Johannesburg's ability to provide bucks and work opportunities. And for a while, lucre won over loveliness, with many of the city's top performers and directors heading upcountry. The local theatre scene is picking up, however. More venues have opened up, community theatre is growing steadily and cabaret venues, usually in restaurants, are increasingly popular.

You'll get a mixed bill of fare, from farce to experimental productions with good musical cabaret productions, one-handers and crowd-pleasers for good measure. Performances to look out for include those by satirists Pieter-Dirk Uys, Robert Kirby and Mark Banks, musicals by David Kramer and Taliep Petersen, Marthinus Basson productions and plays by award-winning playwright Charles Fourie. Many Johannesburg productions come to Cape Town – see any plays by the extraordinary Athol Fugard and the award-winning Sue Pam-Grant, as well as works directed by Janice Honeyman, mime by Andrew Buckland. The University of Cape Town Drama School stages regular student productions, and many are worth watching.

Cape production of Tom Stoppard's *Travesties*.

Check newspaper listings and see box on **Tickets** in section **Arts & Entertainment** for advance bookings.

THEATRE VENUES

The Baxter
Main Rd, Rondebosch (near the UCT Music School). Theatre info and bookings, tel. 685-7880. Restaurant info and bookings, tel. 689-5351. Cinema info and bookings, tel. 685-7880.
Admission: R20-R45.
Credit: all major cards.
The Baxter Theatre complex with its raw brick interior and exterior and Table Mountain backdrop has secured a solid reputation for staging some of South Africa's finest indigenous theatre and it can lay claim to 18 years of involvement with community theatre.

The spacious **Main Theatre** has staged local and international productions, musicals and alternative dance and music. **The Studio**, on the top floor, is small and intimate for experimental and serious productions. For cabaret, food and drink are sometimes served. The **Concert Hall** has hosted dramas, musicals and recitals.

There are also frequent art and craft exhibitions, as well as two cinemas. A restaurant and late-night bar popular with performers give you a good chance of meeting one of the cast after final curtain call.

The Baxter has some facilities for disabled patrons, the Sennheiser System for the hearing-impaired, and Medidrama which provides free medical service to all patrons.

Dock Road Theatre
Dock Rd, Pierhead, Waterfront (next to the Dock Road Café), tel. 419-5522.
Admission: R20-R35.
Credit: major cards.
The Dock Road Theatre is set in the building that housed South Africa's first electric power station (operational from 1882). A small, relaxed and intimate theatre, it opened to box-office success and has kept the crowds coming with a mixture of musicals and well-chosen drama. People in wheelchairs can get into the theatre quite easily, but must be seated in the front rows.

Little Theatre
University of Cape Town, Hiddingh Hall Campus, Orange St (opposite the Labia cinema), tel. 24-2340 or 24-0034 (a/h).
Admission: R7,50-R20.
This UCT-run venue is intimate and comfortable with 245 seats. It's mainly used for UCT Drama School productions, but outside companies perform here occasionally. The 70-seat **Arena** section is used for workshops and productions like children's puppet shows. Wheelchair-friendly.

The Live Theatre
103 Harrington St, City Centre, tel. 45-1608.
Admission: R15-R25. Student and pensioner tickets are R10.
This 50-seat venue is home to the renowned **Theatre for Africa** group, and it also runs productions by other companies. Patrons in wheelchairs should use the side entrance, and be warned that there are some steps into the venue with no wheelchair ramp. Make prior arrangements.

Long Street Theatre
St John's Arcade, cnr Long and Waterkant streets, tel. 418-3496.
Admission: R7-R15. Discounts offered to students and pensioners.
The Long Street Theatre has two performance areas – a 120-seat drama and dance space and an intimate cabaret venue. Wheelchair-bound patrons should be warned that access to the theatre is by stairs.

Maynardville
Wynberg Park, Wynberg, tel. 21-5470.
Admission: R20-R25. Discount tickets can be bought half-an-hour before the show, if available, at R10 to students and pensioners.
Credit: all major cards and cheques.
Shakespeare under the stars is the popular recipe for the Maynardville open-air performances, which usually run annually from January-end of February. Now well into four decades of productions, it's set in a wonder-

ful park, so take a pre-performance picnic, as well as cushions and blankets or warm clothes for the performance (it gets chilly). Watch press for details. Wheelchair-friendly.

Nico Malan Theatre Centre
DF Malan St, Foreshore, City Centre, tel. 21-5470 (theatre switchboard), 21-7839 (box-office). Dial-a-Seat for credit card bookings, tel. 21-7695. Café De L'Opera restaurant, tel. 21-5470.
Headquarters to the performing arts council, CAPAB, the Nico stages theatre, musicals, opera, dance and experimental theatre, and comprises the large **Main Theatre**, the smaller **Arena** for experimental and cabaret productions and the **Opera House**. Once associated with Eurocentric productions and apartheid structures, the Nico is widening its focus to include Afrocentric work. Low-priced previews and matinees, discounts for schools, students and state pensioners. The Nico is wheelchair-friendly, but there are only two wheelchair seats in the Opera House and Main Theatre. Wheelchair access to the Arena by prior arrangement.

Oude Libertas Amphitheatre
Stellenbosch Farmers Winery, Adam Tas Rd, Stellenbosch, tel. 808-7474.
Admission: *average R20. Book at Computicket.*
Open between November and March, this open-air venue outside Stellenbosch is a treat. Performances range from opera and dance to drama, music and mime. A wonderful setting among gardens and vineyards, so take a pre-performance picnic. Wheelchair-friendly.

Theatre On The Bay
Link St, Beachfront, Camps Bay, tel. 438-3301.
Admission: *R31-R37.*
Credit: *all major cards and cheques.*

Local Cape theatre beats New York to the staging of *Boy Meets Boy*.

Originally a tram shed, then a converted cinema, The Theatre on the Bay is now smartly done up with notable 'draped' exterior. It offers a steady stream of farce, revue, drama and light romantic comedies with top South African casts and, thanks to the sharp theatrical insight of owner Pieter Toerien, it's frequently the venue for local versions of hot Broadway and West End productions. There's a pleasant bar and a good restaurant upstairs. Wheelchair-friendly, but prior warning is needed. Use the side door for access and bear in mind that you must book in rows A-H.

CABARET RESTAURANTS

Eauver the Top at The Light Fantastic
3 Kent Bldg, 13 York Rd, Muizenberg, tel. 788-3746.
Admission: *theatre around R20, R3 cover charge for the nightclub.*
This fabulous cabaret venue transforms into a nightclub after the show, as well as a movie club and licensed restaurant. There's a performance every night except Monday. Shows tend towards cabaret and music, and quality is usually high. Wheelchair-friendly.

Upstairs at Elaine's
38 Trill Rd (off Lower Main Rd), Observatory, tel. 47-9425.
Admission: *R20-R25.*
Buzzy restaurant/cabaret venue with bohemian-meets-plush decor (green walls and red velvet drapes), Upstairs at Elaine's is one of the most enjoyable places to catch new and established cabaret talent. Esteemed restauranteur/owner Jacqui Craig is one of a growing band of Johannesburgers to have opted for the Mother City, and both her expertise as an organiser and her enthusiasm show. The 55-seater offers good curries (a three-course meal averages R35), friendly service and some worthwhile acts. Arrive at 7.15pm if you want to eat before the show, which usually starts at 9pm. Book in advance if you can – the place is popular. There's a steep flight of stairs to the theatre, so it's not suitable for wheelchairs.

COMMUNITY THEATRE GROUPS

Watch out for the following at theatres and festivals.

Amabutho Warriors
Internationally successful dance group with a modern and traditional repertoire. They've toured the US and have performed at the BP Showcase of Community Plays. Contact Joyful Cele, tel. 638-5562.

Manyanani
Award-winning theatre and dance group that participated in the 1990 Township Mini-Arts Festival at the Zolani Centre and the Youth Festival at the Baxter Theatre. Contact Thembani Luzipho, tel. 31-6876.

Mbokotho
This group aims to teach drama to township youth and to help expose them to theatre experience. Contact Abbey Xakwe, tel. 34-2343.

New Africa Theatre Project (NATP)
An independent, non-profit educational organisation, NATP's Outreach Programme teaches drama skills to the youth. Contact Dumile Magodla, tel. 47-8792.

Nyanga Theatre Company
Founded in 1982 by drama students at the Nyanga Art Centre, the company holds a variety of workshops, including poetry, drama and story-telling for youth, students and the unemployed. For details contact Douglas Qotywa, tel. 34-5971.

POETRY READINGS

Contact the following for details of poetry readings:

Café Matisse, *76 Main Rd, Kalk Bay, tel. 788-1123.*
Irma Stern Museum, *Cecil Rd, Rosebank, tel. 685-5686.*
Josephine Mill, *Boundary Road, Newlands, tel. 686-4939.*
Natale Labia Museum, *192 Main Rd, Muizenberg, tel. 788-4106/7.*

FILM

From film festivals to box-office hits, nostalgia buff societies to double-bill cheapies ... Where to go, and what to do if you're an aspiring director.

Cape Town is home to a core of obstinately loyal film-makers, many of them award winners, who've resisted moving to Johannesburg, and an increasing number of foreign movie- and commercials makers are discovering the city's scenic, financial and climatic advantages. In case more encouragement is needed, **The Cape Film and Video Foundation** has been established to motivate foreign investment and to market local talent and resources. It's a priority industry on the government's Reconstruction and Development Programme.

Cape Town's three annual film festivals screen European and American fringe and art movies. They are the International Film Festival (April-May), the Weekly Mail & Guardian Festival (September) and the French Film Festival (September-October). The festivals are held at the Labia, the Baxter, the University of Cape Town Campus and, sometimes, special-use Ster-Kinekor and Nu Metro cinemas. Bookings can be made at the cinemas or Computicket (*see box* **Tickets** *in section* **Arts & Entertainment**.)

The movie complex in the Victoria Wharf Shopping Mall at the Waterfront.

MAINSTREAM CINEMAS

Ster-Kinekor and Nu Metro

These are South Africa's major distributors and new movies are released on Fridays. Book at cinemas or **Computicket** (*see box on* **Tickets** *in section* **Arts & Entertainment**.)

Nu Metro admission rates are R10,50 for all shows except 7.45pm screenings, which cost R15. Pensioners pay R4,50 for all screenings except 7.45pm shows, which are normal price.

Ster-Kinekor tickets are R10 and pensioners pay R4 a show until 5.30pm, after which normal prices are charged.

Most cinemas are wheelchair friendly, but check.

Although there are no student discounts at mainstream venues, the budget cinema, The Constantia Rosebank, Main Rd, Rosebank, tel. 686-6649, screens recent releases for R7,50 a ticket.

ALTERNATIVE & INDEPENDENT

Bookings for these can be made at Computicket or the venue.

Baxter Cinema

The Baxter Theatre, Screen 1 and 2, Main Rd, Rondebosch, tel. 689-1069.

Admission: R10 for all shows, subject to the following concessions (at door only): children (under 12) R8, Easy Rider Cards R8, pensioners R4 (except for 8pm and 10pm shows). Discount pre-paid admission tickets are R80 for 10 vouchers.
Part of the Baxter Theatre complex, these cinemas generally show film festival fare. See press for screen times and shows.

BMW Imax Cinema
BMW Pavilion, Waterfront, tel. 419-7364.
Admission: depends on show. Group discounts for 20 or more.
Africa's only giant-format screen boasts a five-storey-high screen and 12 000 watts of six-channel, wraparound Imax digital sound to create a larger-than-life experience. Seating is unreserved so arrive early.

Eauver The Top at the Light Fantastic
3 Kent Bldg, 13 York Rd (opposite Surfers' Corner), Muizenberg, tel. 788-3746.
Admission: R3.
A 32-seater cinema for classic, art and foreign films in one of Cape Town's most 'happening' venues. There's also cabaret, a nightclub, à la carte menu and booze. What more could a movie-lover want? Check venue or press for details.

Luxurama
Park Rd, Wynberg, tel. 797-6152.
Admission: R7 for 10am and 2pm shows, R9 for the 8pm show on weekdays. Sat shows at 10am and 1.30pm (R7), 4pm and 8pm (R9).
This unique bug-house screens double-feature current movies at discount rates. Pensioners pay R2, but there's no student discount.

The Labia
Screen 1 and 2, 68 Orange St, Gardens (near the Mount Nelson Hotel), tel. 24-5927.
Admission: R10 for all shows, subject to the following concessions (at door only): children (under 12) R8, Easy Rider Cards R8, pensioners R4 (except for 8pm and 10pm shows). There are also discount pre-paid admission tickets at R80 for 10 vouchers. Advance booking.

A venerable institution, The Labia shows main-circuit movies, but concentrates on art and foreign fare, film festivals and retrospectives. There are two cinemas and a small, good coffee/snack bar. The main cinema is wheelchair friendly. See press for details or collect a programme from the cinema.

South African National Gallery
Government Avenue, Gardens, tel. 45-1628.
Admission: free.
Lunchtime art and culture-oriented movies are screened in the Annexe adjacent to the Gallery which borders the city's beautiful Company Gardens (*see chapter* **The Sights**). Phone to check screening dates. Annual Weekly Mail & Guardian Film Festival entries are also shown here.

SOCIETIES, ASSOCIATIONS & SCHOOLS

Cape Town Film And Television School
18 Rhodes Ave, Mowbray, tel. 685-4358.
Three-year, full-time and short courses on movie-making. The youth programme, Young Filmmakers, is geared to school children.

Cape Town Film Society
South African Museum, Queen Victoria St, tel. 439-2900.
A veteran of five decades, the Society screens vintage and quality movies. Screenings are on Sundays at 8pm and there's a R60 annual membership fee, although you can pay R10 for a try-out which is deducted from the annual fee. For details phone Peter Katz at 439-2900 or write to PO Box 2232, Cape Town, 8000.

Cape Film and Video Foundation
Tel. 22-2900.
Launched in 1995, this association for entrepreneurs, trade unions, non-governmental organisations and teaching institutions is designed to promote the Cape as a movie-making centre, and to provide training, development and a forum for film-makers and allied industries.

Mayibuye Centre
University of the Western Cape, Bellville, tel. 959-2954.
Mayibuye, a Nguni word meaning 'let it return', aims at protecting the heritage of the anti-apartheid struggle and promoting new avenues for creative expression. The Centre's diverse activities include film festivals, discussions and debates. It also maintains a video library and an archive of 1 000 documentaries and hundreds of hours of news and stock footage.

The National Television and Video Association (NTVA)
PO Box 16140, Vlaeberg, Cape Town, 8018, tel. 23-0975.
Southern Africa's largest association for independent TV producers, manufacturers and distributors.

Players' Film Circle
Foreign movie fans can join the Circle for Sunday screenings at the Metro Cinema, Main Rd, Sea Point or for midweek shows at 12 Ingleside Rd, Camps Bay. The Cannes award-winning advertisements are also screened by the Circle every February. Annual membership of R30 buys you two movies a week and for R25 six movies of your choice are screened. For details, phone Avron Kaplan, tel. 24-2336 or write to PO Box 3057, Cape Town, 8000.

UCT Film Society
The University of Cape Town, Main Campus, Rondebosch.
Alternative films are shown on Wednesdays at 7pm. For details, call Nodi Murphy, 240-7320.

LOOK THIS WAY – CAPE TOWN MOVIE-MAKERS

Cape Town's movie industry is flexing its muscles, but the influx of international movie- and commercials makers and the growing recognition that South Africa needs an authentic movie industry may change that.

Local film-makers to look out for at movie festivals like The Weekly Mail & Guardian festival, on TV and on circuit include: Prolific feature and TV director, the award-winning Dirk de Villiers. Cameraman/director Cliff Bestall, whose work includes the documentaries *Cape Fear*, British Royal TV Award-winner *Maids and Madams*, Emmy Award-winning *Drowning in Blood* and the superb TV series *Ordinary People*. Longtime BBC producer and literary critic, Adam Lowe. Writer/producer/director/cameraman Jimi Matthews (*Suffer the Children, How I'd Love To Feel Free, Where Fragments Are Universe*). Documentary-maker Liz Fish, who has produced and shot some 35 community-based videos and worked for foreign network TV (award-winning *The Long Journey of Clement Zulu*). Bridget Thompson, an independent film-maker with a strong interest in 'third cinema'. Lindy Wilson has made independent documentaries since 1978 and her notable work includes *Robben Island — Our University*.

DANCE

Small but vibrant, Cape Town's dance scene may not be in the league of New York or London, but it does have a distinctive flavour. Many Cape Town-trained dancers have gone on to careers with the world's leading companies. You saw them here first!

Cape Town's dance scene is active and enthusiastic, but restricted by funding shortages. There's one professional classical dance company – **CAPAB** – and one professional contemporary dance company – **Jazzart**, now working together. The city also boasts the highly regarded University of Cape Town Ballet School, which is headed up by Professor Elizabeth Triegaardt. For the rest, dance events are limited to private studio performances staged in school halls, occasionally at theatres or, courtesy of big-business sponsorship, at festivals like the annual First National Bank Vita Dance Indaba.

High flying culture: CAPAB's production of *Carmen*.

Informal street performances are a pleasure though, with buskers in the City Centre around St George's Mall and Greenmarket Square. And although Cape Town audiences traditionally favour ballet over modern dance, the contemporary scene is experimental, progressive and increasingly cross-cultural, with a blend of ethnic African and European/American influences. *Check newspaper listings and* **Computicket** *for dance performances.*

For more on Computicket advance bookings, see box on **Tickets** *in section* **Arts & Entertainment***.*

DANCE VENUES

Agfa Amphitheatre
Cape Town Waterfront, tel. 418-2369.
Entry: *free.*
Situated on the Waterfront, the Agfa Amphitheatre occasionally hosts classical and contemporary dance shows. Information on these is available at Waterfront Information. Facilities for disabled people.

The Baxter Theatre
Main Rd, Rondebosch, tel. 685-7880.
Admission: *R18-R25.*
Credit: *all major cards.*
Smaller than the Nico, but also comfortable, The Baxter tends towards contemporary dance performances. The UCT Ballet School's annual show is staged here. Facilities for disabled people.

The Nico Malan Theatre Centre
DF Malan St, Foreshore, tel. 21-5470 (info/bookings) or Dial-A-Seat 21-7695.
Admission: *ballet matinees R18-R29, evening performances R22-R35.*
Credit: *all major cards.*

The city's biggest theatre complex, the Nico comprises the *Opera House*, *Main Theatre* and the smaller *Arena*. Ballet is generally performed in the Opera House, occasionally in the Main Theatre. Large and well patronised, if somewhat bland, the venue is comfortable and houses a bar and restaurant. CAPAB performs here regularly. Facilities for disabled people.

Oude Libertas Amphitheatre
Stellenbosch Farmers Winery, Adam Tas Rd, Stellenbosch, tel. 808-7474.
Admission: *average R20. Book through Computicket.*
This open-air theatre just outside Stellenbosch is delightful for summertime ballet and Spanish dance performances, which run from end November to end March. Take a picnic basket for a pre-show dinner in the lush garden and vineyard surroundings. Facilities for disabled people.

PROFESSIONAL DANCE COMPANIES

CAPAB Ballet Company
2 Lovers' Walk, University of Cape Town Campus, Rondebosch, tel. 689-4346.
Cape Town's only professional classical dance company, CAPAB has some 50 dancers and a varied repertoire. Performances are usually at the Nico, but there's also a season at the Oude Libertas Amphitheatre (*see* **Dance Venues** *above*) and provincial tours. In addition to professional perfor-

The rhythm of Africa – street dancing in St George's Mall.

mances, CAPAB has been extensively involved in outreach programmes designed to take classical dance to under-privileged communities. *Nico for All*, which is funded by big business and individuals, sponsors the visits by township residents, especially children, to ballet and opera final dress rehearsals. And CAPAB's *Ballet For All* programme has been pivotal in the establishment and running of dance schools in Guguletu, Khayelitsha and Langa townships.

Jazzart Dance Theatre Company
Second Floor, Stella Bldg, 32 Jameson St, City Centre, tel. 24-5349.
The city's only professional contemporary company is directed by award-winning Artistic Director Alfred Hinkel and Company Director Nicolette Moses. Consisting of 15 dancers, it became part of CAPAB in 1992. Jazzart performs regularly in the city and surrounding towns and offers lively jazz, dance theatre and ethnic African dance, including gumboot dancing. Regular studio concerts are around R10 a ticket. Classes available.

CONTEMPORARY DANCE STUDIOS

Private, mainly contemporary, dance studios perform intermittently at the Baxter and Nico theatres (*see* **Dance Venues** *earlier in this chapter*). Performers to look out for include the Full Circle Dance Company, Zama Dance, the Yaku Dance Theatre, Silverleaf, Atlantic Dance, the Barbara Holden School of Dance, North West Dance Company and the Brigitte Reeve Dance Centre.

African influences, rhythms and music frequently inform contemporary choreography, making for an interesting mix.

SPANISH DANCE

Cape Town's leading Spanish dance companies are the Carolyn Holden Spanish Dance Company (headed by Holden whose stage name is Carolina Rosa), Danza Lorca (headed by Mavis Becker whose stage name is Marina Lorca) and the Wilvan Dance Company (directed by Veronica Williams). All three companies perform at the Nico, the Baxter, the Victoria and Alfred Waterfront and the Oude Libertas Amphitheatre Summer Season. For details check newspaper listings or with the venue (*see* **Dance Venues** *earlier in this chapter*).

BALLROOM DANCING

The increasingly popular ballroom scene focuses on regular competitive events. Three annual championships are held at the Good Hope Centre – the Cape Provincial Championship (around April), the Republic Dance Teachers' Association Classic (around July) and the Western Province Championships (around September). For details on ballroom dancing and events, contact former dance champ Albie Matthews, tel. 461-1435.

Ballroom dancing lessons are available at **Arthur Murray Dance Studios,** *The Atrium, Main Rd, Claremont, tel. 61-5069.*

DANCE GEAR SHOPS

Leotards, tights and the like are available at major sports and department stores. For specialised gear try the following:
Balletique, *511 CTC Bldg, Plein St, City Centre, tel. 461-7579* or *57a Regent Rd, Sea Point, tel. 439-3807.*
Turning Point, *Tyger Valley Shopping Centre, Tyger Valley, tel. 945-2651.*

MUSIC

Mozart and Verdi in concert halls or chamber music under the stars, hot rock or cool jazz in smoky dens ... Here's where to find what sets your soul soaring.

CLASSICAL & OPERA

As a gracious setting for music Cape Town takes some beating, and the city boasts established theatres and inspiring outdoor venues. The concert seasons for the Cape Town Symphony Orchestra (CTSO) are Summer/Autumn (January-June) and Winter/Spring (July-December). Recitals are generally on Thursday and Sunday nights at the City Hall. Thursdays are usually for more adventurous classical works and visiting international musicians. Sundays frequently include Beethoven or Mozart. Young local musicians may also get a solo spot. The CTSO also offers a diverse programme of concerts on wine estates, and at civic centres and venues in areas surrounding Cape Town.

Summer heralds outdoor concerts at the Waterfront Agfa Amphitheatre (where they're free) and the Kirstenbosch Botanical Gardens (where all you pay is entry into the Gardens). Along with smaller orchestras, the CTSO also performs at the city's January Proms.

The CAPAB Orchestra, resident at the Nico Malan Theatre Centre, accompanies ballet and opera, and performs independently. Both the CTSO and the CAPAB orchestras are involved in youth and community programmes.

Open-air concert at the Waterfront Agfa Amphitheatre.

The City Hall and the Nico Malan Theatre Centre are the city's most established music and opera venues, but there are seasonal performances at the Baxter Concert Hall, the Josephine Mill in Newlands and the Oude Libertas Amphitheatre in Stellenbosch. Watch newspapers for details. *See also chapter* **Cape Town by Season**.

Opera in Cape Town dates to the early 19th century, when musicals and French *opéras comiques* were performed and by the end of the century, operas were staged regularly by visiting professional and local amateur companies. The South African College of Music established an opera school in 1946, and the first touring production, in association with the University of Cape Town, was in 1964.

The CAPAB opera repertoire includes works by Wagner, Strauss and Weber as well as Italian works and popular musicals.

For booking info, see box **Tickets** *in section* **Arts & Entertainment**.

The Arts Association of Bellville
The Library Centre, Carel van Aswegen St, Bellville, tel. 918-2301.
Admission: *free.*
Musical evenings ranging from chamber music to Latin-American and European folk songs feature in a vibrant, informal art gallery environment. The atmosphere is relaxed and sociable and performances, usually held at 8.15pm on the last Sunday of the month, are free. Wheelchair-friendly.

The Baxter
Main Rd, Rondebosch. Info and bookings, tel. 685-7880. Restaurant info and bookings, tel. 689-5351.
Admission: *R20-R45.*
Credit: *major cards and cheques.*
The raw brick Baxter complex contains a raked concert auditorium, compact theatre, cabaret/experimental studio, small gallery and restaurant. It's the venue for opera, lunch-hour concerts, youth ballet and theatre. Some facilities for disabled patrons, and the Sennheiser System for hearing-impaired patrons.

City Hall
Darling St, City Centre. Bookings, tel. 400-2230. CTSO, tel. 462-1250. Box-office on concert evenings, tel. 461-7084 (7.15pm-8pm).
An impressive, elaborate sandstone creation opened in 1905, the City Hall houses an organ with more than 3 000 pipes, the city library, art collection and a tower with a 39-bell carillon, which is occasionally played by the city carilloneur. The City Hall is headquarters to the CTSO, which rehearses and performs here on Thursday and Sunday nights. It was from the porch at the entrance of the City Hall that Nelson Mandela gave his first public speech, after his release, to crowds on the Grand Parade across the street. Wheelchair-friendly.

Josephine Mill
Boundary Road, Newlands, tel. 686-4939.
Admission: *R12.*
Credit: *major cards and cheques. Credit card phone bookings, tel. 686-4939.*
Cape Town's only surviving and operational water mill, established in 1840, houses a working milling museum, conference facilities and the Threshers Tea Garden. It also produces Josephine stone-ground flour. The Nedbank Sunday Summer Concert Season (early November-end February) features outdoor classical, jazz, folk, swing and choral music in a mellow atmosphere on the banks of the tree-fringed Liesbeek River. Disabled access is extremely limited.

Kirstenbosch Botanical Gardens
Rhodes Drive, Newlands, tel. 762-1166.
Admission: *concerts are free, but entrance to Kirstenbosch is R4 (adults) and R1 (children). Donations welcome.*
The Appletiser Summer Sunset Concerts (December-March) are held in the renowned Kirstenbosch Botanical Gardens on the lawn next to Matthew's Rockery. The concerts last an hour and are 5.30pm-6.30pm (December to February) and 5pm-6pm (March). Occasionally other concerts are held in the Gardens (watch press for details). Bring blankets, pillows and a picnic for this unique experience. The concert venue is moderately wheelchair-friendly, but is being upgraded.

Natale Labia Museum Soirées
Natale Labia Museum, 192 Main Rd, Muizenberg, tel. 788-4106/7.
Admission: *R12. Student and pensioners' concessions available.*
One-hour chamber music performances on the fourth Sunday of the month, in the grand 1929 villa-turned-museum originally built for Prince and Princess Labia. Wheelchair-friendly.

Nico Malan Theatre Centre
DF Malan St, Foreshore, City Centre, tel. 21-5470 (theatre switchboard), tel. 21-7839 (box-office). Dial-a-Seat for credit card bookings, tel. 21-7695. Café De L'Opera restaurant, tel. 21-5470.
Admission: *Lunch-hour concerts: R8 and R5 for students and pensioners. Sunday afternoon concerts: R25. Opera and musicals: R18 upwards. Low-priced previews and matinées, discounts for schools, students and welfare pensioners.*
Headquarters of the performing arts council, CAPAB, the Nico stages theatre, musicals, opera, dance and experimental theatre, and comprises the large **Main Theatre**, the smaller **Arena** for experimental and cabaret productions, and the **Opera House**. The Portofino festival, featuring young soloists, runs every August, and there are seasons of opera and ballet, lunch-hour concerts, musicals, youth ballet and children's theatre. Once associated with Eurocentric productions and apartheid structures, the Nico is widening its focus to include Afrocentric work. The Nico is wheelchair-friendly, but there are only two wheelchair seats in the Opera House and Main Theatre. Wheelchair access to the Arena must be organised by prior arrangement.

Oude Libertas Amphitheatre
Stellenbosch Farmers Winery, Adam Tas Rd, Stellenbosch, tel. 808-7474.
Admission: *R15-R35.*
Bookings: *Computicket.*
Marvellous amphitheatre in gardens and vineyards with seasonal classical, ethnic, rock, ballet, opera and drama performances. Free wine is served and guests are encouraged to bring pre-show picnics. Best during February and March. Wheelchair-friendly.

St George's Cathedral
Wale St, City Centre, tel. 24-7360.
Performances of liturgical masses are held on the last Sunday of each month at 11am. There's a wheelchair ramp from the car park – use the Queen Victoria entrance. A wheelchair can be supplied if needed.

JAZZ

Cape Town has a deserved reputation as one of Africa's major jazz centres. It has produced luminaries like Abdullah Ibrahim (formerly known as Dollar Brand), Basil Coetsee and Robbie Jansen.

Cape jazz is a distinct musical brand and South Africa's social geography and history is traceable in its rhythms and melodies. Its unique blend combines American traditions with powerful local ingredients – the songs of Javanese, Malaysian, Indian and West African slaves who were brought to the Cape in the 18th century, the music bands of coloured minstrels who parade through the city every New Year, church choirs and indigenous township kwela.

For decades Cape jazz, along with countless aspects of life under apartheid, was both an expression and a victim of South Africa's divided society. Many musical veterans recall years when they played behind a curtain because performances by black and white 'mixed' bands were officially taboo. Talents like Abdullah Ibrahim were forced into exile, returning home only after Mandela's release. And, ironically, it took the attention of international musicians like Paul Simon to remind many South Africans of the wealth of local talent. The pressure of commerce being what it is, many clubs continue to steer musicians in the direction of cover versions, rather than original material, so finding good improvised jazz or indigenous compositions may take some work – or fortunate serendipity.

The good news is that the jazz scene is expanding rapidly thanks to the return of exiles, visiting international stars and growing public interest. There's a lively range of jazz venues in the City Centre, suburbs and nearby townships. Cape Town also has its own jazz dancing style – jazzing (pronounced djézzing). To see this mix of strict-tempo ballroom and Latin-American dance, hit Cape Flats jazz clubs like 49 on Flamingo and Club Montreal on Sunday nights.

Big local names, not all permanently based in the Cape, include Abdullah Ibrahim, Morris Goldberg, Tony Cedras, Basil 'Manenberg' Coetsee, Winston 'Mankunku' Ngozi, Robbie Jansen and Jennifer Jones.

As with any music venue, jazz clubs sometimes close or open unexpectedly. In summer there are outdoor concerts and festivals, advertised in the press and via handbills and posters. Cover charges on live music are R10-R20, but may be more, depending on the act.

For updates on jazz, live music events and features on visiting and noteworthy musicians, check the *Cape Times Top of the Times* on Friday, and the *Argus* newspaper. For information on Cape Town's Jazz Route, get the free *Jazz in the Cape Guide* from Captour bureaux. The City Centre branch is at 3 Adderley St, tel. 418-5214.

JAZZ FESTIVALS

Cape Town Annual International Jazz Festival

Africa's largest jazz festival, the massive five-day Cape Town Annual International Jazz Festival is planned for February and aims at featuring international and local musicians in an event along the lines of the Newport and Montreaux festivals. Watch press for details.

JAZZ CLUBS

Blue Note (at Club Galaxy)

Cine 400 Bldg, College Rd, Rylands, tel. 637-9027
Open: *8.30pm-late Thu-Sat.*
Admission: *R10.*
A favourite among serious jazz musicians and one of the places where you're more likely to hear Cape jazz and original, indigenous compositions. No wheelchair access to bathrooms.

Club Montreal

Cnr York St and Third Ave, Sherwood Park, tel. 691-0402 or 694-1780.
Open: *8pm-late Fri-Sun.*
Admission: *R10.*
Top funk and fusion club features great Cape jazz dancing, live music and guest artists, particularly on Sunday nights. The evening begins with standards and proceeds to progressive jazz. With secure parking, light-meal menu and a fully licensed bar, this is a marvellous place to unwind on Sunday nights. Not wheelchair-accessible.

Dizzy Jazz Café

41 The Drive, Camps Bay, tel. 438-2686.
Open: *noon-2am daily. Live music begins at 8.30pm.*
Admission: *R4 on music nights.*
Intimate supper club in a century-old building features classy jazz acts four nights a week. Good food, draughts and wines, and warm atmosphere. Wheelchair-accessible.

Dock Road Café

Victoria and Alfred Waterfront, tel. 419-7722.
Open: *6pm-late daily.*
Admission: *R20-R30 for musical shows, R10 cover when there's a jazz band.*
Dock Road runs popular cabaret and revues with themes like 60s music. In between, there's intermittent jazz featuring rising and established talents. Buzzy restaurant setting. Good wheelchair access.

49 on Flamingo

49 Flamingo Crescent, Lansdowne Rd, tel. 761-3225.
Open: *8.30pm-4am daily.*
Admission: *R10.*
Top musicians star here, as do assorted theme bars, funk and disco areas; à la carte menu, liquor licence and security inside and in the parking area. The best live music is Wed-Sat. Check when there's jazz. There's free transport from here to 49 on Flamingo Jazz Café, its sister club and a noteworthy venue in Paarden Eiland (at 39 Neptune St). Wheelchair-accessible.

168 DayNight • *Cape Town*

Clockwise from top left: Jazz band at The Green Dolphin; buskers in St George's Mall; street musicians in St George's Mall; street theatre in Langa township.

Goodfellas Senior Jazz Club
13 Halt Rd, Elsies River, tel. 591-7379.
Open: *8pm-late Thu-Sat.*
Admission: *R10 (free entrance before 10pm).*
Resident jazz bands at this nightclub, disco and bar are generally jazz-fusion, with special guests on Sundays. Not wheelchair-accessible.

Green Dolphin
Victoria and Alfred Arcade, Waterfront, tel. 21-7471.
Open: *noon-midnight daily. Music starts around 8.30pm.*
Admission: *R10 cover charge in sight of band, R6 out of sight of band.*
Premier, multi-level Waterfront venue for local and guest musicians features wall-to-wall jazz in a classy, relaxed restaurant. The views are great (Table Mountain and the harbour), the extensive menu features excellent seafood and pasta. Wheelchair-accessible.

The Jol
7 Bree St, City Centre, tel. 418-1148.
Open: *6pm-4am Wed-Sun.*
Admission: *R10 on Fri and Sat.*
Jol is local lingo for rave, and that's what this relaxed, traditional African music and jazz venue is. Top bands perform Thu-Sun. Licensed with a snack bar and restaurant. Sunday nights are devoted to jazz suppers with great music and hearty dishes like curry and roast lamb. Very limited wheelchair access.

Manenberg's Jazz Café
1st Floor, Dumbarton House, Cnr Adderley and Church streets, City Centre, tel. 23-8595.
Open: *11am-late Mon-Sat, 6pm-late Sun.*
Admission: *R10.*
Probably Cape Town's best example of a jazz club, Manenberg's provides a notable platform for Cape, Afro and improvised jazz. There's a balcony overlooking the street and traditional Cape meals. Check when there's live music. No wheelchair access.

Riff's Jazz Club
Wetton Road, Wetton, tel. 73-2676.
Open: *4pm-late Mon-Thu, 1pm-late Fri, 2pm-late Sun.*
Admission: *no cover charge.*

What Riff's lacks in plush decor it compensates for with superb live music and a warm, social buzz. The emphasis is on improvisation, it's fully licensed with a light snack menu and on good nights it cooks until morning. Wheelchair-accessible.

ROCK & ALTERNATIVE

Cape rock covers a wide spectrum, from R&B to grunge, rap and hip-hop. A rock sound as distinctive as local jazz has yet to develop, but some local bands are musically and lyrically innovative. Performers to look out for include The Sunshines, The Zaps, Mavericks, The Usual, Robin Auld and, for an outstanding blend of indigenous African and Western music, Tananas. Clubs and venues open and close at a furious pace. The best newspaper listing for live music and parties is the *Argus* newspaper's twice-weekly, laconically written and switched-on *Bandstand* column. *For more music venues, see chapter* **Clubs***.*

Blue Rock Cocktail Bar
251 Main Rd, Three Anchor Bay, tel. 439-1255.
Open: *9pm-late daily, with live music from 11pm onwards.*
Admission: *no cover charge, but 30 cents surcharge on drinks when there's music.*

COON CARNIVAL

The roots of the Coon Carnival are in the late 1800s, when black-face minstrels were popular in the Cape. Thousands of working class coloureds formed performance clubs and the result of this is colourful street parades every New Year. They sing moppies (vaudeville songs) accompanied by banjos, whistles, guitars and drums, and a strong American heritage prevails in costume and song. During the month of January, groups perform and compete in city stadiums. The name 'coon' is controversial; the alternative is Cape Minstrel Carnival.

Small live acts and juggling barmen in trendy atmosphere with live music from 11pm onwards and a massive range of cocktails. Bar environment where the musician provides vibe and background sound. Very limited wheelchair access.

Long Street Theatre
St John's Arcade, 14 Waterkant St, City Centre, tel. 418-3496.
Open: *9pm-3am Thu, 10pm-6.30am Fri-Sat, 8pm-3am Sun. Extended hours when plays are performed.*
Admission: *R10.*
Performance space and open environment with experimental sound and visuals. Anything from erotic theatre to Chekhov goes at this mecca for spaced-out bohemians, students, intellectuals and artists. This alternative venue features synergy games, psychedelic images on big screens, jazz and ambient music. Spontaneity is the name of the game. Delicious late-night snacks and smart drinks. No ramp access for wheelchairs, but plenty of help available.

Muzo's (at Pancho's Restaurant)
127 Lower Main Rd, Observatory, tel. 47-4854.
Open: *8.30pm-midnight Sun only.*
Admission: *R5-R10 (depending on act).*
The upstairs section of South Africa's longest-running Mexican restaurant features live music on Sunday nights and attracts loyal locals, and music and Mexican food fans. Fully licensed with an unpretentious, cheery vibe and the emphasis on original folk, jazz and African rock. Not wheelchair-accessible.

The Purple Turtle
Cnr Shortmarket and Long streets, City Centre (just off Greenmarket Square), tel. 26-2277/8.
Open: *10am-2am Mon-Sat, 4pm-1am Sun. Bands ususally perform Wed, Thu and Sat but watch posters at venue.*
Local, mainly original music of high quality. With a pub, restaurant, lounge, art gallery, big screen videos and bargain spare rib dinners on Sundays, The Purple Turtle offers plenty of distractions. If they aren't enough, down a couple of tequilas and try pronouncing its name four times in a row. Happy hour (with two-for-the-price-of-one drinks) is 4pm-6pm Mon-Fri and 4pm-5pm and 8pm-9pm Sat. Phone for live music details. There are steps at the entrance, but wheelchair assistance is provided by the doorman.

The River Club
Cnr Liesbeek Parkway and Station Rd, Observatory, tel. 448-6117.
Open: *8.30pm-late daily.*
Admission: *R5-R25 for live music events, R5-R7 for the Water Room Disco which operates Wed-Sat.*
This sprawling entertainment centre's Swimming Pool Room is the city's premier live music venue. The River Club also features occasional cabaret and parties, pool competitions on Tuesday nights, movie screenings, pinball machines, several bars, tennis courts, conference facilities and a golf driving range. Whew! Light meals and varied, sociable crowd. Wheelchair-friendly.

The Shebeen on Bree
25 Bree St, City Centre, tel. 21-2951.
Open: *4pm-late Tue-Sun.*
Admission: *R5 Fri-Sat upstairs.*
A visit to Africa wouldn't be complete without visiting the sociable taverns known in the townships as shebeens. Purists regard this one as dubious since it's not set in a township and it's (in every sense) a pale imitation of the real thing. Nevertheless, it's vibrant and fun with bright murals, 'pap' (maize meal porridge) and meat, and booze served, shebeen-style, in measures of 'nips', 'half-jacks' and quarts of beer. Not wheelchair-accessible.

Texas Embassy Saloon
1 Nicol St, Gardens (cnr Kloof and Camp streets), tel. 23-8190.
Open: *5pm-late Mon-Sat. Live music 9pm-2am or later Wed, Fri and Sat.*
Admission: *R5 on Wed and Fri.*
Country-rock venue run by well-known musician Brian Finch, the Texas Embassy

Saloon features a variety of bands, tasty Tex-Mex food, a bar, pool and poker tables, and a happy vibe. If you want more recommendation than that, consider the fact that Shawn Phillips surfaced here when he last performed in South Africa. Superb local venue. Wheelchair-accessible.

FOLK

Considering the small but determined core of die-hard hippies, whole-earthers and new-agers, Cape Town's scarcity of live folk music venues is surprising. What there is, however, is well established and inviting.

Barleycorn Music Club
Constantia Nek Restaurant, Constantia Nek (on the road to Hout Bay), tel. 685-7834 or 72-9503.
Admission: *R5.*
Cape Town's best-known folk club offers varied programmes at 9pm every Monday. Wonderfully warm and sociable with gluhwein and romantic fires in winter. Wheelchair-friendly.

Summer of Love Festival
South Africa's mini Woodstock is crammed with New Age attractions – health-food stalls, smart drinks and craft, but the main attraction is the original, good quality music. Watch the press for details of this successful annual fest.

The Martell Woodstock Festival
The Martell Woodstock Festival features rock as well as folk and original indigenous music. Held on the banks of the Breede River (near Swellendam) it runs for a full weekend in July and January. Bring a tent and camp if you want. Entrance is R110-R150 p/p for the weekend, including a Saturday night barbeque. For details contact 23-1646 or watch press for details.

RADIO

The city's main music stations are Radio Good Hope and Radio KFM. National stations include 5FM, Metro, Xhosa and SAfm. Radio Good Hope plays current hits. KFM plays adult contemporary, basing its mega-successful format on a happy mix of 60s, 70s, 80s and current hits. FMR (Fine Music Radio) plays classical, jazz and world music. With a new broadcasting dispensation, other stations are expected to mushroom. Stay tuned for interesting times.

CLUBS

Everything from acid jazz to African jive, plus insider angles on what's hot, what's not, and where the pretty people are.

Clubs and action bars form the core of Cape Town's night spots, and there's something for everyone – from teenybop ravers to nostalgic rock 'n rollers. No thanks to the apartheid legacy, there are still some racial boundaries, although these will eventually dissolve and they aren't enforced at the door. But geography, economics and different musical tastes still mean that you'll get a different clubbing experience in Guguletu or Athlone than you will in Sea Point.

The Waterkant and Loop street junction, centre of clubs, raves and the source of many happily acquired hangovers.

Central Cape Town offers the best in crossover vibe and cosmopolitan clubbers, and the Waterkant/Loop street junction, in particular, provides non-stop partying seven days a week.

Door fees are generally R5-R10, and while drinks prices vary, they're usually far from outrageous. Most clubs (apart from those around Waterkant St) are open only on Wednesday, Friday and Saturday nights, but they start and finish late, so expect to party seriously and hit a late-night café for a refuel or breakfast (see chapter **Late Night & Early Morning**). The party at clubs listed here usually lasts till 3am, but, depending on the crowd, they can go on much later – end with an early morning walk on Clifton Beach or a meal at one of the eateries listed in the chapter **Late Night & Early Morning**.

Be prepared to queue; if you don't know someone special at the club, you may spend half an hour or more outside. Some venues are also selective. If they think you're uncool, you're unlikely to get in. These venues are easy to spot though; loads of expensive cars outside and jam-packed with pretty bimbettes.

Gay clubbing is also the rage. Even if you're straight, these venues should offer you a rave (see chapter **Gay Cape Town**).

Because trendiness is a temporary condition, venues go in and out of fashion, so watch the press. The summer season means a host of new clubs and extended hours in old ones. Dress fancy but leave valuables at home.

Public transport in the early hours is rare and inadvisable and taxis aren't cheap (for details see chapter **Getting Around**). If you're driving, be warned that South Africa has strict drink-drive rules and roadblocks are common, particularly during holiday seasons.

See chapter **Music** for live music venues. And if you run into trouble, see chapter **Survival** for emergency numbers and helplines.

Browne's
Cnr Waterkant and Loop streets, City Centre, tel. 21-1951.
Open: 9am-3am Wed-Sat.
Admission: R10 from 9pm onwards Fri-Sat.
Acid-jazz venue with Parisian feel, smart drinks and lively street life to alleviate the boredom of standing in line outside. Sunday nights, with live jazz, are particularly good.

Café Comic Strip
Loop St, City Centre, tel. 419-1123.
Open: 9pm-sunrise daily.
Admission: R5 after 9pm.
This strip-club turned party-place is one of the city's most 'happening' venues. There's always a queue and a good time is pretty much guaranteed. Once you've queued to get in, you'll queue again to get to the upstairs dance floor, but it's worth it.

Club Galaxy
College Rd, Rylands, Athlone, tel. 637-9027.
Open: 8pm-4am Thu and Fri, 3pm-4am Sat.
Admission: R10.
Get a local to take you to this veteran venue famous for its jazzy sounds and vibrant atmosphere. The mostly coloured crowd really parties. Thursday and Saturday are the best nights.

Club Lenin
2-14 Old Klipfontein Rd, Athlone, tel. 696-4144/5 or 696-0528 (daytime).
Open: 9pm-late Thu-Sat.
Local and original music, light shows and nostalgic rock star at this vibey club in the coloured suburb of Athlone. Regulars are 21-35 and they know how to have a good time.

Crowded House
26 Main Rd, Rondebosch, tel. 686-7000.
Open: 8.30pm-3am Tue-Sat.
Admission: R5 Wed-Sat.
Mainly supported by university students, this unpretentious, sociable southern suburbs venue offers a separate VIP bar and varied music, from Top 20 to techno. Tuesday nights are for alternative music, Thursdays are ladies/gents nights and Friday and Saturday offer party music.

49 on Flamingo
49 Flamingo Crescent, Lansdowne, tel. 761-3225.
Open: 8.30pm-3am Wed-Sat.
Admission: R10.
Another one to visit with a local, this expansive venue is modelled on Amsterdam's Roxy with loads of erotic shows. It feels like a zillion people have jammed onto the dance floor and the undercurrent is strong and sexy. Good club nights are Wednesday, Friday and Saturday. Live music Wed-Sat. There's free transport from here to the sister club in Paarden Eiland (at 39 Neptune St).

Gecko Lounge
29 Loop St, City Centre, tel. 419-8423.
Open: from 10.30pm onwards Wed, Fri-Sat.
Admission: R10.
Ultra-trendy venue in a former whorehouse. Come equipped with designer smile, designer wallet and designer personality and watch that you don't trip over anyone's attitude.

The George
32 Waterkant St, City Centre, tel. 25-3636.
Open: 8pm-4am daily. Music from 9pm.
Admission: R5.
Tiny and jam-packed, this casual venue offers hot, sweaty vibes with lots of body contact. Wear something clingy. Dancing on the bar counter is the norm. Pop sounds abound.

Havana
45 Waterkant St, City Centre, tel. 419-7041.
Open: 11am-3pm and 8pm-late Tue-Sat. Music Wed, Fri-Sat.
Admission: R5 on Sat.
Ultra-cool rave with cocktails and a balcony overlooking the heart of clubland. Wear something pretty, preferably designer, to handle the exclusive door policy. The party's usually over by 3am.

The Jol and Gimba's
7 Bree St, City Centre, tel. 418-1148.
Admission: R10.
The Sunday supper club is particularly good, with Cape food and live music or disco on Wed, Fri and Sat. Open 6pm-4am.

Nexus
2 Leslie Lane (off Waterkant St), City Centre, tel. 082-444-5908 (cellphone).
Open: *10pm-late Wed, Fri-Sat.*
Techno Rave club with explosive vibe in a hugely popular venue (previously home to Eden, the city's first rave club). Nexus packs a mean punch. Jungle room, sublime chill-out zone, huge dance floor and pool tables.

Oxygen/West End
11 Port Rd, Waterfront, tel. 21-5355.
Open: *6.30pm-2am Wed-Sun.*
Admission: *R10 or depending on live entertainment.*
Two clubs in one sprawling complex. Oxygen with its New York-style decor and Aramis-drenched dudes offers commercial and jazz/fusion sounds and comprises three bars and a large dance floor. Pop acts often use it as a performance venue. The elegant, upmarket West End upstairs caters for more mature dine-and-dance crowds and offers smart wooden decor and good food.

Raffles
105 Voortrekker Rd, Bellville, tel. 948-9250.
Open: *7pm-4am Tue-Sun.*
Admission: *free until 8pm, thereafter R10 except for Thu when guys pay R20, and gals pay R10.*
Don't be misled by this venue's international namesakes – there's no connection. It's a former furniture store, mainly for conservative northern suburbs ravers and the vibe can be aggressive. This is not the place to spill your beer on anyone. Varied music and frequent hard-core rock and metal sounds. There are also nights for karaoke, strip shows and live bands. The restaurant/cocktail bar is slightly more upmarket.

The Shebeen on Bree
25 Bree St, City Centre, tel. 21-7147.
Open: *3.30pm-late Tue-Sat, 6pm-2am Sun.*
Admission: *R5.*
A visit to Africa wouldn't be complete without a trip to one of the sociable club-cum-bars known in the townships as shebeens. Purists regard this one as dubious since it's not set in a township and it's (literally and figuratively) a pale imitation of the real thing. Nevertheless, it's vibrant and happening with specialised African jazz. It features bright murals, 'pap' (maize meal porridge) and meat, and booze served shebeen-style in measures of 'nips', 'half-jacks' and quarts of beer.

Yeah-Bo
139 Main Rd, Sea Point, tel. 45-2532 (daytime only).
Open: *10pm-4am Fri-Sat.*
Admission: *R10.*
Worth investigating, this venue is still squeaky clean in parts, but once the sound system gets going the walls sweat. Non-aggressive vibe and you're assured of a party. Hooded sweatshirt turf.

LATE NIGHT & EARLY MORNING

For post-party munchies and emergency milk and cigarette supplies, these options range from *haute*-trendy to seriously downmarket.

See also chapter **Music** *for live music venues, many of which are still hopping well after midnight, and chapter* **Where to Eat** *for fast food. And if you run into trouble, chapter* **Survival** *contains emergency numbers and helplines.*

RESTAURANTS & EATERIES

Ardi's
Milnerton, tel. 551-6402. Rondebosch, tel. 685-1547. Sea Point, tel. 439-7322 or 448-2266. Waterfront, tel. 25-4606.
Take-out and sit-down sandwiches, pita breads, burgers and the like – the food won't drive you wild with desire, but it's solid, well-priced, and at 3am what do you want? The Waterfront branch is open daily until 1.30am. The Rondebosch branch is open until 3.30am Mon-Sat and until 1.30am Sun. The Milnerton branch is open until midnight Mon-Sat and until 10.30pm Sun. But, best of all, the Sea Point branch is open 24 hours a day. Every day.

A Touch of Madness
42 Trill Rd, Observatory (just off Main Rd), tel. 448-2266.
Gilt- and velvet-decorated café with pub food, soups, casseroles and notable cheesecake. Owned by a flamboyant former CAPAB wigmaster. Open 7pm-2am daily.

Café Casablanca
269 Main Rd, Sea Point, tel. 439-9839.
This vibey longtime landmark on Sea Point's changeable Main Rd offers super burgers and the non-pork kitchen delivers everything from steak rolls to spare ribs, all under R40. It's open daily 11am-late.

Café Manhattan
74 Upper Waterkant St, City Centre, tel. 21-6666.
Friendly staff, a wooden bar and sociable vibe make this a very good place to eat until at least 2am, or drink until 6am. The best access to Upper Waterkant St is via Dixon St.

Carlos O'Brian's
34 Loop St, City Centre, tel. 419-6950/1/3.
Tex-Mex food, tequilas and a generally wild time are on offer at this very happy venue in the heart of clubland.

Dizzy Jazz Café
41 The Drive, Camps Bay, tel. 438-2686.
This outstanding jazz restaurant and bar closes its kitchen at around 1am. Well worth a visit. *For more info, see chapter* **Music**.

Don Pedro's
113 Roodebloem Rd, Woodstock, tel. 47-4493.
This brilliant value-for-money late-night spot attracts trendies, intellectuals, politicos and creative folk, and it offers tasty pizza bread, good mezze, moussaka and well-priced boozy coffees. It opens at 7pm and closes well after midnight.

i Café
273 Long St, City Centre, tel. 24-6576.
Send your mind into cyberspace, munch on brain food and cocktails and use the continuous on-line connection to the information highway. Open daily 10am-2am.

Kuzmas
91 Main Rd, Rondebosch, tel. 689-3762.
Take-out and sit-down Mediterranean food venue, popular with students and bohemians. Open daily till early morning.

The Magnet
101 Bree St, City Centre, tel. 24-1224.
Open: *7pm-3am daily.*
Credit: *cards and cheques.*
Laid back and trendy. The Magnet is a sophisticated alternative to noisy, rough and ready joints. There's a pool table at the back, good coffee and the music tends towards jazz. This is one of *the* hot spots for late-night snacks, easy socialising and a game of pool. Very Cape Town – give it a serious whirl.

La Med
Glen Country Club, Victoria Road, Clifton, tel. 438-5600.
Favourite watering hole and tapas bar for the Cape's ageing hippies and surfing yuppies, La Med gets full marks for location (on the bluffs, overlooking the sea). It's fully licensed and serves food (sort of). The kitchen closes at midnight.

Micky Finn Cocktail Bar and Diner
The Courtyard, 100 Main Rd, Sea Point, tel. 439-9011.
Cocktails, table-hopping, videos and everything from breakfast and light meals to coffees and cakes. Slick, off-beat decor, well-priced cocktails and there's a happy hour (5pm-7pm) when all cocktails are R7. Open 5pm-late Tue-Sun. Jazz on Wed-Sun.

Mr Pickwick's
158 Long St, City Centre, tel. 24-2696.
Terrific value-for-money oversized sandwiches, soups, cakes, pastas and hefty, homey meals served on tin plates. It's fully licensed with friendly staff, a great vibe. Open 8am-2am Mon-Tue and 8am-4am Wed-Sat. Great for backgammon too.

The Purple Turtle
Cnr Shortmarket and Long streets, City Centre (just off Greenmarket Square), tel. 26-2277/8.

The city never sleeps – late-night refreshment at the Roxy.

Late Night & Early Morning

With a pub, restaurant, lounge, art gallery, big-screen videos, bargain spare-rib dinners on Sundays and terrific fish and chips, The Purple Turtle offers plenty of distractions. Open 10am-2am Mon-Sat and 4pm-1am Sun. Happy hour (with two-for-the-price-of-one drinks) is 4pm-6pm Mon-Fri and 4pm-5pm and 8pm-9pm Sat. Phone for details of live music.

Rick's Café Americain
196-198 Loop St, City Centre, tel. 22-2378.
You've seen the movie now visit the bar/restaurant ... Rick's attracts pretty people and offers everything from coffees to full meals. The dress code is that peculiarly South African anomaly, 'smart casual'. This means no shorts or sneakers. Open 7pm-2.30am Mon-Fri and 7pm-4am Sat. Very popular.

Rock Spider Opera
81 Main Rd, Green Point, tel. 439-7392.
So unpretentious they don't even have a street sign, Rock Spider Opera is eclectic, eccentric and renowned for hefty servings of wholesome food. Not cheap, but a good deal nevertheless. There's a minimum bill of R10 per person after 2am, and it closes late – sometimes around sunrise.

Roxy Coffee
14 Wandel St, Gardens, tel. 461-4092.
Unmissable, bohemian eatery decorated with B-grade movie posters, crowded tables and a Dinky car-decorated ceiling for the amusement of strenuously partied-out diners. Try the salads, hot meals, coffees and cakes. It's open 7pm-2am daily.

Spanish Gardens Bistro
Tex Arcade, Main Rd, Claremont, tel. 61-0441.
The only concession to Spain in the Spanish Gardens is bullfighting posters. This eatery, accessed via a little alley, is kitchen chairs and paraffin lamps territory. But the vibe is warm, and the food is great value for money – generous portions for under R20. There's also an extensive range of liqueurs, boozy hot chocolates and coffees. Open 7pm-2.30am daily. Olé!

For more late-night venues see box **Waterfront** *overleaf.*

CAFÉ SUPPLIES & SNACKS

Bimbo's Fast Foods
Cnr Main and St John's roads, Sea Point, tel. 434-3900.
With videos for hire and fast food like burgers and shwarmas, Bimbo's is heaven for insomniacs and night owls. Open 24 hours a day, every day of the year.

Cadiz
Cnr Longmarket and Loop streets, City Centre, tel. 24-3904.
This corner café caters to a clientele which ranges from video-game-playing sleazeballs to chic clubbers on the prowl for nicotine and takeouts. It's open all night. The takeout food includes fish and chips, but isn't as cheap as the decor.

Imperial Café
67 Dock Rd, City Centre, tel. 25-1943.
According to urban legend, the highway near the Imperial couldn't be completed because the Imperial's owner refused to sell. In fact, the highway is uncompleted because of a bureaucratic row, but the Imperial is an oasis to sailors and late-nighters in search of everything from cards, underwear and groceries to sandwiches. It's convenient to the Waterfront and the City Centre, and where else will you find milk and pantyhose at 3am?

Snack Shop
Oranje Motors, Annandale St, Gardens, tel. 461-4320.
Open 24 hours for petrol, bank machine, cigarettes, and corner-shop food.

WATERFRONT

There's an unbeatable choice of late-night eateries and bars at the Waterfront and these really hum during holiday season. The best way to find one that takes your fancy is to walk around – all that fresh air will do you good, the vibe's terrific and security is very good.

Just for starters, try one of the following for food that fills the gap between dinner and breakfast ...

Cantina Tequila
Shop 4, Quay 5, Victoria Wharf, tel. 419-8313.
Open seven days a week until about 1am, the Catina is where you go for authentic Mexican food, spicy fish dishes and (natch) tequila.

Den Anker
Pierhead, Waterfront, tel. 419-0249.
Water's edge Belgian brasserie with four Belgian beers on tap and good mussels and chips. Open 11am-1am daily.

La Playa Coffee Shop
Shop 224, First Floor, Victoria Wharf, tel. 25-2867.
Open weekdays until 1am and weekends until 2am, La Playa is a good blend of social and soothing, with light meals, coffees, wine, beer and views – both architectural and human.

Quay Four
Pierhead, tel. 419-2008/9 or 21-2088/9.
There's a fantastically popular tavern on the water's edge downstairs for drinks, value-for-money light meals and a buzz of people. Upstairs, the airy restaurant is smart, with an excellent selection of seafood, meat and poultry. It's all open daily from 10.30am till late and it has one of the city's most spectacular views.

San Marco
128 Victoria Wharf Centre, Waterfront, tel. 418-5434.
This is *the* place to shmooze at the Waterfront. The outdoor views are particularly good, by which we don't mean only the water and seagulls, but the people-parade as well. Cappuccino, good salads, sandwiches, pastas and great ice-creams. Lovely for light lunch or dinner. It's open 8am-12pm Sun-Thu and 8am-1am Fri-Sat.

Santa Ana Spur
Shop 280, First floor, Victoria Wharf, tel. 418-3620.
South African steakhouses are generally excellent, and after all that raving, you'll need the vitamin B in a burger or steak. The menu here isn't limited to meat – try chicken, salads or quesadillas. Open until midnight Mon-Thu and to 2am on Fri-Sat. Closes at 11pm on Sun.

Sports Café
Shop 259, First Floor, Victoria Wharf, tel. 419-5558.
Fifty-nine TV sets devoted to sports, late-night disco, noisy socialising and an extensive range of meat, fish, poultry and snack meals, as well as a full licence make this one of the city's most popular joints. It's open daily from noon-2am, and during season on Sun as well.

St Elmo's Restaurant and Pizzeria
Shop 156, Ground Floor, Victoria Wharf, tel. 21-7005/6.
Takeout pizza, starters, pastas and desserts at restaurant tables with some of the best people-watching at the Waterfront. It's open daily until 11pm.

The Edge
Pierhead, tel. 21-2583/4.
Open daily until 2am, the Edge has indoor and outdoor seating, brilliant views and a cocktail bar. Food ranges from pub menus to smarter dishes like honey-and-ginger-glazed duck and sole fillets with mustard seed and tarragon sauce.

SPECIAL INTERESTS

The focus here is on specialities – children, students and budget travellers, business, gay and women's Cape Town. So whether you're looking for a day outing for Junior, a night at a hostel, a translator, a sexy steam bath or a women-only sauna, this is the section you're looking for. As they say in Cape Town when they're in a good mood or it's summer – enjoy.

CHILDREN'S CAPE TOWN

From sun 'n sand and scratch patches to mountains and museums, Cape Town aims to entertain, edify, delight and distract Junior.

The laid-back atmosphere of Cape Town is, by its very nature, one that appeals to children – their curiosity and energy can be given full rein in this city of wonders. With sunny beaches, gentle seas, mountains and numerous natural attractions, it's not difficult to see why junior Capetonians grow up to be senior ones with a seriously chilled-out attitude.

The spectacular scenery that accompanies many excursions is a bonus, as is interaction with a variety of animals, from environments like farms and game drives to the baboons all over the Peninsula. (Don't touch or feed the baboons.) Zoos, an aquarium and bird-watching parks add education to entertainment.

The Waterfront offers a host of imaginative and well-run children's activities. Programmes are available from the Waterfront Information Centre or the Waterfront Information Kiosk (both at tel. 418-2369). Even without special events and promotions, it's a wonderful family and children's environment, offering variety, safety, a massive range of eateries, shops and the experience of being in a working harbour. Don't miss the seals.

Most libraries have a regular weekly children's hour, school holidays are catered for on a grander scale with theatre, shopping-centre entertainment, kids' movies and mini-amusement parks set up temporarily, often close to

Fun and games in a city which has plenty in the way of kids' stuff.

Muizenberg beach with its trademark pavilions, ocean vistas and sun worshippers.

CREATIVE COLOUR

210 LOOP STREET
CAPE TOWN
TEL: 231430/1/2/3/4
FAX: 231435

USE THE LAB TRUSTED BY THE MAJORITY OF PROFESSIONAL PHOTOGRAPHERS FROM EUROPE.

STOCKISTS OF THE COMPLETE FUJI RANGE OF PROFESSIONAL PRODUCTS.

CONTACTABLE PERSONS DENNIS OR TERRY.

FUJI Professional

OASIS GREEN LABORATORY

popular beaches. Also to be found are several lovely public gardens, many equipped with a playpark area. And, of course, there's sand, sea and sun in a city surrounded by some true beach jewels.

Captour bureaux provide free 'What's On' guides (*see chapter* **Essential Information**). For other outings, see also chapters **Cape Town by Season, The Sights, Museums, Art Galleries, Day Trips** *and* **Wet, Wet, Wet**.

ACTIVITIES: INDOOR

See also chapter **Museums**.

Cape Peninsula Ice-Skating Club
Goodwood Showgrounds Rd, Goodwood, tel. 54-4919.
Open: *daily, phone for session times.*
Admission: *R10 including skate hire.*
Credit: *cards and cheques.*
A popular rink with a resident instructor. Fast food kiosk on premises.

The Chequered Flag Indoor Go-Karting
Cnr De La Rey and Jean Simonis roads, Parow, tel. 930-1477.
Open: *10am-10pm Sun-Thu, 10am-midnight Fri-Sat.*
Admission: *R20 (includes helmet and race suits).*
Computer-timed races and a junior championship (ages 12-16) on the third Saturday of every month. It's noisy and no under-12s are permitted to race.

The Castle
See chapter **The Sights**.

Imax Big Screen Theatre
BMW Pavilion, Waterfront, tel. 419-7364.
Open: *first screening at 11am, last screening at 8pm.*
Admission: *depends on movie, but expect to pay at least R13 for children and R18 for adults.*
Colossal screen with six-channel wrap-around digital sound and frequently info-tainment-oriented movies.

Koeberg Visitors' Centre
Off West Coast Rd, Melkbosstrand, tel. 553-2133.
Open: *8.30am-4.30pm Mon-Fri, 2pm-4.30pm on the second and last Sun of the month.*
Admission: *free.*
Here kids can have a literally hair-raising experience on the static-transmitting fun generator and learn about energy and electricity at an operating nuclear power station. Enquire about walking trails.

The Pines Entertainment Centre Ten Pin Bowling Alley
Jean Simonis Ave (off Voortrekker Rd, opposite Shoprite Park), Parow, tel. 930-4795/6.
Open: *8am-midnight daily.*
Admission: *R9 children (over 6), R11 adults. This includes balls and shoes.*
The 22-lane bowling alley is enjoyed by older children, while pre-schoolers are catered for with short putters on two 18-hole miniature golf courses. Snacks, pizzas and drinks at the restaurant.

Miniature Golf
Tyger Valley Centre, Tyger Valley, tel. 949-0192.
Open: *10am-10pm Mon-Fri, 9am-11pm Sat-Sun.*
Admission: *R6 per player. Boats R3 per child up to 10 years old (2pm-6pm Fri, 9am-6pm Sat, 10am-6pm Sun).*
In contrast to the dreariness of Mini-Cape across the road, the sparkling waters and lush indoor greenery of this 18-hole golf course will delight children with its many distractions. You can also hire a boat to paddle through the fun waterways around the course. Overhanging the course in this children-friendly shopping centre and fast food hall, a giant 8 x 6 metre screen entertains you while you eat. A Mississippi River Boat theme dominates the mall's centre.

The Scratch Patch
Dock Rd, Waterfront, tel. 419-9429.
Open: *8.30am-4.45pm Mon-Fri, 9am-5pm Sat-Sun and public holidays.*
Dido Valley Rd, Simon's Town, tel. 786-2020.
Open: *8.30am-4.45pm Mon-Fri, 9am-5pm Sat-Sun and public holidays.*

An absolute delight for children, the Scratch Patch provides bags from R3-R26 to be filled with semi-precious stones. It's a distraction that works on all but the most churlish and jaded junior. An indoor 18-hole miniature golf course is ideal for winter days and costs R5 p/p per game.

The Waterfront branch has a Party Cave in the style of a medieval cave with TV screens, which can be hired as a party venue, with food and fun provided for up to 25 kids. This includes a Scratch Patch bag. Cost: R15-R20 p/p.

Simon's Town Museum
The Residency, Court Rd, Simon's Town, tel. 786-3046.
Open: 9am-4pm Mon-Fri, 10am-1pm Sat.
Admission: 50c children, R2 adults, R1 students and pensioners. Demonstration and talk on penguins/whales must be booked in advance (R1).
Kids will love the museum's Just Nuisance slide show accompanied by a story about the Great Dane who was enlisted as a canine seaman during World War II.

South African Naval Museum
Access from Court Rd, Simon's Town, tel. 787-4635.
Open: 10am-4pm daily.
Admission: free.
Hands-on exhibits, a mock-up of a Daphne-class submarine's operations room and control centre, and air-raid shelters.

Stellenbosch Toy and Miniature Museum
Cnr Market and Herte streets, Stellenbosch, tel. 887-2937.
Open: 9.30am-5pm Sun-Fri (closed lunch-hour on Sat).
Admission: 50c children, R2 adults.
Exhibition of antique dolls and toys. See a backyard scene changing from day to night. Unique miniature rooms include an Old Cape Kitchen and a Cape Fisherman's Hut.

Telkom Exploratorium
1st Floor, Union Castle Bldg, Waterfront (entrance between Trust and Standard Banks), tel. 419-5957.
Open: 9am-6pm daily. Extended hours during school holidays.
Admission: R2 children, R5 adults. Special group rate.
A large range of communication tools awaits discovery here and inquisitive little fingers are encouraged by hands-on exhibits. The display extends from the first telephone used in South Africa to satellite and cellular communications. A daily smoke, laser and light show depicts how far we've come since homing pigeons.

Hout Bay Rock Shop
Beach Crescent, Hout Bay, tel. 790-5637.
Open: 9am-5pm daily, except Christmas and New Year's Day.
Credit: cards and cheques.
Children can have fun exploring interesting old equipment previously used on the Northern Cape mines. Fill your bag with gemstones from the shop's garden. Bags start at R4.

South African Museum, Planetarium & Whale Well
25 Queen Victoria St, City Centre, tel. 24-3330.
Open: 10am-5pm daily.
Admission: Museum: free for children, R2 adults. Planetarium: R3 children, R5 adults. Combined tickets are available.
Planetarium programme changes regularly. Demonstrations and workshops for children are some of the additional activities offered during summer and school holidays. There are also lunchtime and weekend shows throughout the year – check the programme with the venue. The Discovery Room at the Museum explains natural history and anthropology while children can enjoy a hands-on experience. Enquire about Sunday videos on the same subjects.

The Victoria Treasure Ship
Pierhead, Waterfront, tel. 25-4127.
Open: 8am-5pm Mon-Fri, 10.30am-5pm Sat-Sun. Extended summer hours.
Admission: R3 children, R6 adults.
Treasure rooms filled with coins and jew-

ellery from shipwrecks, and an effigy of a 1770 British East India seaman. Also caters for private parties.

ACTIVITIES: OUTDOOR

Adventureland
Beach Rd, Mouille Point, tel. 434-7655.
Open: *11am-6pm Sat-Sun, school and public holidays.*
Mini-adventure park for under-12s, including train rides on a mini-track. Rides are R2,50-R5.

Epping Market Choo Choo
Epping Market, Epping, for info contact Captour, tel. 418-5214/5, or Ian Gilmore, tel. 64-2447, or John Hilton, tel. 591-5708.
Rates: *R5 children (ages 2-12), R10 adults.*
Full steam ahead in a 1920s train. The 55-minute trip is on the second Sunday of the month at 11am, 1pm and 3pm.

The Blue Train
Beach Rd, Mouille Point, tel. 434-8537.
Open: *weekends, public holidays and school holidays.*
Not quite like its renowned namesake, this 40-year-old local landmark puffs around a mini-track and through a tunnel, close to the sea wall. R3 per ticket.

From Ship to Shore
Pierhead, Waterfront. Check times and details with the Waterfront Information Office, tel. 418-2350.
Starting at the Pierhead, the Waterfront's weekday introduction to the intrigues and workings of the harbour costs R4,50 and is for ages 9-16. The one-hour walking tour includes historic accounts of landmarks by actors. Children must be accompanied by adults. Operates in summer only.

Kirstenbosch Botanical Gardens
Rhodes Drive, Bishopscourt, tel. 762-1166.
Open: *daily 8am-7pm (Sep-Mar), 8am-6pm (Apr-Aug).*
Admission: *R1 children, R4 adults. Free entry for pensioners on Tue and for members of the Botanical Society. Donations appreciated.*

Close to 6 000 indigenous plant species, including notable proteas, are cultivated on these 528 ha of renowned indigenous beauty. Wonderful walks and views, otters and porcupines and a tea garden/eatery make it a delight for children, and the Appletiser Summer Sunset Concerts (Dec-Mar) are wonderful. *See also chapters* **Music, Where to Eat** *and* **The Sights**.

Maritime Adventure
Waterfront, tel. 418-2350.
One-and-a-half-hour maritime educational adventure for ages 3-8. It's supervised, costs R3 and runs on Thu-Fri. Only for groups of more than 30 children. A boat trip and visits to other educational venues at the Waterfront are included. Storytelling sessions are often provided.

Mouille Point Miniature Golf Course
Beach Rd, Mouille Point, tel. 434-6805.
Open: *9am-10.30pm daily (subject to the weather).*
Admission: *R6 p/p.*
Under-4s can hire small plastic putters (R2) to try their luck on these two 18-hole courses on the seafront.

ANIMAL CRACKERS

Adventure Farm
Weltevreden Rd, Philippi, tel. 31-5246.
Open: *9am-5pm daily.*
Admission: *R4,50 children, R7,50 adults, R4,50 pensioners and students.*
About 450 touch-tame farmyard animals housed in attractive surroundings. Feeding and brushing of animals permitted, and price includes a pony ride. Playpark on premises. Barbecue and picnic facilities.

Firlands Farm Stall
On the N2 between Somerset West and Sir Lowry's Pass, tel. (024) 56-3130.
Open: *9am-6pm Mon-Fri, 8am-8pm Sat-Sun.*
A farmyard with a tame cheetah, mini-steam-train rides (R3 kids, R5 adults), tractor rides (R1) pony rides (R2), miniature golf (R6) and playpark.

Le Bonheur Crocodile Farm
Franschhoek Rd, Paarl, tel. (02211) 63-1142.
Open: *9.30am-5pm daily. Extended hours in summer.*
Admission: *R4 children, R10 adults. Family rates available.*
A video introduction to the Nile crocodile is followed by a tour to the dam where the croc population includes a 500-kg, 4-m-long beast. For the peckish and curious, the café-menu includes crocodile pie.

Nature Park
Ocean View, Imhoff Gift Farm, Kommetjie Rd, Kommetjie, tel. 783-2309.
Open: *9am-5pm daily.*
Admission: *R3,50 children, R7 adults.*
A breeding park for the endangered African blue and crowned cranes, Nature Park also has a large selection of birds like ostriches, emus, New Zealand cassowaries and South American rheas, all housed in shady pens. Children can also interact with animals in a farmyard setting.

Redhill Farmyard
Cnr M65 and M66, Scarborough Junction, Scarborough, tel. 780-1209.
Open: *9.30am-5.30pm daily.*
Admission: *R5 children, R7 adults.*
There are 150 friendly animals, tractor and pony rides and a chance to feed the cows, horses, sheep and watch the 4pm milking of cows.

SANCCOB
22 Pentz Drive, Table View, tel. 557-6155.
Open: *9am-4pm daily.*
SANCCOB stands for South African National Foundation for the Conservation of Coastal Birds. Sick, oil-covered and injured penguins, gannets, cormorants and gulls are rehabilitated and cared for here. Feeding times: 10am and 3pm. No entrance fee, but donations are appreciated.

Two Oceans Aquarium
Dock Rd, Waterfront, tel. 418-3823.
Open: *10am-6pm daily.*
Admission: *R8,50 children, R15,50 adults.*
Credit: *cards and cheques.*
The theme of 'Two Oceans around the Cape Coast' is explored via two huge tanks in this celebration of sea life. Local fish such as snoek, tuna, yellowtail and sharks can be seen. A kelp forest, with plants up to 6 m high, grows in the watery wilderness of the second tank, and 29 smaller tanks house different invertebrates. Also a seal and penguin pool. Children will especially enjoy the touch pools, computer touch screens and the interactive exhibits.

Tygerberg Zoo
Waarburgh Rd, Joostenbergvlakte (exit 39 off the N1), tel. 884-4494.
Open: *9am-5pm daily.*
Admission: *R6 children, R14 adults. Group rates available.*
A fine zoo which houses 1 200 birds, reptiles and mammals including brown bears, kangaroos and some endangered species. The bears are fed at noon, the chimps at 11.30am and the cheetahs at 3pm. There's also a children's farmyard.

Wiesenhof
On the R44 (Stellenbosch/Klapmuts turn-off), Winelands, tel. (02211) 5181.
Open: *9.30am-6pm Tue-Fri, 8am-6pm Sat-Sun.*
Feeding time for the cheetahs is 11am. Other animals that may be spotted on the 120 ha of fynbos-covered hills include eland, wildebeest, gemsbok, ostrich and the zeedonk (zebra/donkey cross). A look-out tower offers a 360-degree view of the Boland. Four swimming pools and boating on the lake are included in the ticket price of R4 for under-10s and R8 for adults. R5 per car at the entrance.

World of Birds
Valley Rd, Hout Bay, tel. 790-2730.
Open: *9am-5pm daily.*
Admission: *R7 children and pensioners, R14 adults (subject to price reviews).*
An extraordinary experience, the World of Birds provides close encounters with 3 000 birds and other animals (including monkeys and meerkats) in natural settings and walk-through aviaries.

BOAT TRIPS

See also chapter **Wet, Wet, Wet**.

Circe Launches
Hout Bay Harbour, tel. 790-1040.
One-hour cruises to Seal Island. Under-2s are free, children under 14 pay R8 and adults pay R17,50. Operates weekends only in winter. Phone for cruise times.

Penny Ferry
Pierhead, Waterfront, tel. 418-2350 ext. 265.
The Penny Ferry was introduced in 1871 to row harbour staff across the Cut (the original entrance to the Alfred Basin). It was opened to the public in 1880 for a penny fare. The best sailing bargain in Cape Town, the Penny Ferry is rowed from the Pierhead to Bertie's Landing providing a soothing, brief sail with harbour, seal and mountain views – all for R1. Great fun.

Sealink
Quay 5, Waterfront, tel. 25-4480.
Boats operate daily throughout the year and R8 gets you an enjoyable half-hour harbour trip.

Waterfront Charters
Pierhead, Waterfront, tel. 25-3804.
For R2, a water taxi will take you on a short trip to see the seals. Alternatively, go for the 25-minute Seal Cruise for R8 p/p.

CHILDCARE & BABYSITTERS

Bilbo Baggins Nursery School & Day Care
43 Cheviot Place, Green Point, tel. 439-1575.
For pre-schoolers 2-5 years old. Qualified staff for 70 children in a happy environment. Half-day is 7.30am-2pm at R20. Full-day until 5.30pm is R25. This includes meals, a snack and juice. The hourly rate is R6. Cheques accepted.

Rent-a-Student
7 Murray House, 25 Hout St, City Centre, tel. 24-6666.
Reliable male and female students (18-22 years old) for babysitting or au pair work at R12 per hour or R60 per day (excl. travelling costs). The agency is open 10am-4pm Mon-Fri.

Sunshine Playgroup
13 Orchard Rd, Milnerton, tel. 52-1466.
Open: *8.30am-noon.*
Kids from 20 months to 4 years. R15 daily rate. No meals included.

Supersitters
30 Ave De Longueville, Fresnaye, tel. 439-4985.
Established agency for child-minding, lift schemes, entertaining at kids' parties, live-in child-minding, homework supervision, tutoring and au pairs. Babysitting per hour (minimum 2 hours) is R12,54 (1pm-midnight) and R18,81 (after midnight). Live-in child-minding costs R163,02 per day. Registered nurses and French, German and Hebrew speaking staffers available. Weekend bookings must be made by lunchtime on Fri.

CREATIVE CLASSES

Bellville Arts Centre
Carel van Aswegen St, Bellville (part of library complex), tel. 918-2293.
School-holiday craft class programmes are extensive and there are ongoing classes in art (ages 3-15) and pottery (ages 4-15). R6 per art lesson and R8 per pottery lesson (payable in advance). Call for times.

Durbanville Cultural Society
Rust-en-Vrede, Wellington Rd, Durbanville, tel. 96-4691.
Varied children's activities, including ballet, drama and art. Ballet for preschoolers and older. For details, call Gillian Saffrey, tel. 913-4582.

Weekly speech and drama classes (ages 6-16). For details call Gail Peterson, tel. 975-4120.

Art classes (ages 4-17) cost R20 per two-hour weekly class for casual pupils. For details, call Francine Nepgen, tel. 96-9874.

Julia Joynt Art & Crafts
Ebenhaizer, Spaanschemat River Rd, Constantia, tel. 794-2279 (after 3pm).
Qualified Waldorf teacher offers classes in painting, drawing, pottery, clay modelling, basketware, batik, candle-making and puppetry. The 90-minute classes cost R20 (incl. materials). Children are encouraged to stay till completion of item. Phone for times and days.

DAY TRIPS

See also chapter **Day Trips**.

Berg River Resort
Simondium Rd, Paarl (exit 55 off the N1), tel. (02211) 63-1650.
Open: *8am-5pm Mon-Thu, 8am-6pm Fri-Sun.*
Admission: *R5 under-16s, R10 adults.*
Lovely swimming in the river, two swimming pools, pony and tractor rides on weekends and a waterslide (at extra charge).

Bien Donné Fruit Farm
Simondium (R45 between Paarl and Franschhoek), tel. (02211) 4-1684/13.
Open: *tours early morning and late afternoon by reservation.*
The one-hour tours on this 60-year-old fruit research farm cost R5 for children, R10 for adults and include fresh fruit, fruit juice and hamburgers for the kids. Other highlights are a demonstration of fruit tree grafting and an introduction to cultivars, packing and fruit exporting.

Jonkershoek Trout Hatchery
Jonkershoek Rd (opposite Okkie Jooste Campsite), Stellenbosch (take the Stellenbosch/Klipheuwel exit on the N1), tel. 887-0180.
Open: *8am-4pm Mon-Fri.*
Admission: *free.*
Part of a University of Stellenbosch research programme, the hatchery provides an opportunity to watch a bass-feeding demonstration and a visit to a freshwater aquarium. The best months are June to September (breeding time). A minimum of four people per group is required for a visit.

Rondevlei Nature Reserve
Fisherman's Walk, Zeekoeivlei, tel. 706-2404.
Open: *8am-5pm daily.*
Admission: *free for under-5s, R3 for older children and adults.*
This 200-ha reserve contains 226 recorded bird species and a field museum documenting local birds.

Safariland Holiday Resort & Game Park
Wemmershoek Rd, Paarl, tel. (02211) 64-0064.
Open: *7am-5.30pm daily.*
Admission: *R5 under-12s, R10 adults, R5 per car.*
A small-scale game park less than an hour's drive from the city, Safariland provides close-up views of animals like giraffe, camel, fallow deer, eland, zebra, blue wildebeest, zeedonk, ostrich, dwarf zebu cattle and crocodile. The circular drive around the park takes approximately 45 minutes. Stop at the shaded swimming pool and picnic area.

Tweede Tol
Bainskloof (on the pass between Wellington and Wolseley), tel. (02324) 607.
Open: *7.15am-4.15pm Mon-Fri.*
Admission: *R2 p/p, R5 per vehicle.*
A cooling series of interconnected natural rock pools in which to swim, located in the beautiful valley of the Witte River.

ENTERTAINMENT

The Birthday Party Centre & the Hooley Hooley Store
Union Castle Bldg, Waterfront, tel. 419-0672/3.
Open: *9am-5.30pm daily.*
Credit: *cheques but no cards.*
A very popular supervised fun complex comprising theme rooms like the Neptune, Camelot and Chief Seattle, where kids can select costumes related to their theme choice, followed by a storytelling session. There are distorting mirrors and a Punch and Judy stand upstairs. It's a tremendously popular birthday venue. Drop off Junior and the

gang for 90 minutes of fun, which includes a clown and snacks, at R15 per child. Birthdays are catered for at R20 per head.

Circuses & Carnivals
Boswell-Wilkie's Circus comes to town in April. Enquire at Captour for further details. **The Chinese State Circus** comes to town intermittently (watch press for details). And the **Community Chest Carnival** at Maynardville at the end of February or in March is four days of music, entertainment and food at international stalls.

HIRE SERVICES

Carol Wener Baby Hire
36 De Grendel Rd, Cambridge Estate, Milnerton, tel. 52-1466 (am) and 551-3859 (pm).
Good-condition cots, prams, car seats and high chairs are rented out on a weekly basis. Free delivery and assembling. R30 per week per item.

Cots and Prams
York Rd, Muizenberg, tel. 788-8064.
Car seats, cots, camp cots, prams and baby accessories for hire.

The Hutt
Recreation Rd, Fish Hoek, tel. 782-1977.
Car seats, cots, camp cots, prams and baby accessories for hire.

LIBRARY ACTIVITIES

Check updated times and details at libraries.

Bellville Central Library
Carel van Aswegen St, Bellville, tel. 918-2300.
Storytelling on Fridays at 10.30am and occasional video screenings.

City Library
City Hall, Darling St, City Centre, tel. 462-4400.
Open: *Children's Library: 1pm-5pm Mon-Tue, Wed and Fri, 9am-4pm Sat.*

Storytime at 11am on Fridays and there are holiday programmes at suburban libraries. Residents of six months or more are entitled to free membership. Visitors pay R20 for two books. Bring ID.

Sea Point Library
Cnr Main and Glengariff roads, Sea Point, tel. 439-7440.
Storytelling every Thursday 3.30-4pm (ages 3-8).

PARKS & GARDENS

Government Avenue in the Company Gardens, between Adderley and Orange streets, is an almost failproof winner, with squirrels to feed, oak trees, fishponds and plenty of lawns for running around. Arderne Gardens, Main Rd, Claremont, have fishponds, walkways, ducks and wooden bridges. Wynberg Park (off Travato Link) has plenty of space, as do Rondebosch Common and Rondebosch Park. Maynardville (bordered by Piers, Wolfe and Church streets, Wynberg), is tree-filled and lush. And there are playparks and comfortable strolls to be had along the Sea Point Promenade.

RESTAURANTS & EATERIES

CJ's Bar-B-Que
165 Main Rd, Rondebosch, tel. 689-3010.
Open: *noon-2.30am Mon-Fri, 6pm-midnight Sat-Sun.*
Credit: *cards and cheques.*
If one adult eats a main dish, one kid gets a free hot dish, coke and ice-cream.

Dodge City Diner
Shop 130A, Victoria Wharf, Waterfront, tel. 418-1445.
Open: *9.30am-midnight daily.*
Credit: *cards and cheques.*
American-style diner with jukeboxes, high stools and bright decor. Fast food from kiddies' Dinky Burgers and appealing puddings to specialty milkshakes that are big enough for two.

Greek Fisherman
Shop 157, Ground Floor, Victoria Wharf, Waterfront, tel. 418-5411.
Open: *noon-3pm and 6pm-11pm daily.*
Credit: *cards but no cheques.*
Prams are welcome, high chairs are available, and a children's menu can be co-ordinated from the large selection of tasty mezze dishes, many of which are suitable for vegetarians.

Saddles
92 Beach Boulevard, Blouber150 strand, tel. 56-1877.
Open: *noon-11.30pm Mon-Thu, noon-midnight Fri, 9.30am-10pm Sat-Sun.*
Credit: *cards but no cheques.*
Part of a Peninsula-wide chain, this eatery has spectacular sea views and good value-for-money meals. Average dishes on the kiddies' menu are R10, and lucky packets are handed out as bonuses.

St Elmo's
79 Victoria Rd, Camps Bay, tel. 438-2690.
Open: *noon-late daily.*
Credit: *cards and cheques.*
This branch of the popular pizza and pasta chain offers easy proximity to the beach and caters extensively for children with a kiddies' menu (pizzas R9 and pasta R6) and special offers for kids.

SERVICES & SUPPORT

Department stores like Stuttafords offer facilities for breastfeeding and compactums for nappy-changing. The Waterfront offers two breastfeeding and nappy-changing rooms in the Victoria Wharf shopping centre and the Art & Craft Market. (The ones in the Market are open during Market hours only.) Baby strollers can be booked at the Information Kiosk, which also carries emergency supplies of diapers, powder and creams.

The Child Care and Information Centre
46 Sawkins Rd, Rondebosch, tel. 685-4103 or 689-1519 (a/h).
A resource centre that focuses on parenting, with an emphasis on health care.

The Parent Centre
31 Eden Rd, Claremont, tel. 61-9142.
An excellent resource centre for information and parent support. The coffee mornings (10am-noon Wed-Thu) are particularly good for travelling moms. Also provided: counselling, parenting workshops and the best library on the subject of child-raising in Cape Town. Payment by donation.

SHOPS

Afro Dizzy
Shop 13, Victoria and Alfred Mall, Waterfront, tel. 419-9511.
Open: *9am-9pm Mon-Sat, 10am-7pm Sun.*
Credit: *cards and cheques.*
Fun, casual and instantly recognisable range of adults' and kids' clothes and accessories, all emblazoned with trademark prints of chameleons, crocodiles and chickens. The clothes are durable and comfortable and an average kid's garment is R70.

Bear Basics
The Railway Station, Simon's Town, tel. 786-1994.
Open: *9.30-5pm Mon-Fri, 2pm-6pm Sun. Closed Sat.*
Credit: *cards and cheques.*
Paradise for kids and cultists, Bear Basics is crammed with teddy bears, teddy bear badges, books, slippers, cards. Find it in the Simon's Town railway station by following the paw prints.

Beeline Factory Shop
Castor Rd, Lansdowne, tel. 761-0133.
Open: *9am-4pm Mon-Thu, 9am-3pm Fri, 9am-noon Sat.*
Credit: *cheques but no cards.*
Good quality children's clothing factory shop with emphasis on boys' clothes at reasonable prices. Smart, casual and practical clothes with gun prints on cottons and thermal fabrics. For ages 6 months to 14 years. Suppliers to chain stores.

Dooby Scoo
4 The Odeon Centre, Regent Rd, Sea Point, tel. 434-2854.
Open: *8.30am-6pm Mon-Fri, 8.30am-2pm Sat.*

Credit: cards and cheques.
Large collection of interesting and original toys, including beach equipment and ethnic puppets for children up to eight years old.

French Connection Factory Shop
Orion Rd, Lansdowne, tel. 797-6144.
Open: 9am-4pm Mon-Fri, 9am-noon Sat.
Ages 2-14 are well catered for with winter and summer wear (more for girls). The matching co-ordinated sets for moms and daughters are popular and these leisurewear specialists offer mainly fashionable knit designs.

Just Ashleigh
17 Fountain Centre, Main Rd, Rondebosch, tel. 689-3600.
Open: 9am-5pm Mon-Fri, 9am-1pm Sat.
Credit: cards and cheques.
Handmade toys and exclusive, versatile clothes. Average: R50 per garment.

Kids Kuts
Shop GB5, Cavendish Square, Claremont, tel. 61-8014.
Open: 9am-5pm Mon-Sat.
Credit: cards and cheques.
Bright, children's oriented hair salon with tractor, Noddy car and motorbike chairs and duck-shaped driers. For up to 12 years old. Cuts are R27 (weekdays) and R29 (Sat).

Naartjie
Shop 117, Victoria Wharf, Waterfront, tel. 21-5819.
Open: 9am-7pm Mon-Tue and Thu-Fri, 9am-9pm Wed, 9am-5pm Sat, 10am-5pm Sun.
Credit: cards and cheques.
Overdyed, baggy, bright printed gear in assorted fabrics. The shop is funky and sizes go from babies to adult. Kids' clothes are R15 upwards and shoes are around R100.

Nursery Classics
4a Cavendish St, Claremont, tel. 61-2635.
Open: 9am-5pm Mon-Fri, 9am-2pm Sat.
Credit: cards and cheques.
Interior designers for continental and English-style nurseries and children's rooms, including custom-made furniture, murals, blinds and lovely fabrics. There are also some pretty clothes for kids up to age six.

Prima Toys Factory Shop
Cnr Grenville Ave and Gunners Circle, Epping, tel. 531-7430.
Open: 9am-4pm Mon-Thu, 9am-3.30pm Fri.
Credit: cards and cheques.
A huge range of toys, including puzzles and bikes at an average saving of 25%.

The Red Shed Craft Market
Waterfront, tel. 418-2850.
Open: 10am-5pm weekends and public holidays only. Extended hours in season.
Unusual children's clothes and toys, including wooden lettering at The Outrageous Name Company, simple, bold designs at Hippo Clothing and colourful animal and floral prints for ages 2-11 at Walrus.

Reggies
Shop 53, Golden Acre, City Centre, tel. 419-2955.
Open: 8.30am-5pm Mon-Thu, 8.30am-5.30pm Fri, 8.30am-1pm Sat.
This is the central branch of a chain of six Peninsula-wide stores. Equipment for new moms and babies and a good range of toys for ages 6 months to 12 years.

The Rocking Horse Shop
Red Shed Craft Market, Waterfront, tel. 696-3227.
Open: 9am-7pm Mon-Tue and Thu-Sat, 9am-9pm Wed, 10am-6pm Sun. Extended hours in summer.
Credit: cards and cheques.
Pine rocking horses (R350) and pretty, hand-crafted painted toys.

Tasha Pasha
Shop 112, Victoria Wharf, Waterfront, tel. 25-1742.
Open: 9am-7pm Mon-Fri, 9am-5pm Sat-Sun. Extended summer hours.
Credit: cards and cheques.
A very popular range of kids' clothes for up to age nine. Look out for the jungle and ethnic designs. Around R60 for dresses, R90 for denim jackets.

Toy Exchange
Sherwood Shopping Centre, Dreyersdal Rd, Bergvliet, tel. 72-2114.
Open: *9am-5pm Mon-Fri, 9am-1pm Sat.*
Credit: *cards and cheques.*
New and second-hand toys, including rollerskates, bicycles, dolls, books, mobiles, trains, games. Also buys used toys.

Xtra Shoes
120 Buitengracht, City Centre, tel. 23-0318.
Open: *8.30am-5.30pm Mon-Fri, 8am-1pm Sat.*
Credit: *cards and cheques.*
A good range of leather and synthetic shoes for adults and children from around nine years up. Prices are excellent and this is a very good source of instant fashion shoes and boots as well as more conservative styles.

SWIMMING

For beaches and public pools, see also chapter **Wet, Wet, Wet**.

Long Street Baths
Long St, City Centre, tel. 400-3302.
Open: *7am-8.30pm Mon-Fri, 7am-7pm Sat, 8am-6pm Sun.*
Admission: *R1,80 children, R4 adults.*
Heated indoor pool in a landmark Victorian building. Locker rooms and hot showers.

Muizenberg Pool
Beach Pavilion, Muizenberg, tel. 788-7881.
Open: *8am-5pm Mon-Fri, 8am-6pm Sat-Sun. Extended hours during summer season.*
Admission: *R2,30 children, R5 adults.*
A kiddies' pool, splash pool with fun slide and a big pool in green grass setting close to the beach. The Muizenberg Pavilion offers a waterslide, boats, a playground and fast food outlets.

Newlands
Cnr Main and Sans Souci roads, Newlands, tel. 64-4197.
Open: *7am-7pm daily in summer. Shorter hours in winter.*
Admission: *R2,20 children, R5 adults. Reduced rates in winter.*

Set among shady hibiscus trees, this venue is one of the more attractive places to cool off. In addition to two big swimming pools, there's a children's pool and playpark.

THEATRE & MUSIC

Theatres
The Baxter, *Main Rd, Rosebank, tel. 685-7880.*
The Nico, *DF Malan St, Foreshore, City Centre, tel. 21-5470.*
Dock Road Theatre, *Waterfront, tel. 419-5522.*
Children's theatre productions during school holidays and summer. Watch press or call venues for details.

Sea, sun and fun on St James beach.

Beau Soleil Music School
12 Salisbury Rd, Kenilworth, tel. 761-1894.
Open: *Wed 5.15pm.*
One-hour chamber music concerts are presented by the Music School pupils and staff. Not suitable for children under nine. Donations appreciated.

Music is Fun
Run by the University of Cape Town Music School at the Baxter Theatre, tel. 650-2620, this holiday programme usually starts at 3pm on Saturdays. Admission is R6,50. Productions by juniors focus on myths, music and dance as well as an exploration of African instruments. Runs April to September. Phone for details.

The Puppet People
Intermittent shows through the year involving some child-sized puppets and muppets. Usually at the Waterfront and the University of Cape Town Arena. Tales are African and Native American in origin and often have an ecology theme. Call 697-4653 for details of venues, prices and times.

The Rainbow Puppet Theatre
Waldorf School, Spaanschemat River Rd, Constantia, tel. 61-9646/ or 794-2103.
Admission: *R5 children, R8 adults.*
A charming theatre located in a lovely setting. Saturday puppet shows at 10.30am (ages 4 and up). There's also a health shop and health food/organic store.

Stagecraft 2
Productions at Cavendish Square and the Nico Theatre mainly during school holidays. One-hour animal and fairy stories for ages 3-9 cost R10 per ticket. For more information, tel. 23-2675.

The Story Spinning Theatre
Baxter Theatre, Main Rd, Rosebank, tel. 685-7880.
Four annual productions focus on well-known fairy tales adapted for an authentic, cross-cultural appeal. Usually held at 10.30am and 2.30pm. R11 per ticket.

STUDENTS & BUDGET TRAVELLERS

Cape Town is a glorious city for students. In fact, its only disadvantage as an academic option, is the number of distractions. Budget travellers may also find some useful information in this chapter.

Foreigners who are set on becoming full- or part-time students in Cape Town may have to deal with some red tape to do so. The Cape's universities must comply with the stringent regulations of the Department of Home Affairs and requirements for foreign students vary according to the background, education and country of origin of the applicant. Courses like the MBA, offered by the Graduate School of Business, however, encourage foreign students and offer tuition of a high standard.

Apply for a student visa at your nearest South African embassy or consulate at least three months in advance. Tourist visas are issued free of charge and take about a month. The maximum stay is generally three months, after which you may renew the visa. The Department takes a serious view of travellers working illegally in the country, and can issue fines of up to R20 000. However, this has not deterred plenty of visitors from doing just that. Once here, you can apply for a work permit, which takes 6-8 weeks to be finalised and is valid for six months. And despite the warnings of the Department of Home Affairs, many would-be students enter the country on tourist visas and then apply at an institution. Should you make the grade, the University of the Western Cape and the University of Cape Town have a full-time Medical Unit in operation for registered students.

The stately columns of the University of Cape Town.

There are few subsidies and generally little help in finding accommodation through the small, private institutions. Noticeboards of the institutional residences attached to UCT or the Technikon could help in your search. Alternatively, try community boards at shopping complexes and the newspaper classifieds. Most of the accommodation listed in this chapter is either for women only or for *bona fide* students.

SERVICES

Hostelling International SA
Tourist Rendezvous Centre, 3 Adderley St, City Centre, tel. 418-5202.
Open: 9am-5pm Mon-Fri, 9am-1pm Sat.
An invaluable resource desk for budget travellers in Cape Town, this service provides clued-up information on all aspects of travel and short-term accommodation, discounted day trips and pubs. It can also make bookings at the hostel of your choice, and making it your first stop is usually a good move. The Go 25 Youth Card and ISIC Student Cards (R25) are sold here. A legal and medical aid service is available through the 24-hour ISIC (card-holders) helpline. Call collect on 90-44-816669205.
Information about jobs, lifts, accommodation and the buying or selling of goods or cars is networked through the Tourist Rendezvous Centre's popular noticeboard.

STUDENT TRAVEL

SASTS
Leslie Bldg, University of Cape Town (UCT) campus, tel. 685-1808.
Open: 8am-3pm Mon-Fri.
SASTS offers a full range of services to student travellers, including bookings, insurance and visas. Good transport discounts are provided by the ISIC Student Card (valid for a year to full-time *bona fide* secondary school or tertiary students only). Discounts include considerable reductions on rail and bus services.

UNIVERSITIES & TECHNIKONS

Cape Technikon
Keizergracht St, District Six, tel. 460-3911.
The Cape Technikon has been around for a decade and boasts the Western Cape's only optical dispensing unit. There are 7 000 to 10 000 students annually. For information on student life, social events and useful services, try the noticeboards around the seating areas of the four cafeterias and in the passageways to buildings. Alternatively, the PR office can direct you to the relevant department or provide extra information. *Technique,* the monthly student newspaper, obtainable free of charge at the cafeterias, carries classified ads and 'What's On' listings.

Peninsula Technikon
214 Durban Rd, Bellville, tel. 946-1425 or 959-6911.
Courses at the Peninsula Technikon include marketing and journalism and the campus life is informal and relaxed. For information on student events, social happenings and sports, head for the two noticeboards at the Student Centre on the ground floor. There are also noticeboards in front of the main Sports Centre and the various departments have their own noticeboards.

University of Cape Town
Rhodes Drive, Rosebank, tel. 650-9111.
Set in magnificent surroundings on the mountain slopes, the University of Cape Town has a liberal tradition and some first-rate arts faculties, as well as a notable science research faculty. Its imposing buildings provide commanding views over Cape Town's southern suburbs and the Cape Flats. There are some 14 500 students annually.
The social and student life at UCT is very active and you'll find information on the noticeboards on each level in the Students' Union Building – the Red Level carries miscellaneous notices, the Yellow Level specialises in accommodation, and you'll also find the bursary board here. The Blue Level noticeboard carries sports club and society notices. There are also boards in the vicinity

of the bookshop, the Leslie Social Sciences Building and around the cafeteria. Each department also has its own noticeboard.

University of Stellenbosch
Victoria St, Stellenbosch, tel. 808-4515.
Stellenbosch University is the Harvard of Afrikanerdom, set in an historic university town. It occupies an unassailable position as the alma mater of the Afrikaans intelligentsia and its sprawling campus gives a unique atmosphere to the town of Stellenbosch. (*For history of the University, see chapter* **Day Trips**.) Its outstanding faculties include jewellery design, the only agricultural sciences faculty in the Western Cape, viticulture (the study of vine-growing) and the only forestry faculty in South Africa. There are some 14 500 full-time students.

Noticeboards for information on social events, accommodation and the like are located in the Langenhoven Students' Centre (also known as the Neelsie Centre). The Commercial Students' Centre, housing 40 businesses aimed at students, including theatres, restaurants, pharmacies, etc., is also a good source of services and noticeboard information. Outside the library in the centre of the campus, between the Student Centre and the Admin Building, are noticeboards carrying general notices. Each of the 25 residences on campus has noticeboards as does each faculty.

University of the Western Cape
Rotterdam Rd, Bellville, tel. 959-2911.
UWC has grown from small beginnings into one of South Africa's most substantial academic institutions and it attracts students and staff from a wide spectrum of ethnic communities. There are some 14 500 students annually. Its track record in political studies is very good and it houses the Mayibuye Centre, a unique record of the anti-apartheid struggle (*see chapter* **The Sights**). With a steady growth in student numbers, the modern campus and extensive student facilities are humming with student life.

Noticeboards are concentrated in the Student Centre (opposite the Main Library, off the Student Square), but there is also one on the ground floor of the Admin Building and one in the library foyer. In addition, all faculties have noticeboards.

PRIVATE COURSES

There are several private colleges for post-matriculation studies. Foreigners should possess a study permit when applying.

Academy of Learning
4th floor, Saambou Bldg, cnr Burg and Castle streets, City Centre, tel. 22-2507/8.
Specialists in secretarial, computer, accounting and management studies, the Academy offers courses of six months to one year. The cheapest course is around R870 (basic two-month typing and computer course). Computer courses extend from two weeks to a six-week Computer Literacy course for R1 485.

Graduate School of Business
Portswood Rd, Green Point, tel. 406-1324.
The Graduate School of Business offers a highly regarded one-year MBA as well as short courses on management, marketing, finance and human resources. Accommodation is available.

Intec College
1st and 3rd floor, Scotts Bldg, cnr Plein and Darling streets, tel. 462-4510.
Business, technical and creative courses, such as hotel management, fashion marketing and journalism are offered here. Courses range from four months to a year and fees are R5 200-R7 300. The minimum qualification needed to study here is a matric certificate (with university exemption).

Damelin College
4 Park Rd, Gardens, tel. 24-4344.
This private college offers part-time adult education studies in business disciplines. Courses last six to nine months and fees range from R1 000-R3 500. Full-time students on campus are under 24 and diplomas include travel and public relations. Computer courses and business degrees are also offered. Weekly social

events with the focus on sports are arranged and the Damelin Student Card offers discounts at leisure venues.

ACCOMMODATION

In addition to university residences, private student accommodation is advertised on noticeboards, and for travellers there's a wide choice of short-term budget hostels, some of which take residents for up to six months.

Ascot Manor
369 Main Rd, Sea Point, tel. 439-3885.
The maximum stay here is six months at R65 per day for bed and breakfast. Doubles are R120. There are well-priced, home-cooked meals and the Manor is a block away from Sea Point's Beach Rd. No credit cards.

Spes Bona
44 Hof St, Gardens, tel. 23-3505.
A deposit of R750 is required at this women-only hostel which caters for students only. Three-fifths of the annual fee of R8 700 (incl. all meals) is payable at the beginning of the year, and the balance is required in the middle of the year. Foreign students must pay the full fee in advance. Credit cards are not accepted, but cheques are. The hostel accepts mainly Technikon students, preferably under 21, and fully registered at an institution. Applying students should submit a testimonial, medical certificate and a parent-signed contract.

Villa Maria
1 Kloof Nek Rd, Tamboerskloof, tel. 23-8136.
Open to working people and students of all ages, this women-only residence has several house rules – no visitors are allowed in rooms, no house keys, and curfews. The monthly rate of R680-R800 includes meals. No credit cards. Founded and owned by a group of Catholic nuns, this institution is conveniently located near shops and bus routes.

YMCA
Burnham Rd, Observatory, tel. 47-6217.
Many students take this more relaxed option, open to both sexes and available short-term to travellers at R60 per person per day including meals. The monthly rate is R800-R925 for a room (incl. meals and limited laundry). No credit cards.

TRAVELLERS' HOSTELS

The hostelling information desk at the Tourist Information Centre, 3 Adderley St, City Centre, tel. 418-5202, provides information on Cape Town hostels. Hostels sleep 4-12 in a room, often on bunk beds, with shared bathrooms and kitchens. Most hostels discourage long-term residents (longer than a few weeks), particularly in the busy summer months. However, some hostel owners accommodate longer-term guests in winter off-season months.

Albergo
5 Beckham St, Gardens, tel. 22-1849.
A popular initial stop for students with no limit on length of stay, Albergo offers plenty of social activity, such as barbecues, hikes and beach parties. From R25 p/p per night. No credit cards.

Bunkers
15 Graham Rd, Sea Point, tel. 434-0549.
Both travellers and long-term students are welcome at this hostel, which has full kitchen facilities and free tea/coffee. High season rates are R30 p/p per night. The out of season rate is R25 p/p per night. Out of season there's also a monthly rate of R500 in dormitory accommodation.

Green Elephant
57 Milton Rd, Observatory, tel. 448-6359.
A large Victorian house with a swimming pool, Green Elephant provides spacious living in a lively student area. Dorms are R25 p/p per night; double rooms are R70 p/p per night. Weekly discount.

Oak Lodge
21 Breda St, Gardens, tel. 45-6182.
Warm, friendly and communal, this travellers-only hostel has a fax service, laundry,

fans in all rooms, a private club and pool room and is centrally located. Dorms are R25 p/p per night or R150 p/p per week. Double rooms are R70 per night for two people sharing. This hostel ranks high on the list. No cheques or credit cards.

St John's Lodge
Cnr St John's and Main roads, Sea Point, tel. 439-9028.
St John's Lodge is one of the best hostels in town. Long-termers are welcome during quiet times; the hostel is on taxi and bus routes and is a stone's throw from the beach. Rates are R50 p/p for single rooms and R90 for double rooms daily. A flat that sleeps three costs R140 a night. The sister lodge, St John's Waterfront Lodge, 6 Braemar Rd, Green Point, tel. 439-1404, is about seven minutes' walk from the Waterfront. Single rooms are R70, doubles R90 and dorms R25. No credit cards.

RESTAURANTS & PUBS

Besides chains like the Spur Steak Ranches, Saddles and St Elmo's for pizzas and pasta, a range of budget-conscious eateries are dotted all over the city. Some student-oriented pubs in Observatory and the City Bowl also have excellent pub grub.

For more information, see section **Cheap & Cheerful** *in chapter* **Where to Eat**.

CLUBS & MUSIC

See chapters **Music, Clubs** *and* **Late Night & Early Morning**.

ADVENTURE ACTIVITIES

The Tourist Information Centre, 3 Adderley St, City Centre, tel. 418-5214, can provide additional information. *See also chapters* **The Sights, Sport, Fitness & The Great Outdoors** *and* **Wet, Wet, Wet**.

TRANSPORT

See chapter **Getting Around**.

BUSINESS

Handy connections and numbers for those who'd rather work than surf.

Cape Town is more envied for its lifestyle than renowned for its business efficiency. That, of course, is part of its appeal and an increasing number of business people are choosing to relocate or commute between Cape Town and Johannesburg.

Don't expect speed to be the order of the day. Friendly though the Capetonians are, they seem to know that tomorrow is another day and when the surf's up, well ...

Cape Town is, however, the centre of several national industries, particularly the large insurance groups like Old Mutual, Sanlam, Southern Life, Metropolitan Life and Norwich. It houses the head offices of most of South Africa's petroleum companies, including British Petroleum, Shell and Engen (formerly Mobil). It's also home to several leading retail groups such as Pick 'n Pay (one of the country's largest food-based retailers) and Wooltru (whose Woolworths stores are modelled on the UK's Marks and Spencer).

Cape Town and the surrounding areas are the centre of South Africa's wine and liquor industry. Clothing manufacture and textiles are also largely centred here. One of South Africa's most successful multinationals, Rupert International, the tobacco and luxury goods giant, is headquartered in Stellenbosch.

South Africa has a large and sophisticated banking sector. The four main banking groups, First National, Nedbank, ABSA and Standard

Contrary to popular opinion, Cape Town business people do take time off from surfing.

Bank are well represented in the city. All offer a complete range of commercial, private, investment and merchant banking services.

Telecommunication in South Africa is controlled by Telkom, formerly the Department of Posts and Telecommunications. It's trying hard to rid itself of its old stodgy image and habits, but it has a long way to go. It can still often take months to get a telephone installed, and many of the exchanges are mechanical not electronic, so dialling is slow and painful. Telkom's rates are set, and although there are cheaper after-hours rates, the company doesn't make much effort to advertise the fact. Telkom has introduced 'Smart Cards', which can be purchased at most cafés, tourist bureaux or post offices, in various denominations, for use at public call boxes. A number of the public phone services listed in this chapter are cheaper than using call boxes.

The biggest revolution in telecommunications has been the cellphone. There are now more than 300 000 cellphones in South Africa since their initial launch just over a year ago. Cellphone rates are higher than Telkom's for in-city calls, but intercity rates are competitive.

USEFUL ADDRESSES

The Cape Town Chamber of Commerce
Chamber House, 19 Louis Gradner St, Foreshore, tel. 418-4300.
Open: 8.30am-4.45pm Mon-Fri.
Information on the ins and outs of importing/exporting, local business information, labour relations as well as sourcing of products through their members. Input on local and regional affairs and taxation is also available.

Customs and Excise
9 Table Bay Boulevard, tel. 21-1930.
Open: 7.30am-12.30pm and 1.15pm-4pm Mon-Fri.
Information on tariff classification, import and export.

Department of Labour
Thomas Boydell Bldg, Cnr Parade and Barrack streets, City Centre, tel. 460-5911, fax 45-7318.
Open: 8am-3.30pm Mon-Fri.
Advice on labour legislation, including that pertaining to domestic employees.

Department of Trade and Industry Export Promotions
Plein Park Bldg, Plein St, City Centre, tel. 45-1508, fax 45-1508.
Open: 8am-1pm and 1.30pm-4pm Mon-Fri.
Deals mainly with export legalities, but the Department also offers services to exporters, including marketing advice, advertising and exhibition services. Financial assistance is also possible.

The South African Foreign Trade Organisation (SAFTO)
21st Floor, Trust Bank Centre, Adderley St, City Centre, tel. 25-1531, fax 418-1366.
Open: 8.30am-4.30pm Mon-Fri.
Among the services offered to foreigners – at a fee – are consultations, international trade information and business contacts. Additional international trade services can be provided with SAFTO Head Office support.

The Small Business Development Corporation (SBDC)
60 Sir Lowry Rd, City Centre, tel. 462-1910, fax 461-8720.
Open: 8.30am-4.30pm Mon-Thu, 8.30am-4pm Fri.
Aimed at encouraging local entrepreneurs, the SBDC offers financial services, industrial premises, consultation and business training for those wanting to develop small and medium-size businesses.

Wesgro
City Hall, Darling St, City Centre, tel. 461-6161, fax 461-5994.
Open: 8.30am-5pm Mon-Fri.
The Association for the Promotion of the Economic Growth of the Western Cape: services provided free of charge include general and preliminary information on establishing a business, advice on concessions (government relocation schemes, export incentives, etc.), introductions to relevant people/organisations, access to a database linked to products/services in industrial mar-

keting, and assistance with project-feasibility studies.

PROPERTY BROKERS

Pam Golding
180 Main Rd, Kenilworth, tel. 797-5300, fax 797-5310.
Open: *8am-5.30pm Mon-Fri.*
This reputable national company specialises in residential properties, but also provides services such as letting of property, development projects, valuations, auctions, commercial and industrial investment and business broking. Office space is approximately R40 per square metre for A-grade space, shop space in the CBD is approximately R70 per square metre, space at the Waterfront goes up to R130 per square metre.

Permanent Trust Association
11th Floor, Southern Life Centre, 8 Riebeeck St, City Centre, tel. 25-1670, fax 419-3315.
Open: *8.15am-5pm Mon-Fri.*
The Permanent Trust Association specialises in the letting of commercial and industrial space and sales of commercial, industrial and investment properties. Rented A-grade office space in the City Centre is approximately R25-R30 per square metre. A-grade factory space is approximately R12,50 per square metre.

Seeff Residential Properties
Seeff House, 42 Hans Strydom Ave, Foreshore, tel. 419-0920, fax 419-7547.
Open: *8.30am-4pm Mon-Fri.*
South Africa's largest independent residential real estate company is a member of the Seeff Holdings Group. With some 40 branches nationally, the company also specialises in business broking and commercial property, and can provide assistance in all aspects of buying, selling and renting of residential, industrial and commercial properties. The residential division is situated in Sea Point, tel. 434-9175.

Stocks and Stocks Properties
1st Floor, Block B, Portswood Square,
Portswood Rd, Waterfront, tel. 418-4733, fax 418-4754.
Open: *8am-4.30pm Mon-Fri.*
Property developers who can provide help in sourcing development opportunities. Office space is let at approximately R45 per square metre for super A-grade office accommodation in the prestigious Waterfront.

BUSINESS SERVICES

Copy Wizardz
Lower Level, Gardens Centre, Mill St, Gardens, tel. 461-9334, fax 461-7456.
Open: *8am-8pm Mon-Thu, 8am-7pm Fri, 9am-4pm Sat, 10am-1pm Sun.*
Level P3, Portswood Square, Waterfront, tel. 419-7153, fax 419-7154.
Open: *8am-5pm Mon-Fri.*
Colour laser copying, presentation packages, overhead transparencies, photocopying, typesetting, faxing, international phoning, ring binding, laminations and printing from disks can be accommodated by this efficient business. Printing on T-shirts and caps is a specialty here – flags and photographs are the most popular designs.

COMPUTER RENTALS

Dial-a-PC
206 Durban Rd, Bellville, tel. 949-5600, fax 949-5602.
Open: *8.30am-5pm Mon-Fri.*
Computers, printers and faxes for rent. The minimum rental period is a week. An SBM 386 SX starts at R108,30 for one week, an SBM 486 notebook is R296,40 for one week. Monthly and longer rentals available. Rentals include VAT, insurance and equipment maintenance. Printer rentals start at R39,90 for one week.

Rent-a-Micro
185 Buitenkant St, City Centre, tel. 462-1265, fax 461-2966.
Open: *8.30am-5pm Mon-Fri.*
A full range of PCs and faxes with a minimum rental period of one week. From the

386 SX (R105-R400 per week) to the 486 DX4 (IBM compatible). Top-range notebooks are also available for rent (a week's rental is R185-R400, excl. VAT).

Ultra Technology
127 Alexander Rd, Parow, telefax 930-2859.
Open: 8.30am-5pm Mon-Fri.
Computers, notebooks, printers and computer accessories for rent on a daily, weekly or monthly basis. Notebooks are R220-R430 per week, PCs from R240 per week, printers from R30 per week (excl. VAT and insurance). Delivery is R40.

COMPUTER SALES

Microdata
7th Floor, Nedbank Bldg, Heerengracht, City Centre, tel. 21-4570, fax 21-4377.
Open: 8am-5pm Mon-Fri.
A leading computer hardware distributor and service provider, including expertise in electronic publishing, point-of-sale technology, software support and development, engineering, Lotus notes, consulting and touch-screen technology.

Computermania
Shop 19, Maynard Mall, Wynberg, tel. 797-9457, fax 797-0183.
Open: 9am-5.30pm Mon-Fri, 9am-3pm Sat.
Specialists in sales and repairs of computer systems, with emphasis on Mecer computers. Stockists of Epson and Panasonic printers. The two other branches in the City are at N1 City Shopping Mall (tel. 595-2602, fax 595-2725) and Tyger Valley Centre, Tyger Valley (tel. 948-0510, fax 948-0580).

Mac's Computers
Victoria Wharf, Waterfront, tel. 25-2320, fax 25-4355.
Open: 9am-7pm Mon-Fri, 9am-5pm Sat, 10am-5pm Sun.
Specialises in AppleMac hardware and software, but also caters for IBM users – both hardware and software. Cellular accessories offered. Rentals of Apple computers are available from a week to a month.

CONFERENCE CENTRES

Major hotels offer conference facilities (*see* **De Luxe** *and* **Good** *listings in chapter* **Accommodation**. Captour (*see chapter* **Essential Information**) carries a *Cape Conference & Venue Guide* listing conference facilities and support services.

Conferences and Promotions Unlimited
33 Margaret Ave, Pinelands, tel. 531-0451, fax 531-0529.
Open: 8am-5pm Mon-Fri.
Experts in finding suitable conference venues locally and nationally. They also arrange secretarial services for conventions, transport, entertainment and decor. Broking and co-ordinating services, quoting and booking are free – the fee is paid by the venue.

The Waterfront
Waterfront Information, tel. 418-2369, fax 25-2165.
Open: 9am-5pm Mon-Fri.
Ten conference venues and a variety of restaurants serving as conference facilities are located in the Waterfront. The free *Waterfront Conference Guide* is available at the Waterfront Information Centre.

COURIER SERVICES

From urgent business contracts to birthday gifts you remembered at the last minute ... here's how to get it there fast. Rates depend on destination and type of article.
DHL International, *tel. 511-9550.*
Sun Couriers, *tel. 386-2100.*
Sky Express Deliveries, *tel. 439-3309 or 21-5420 code 87190 or 083-253-4444.*

DESKTOP PUBLISHING

The Computer Room
3 Rondebosch Shopping Centre, Main Rd, Rondebosch, tel. 686-8353, fax 685-4260.
Open: 8am-5pm Mon-Fri, 9am-12am Sat.

A reputable company for book, magazine and document layouts, flyers and posters. Laser printing, scanning, typing and photocopying services also available.

D&R Graphics
3rd Floor, Earlgo Bldg, Park Rd (off Kloof St), Tamboerskloof, tel. 24-5949, fax 24-5826.
Open: *8.30am-5pm Mon-Fri.*
Design work includes layout, brochures, catalogues, presentations and documents.

Graphix Design
2 Bramber Court, St John's Rd, Sea Point, telefax 439-1563.
Open: *24 hours daily.*
Typesetting, design and layout, and printing of business cards, letterheads, invoice books, memos, package design and general typing at competitive rates.

LAMINATING

The Plastic Sandwich
94a Shortmarket St, City Centre, tel. 24-1655, fax 24-8542.
Open: *8.30am-4.50pm Mon-Fri.*
Laminating specialists for documents, posters, cards, etc.

PHONE SERVICES

So far, there is only one phone company in South Africa – Telkom. The lack of competition means that rates are set, but there are cheaper after-hours calls, and in the case of national calls, it's sometimes cheaper to use a cellphone. A number of the public phone services listed here are cheaper than using call boxes.

CELLPHONE HIRE

Cellu City
Kiosk 5, Victoria Wharf, Waterfront, tel. 418-1307.
Open: *9am-7pm Mon-Tue and Thu-Fri, 9am-9pm Wed, 9am-5pm Sat, 10am-5pm Sun.*

Daily rates start at R39,95, weekly rates start at R25 per day, and monthly rates at R12,50 per day. Credit card payment preferred as security. Rates exclude VAT, insurance and calls.

Unicell
76C Voortrekker Rd, Bellville, tel. 949-1094/5.
Open: *8am-5pm Mon-Fri, 8.30am-12.30pm Sat.*
Daily rentals start at R39, weekly rates are R25 per day, and monthly rates R12,50 per day. Deposit of R2 000 required in advance. Rates exclude VAT, insurance and calls.

PHONE AND FAX SERVICES

International Call Office
Main Post Office, Parliament St, City Centre, tel. 461-5710. General enquiries, tel. 409-2312 or tollfree customer care line, tel. 0800-11-4488.
Open: *8am-9.45pm Mon-Sat, 9.30am-8.30pm Sun.*
Despite its rather worn setting, this Telkom service is up to date and offers a collect or cash call service. The following are some of the countries that do not accept collect calls from South Africa: Austria, India, Mozambique, Pakistan, Zambia and Zimbabwe.

A post restante and enquiry desk is situated in the Main Hall. Interior wall paintings depict scenes from South African history. For faxing, buy a phone card (in the Main Hall during office hours) and use the fax machine day or night in the foyer on the Parliament St side of the building.

Pronto Phone
The Tourist Information Centre, 3 Adderley St, City Centre, telefax 25-3897.
Open: *8am-7pm Mon-Fri, 8.30-5pm Sat, 9am-5pm Sun.*
Shop 42, The Pavilion, Thibault Square, City Centre, tel. 419-2959.
Open: *8am-5pm Mon-Fri.*
A local telephone unit constitutes three minutes, a national call 8,4 seconds and an international call 1,5 seconds. Calls are charged at around 65c per unit (local phone

rates are sometimes subject to rapid price hikes). Also offers a photocopying service (25c-30c per copy), and a phone-answering service at around R30 per month.

Telinternational
263c Main Rd, Sea Point. telefax 434-2162.
Open: 8am-11pm daily.
A strange but workable combination of a gift-cum-phone shop, offers international and local calls at considerably cheaper rates than ordinary phone booths. Copying, faxing and a phone/fax message service are also offered. Charges are 60c per local call and 40c per unit for international calls. (Prices are subject to change.)

Waterfront Photo
Alfred Mall, Waterfront, tel. 25-4868.
Open: 8.30am-9pm daily.
Faxing, photograph developing and printing, and photocopying (25c-30c per copy).

PRINTERS

Multipress Printers
273a Main Rd, Sea Point, telefax 434-8418.
Open: 8.30am-5pm Mon-Thu, 8.30am-4.30pm Fri, 9am-12.30pm Sat.
Printing, photocopying, a worldwide fax service and the purchase of address labels and rubber stamps are offered at this small but efficient and well-located company.

Omniprint
20 Loop St, City Centre, tel. 21-2130, fax 25-2504.
Open: 8.30am-5pm Mon-Fri.
Services at this 27-year-old establishment include binding, photocopying, collating, perforating, and the printing of invoice and order books. Competitive rates.

Ozalid
19a Woodlands Rd, Woodstock, tel. 448-5950, fax 448-2040.
Open: 8am-4.30pm Mon-Fri.
Drawing-office equipment and supplies, including plain paper copiers, microfilm and plotters.

Print Works
166 Bree St (cnr Bloem St), City Centre, tel. 24-6045, fax 24-5153.
Open: 8.30am-5pm Mon-Fri.
Fast, colour laser printing from disk, colour laser copying, DTP design and origination, promotional items like keyrings and badges. Lamination and overhead transparencies also available.

Quickprint
94 Strand St, City Centre, tel. 25-4544, fax 25-1625.
Open: 8am-5pm Mon-Fri, 9am-noon Sat.

3 Corwen St, Claremont, tel. 61-9270, fax 61-8450.
Open: 8am-5pm Mon-Fri.

155 Durban Rd, Bellville tel. 949-0210, fax 949-0055.
Open: 8am-5pm Mon-Fri.
Full printing and photocopying (incl. colour) services are offered at this reputable and established company. Guaranteed deadlines on all services. Business cards and letterheads done in 24 hours.

Sigma Graphics
58 Loop St, City Centre, tel. 24-7200, fax 262-2472.
Open: 8.30am-5pm Mon-Fri, 8.30am-noon Sat.
These suppliers to the drawing-office industry and the graphic design market offer services like printing and photocopying (incl. colour), binding and a range of paper, portfolios, stationery, pens, graphic design and drawing office equipment and computer consumables.

PR CONSULTANCY

Home Run Promotions and Marcus Brewster Publicity
5 Arundel Gardens, Leeuwendal Crescent, Tamboerskloof, tel. 24-0470, fax 23-1594.
Established, inventive and professional concern with clients ranging from celebrities to business.

Lange Public Relations
12 Vine Park, Vine Rd, Woodstock, tel. 448-7407, fax 448-0309.
Public relations and marketing for top-notch companies and individuals; well known for corporate PR.

TWS
The Terraces, 7th Floor, 34 Bree St, City Centre, tel. 21-6584, fax 21-2450.
The Cape Town office of a major national PR organisation.

STAFF HIRE

Drake Personnel
Shell House, Riebeeck St, City Centre, tel. 25-3300, fax 419-8002.
Open: 8am-5pm Mon-Fri.
This international company can find a secretary who speaks a language of your choice, as well as assistants, typists and general office staff. The hourly salary of R19,50-R25 includes the agency's commission.

Kelly Girl
1st Floor, Norwich House (on St George's Mall), City Centre, tel. 21-7080, fax 419-5906.
Open: 8am-5pm Mon-Fri.
Short- and long-term secretaries, typists, general office staff at an hourly R20,50-R25,20 on a cash-upfront basis.

Status Personnel
14 Foregate Square, Harbour Rd, Foreshore, telefax 21-1917.
Open: 8am-5pm Mon-Fri.
Short- and long-term secretaries, typists and general office staff at an hourly R15-R23 (incl. agency commission).

STATIONERY

See also chapter **Shopping**.

Waltons Stationery
Dock Rd, Waterfront, tel. 448-5060.
Kort Street, Bellville, tel. 946-1770.
Gunners Circle, Epping, tel. 54-3351.
4 Dawn St, Montague Gardens, tel. 52-4466.
Shop 2, Stegmann Rd, Claremont, tel. 61-3123.
Stationery Centre, 13 Beach Rd, Woodstock, tel. 448-5060.
Open: 8.15am-4.45pm Mon-Fri, 9am-noon Sat.
Credit: cards and cheques.
Wide range of office and personal stationery, office furniture and briefcases.

TRANSLATIONS

Cape Communication Centre
The Strand Tower, 66 Strand St, City Centre, tel. 419-1967.
Open: 8am-5pm Mon-Fri.
Translations at R40 per 100 words (excl. VAT) in a variety of languages, including English, Afrikaans, Xhosa, Zulu, German, French, Japanese and Italian. Interpreting services during office hours (minimum of 4 hours) cost R300 for the first hour and a negotiable rate thereafter. After 5pm, the hourly rate is R110.

Herman Fourie
Telefax 461-2369.
Sworn translator (meaning that he's been admitted in the Supreme Court as a translator) for German and English official translations, and interpretation of German, Dutch and French into English.

GAY CAPE TOWN

Cape Town is probably Africa's gay capital and it offers a laid-back, tolerant lifestyle and beaches full of god-like beings.

Cape Town is reputed to have approximately five women to every man, and many of those women believe that most of the men are gay, possibly making this Africa's gay capital. For gay visitors it's a feast.

In 1994 the city saw a coming-out of gay venues with bath-houses opening and gay clubs advertising in mainstream media. New-found freedom has led to a frenzied activity in clubs and public cruising.

The annual Gay Pride March, held on the second Saturday of December, is a popular, successful event. Capetonians are generally accepting. A gay couple walking hand in hand around the City Centre shouldn't attract more than some smiles or occasional comments. In more conservative areas, however, they could be beaten up. Soliciting is illegal, but discrimination based on gender or sexual orientation is forbidden by the Interim Constitution. Sex with a minor is illegal, and while the controversial difference between the ages of consent for heterosexual sex (16) and gay/lesbian sex (19) is under legislative review, anyone under 19 is regarded as a minor when it comes to homosexual sex.

Check the daily *Argus* newspaper's *Adult Entertainment*, *Personal*, *Social* and *Massage* classified columns for health services and social pleasures. Most men advertising here are looking for gay clients, but check. *See chapter* **Women's Cape Town** *for lesbian info.*

SERVICE ORGANISATIONS

AIDS Help-Line
Tel. 21-5420.
Gay, lesbian and bisexual counselling. Leave your name and number and a counsellor will call you back with confidential information and free advice on HIV- and AIDS-related issues.

AIDS Support and Education Trust (ASET)
41 Salt River Rd, Salt River, tel. 21-5420 (24-hour paging) or 448-3812 for appointments.
Advice and information as well as counselling.

AIDS Training and Information Centre (ATTIC)
Podium Block, Civic Centre, Foreshore, tel. 400-3400.
AIDS education, training, prevention, testing, clinic and counselling.

Belville Community Health Project
Dammert St, Kasselsvlei, Bellville South, tel. 951-5928.
Straight-friendly health care, education and AIDS prevention. Body Positive, a support group for HIV-positive people, meets here on the first and third Thursday of every month.

Gay, Lesbian and Bisexual Helpline
Tel. 21-5420.
24-hour service. Leave your name and phone number.

Northern Areas AIDS Action Group
Tel. 92-9120.
Care-givers and support.

SA Red Cross Society
21 Broad Rd, Wynberg, tel. 797-5360.
HIV home-care and related help.

Sexually Transmitted Disease Clinics
Spencer Rd, Salt River, tel. 400-2047.
Chapel St Clinic, Woodstock, tel. 462-4400 ext. 261.
Lower Maynard Rd, Wynberg, tel. 797-5190/1/2.
De Villiers St, Durbanville, tel. 96-1418.

Triangle Health Care Centre
Ground Floor, Community House, 41 Salt River Rd, Salt River, tel. 448-3812 for an appointment.
Open: *10.30am-9pm Mon-Tue, 10.30am-4.30pm Wed-Fri.*
The Centre's professional counsellors and medical practitioners deal with sexual problems and sexually transmitted diseases.

Gay Christian Church
Meetings are held every Sunday at 6pm at Quaker House, cnr Hornsey and Rye roads, Mowbray, tel. 531-7171.

CLUBBING

The Cape Town gay scene is small and changeable; this month's hot spots are next month's no-go zones and summer heralds new clubs or new decor in old ones. See *Exit* newspaper, available from clubs and Exclusive Books, for updates. These are the venues at time of printing. Pay your money and take your chances.

Angels
27 Somerset Rd, Green Point, tel. 21-2958.
Open: *9pm-yawn Wed, Fri and Sat.*
Admission: *R10.*
If you hit only one club in town, make it this large-scale, hot, body-packed turn-of-the-century warehouse which has Detour upstairs and Angels bar downstairs. Wooden floors and stone walls give an historic feel. Techno sounds upstairs, with commercial and golden oldies downstairs. The outdoor area with balconies overlooking Somerset Road is a major attraction. So is the 'dark' room.

The Bronx
Cnr Somerset Rd and Napier St, Green Point. Adjacent to Angels.
Open: *noon-late Mon-Sun.*
Admission: *R5 on cabaret nights (Sun).*
Cabaret venue and bar with live entertainment Sunday to Tuesday and Thursday. Sunday is the time for cabaret – anything from drags to torch singers.

Hot, sweaty and sexy, Angels club attracts a mixed crowd that dances 'til dawn.

4 Play
41 Riebeeck St, City Centre, tel. 419-8798.
Open: *8.45pm-late daily.*
Admission: *R10 on Sun and Thu.*
Two levels with disco and bar on street level and 'dark' room upstairs. Pretty venue but frequently tacky crowd.

BARS & EATERIES

Although none of these are gay-only they are gay-friendly, in some cases very much so.

Aladdin Coffee Shop
Nedbank Centre, Kloof Rd, Sea Point, tel. 439-4428.
Open: *8pm-6pm Mon-Fri, 8am-4pm Sat, 9am-4pm Sun.*

Daytime coffee shop with a quaint vibe, value-for-money sandwiches and pita bread.

A Touch of Madness
42 Trill Rd, Observatory (just off Lower Main Rd), tel. 448-2266.
Open: 7pm-2am daily.
This gilt and velvet-decorated eatery is owned by a flamboyant former wigmaster and it serves good light meals and notable cheesecake.

Brunswick Tavern
17 Bree St, City Centre, tel. 25-2739.
Open: 11am-midnight Sun-Wed, 11am-3am Thu-Sat.
An unpretentious, casual survivor with friendly staff and generally ordinary clientele. If the pretty-boy meat-market isn't for you, the Brunswick is.

Café Erté
265 Main Rd, Sea Point, tel. 434-6624.
Open: 7pm-late daily.
A comfortable, inviting haunt with board games, light meals, music videos, cocktails and slightly tacky, OTT decor, this coffee bar and eatery is a terrific place to tête-à-tête. Gay-, lesbian- and straight-friendly. Grab a corner couch.

Henry's
66a Loop St, City Centre, tel. 24-3944.
Open: 9pm-late daily.
People just walk from one side of this venue to the other to get a kinky buzz and it's very cruisy with loads of pretty boys. Parking is problematic so keep the high heels in your handbag.

STEAM

If you want to work out, try the city's Health and Racquet Clubs. If you want another kind of sweat, here's where to indulge.

Club Welgelegen
51 William St, Mowbray, tel. 448-6202.
Open: 4pm-late Mon-Fri, 2pm-late Sat-Sun.
Admission: R20.
Cape Town's first steam bath is now one of the smallest and least sophisticated. Large, dark steam room, sauna, interleading cubicles and two communal 'rest' rooms. Private and drug-free.

Steamers
Cnr Solan Rd and Wembley St, Gardens, tel. 461-6210.
Open: 3pm-late Mon-Thu, 3pm-onwards Fri, 24 hours Sat-Sun.
Admission: R40.
The city's most upmarket venue is a sprawling pleasure zone with a nautical theme. Swimming pool, spa, sauna and steam in pristine conditions. Private 'rest' rooms, video lounge and pool table add to this notable venue.

Steam Zone
Caris House, Cnr Jamieson and Carisbrook streets, City Centre, tel. 23-3446.
Open: noon-late daily.
Admission: R40.
Three-level sauna, steam and spa. Video bar, coffee lounge and 18 private 'rest' rooms. Totally professional and slick. Included in your pristine white towel are two condoms and lubricant. Overnight facilities available.

BEACHES

Cape Town's renowned beaches offer assorted pleasures. The Atlantic Ocean is beautiful but cold, so if you want to swim, head for the Indian Ocean. *For general information on beaches, see chapter* **Wet, Wet, Wet**. The following are the best for gays.

Graaff's Pool, Sea Point
This idiosyncratic, men-only nudist beach is a tidal pool just off Beach Rd, across the street from the Bordeaux Flats, formerly manorial home to one Mr Graaff, who is rumoured to have had a tunnel under the road to *his* pool. In the past the left side was straight and the right side gay, but now it's a free for all with a core of straights and lots of under-40 gays.

After dark, Graaff's becomes the Wall, renowned as a cruising and doing area. During the last few years hustlers have plied their trade here too. If someone looks like a rent boy, assume he is and ask the price. Once you're behind the wall, you're secluded, which also means potential danger. Take care. Like anywhere in the world, cruising in public places must be treated circumspectly.

For the less adventurous, cruising but no doing takes place along the promenade in the area from the front of Graaff's Pool to outside the SABC. A campaign to close Graaff's at night is being battled by the gay lobby.

Sandy Bay, Llandudno
This multi-gender nudist beach is one of the Cape's most beautiful, but a half-hour walk is needed to get there. Take the Llandudno turn-off on Hout Bay's Victoria Rd and follow the signs to Sandy Bay. Cruising and action happens around the rocks and in the bushes. Muggings and gay-bashing have occurred. There's a small strip of beach which seems to be, unofficially, exclusively gay. You can't miss it.

SEX WORKERS

Avoid hustlers on Green Point's Somerset Rd and the Burg St and Hout St area. Known as Pick and Pay by locals, the rent is generally dangerous and tacky. Rather consult local papers' 'massage' columns. R80-R120 is the average fee, including a 'happy-ending'.

HAPPENINGS

Gay Pride March
Scheduled for the second Saturday of December, the event attracts hordes of supporters and combines both political statement and a good time. See press for details.

The Secret Garden Project
An annual event by Mother City Queer Project, this gay-, lesbian- and straight-friendly party is scheduled for December. If previous events are anything to go by, you can expect an incredibly wild bash. Set aside two days for recovery. Contact André Vorster, tel. 685-6064, or Andrew Putter, tel. 685-6319, for details and venue.

WOMEN'S CAPE TOWN

Gender equality and lesbian and women's venues have a way to go. But there's still a good time to be had.

'Mother City' (a description to denote Cape Town's status as South Africa's first modern city) makes a pleasant change from labels like 'the Fatherland' and 'Uncle Sam'. It also has a deeper resonance, considering that there are roughly five women to every man in Cape Town. But there's more to it than that. Women here have played a significant role in South African politics. Although the women's movement has been divided over strategy issues, the country's first democratic election featured parties like the Women's Rights Peace Party and the South African Women's Party, both of which focused on issues like women's health, violence against women and discriminatory customary law. And although none of these parties won enough votes to send MPs to parliament, it's telling that when South Africa's first democratically elected parliament sat in Cape Town in 1994, 106 parliamentarians were women, meaning that in terms of the ranking of women in government, South Africa is placed seventh in the world. South Africa's first democratically elected parliament also boasted a noted feminist, Dr Frene Ginwala, as Parliamentary Speaker.

Feminism isn't merely academic; it has emerged from grassroots level upwards, alongside the struggle against apartheid. One of the first, most compelling events illustrating the organised strength of South African women was the anti-pass-law campaign organised by the Federation of South African Women (FEDSAW). This culminated in a march on Pretoria's Union Buildings on August 9, 1956. The rallying cry – 'Strike the woman, strike the rock!' remains popular and the march is commemorated on National Women's Day.

Gender equality still has a long way to go. Most South African women still live in poverty. Few ministerial and cabinet posts and no regional premierships are occupied by women. And South Africa has one of the world's highest incidences of rape. But organisations like the ANC Women's League, and the Black Sash, a women's group that was dedicated to fighting apartheid, have historically given women a voice, and many of the country's most notable political forces emerged from these organisations and their predecessors. The ANC's Cheryl Carolus, for example, was a leading light in the United Democratic Front, effectively the front for the then-banned ANC.

The new government has improved things by introducing free healthcare for pregnant women and children under six years old. Non-governmental organisations continue to lobby for change and significant headway has been made by Rape Crisis, which played a pivotal role in instituting the world-first rape courts. In the absence of a state facility, Rape Crisis provides free counselling for sexual-assault survivors. The Abortion Rights Action Group lobbies for free abortion on demand. The Gender Equity Unit addresses affirmative action and

South African sisterhood.

sexual harassment. And there's increasing pressure on business organisations to hire and promote women.

South African women who've made their mark internationally include Nobel Prize winner Nadine Gordimer, political veteran Helen Suzman, Winnie Mandela, movie director Elaine Proctor, academic and activist Dr Mamphele Ramphele and actresses Embeth Davidtz, Janet Suzman and Yvonne Bryceland.

Gay men have infinitely more choice of clubs and meeting places than lesbians. But Cape Town's lesbians are coming out increasingly and the annual Gay Pride March is a political statement and a fun event. Thanks to the lesbian community, grassroots women's organisations and some canny entrepreneurs, new venues are popping up increasingly. But so far, with the exception of *ad hoc*, privately organised events, there are lamentably few women/lesbians-only venues, parties or clubs. The places listed in this chapter are women- and lesbian-friendly. Check *Exit* and *Outright*, available from clubs, most CNA stores and Exclusive Books for updates on lesbian activities.

WOMEN-ONLY ACCOMMODATION

Villa Maria
1 Kloof Nek Rd, Tamboerskloof, tel. 23-8136.
Rates: *R680-R800 per month including meals.*
Credit: *cheques but no credit cards.*
Well located, near to shops and bus stops, this women-only residence is owned and funded by Catholic nuns. House rules are strict – no visitors in rooms, no house keys issued and curfews (it closes at 11pm Sun-Thu and at 11.45 Fri-Sat).

It's popular with Technikon students, but working women and tourists can also book in.

Young Women's Christian Association
20 Bellevue St, Gardens, tel. 23-3711.
Rates: *R59,50 p/p per day (incl. dinner, bed and breakfast) or R400 per week.*
Credit: *cheques and travellers' cheques but no credit cards.*
Christian-oriented residence for students (18-25) and working women from outside Cape Town, the YWCA offers budget accommodation (five double rooms and one single room). Rules are strict – closing time is 11pm Mon-Fri and midnight Sat-Sun.

WOMEN-ONLY SWIM & STEAM

Long Street Turkish Baths
Cnr Orange and Long streets, City Centre, tel. 400-3302.
Don't expect a spanking new environment at the Long Street Turkish Baths, but they do provide great relaxation after an amble through Long Street's appealing book and antique shops. There's a heated swimming pool, Turkish bath and massage service. Monday and Thursday (8.30am-8.30pm) and Saturday (9am-6pm) are ladies-only days. The Turkish bath costs R31; Turkish bath plus massage is R44,50 on a first-come, first-served basis.

SERVICE ORGANISATIONS

AIDS Help-Line
Tel. 21-5420.
Gay, lesbian and bisexual counselling and info on HIV- and AIDS-related issues.

Cape Organisation for Gay Sport (COGS)
Tel. 689-2551 or 557-7195.
Regular sporting get-togethers for gays and lesbians.

Gay, Lesbian and Bisexual Helpline
Tel. 21-5420.
24-hour service. Leave your name and phone number.

The Gender Advocacy Project
2 Lente Rd, Sybrand Park, tel. 696-2810.
This non-aligned women's lobbying organisation has strong links with local political organisations. It networks between civic and religious groups to help women define common needs, analyses and researches community requirements and lobbies policy-makers.

The Lesbian Action Project (LAP)
For info, contact Viv at 685-1356 or Lynne at 788-4895.
Lesbian networking, information and politically slanted support organisation that also provides a fun alternative to socialising in clubs, as well as outdoor activities.

National Association of Women's Business Owners (NABO)
Tel. 788-4815.
A networking organisation for businesswomen, NABO runs monthly breakfast meetings. It also offers business training, education mentorship, a training committee, brochures and advice. Outsiders are encouraged to participate.

Rape Crisis
4 Bishop Rd, Observatory, tel. 47-9762.
A counselling service for sexual-assault survivors, Rape Crisis has grown from a voluntary body to a professional, highly regarded organisation. It was a major player in the reform initiatives of the pioneering Sexual Offences Court, which offers streamlined and specialised legal procedure aimed at reducing the 'secondary victimisation' of sexual-assault survivors. Other notable organisations that were involved in this reform include Lawyers for Human Rights Women's Desk, tel. 47-6168, and the Institute of Criminology, UCT, tel. 650-2988.

SA Red Cross Society
21 Broad Rd, Wynberg, tel. 797-5360.
HIV home-care and related help.

Sexually Transmitted Disease Clinics
Spencer Rd, Salt River, tel. 400-2047.
Chapel St Clinic, Woodstock, tel. 462-4400 ext. 261 (Mon mornings only).
Lower Maynard Rd, Wynberg, tel. 797-5190/1/2 (Thu 1.30pm-4pm).
De Villiers St, Durbanville, tel. 96-1418.

Triangle Health Care Centre
Ground Floor, Community House, 41 Salt River Rd, Salt River, tel. 448-3812.
Open: *10.30am-9pm Mon-Tue, 10.30am-4.30pm Wed-Fri.*

The Centre's professional counsellors and medical practitioners deal with sexuality and sexually transmitted diseases.

Women 2000
For info, contact Angelica at 683-3397 (6pm-9pm).
Women 2000 aims at creating an awareness of social and political issues. Meetings take place on the first Wednesday of every month and operate on a workshop format. Typical subjects for discussion: sexual harassment, religion, romantic love.

Gay and Lesbian Christian Church
Meetings are held every Sunday at 6pm at Quaker House, cnr Hornsey and Rye roads, Mowbray, tel. 531-7171.

WOMEN'S READING

BOOKSHOPS
There are no bookshops devoted solely to women's literature, but the following have the best selection.

The Book Warehouse, *20 Main Rd, Rondebosch, tel. 686-4795.*

Exclusive Books, with branches at:
Constantia Village, Constantia, tel. 794-7800.
Lower Level, Cavendish Square, Claremont, tel. 64-3030.
225 Victoria Wharf, Waterfront, tel. 419-0905.

WOMEN'S PUBLICATIONS
The leading women's glossies are *Fair Lady, Cosmopolitan* and *Femina*. All offer features, profiles, fashion, decor and cooking. They're available at newsagents and cafés.

For specialist publications, check out *Agenda* (a gender-issues journal), *Speak* (whose motto is 'Putting Women First'), *Exit* newspaper and *Outright* magazine (gay and lesbian publications). All are obtainable from specialist bookstores.

SPECIALISED LIBRARY SERVICE

For books on gay- and lesbian-related subjects, meet at the *Community Centre, cnr Victoria and Bree streets, City Centre, 7.30pm-9pm every Wednesday, tel. 701-1257.*

CLUBS & PARTIES

Angels
27 Somerset Rd, Green Point, tel. 21-2958.
Open: *9pm-dawn Wed-Sat.*
Admission: *R10.*
This festive, decadent bar-cum-disco is a 'gay fantasia' and it attracts gays, bisexuals and straights. The dance floor offers current hits and there are three floors. Women usually congregate downstairs and men upstairs. The roof balcony offers refreshments, snacks and street views.

Brenda's Bash
Goodwood Sports Club, Milton Rd, Goodwood, tel. 551-4813 or 551-4860.
Renowned, monthly women-only party with great music and vibe. Bring your own booze and glasses and party the night away. Check dates at number above.

Dizzy Creations
Venues vary, check details at tel. 448-3614.
Celebrations to promote live, mostly original, women's music, commemorate dates like International Women's Day and raise funds for women's organisations. Lesbian-friendly.

Knights Bar
Caris House, Jamieson Rd, City Centre, tel. 23-3446.
Open: *noon-midnight daily.*
Comfortable cocktails and coffee chat bar for lesbians and gays.

RESTAURANTS & EATERIES

These aren't exclusively for women, but they're lesbi/gay-friendly. Even if you don't find the woman of your dreams, you should have a good time.

A Touch of Madness
42 Trill Rd, Observatory (just off Main Rd), tel. 448-2266.
Open: *7pm-2am daily.*
Gilt and velvet-decorated café with pub food, soups, casseroles and notable cheesecake.

Café Erté
Main Rd, Sea Point, tel. 43-46624.
Open: *7pm-5am daily.*
A 'homo-age' to artist Erté, with board games, light meals, music videos, cocktails and slightly tacky OTT decor, this coffee bar/eatery is a terrific place to tête-à-tête. Gay-, lesbian- and straight-friendly. Grab a corner couch.

The Caz/bah
Castle Bowling Club, Melbourne Rd, Woodstock, tel. 26-1632 (a/h).
Open: *8pm-2am Wed and Fri, and in summer 8pm-2am Sat.*
Lesbian bar with dance and barbecue facilities and pool tables.

Elaine's Curry Bistro
105 Lower Main Rd, Observatory, tel. 47-2616.
Open: *12.30pm-2.30pm Mon-Fri, 6.30pm-midnight daily.*
Lesbian-owned, established, laid-back restaurant with Indian decor for superb curries (*see also chapter* **Where to Eat**).

Fiddlewoods
40 Trill Rd, Observatory, tel. 448-6687.
Open: *8am-5pm Mon-Fri, 7pm-late Fri, 8.30am-2pm Sat-Sun.*
Mediterranean-style light meals, breakfasts and bistro cooking in a cheerful setting. Reserve a table in advance (*see also chapter* **Where to Eat**).

Theresa's Restaurant
11 Palmer Rd, Muizenberg, tel. 788-8051.
Open: *8.30am-4.30pm and 7pm-10.30pm Tues-Sun.*
Bohemian budget decor with odd metal and wooden chairs, sackcloth ceiling and yellow walls. The menu – homey, huge servings –

includes enormous English breakfast (R10,95), daily specials and excellent casseroles, lamb curry and salads. Owner Theresa has created a sociable hangout for local writers, artists, surfers and professionals. Licensed.

HAPPENINGS

For information on the *Gay Pride March* and the *Secret Garden Project,* see Chapter **Gay Cape Town.**

WET, WET, WET

Surf's up! Beaches, watersports, sailing and more ...

You've got your swimsuit, suntan oil, hat, bucket and spade and you're ready to explore Cape Town's world-renowned beaches. Now the question is – where to go?

Water on the False Bay side of the coast is generally five degrees warmer than that on the Atlantic side, where the cold Benguela current heading northwards from the Antarctic makes for bone-chilling bathing. So the choice is icy water, breathtaking scenery and beautiful trendies (at beaches like Clifton, Camps Bay and Llandudno) or less glamorous beaches with infinitely better bathing and a good spread of tidal pools.

Windy most afternoons, the False Bay beaches are best visited in the mornings. For afternoon beaching, the Atlantic coast beaches are more sheltered.

SURF REPORTS & BEACH FOOD

Information on surf conditions, tides and wind is available on the Surf Report, tel. 788-5965. Radio KFM also offers a daily 7.15am surf report. And, of course, a city famed for its laid-back attitude has to have a beach takeout delivery service. So if you're yearning for pizza, burgers or even sushi, but are too lazy to get it for yourself, Mr Delivery, tel. 439-9916, will bring the victuals to your towel.

BEACHES

Beaches listed here are divided according to the warm-water False Bay, cold-water Atlantic coast, and west coast in the sequence in which they appear by road.

HEADING SOUTH: THE FALSE BAY COAST

Muizenberg Beach
Take the M5 and Prince George Drive, or the M4 past Lakeside, and follow the Muizenberg signposts.
Once the darling of resorts among the wealthy, Muizenberg was home to the likes of Rhodes, Oppenheimer and Robinson and even appeared in a poem by Rudyard Kipling, 'as white as the sands of Muizenberg'. But the old glory is much faded and the seafront area has become tacky, despite the charm of the old village.
The beach, however, far from being charmless, offers lovely swimming and such easy surfing that it's known as a surfing nursery for beginners. Favoured by picnick-

ing families who come for the safe swimming and the fast food joints, miniature golf, pavilion, promenade, waterslide, fun fair and Sunday flea-market.

Multi-coloured changerooms and mountain views characterise this beach, and there's also a great walk along a rocky promenade from here to St James. Late winter and spring are also good for whale-watching. If the surf looks dirty, don't worry – it's algae build-up more than pollution.

St James
Some 6 km south on the coastal road past Muizenberg.
Rock pools, protection from the wind and proximity to facilities, cafés and eateries make this cosy and reliable beach popular with families. The Gordon's Bay mountains can be seen across the dreamy vista of the Indian Ocean from this appealing spot.

The distinctive, bright changerooms of Muizenberg beach.

Kalk Bay
Pass St James, south along the railway line to the signposts. An alternative and equally scenic route is via Boyes' Drive.
Kalk Bay village, with its antique and junk shops, bistros and coffee bars, has a distinctly bohemian air and it attracts everyone from die-hard hippies and students to families. If that's not enough to tempt you, the beach offers tidal pools, good waves for experienced surfers and a small harbour (with an established fishing community).

Buy fresh fish from the fishermen or the harbour kiosk, or, if you're serious about fishing and prepared to set out at around

SAND BETWEEN YOUR TOES: BEACH ETIQUETTE & TIPS

Just in case you weren't listening to mom, sunshine can be dangerous. You need all the blockout lotion you can get at this end of the globe. Bluebottles usually appear only after a very strong south-easter, but don't play with them — they can hurt. In case you intend ignoring this advice, see chapter **Survival** for medical emergency numbers.

Bottles are banned on the beaches for safety reasons and offenders can be fined. Four-wheel drive vehicles are prohibited on beaches. Beachfront parking is scarce during summer, but traffic cops are plentiful, so expect a ticket if you park illegally. Topless tanning is not yet *de rigueur* but you're welcome to go ahead. Those offended by the public display should complain to a public officer. If topless is too tame for you, head for the wonderfully scenic naturist Sandy Bay beach. There's also the men-only naturist Graaff's Pool (*see chapter* **Gay Cape Town**).

Shell collecting is best at Muizenberg, Glencairn or, with a permit only, in the Cape of Good Hope Nature Reserve.

3am, some fishermen will take you along for R30-R80.

Across the bay is Seal Island, home to hundreds of seals and birds and one of the few breeding grounds for the great white shark.

In a truly exotic setting, so close to the tidal pool that you can almost dangle your feet in the water, is the landmark Brass Bell, a sociable, popular restaurant-cum-bar with a sundeck and clear sea views (*see chapter* **Where to Eat**).

Fish Hoek

Drive towards Cape Point along the coastal road from Muizenberg. Alternatively, take the Ou Kaapse Weg and turn right where the M3 freeway forms a T-junction with the M42 and watch for the signposts.

Fish Hoek is blandly suburban, but its beaches offer warm water and excellent sailing, surfing, kite-flying and hobiecatting. The crowd includes windsurfers and sailors, and the beach restaurant and tearoom make it popular with families.

Fishing shops on Main Rd and Recreation Rd hire out fishing tackle and the stretch of shops and cafés between Fish Hoek and Simon's Town harbour has a colonial, conservative air. Sailors, sailors everywhere. Jaeger Walk, named after an ex-mayor, forms a magnificent promenade between the sea and rocks – a worthwhile walk. In the distance, across the bay, lie the Hottentots-Holland Mountains.

You won't be far from the maddening crowd, but there are changerooms, showers, a kids' playground and restaurant. It's also great for whale-watching in late winter and spring.

Seaforth Beach

Take St George's Rd through Simon's Town and turn left into Seaforth Rd.

Safe swimming, shelter from the wind, lawns, car parks, picnic spots and a waterslide.

Boulders

Drive past Simon's Town towards Cape Point and, just after Seaforth, the beach is signposted down Bellevue Rd.

Boulders is a gem – warm, sheltered, stun-

Fisherman at Kalk Bay Harbour.

ningly pretty with nooks, coves, safe swimming, snorkelling and the giant boulders from which it derives its name. It's also home to endangered African jackass penguins and the odd octopus.

This is one of the few Cape beaches with an entrance fee, but it's worth every cent – R3 for adults, and R1,50 for children under six on weekends and during season (November to mid-April). Season tickets (R15 for adults and R7,50 for children) are sold by the Simon's Town Municipality, tel. 786-1551. Take your own food and drinks and go early if you want a good spot.

Buffelsbaai

Drive along the M4 or M65 to the Cape of Good Hope Nature Reserve, which is where you'll find Buffelsbaai. The only public transport to the area is by daily coach tours. For info on these call Captour, tel. 418-5214.

You can take a rikki from Simon's Town station. Rates vary according to the number of passengers. For info, tel. 786-2136.

Buffelsbaai, inside the Cape of Good Hope Nature Reserve, offers marvellous walks among the Cape wildflowers (fynbos) and crags, a deep-sea fishing-boat launching slip, white sands, a shipwreck and easy swimming in the huge, safe tidal pool. Cape Point is also one of the few areas suited to deepwater angling from the rocks. And what it loses in easy accessibility, it compensates for in the unusualness of the setting and absence of fast-food chomping crowds. Unsheltered from the south-easter, it's best visited in calm weather.

For info on the walks and weather, phone the Cape of Good Hope Nature Reserve, tel. 780-9526 or 780-9100 (main gate).

HEADING EAST: THE (WARM) GORDON'S BAY SIDE

Strandfontein
Head east from Muizenberg along Baden Powell Drive.
Seven kilometres of beach with a tidal pool and good walks, Strandfontein offers a mural-decorated pavilion with shops and restaurants and a popular supertube. Lifeguards are on duty during season, and, as with Muizenberg, the crowd tends towards picnicking families.

Mnandi and Monwabisi
Khayelitsha, False Bay Coast. Pass Strandfontein beach along Baden Powell Drive and watch out for the signposts.
Although apartheid laws that segregated beaches have gone, Mnandi and Monwabisi are still mainly frequented by nearby residents, and they regularly attract crowds of up to 50 000 people. Mnandi has basic facilities, good angling and it's best in the morning. Monwabisi has Africa's largest tidal pools, lawns, refreshment kiosk, kiddies' pool and barbecue areas. Its recreation complex, an innovative architectural design, features a central pavilion and brick amphitheatre with striped blockwork, timber fins, primary colours and murals. Occasional live bands and evangelical baptisms in the water may feature. Entry fee is R1 p/p and per vehicle.

Strandfontein's curious pavilion.

The Strand
Take the N2 from Cape Town or drive along the coastal road from Strandfontein.
Around half an hour's drive from Cape Town, Strand beach is long and wide with safe swimming in warm water, but it can be ferociously windy. There's a good range of shops, restaurants and cafés in the area.

Gordon's Bay
Reach Gordon's Bay beach via the N7 if you fancy a leisurely, 30-km scenic drive from Cape Town. Alternatively, take the N2 and head off at the Gordon's Bay turn-off.
Labelled 'Sea Point for Afrikaners' on account of its tourist amenities and Boland and Somerset West fans, Gordon's Bay's once-conservative atmosphere is giving way to an integrated crowd and the beach is lovely, but it can be windy.

Gordon's Bay beach is divided into two sections – Bikini and Main beaches – linked by an easy path. Bikini beach is best for sheltered tanning and Main beach is good for watersports. There are shops, restaurants and cafés in the area.

GO WEST: HOUT BAY AND SURROUNDS

Hout Bay
From the Sea Point side, follow the M6 from Camps Bay and drive south for 15 km. From the southern suburbs, drive over Constantia Nek (take the M41 off the M3 freeway) following the Hout Bay signposts. The drive should take around half an hour.
Wide and long, Hout Bay beach is flanked by Sentinel mountain and Chapman's Peak and it's reached via quaint, oak-shaded Hout Bay village. (The name Hout means 'wood' and is derived from the forests that supplied the Cape settlement with timber in Van Riebeeck's time.)

The crowd ranges from surfers, paddle-skiers and suntanners to families. The cold water's best for windsurfing, hobiecats, paddle-skiers and surfers and the walking's good.

Hout Bay harbour boasts Mariner's Wharf Seafood Emporium (South Africa's first harbour-front fresh-fish emporium), for fresh fish, takeouts, seafood eateries, lobster markets, craft, curio and collectables shops. (For info on Mariner's Wharf, tel. 790-1100.) Parking is relatively easy.

Noordhoek
From Hout Bay, drive along Chapman's Peak Drive onto the M6. Noordhoek will be signposted as you enter the valley.
This eerily pristine, 8-km beach is a dazzling sight from Chapman's Peak Drive and it's surrounded by a marsh with abundant birdlife and flora. (Look for Egyptian geese, sunbirds, gulls, egrets, ibis and cormorants.)

Better suited to surfing, walking and horse-riding than swimming, Noordhoek offers superb views of Hout Bay and mind-clearing space.

Southwards towards Kommetjie lies the wreck of the *Kakapo*, a steamship that ran ashore during the 1900s. The vessel's ribs, boiler and rudder posts are clearly visible. The walk along Long Beach to the wreck takes about 45 minutes.

There's no café within walking distance of Noordhoek, but The Red Herring craft-restaurant complex on Beach Rd is about ten minutes' walk from the parking lot.

Kommetjie
From Noordhoek, drive along the M6 and just after Sun Valley turn right into the M65. Alternatively, Kommetjie can be reached via Fish Hoek along the M65. The landmark lighthouse is visible from Noordhoek.
Famous for its surfing and crayfish, Kommetjie's name, meaning 'little bowl', refers to its natural tidal pool (now walled off and polluted). Surfers gravitate to the south end of the beach, where breaks have idiosyncratic names like 'kitchen windows', 'bone yards' and 'paper pipe'. The swimming's cold, but there are superb walks from Kommetjie to Noordhoek or on the Catwalk to the lighthouse. (Avoid walking alone – muggings have occurred.)

For fishing, Kommetjie is known for its concentration of galjoen, mostly netted from boats, and crayfishing from kelp beds off the lighthouse at Slangkoppunt.

Nearby Kommetjie village is rustic, with shops, eateries, beautiful milkwood trees and beach houses dating back to the early 1900s.

White Sands, Scarborough and Misty Cliffs

Heading south on the M65 along the coast, you'll see the signposts and the long stretches of these three powdery white, underpopulated beaches.

Beautiful sunsets, good surfing, fishing, and space are the main attractions at these beaches. Overdeveloped they ain't.

Between Misty Cliffs and Scarborough is 365, a surf spot where waves are apparently great all year round, and Scarborough's rock pools are great for mussel-picking, provided you stick to the quota, which varies seasonally. For details of safe mussel-picking and regulations, call the Sea Fisheries Institute, tel. 402-3911. Don't pick mussels without checking whether there's a poisonous red tide. (Newspapers carry details, or call Red Tide Hotline, tel. 439-4380.)

Graaff's Pool, a nudist and men-only enclave on the Sea Point promenade.

There's a campsite and barbecue area just outside Scarborough village, which is also home to resolute hippies, alternative lifestylers and summer music festivals.

TRENDY ATLANTIC SEABOARD

Sea Point

Beach Rd, Sea Point.

Sea Point beaches (although there's not much beach *per se*), include Rocklands, Saunders' Rock, Sunset Pool, Milton Pool and Graaff's Pool (*see chapter* **Gay Cape Town**). They're small and easily accessible with tidal pools and nearby shops, eateries, playgrounds, miniature golf and buzzy atmosphere.

The promenade is wonderful for walking, jogging and rollerblading and it attracts everyone from octogenarians to trendoids. Swimming is cold but relatively safe. There's a cycle and rollerblade hiring service at Rent 'n Ride, Park Rd, Mouille Point, tel. 434-1122.

Clifton

Follow the coastal road past Sea Point in the direction of Camps Bay. Clifton's beaches, (1st, 2nd, 3rd, 4th) are signposted.

South Africa's most glamorous beach is set below some madly expensive real estate and it's accessed via steep steps. Clifton is truly unmissable – renowned for its horribly cold water and gorgeously hot bodies, which are as much part of the scenery as the stunning ocean view.

Granite boulders divide Clifton into four separate areas, each with its own crowd – 4th Beach is for families and sports, 3rd for playboys and girls, 2nd for teenagers and 1st for trendies. Tucked away beyond 1st Beach is Moses Beach where the alternative, sophisticated set hang out. Parking is hellish, but it's worth the struggle.

Camps Bay

Take Victoria Rd past Clifton towards Llandudno. Camps Bay beach is opposite sidewalk cafés and the large Bay Hotel.

Palm tree-lined Camps Bay beach is kelp- and rock-free and good for body surfing. There's also beach volleyball and splendid views of Table Mountain and the Twelve Apostles. Don't expect natural splendour alone. The convenience of nearby shops and outdoor cafés comes at the price of parking hassles and crowds.

Regulars range from families picnicking on the grassy verge to trendies, yuppies and sporting types, and there are huge crowds during summer and on public holidays.

Over the rocks, towards Clifton is surfers' haven, Glen Beach.

Bakoven

Drive a little way past Camps Bay in the direction of Llandudno and take the Bakoven signpost to the right.

Bakoven is small, secluded, popular and very pretty with marvellous mountain views, spectacular sunsets and icy water. It's not as flashy as Clifton (what could be?), but it does have discreet cachét. There are no shops or eateries within easy walking distance.

Oudekraal

Take the coastal road from Camps Bay towards Llandudno and, approximately half way between the two, you'll see Oudekraal, with its ablution blocks and barbecue sites.

A favourite with families and divers, Oudekraal offers deep rock pools, a shipwreck and small enclaves of beaches separated by rocks.

There's a daily entrance fee in season: adults R4 and children R2. The gates close at 6pm but you can buy a late night permit from the cash desk at the entrance for R30 per group if you want to stay until 11pm.

Llandudno

Travel 10 km south from Camps Bay along the M6, or head north from Hout Bay.

Set below steep hills and flanked by luxury houses, spectacular Llandudno beach has huge granite rocks, sheltered tanning areas, good picnicking and surfing, and gorgeous sunsets and mountain views. It's also wonderful for walking. There are no shops nearby, so stock up beforehand.

Sandy Bay

Take the M6/Victoria Rd. Turn right into

Blondes, bikinis, bods – Clifton's stock in trade.

Llandudno and stick to the Llandudno Rd, which becomes Fisherman's Bend, then turn right into Oakburn and left into Leeukoppie which leads to Sandy Bay parking. From there, take the 20-minute walk along the natural path.

Cape Town's unofficial but long-established nudist beach is superbly set between dense mountains and rocks. It has white sands, lovely walks and a beautiful, if cold, bay. Apart from occasional creepy voyeurs, the vibe is extremely relaxed.

No facilities or nearby shops (besides an occasional cool-drink vendor in the parking lot). Take your own refreshments. Stripping off is not *de rigeur*.

WEST COAST

Milnerton

On the N1 from the City Centre take the Milnerton/ Paarden Eiland turn-off.
This 10-km beach is great for walking, kite-flying, mussel-picking and frequently photographed views of Table Mountain. Cold water. Check mussel quotas with the Sea Fisheries Institute, tel. 402-3911.

Milnerton Lagoon is safe with fairly calm windsurfing. No refreshments are sold at the beach but there are shops nearby. Good changerooms and facilities.

Blouberg

Take the Milnerton/Paarden Eiland turn-off on the N1 from the City Centre. Go north past Milnerton and follow the signposts to Blouberg.
Beautiful Blouberg beach comprises Big Bay, a renowned surfers' paradise, and Little Bay, a family favourite. The water's freezing, but walking and jogging are good and Big Bay has regular windsurfing, surfing and paddle-skiing competitions. Some quaint cafés and restaurants overlook the beach.

Beach volleyball on Camps Bay, one of the city's most popular beaches.

Table View

Take the coastal road past Milnerton lighthouse.
Magnificent views of Table Bay and Robben Island, accessible parking, shops, clean, white sand and sand dunes are the attractions here. The water's icy and there's not much shelter from the wind, but surfing's good as are beach facilities and local cafés and restaurants.

TRANSPORT TO BEACHES

TRAINS

A network of trains connects the False Bay coast with the City Centre and provides one of the most enjoyable ways to get to the Muizenberg side. (There are no trains to the Clifton side.) Timetables are obtainable from station ticket offices. For arrival and departure times:
Muizenberg, tel. 507-2603.
Simon's Town, tel. 507-2586.
Metro enquiries, tel. 405-2991
Mainline reservations, tel. 405-3871.

The ride between Cape Town Station and Muizenberg is R4,60 first class and R2 third class.

Most trains stop running after 9pm and third class can be dangerous especially after dark, when first class is recommended. Station security is being stepped up, but don't stand alone, and watch your belongings.

BUSES

Buses run from Muizenberg, Fish Hoek and Simon's Town stations to adjacent villages.

For information on metropolitan bus services, call Golden Arrow, tel. 0801-21-2111 or the Simon's Town depot, tel. 786-1377.

Buses to Milnerton and Blouberg depart from the Golden Acre Terminus, Adderley St, City Centre, and they're labelled Killarney or Atlantis. A single ticket to Milnerton is R2,30 and to Blouberg R7,90.

Take the Hout Bay bus to get to Llandudno and Hout Bay from outside the OK Bazaars, Adderley St, City Centre. A single ticket is R4,40.

MINIBUS TAXIS

Considerably cheaper, if less sedate than conventional taxis, minibus/combi taxis are crowded and fast, and they cover major Cape Town routes. You can catch one outside the Cape Sun Hotel in Strand St, along Sea Point and Green Point Main roads, at bus stops or along most main roads. Simply lift your arm to signal that you want a ride. Average fare is R1-R3. Expect a frequently jostling, sociable ride, often with blaring music.

PUBLIC SWIMMING POOLS

Cape Town has some 15 public swimming pools and the average entry is about R3 per adult. Monthly tickets are also available at around R50. Most public pools offer discounts to pensioners, coaches and members of recognised aquatic clubs, but tariffs rise during high season (Dec-Jan), and fees are reviewed annually, meaning that prices listed here may increase. The following are open all year.

Long Street Baths

Cnr Long and Orange streets, tel. 400-3302.
Open: *7am-10pm Mon-Fri, 7am-7pm Sat, 8am-7pm Sun.*
Admission: *R4 adults, R1,80 for under 16s. (The last ticket is sold an hour before closing time.)*
Heated indoor pool in Victorian building with 27-m-long mural by local artist Gregg Smith. There's also a Turkish steam bath with resident masseur and sauna for R44,50. Women's days for the steam baths are 9am-8.30pm Mon and Thu, and 9am-6pm Sat. Men's days for steam baths are 9am-8.30pm Tue, Wed, and Fri, and 8am-noon Sun. Wheelchair-friendly (but not in the steam baths).

Muizenberg Seawater Pool

Muizenberg Beachfront, Muizenberg, tel. 788-7881.
Open: *In summer: 8am-5pm Mon-Fri, 8am-6pm Sat-Sun. In winter: 8am-4.30pm daily.*
Admission: *R3,30 adults, R1,30 children. During Dec and Jan: R5 adults, R2,20 children.*
Large seawater pool set amid fast food stores, playground and fun fair. Wheelchair-friendly.

Newlands Pool

Cnr Main and Sans Souci roads, Newlands, tel. 64-4197.
Open: *daily 7am-7pm (Nov-Mar) and 8.15am-5pm (Apr-Oct).*
Admission: *R3,30 adults, R1,30 children. During Dec and Jan: R5 adults, R2,20 for children.*
Outdoor pool. Seasonal snack kiosk, jungle gym and children's pool. Wheelchair-friendly.

WATERSPORTS

Cape Town has much to offer waterbabies – from charters, fishing, scuba diving, sailing and surfing to yachting, canoeing and horse-riding on beaches. Watch out for the South Atlantic swell though – it's rumoured to have been a cause of some concern to visiting royals. Here are some of the best watersports options. *See also chapter* **Sport, Fitness & The Great Outdoors**.

BOAT CHARTERS & CRUISES

Prices and times are subject to seasonal change.

Champagne Sunset Cruise

Quay 5, Waterfront, tel. 25-3578.
Splendidly romantic two-hour trip to Clifton and back to the Waterfront includes a bottle of sparkling wine per couple and costs R35 per adult and R20 per child under 12. Pre-dinner, one-hour harbour cruise sets off before sunset at R25 per adult.

Circe Launch Trips

Hout Bay Harbour, tel. 790-1040.
Two-hour, champagne sunset cruises into Table Bay include sparkling wine and snacks; R63 per person. One-hour cruises to Seal Island are R17,50 per adult, R8 per child. Half-hour trips to Seal Island depart

daily at 10.30am and cost R22 per adult, R10 per child under 14. Operates weekends only in winter. Phone for cruise times.

Condor Charters
Quay 4, Waterfront, tel. 448-5612.
One-and-a-half-hour sunset sea cruise includes harbour lights and sparkling wine; R50 per person. Daytime 45-minute sea cruises are R20 for adults, R10 for children under 12, free for toddlers. Robben Island cruises on Wednesday, Saturday and Sunday depart at 8.30am and last two-and-a-half hours; R75 including refreshments and food. The vessel accommodates 70 people and has a lounge, covered deck and viewing deck. Fully licensed. Conference facilities also available.

Le Tigre Catamaran Charters
Front of Victoria and Alfred Hotel, Waterfront, tel. 419-7746.
Sail in Table Bay in a 54-foot luxury catamaran, sail- and motor-powered, cash bar on board. The two-hour Robben Island cruise is a fully guided tour along the east coast of the island. (Landing is prohibited.) Cost: R70 per adult, R35 per child under 16. It departs at 11am and 1.30pm and booking is advisable. Two-hour sunset cruises are R60 per adult, R30 per child under 16. One-and-a-half-hour cruises are R45 per adult, R25 per child under 16. One-hour cruises around Table Bay, suitable for families, depart three times a day in summer and twice a day in winter at R30 per adult and R15 per child under 16. *Le Tigre* can be privately chartered from R750 per hour in low season to R1 175 per hour in high season for a maximum of 47 passengers. Catering can be arranged.

Penny Ferry
Pierhead, Waterfront, tel. 418-2350 ext 265.
The Penny Ferry was introduced in 1871 to row harbour staff across the Cut (the original entrance to the Alfred Basin). It was opened to the public in 1880 for a penny fare. The best sailing bargain in Cape Town, the Penny Ferry is rowed from the Pierhead to Bertie's Landing providing a quick, soothing sail with harbour, seal and mountain views – all for R1. Great fun.

En route to Seal Island on *The Circe*.

Pommery Charters
North Quay, Alfred Basin, Waterfront, tel. 25-4277.
The *Pommery*, a luxury motor cruiser, offers tailor-made cruises starting at R650 an hour.

Sea Link Tours
Quay 5, Victoria Wharf, Table Bay Harbour, tel. 25-4480.
Relaxed, one-and-a-half-hour harbour cruises run throughout the day for R5 p/p. The one-hour harbour and sea cruise is R10 p/p.

Spirit of Victoria
Pierhead (in front of Piers Restaurant), Waterfront, tel. 25-4062.
A 58-foot schooner for a variety of trips – into Table Bay towards Robben Island or Clifton. Two-and-a-half-hour trips are R70 per adult, R35 per child. One-and-a-half-hour sunset cruise, including sparkling wine, is R45 p/p. One-hour breakfast cruises can be arranged, and private charters with a maximum 45 passengers are R800 per hour. Arrive 20 minutes before departure time.

Teacher's Spirit of Adventure
Jetty 2, Waterfront, tel. 419-3122 or 419-2749 or 419-5646.
Continental or English breakfast, cocktail, three-course lunch, and romantic dinner cruises with free welcome cocktails. Cruises last between two and three hours and sail around the harbour. Phone for booking info and prices.

Waterfront Charters
Old Port Captain's Bldg, Pierhead, Waterfront, tel. 25-3804 or 25-4292.
Three-hour trip to Robben Island coast (landing is prohibited) is R70 p/p. Drinks are available, and for large groups, snacks can be arranged. One-and-a-half-hour champagne sunset cruise around Table Bay, including bubbly and snacks, is R45 per person. Departs 6.30pm daily in summer. Phone to check times in winter. One-hour harbour tour into the international docks is R20 per adult and R10 per child. Departs 2.30pm daily. Guided tours of the Waterfront and docks depart every half-hour daily for R8 p/p.

CANOEING & RIVER ADVENTURES
To hire or buy canoes, try *The Boardsail Inn, Sandvlei, tel. 788-4697.* The following offer adventurous river trips with overnight stops as well as white-water rafting. Four- or five-day river trips are around R400 p/p and one-day trips are around R100-R175 p/p, depending on catering arrangements and distances. You can also combine river-rafting with a trip to wine route areas, usually with farm lunches and wine-tasting.
Breede River Adventures, tel. 762-6935/6/7.
Cape Canoe Trails, tel. 789-2136.
Felix Unite River Adventures, tel. 762-6935/6/7.
Orange River Adventures, tel. 419-1705.
River Rafters, tel. 72-6935/6/7.
River Runners, tel. 762-2350.
Southern Journeys, tel. (0291) 4-2466.

FISHING
There are two types of fishing in the Cape – bay and deep-sea fishing. Bay fishing (in False Bay area) is where you'll catch kabeljou, geelbek, white stumpnose and snoek. Deep-sea fishing, 20 to 40 miles offshore, is best for catching yellowfin and longfin tunny, dorado, skipjack and the odd elusive marlin.

There's a range of deep-sea, game-fishing and boat-chartering services, most of which exclude food and drink (except by prior arrangement at extra cost) but include fishing tackle, rods, bait, skipper and co-skipper.

Strict rules govern the catching of crayfish (Cape rock lobster), perlemoen (abalone), mussels and other shellfish. For information on marine reserves and regulations, contact the Sea Fisheries Institute, tel. 402-3911, or the Marine Conservation Inspector, tel. 788-8313 (Kalk Bay) or tel. 783-2295 (Kommetjie). Fishing permits are obtainable from the Magistrate's Office, St George's Rd, Simon's Town, tel. 786-1561/2.

Angling rules for a *vlei* (marshy area) include fishing only by hook and line, no fishing at night with a light, no cleaning, selling or disposing of fish on the vlei banks, and no unauthorised removal of shrimp and prawns.

The best rock and surf angling areas around Cape Town include Paternoster (on the west coast), Langebaan Lagoon, Strandfontein and Swartklip (near Muizenberg), Cape Hangklip, Kleinmond, Gansbaai, Pearly Beach, Struisbaai, Arniston and Cape Infanta, as well as Rooikrans, one of the world's superb angling spots.

For boat hire, guides and tours, try the following:

African Fishing Safaris
Tel. 438-5201.
Deep-sea fishing and tailor-made fishing safaris, trout and fly-fishing.

Big Game Fishing Safaris
Tel. 64-2203.
Game-fishing off Cape Point, including gear for tunny and marlin catching.

Waiting for the big one.

Bluefin Charters
Tel. 783-1756 or 786-1463 or 23-3333 code 7813.
Deep-sea game-fishing.

Captain Rob's Tours
Tel. 788-5261.
Kalk Bay tours and fishing trips.

Game Fish Charters
Tel. 790-4550 or 790-1388.
Trips to the tunny-rich fishing grounds near Hout Bay. Bait, tackle and soup, lunch or refreshments (and alcohol on return trip) included.

Neptune Deep Sea Game Fishing
Ron Davis, tel. 782-3889.
Fishing in False Bay and game-fishing off Cape Point in fully equipped boats.

Trout Adventures
Tel.26-1057.
Freshwater fishing.

HORSE-RIDING IN BEACH AREAS

Horse Trail Safaris
Indicator Lodge, Skaapskraal Rd, Ottery, tel. 73-4396.
Rides on Kommetjie and Noordhoek beach (R75 p/p for a two-hour ride) and Ottery Dunes (R40 p/p for a one-hour ride). Also offers weekend trails up the west coast and Cederberg Mountains, lessons and children's riding holiday camps.

Sleepy Hollow Horse Riding
Sleepy Hollow Lane, Noordhoek, tel. 789-2341.
Sunset, day and moonlight rides, beach and bush rides and lessons with guided trails are on offer here. In the Noordhoek area, there are breathtaking Chapman's Peak views, birdlife and shipwreck viewing. Two-hour sunset rides (R85), day rides (R65 for two hours), lessons (R35 for half hour privately, R35 per hour for two people). All rides are down an access path via the wetland/marsh. Booking advisable.

St James beach on the False Bay coast.

SCUBA DIVING

The Atlantic Underwater Club, Bay Rd, Mouille Point, tel. 439-0701 or 439-9322 is open from 5.30pm except Mondays, and the False Bay Underwater Club, Connaught Rd, Wynberg, tel. 761-2763, caters for members only, but can provide info on diving conditions.

Blue Print Diving
Shop 5, Quay 5, Waterfront, tel. 418-5806.
Courses, equipment hire, repairs, sales and boat charters. The beginners' course costs R550 and includes lectures, pool training, registration, equipment hire and four sea dives, either on a four-day full-time or two-week part-time basis. There's a boat charter service for experienced divers at R50 per dive. Full equipment hire costs R100 per day. Guided shore entries are R50 for a day.

Ocean Divers International
Protea Ritz Hotel, Main Rd, Sea Point, tel. 439-1803.
Professional instruction and equipment hire with full- and part-time courses. Beginners' course costs R650. Full equipment hire costs R100.

Scuba Venture
Avalon Bldg, 8 Mill St, Gardens, tel. 461-2709.
This equipment shop offers courses, boat charters and equipment hire. Three-week part-time, or one-week full-time courses comprise lectures, pool sessions and sea dives for R695. A full boat charter costs R45 per person, a refresher course for those wanting to consolidate their diving experience costs R295 per day. Scuba gear hire is R65 per day. Student discounts available.

SURFING

The best surfing is at Long Beach, Kommetjie, Noordhoek, Llandudno, Kalk Bay, Muizenberg, and Big Bay at Bloubergstrand. There are competitions during summer at Bloubergstrand. *For info on surfing conditions, tel. 788-8218.*

For surfboard stores and hire, try the following:

The Corner Surf Shop
143 Main Rd, Muizenberg, tel. 788-1191.
Surfboards for hire at R35 per day or part thereof. Not always available.

Fish Hoek Sport
Recreation Rd, Fish Hoek, tel. 782-2123.
Paddle-ski and surfing equipment for hire.

Lifestyle Surf Shop
Donkers Bldg, York Rd, Muizenberg, tel. 788-8218.
Bodyboards are R7 an hour; surfboards are R12 an hour and wave-skis are R15 an hour.

Suntrax Sail, Surf & Street
7 Bree St, City Centre, tel. 419-3772.
Latest models from learner to expert, board and sail repairs and trade-ins.

Side Surf Shop
Shop 578, Tyger Valley Centre, Tyger Valley, tel. 948-9565.
Latest models, advice and an exceptional range of sports goods.

YACHT CLUBS & SAILING

Cape Town's major yachting events are the Cape to Rio Yacht Race every two years (the next race is in January 1996) and Rothmans' Week Regatta, which begins annually on 16 December.

Keel boats are harboured at Simon's Town, and the best spots for hobiecatting are Fish Hoek and Hout Bay. For dams, lagoons and river sailing, try Zeekoeivlei and Langebaan Lagoon.

For information on sailing, contact the Western Province Sailing Association, tel. 439-7976.

Cape Town's major clubs are the False Bay Yacht Club, tel. 786-1703, the Royal Cape Yacht Club, tel. 21-1354, and the Hout Bay Yacht Club, tel. 790-3110. Although these are for members only, visitors can be accommodated by arrangement if they're crew members, guests of a club member or a member of an affiliated international club.

For information on boat registration and handicapping, contact the Western Province Sailing Association, tel. 439-1147.

DAY TRIPS

Get out of town – and head for pastures green, vineyards, valleys and great escapes.

Cape Town is surrounded by sensational natural attractions, wine routes, cultural landmarks and great country restaurants – many of them well under an hour-and-a-half's drive from the City Centre. This chapter includes truly memorable ones, but they're just a few of your many options. Contact Captour bureaux (*see chapter* **Essential Information**) for information, maps and excellent specialised brochures on the Wine Route, the Whale Route, the Antique Route, the Fruit Route, the Shipwreck and Lighthouse Route, the Arts and Crafts Route, Treasure Coast Art Route, the Paarl Language Route, Fynbos Route, the Fireside Guide and the Birdwatchers' Guide. Major wine routes in this chapter include Stellenbosch, Franschhoek and Paarl. For trips further afield, try Wellington, Worcester, Robertson, Tulbagh, Greyton and the Klein Karoo wine area. The Constantia and Durbanville wine routes are situated within the Cape Peninsula (for more info, contact Captour, tel. 418-5214/5 or 418-5202).

The Huguenot Memorial in Franschhoek commemorates the 250th anniversary of the arrival of the Huguenots in South Africa.

FRANSCHHOEK

A trip to Franschhoek is one of the Cape's most rewarding outings. Apart from the natural splendour of valleys, vineyards and mountains, the area is rich in culinary and cultural pleasures, offering some of the country's finest restaurants and great opportunities to sample and invest in wine and to view historic architecture.

Franschhoek (meaning French corner), was founded in 1688 on land granted by Governor Simon van der Stel to French Huguenots who had escaped religious persecution in Europe. These 200 settler families had a profound influence on Cape culture. They brought expertise in agriculture and wine-making, and during the three centuries since their arrival on South African soil, the wine cultivars introduced by the Huguenots have matured to produce a notable range of red and white wines, sparkling wines and port. The nine original farms that belonged to the first Huguenot settlers – La Dauphine, Burgundy, La Bri, Champagne, Cabrière, La terra de Luc, La Cotte, La Provence and La Motte are still associated in some way with wine-making.

For an introduction to Huguenot history, visit the Huguenot Memorial Museum in Lambrecht St, (next to the Huguenot Monument), tel. (02212) 2532 or 2673. Admission is R2 for adults and 50c for children and guided tours can be arranged in advance.

The best way to explore the outstanding estates in the area is via the excellent brochures and advice provided by the Vignerons de Franschhoek, an association that comprises the 16 wine producers who collectively make up the Franschhoek Wine Route.

Estates on the route range from modern, sophisticated establishments to smaller, family owned producers. All welcome visitors and many have restored splendid traditional Cape Dutch architecture.

Local estates that won awards at the 1994 Veritas, the highest South African honours for excellence in wine-making, are Bellingham (tel. (02211) 4-1011), Boschendal (tel. (02211) 4-1034), Chamonix (tel. (0221) 2-2498 or 2-4940), La Bourgogne (not generally open to the public, but visits by appointment, tel. (02212) 2115), La Cotte (whose wine is produced by the Franschhoek Vineyards Co-op, tel. (02212) 2086/7), Mouton-Excelsior (tel. (02212) 3316), Haute Provence (tel. (02212) 3195), La Motte (tel. (02212) 3119), Dieu Donné (tel. (02212) 2493) and L'Ormarins (tel. (02211) 4-1026 or 4-1024).

When it comes to restaurants and eateries, you'll seldom go wrong in this area. The choice ranges from charming delis to serious restaurants (*see chapter* **Where to Eat**). It's also worth dropping in at La Cotte Inn Wine Sales, just off Main St, on the corner of Huguenot and Louis Botha streets. This shop offers local wines for tasting and prices are only a fraction higher than those at the estates. The 5-km Wine Walk offers wine-tasting tours in the area. Maps are available at the Tourism Information Centre, tel. (02212) 3603.

Winelands Cycle Tours caters for children and adults and the morning tasting route concludes with a picnic lunch, tel. (02212) 2416 or 082-555-3387 for details. Franschhoek Fish House sells smoked and cured salmon trout, caught nearby, and deli seafood products. To find it, turn left onto the Wemmershoek Rd to Paarl, after crossing the Berg River on the R45 to Franschhoek, tel. (02211) 64-0192. The Three Streams Smokehouse also sells smoked and fresh fish, including local trout. Find it at the top of Main St, opposite the Huguenot Monument.

The Franschhoek Tourism Association, tel. (02212) 3603, supplies free brochures providing details on the wine estates and co-operatives in the area. The Vignerons de Franschhoek, tel. (02212) 3062, also provide excellent information on the local wine route. On Huguenot Rd, Franschhoek, it's open 9am-5pm Mon-Fri, 10am-4pm Sat and 10am-2pm Sun.

HERMANUS

Hermanus – the nursery of the southern right whale – is easily reached from Cape Town, and is a favourite weekend getaway for Capetonians. Although the town has patchy architecture, quite unlike the consistent charm of an area like Franschhoek, its setting – between mountain and ocean – is beautiful, its beaches are excellent, its lagoon offers boating and sailing, the golfing is notable and the hiking in the area, particularly in the Fernkloof Nature Reserve, is outstanding.

Interesting visits include the old harbour that served the fishing industry for more than a century, now a museum and national monument. The new harbour at Westcliff offers charter trips for deep-sea fishing. The 1 500-ha Fernkloof Nature Reserve, tel. (0283) 2-1122, north of the town, has magnificent indigenous flora and wonderful walks, and the Orothamnus Reserve, a 12-hectare area specifically proclaimed to protect the rare marsh rose *Orothamnus zeyheri*, is worth a visit. Fick's Pool, a tidal pool on the southern side of Hermanus, is safe for swimming, while Langbaai, Voëlklip and Grotto beaches are recommended. Angling is popular at the mouth of the lagoon and along Die Plaat.

Hermanus offers the best land-based viewing of whales anywhere in the world. A 12-km-long cliff path, following the contours of the coast and stretching from one side of town to the other, offers whale-watchers unlimited opportunities. At the old harbour, the world's first whale-crier keeps visitors informed of where whales are likely to be seen, by sounding a kelp horn. Southern right whales begin arriving in Walker Bay in June and leave in

December or January. The peak whale season, when daily sightings are practically guaranteed, is September and October. Calving season is August and September, with peak whale population in Walker Bay in October.

In September, Hermanus's Whale of a Festival, an annual arts festival, provides a week of theatre, music, cabaret, art, sport and craft. It coincides with the Spring Flower Show in the Fernkloof Nature Reserve.

Hermanus has plenty to please the palate. There are some very good restaurants (*see chapter* **Where to Eat**) and two excellent wine estates – Bouchard Finlayson (tel. (0283) 2-3515) and Hamilton Russell (tel. (0283) 2-3595).

If you want to drive further, take a trip to Gansbaai where fresh fish is sold in the harbour. Nearby is Danger Point where the British troopship HMS *Birkenhead* went down in 1852 with the loss of 445 soldiers bound for the eastern Cape frontier. Further on is Die Kelders, a group of caves through which an underground stream flows and where swimming in the clear pools is a pleasure.

West of Hermanus, on the road from Cape Town, is the small village of Onrusrivier, home to a number of artists and writers. Onrus also offers some good eateries, an inviting art gallery (*see chapter* **Art Galleries**) and long, unspoiled beaches.

Take the R43 back towards Cape Town and turn left onto the R44 to Kleinmond, a small town situated between the mouths of the Palmiet and Bot rivers. The Palmiet River is superb for swimming and canoeing and there are fine picnic spots along its banks. Further down the road are Betty's Bay and the Harold Porter National Botanical Reserve, tel. (02823) 2-9311. Turn right at the Gardens signpost into Broadwith Road and continue along the R44 to Rooiels where adventurous visitors can take the dirt road around the coast to Cape Hangklip and Pringle Bay. The road continues to the seaside resort town of Gordon's Bay (*for info on the beaches, see chapter* **Wet, Wet, Wet**).

For tourist information on Hermanus, contact the Hermanus Publicity Association, Main Rd, Hermanus, tel. (0283) 2-2629. Open 8am-4.30pm Mon-Fri, 9am-3pm Sat and 11am-3pm Sun.

Main Road, Paarl.

PAARL

In 1657, when Abraham Gabbema was dispatched by Jan van Riebeeck to explore the hinterland of Table Bay, he found a beautiful valley surrounded by mountains, and filled with animals such as hippo, rhino and zebra. The country's third-oldest proclaimed town no longer offers wild animals but, at a mere half-hour drive from Cape Town along the N1, it offers much by way of history, wine and natural beauty. Paarl is named after the huge granite rock that towers above it, because, according to the first settlers, the rock shines like a pearl in the rain.

Begin in the centre of town, where the diverse architecture, including Cape Dutch, Victorian, Georgian and Art Deco, can be seen on a walk along Main St. Die Oude Woning, on

Main St, is one of the earliest surviving houses in Paarl (dated 1784). The first farms were granted to Dutch settlers and French Huguenots in 1687 and many of the original farms, including La Concorde, Laborie, Picardie, Zandwijk, De Hoop and Nantes, can still be seen.

If you prefer natural wonders to architecture, the Arboretum contains 700 species of local and exotic trees on the eastern bank of the Berg River. Alternatively, head for Paarl Rock, which is within easy walking distance of Mountain Rd. It offers wonderful vistas, and is the site of the cannon used to announce the arrival of merchant ships in Table Bay. To reach Gordon Rock, with its marvellous views, use the chain ladder to get to the summit. Alternatively, Jan Phillips Mountain Drive, an 11-kilometre drive along the eastern slopes, provides easy access to the mountain. Don't miss Millwater Wildflower Garden, a showcase of indigenous flora.

The Paarl Wine Route has 17 members, one of which is the KWV (Co-operative Winegrowers' Association) headquarters, tel. (02211) 7-3007/8. With its magnificent Cathedral Cellars and the five largest vats in the world under one roof, KWV is smoothly run with fine tasting facilities. Other estates and wineries worth visiting include Zandwijk, tel. (02211) 63-2368 (South Africa's only kosher winery), Fairview, tel. (02211) 63-2450, which produces excellent goats' milk cheese, Paarl Rock Brandy Cellar, tel. (02211) 62-6159, which offers brandy-tasting and an audio-visual presentation, the notable Backsberg estate, tel. (02211) 5141, and the big-name Nederburg estate, tel. (02211) 62-3104, which has the biggest-selling range of quality wines in South Africa and is also the venue for the annual Nederberg Wine Auction.

For a first-hand experience of the town's atmosphere and wines, try the festivals. On the first weekend of April, the harvest's first wines are celebrated at the **Nouveau Wine Festival** with music, wine-tasting and food (seafood is the main attraction). Entrance: R25. For more info, tel. (02211) 2-3605. The **Paarl Sparkling Wine Day,** on the first Saturday of September, focuses on local sparkling wine with good food.

You won't go hungry in Paarl – there's a fine range of restaurants (*see chapter* **Where to Eat**). And if you're looking for aesthetic pleasure, Non Pareille (near the town hall) houses a group of artists who exhibit their work from time to time.

The Paarl Wine Route office on Main St, tel. (02211) 2-3605, supplies brochures and a map of the area. For more information, contact the Paarl Publicity Association, also in Main St, tel. (02211) 2-4842 or 2-3829.

SOMERSET WEST

About thirty minutes west of Cape Town, along the N2 and overlooking False Bay, lies Somerset West, one of the first areas developed beyond the present-day Cape Town by Willem Adriaan van der Stel, Governor of the Cape from 1700 to 1706. Van der Stel granted himself huge tracts of land extending from the Hottentots Holland mountains to False Bay, and the Golden Bowl – the windfree valley that overlooks all of False Bay and contains the remnants of Van der Stel's estate Vergelegen (Far Away Place) – is not to be missed.

A brilliant horticulturalist, but basically a rogue, Van der Stel poured the Cape's resources into building up the estate during his brief tenure as Governor. When the Dutch East India Company, which administered the Cape at the time, got wind of his activities they had the estate confiscated, divided into four and sold to the highest bidder. The remaining sections (which amount to about 10 000 ha) still house those four estates (Vergelegen, Morgenster, Lourensford, and Land en Zeezicht), though only Vergelegen is open to the public.

In 1917, Lady Florence Phillips, wife of Transvaal mining magnate Sir Lionel Phillips, bought the estate and restored it, adding a typical English garden and converting the old winery into a library reminiscent of Vita Sackville-West's Sissinghurst in Kent. In 1986 Vergelegen was acquired by the Anglo-American Corporation, with the objective of making Vergelegen South Africa's finest wine-producing estate. The Rothschilds have consulted on the winemaking and Patrick Dillon and Jean de Gastines were brought out from

Bordeaux to design the state-of-the-art wine cellars. To date, their efforts have produced light but very drinkable white wines and a rather coarse red, though in fairness the recently planted vines have only just begun to mature and the Anglo American commitment is substantial.

Of all the wine estates in the Cape, the Vergelegen experience is probably the most gracious, giving the best idea of how enchanting Cape country-life among the well-heeled could be. The view across the lawns, magnificently shaded by 300-year-old camphor trees, which are now national monuments, is spectacular. The Lady Phillips Tea Garden offers a very pleasant lunch in a delightful setting, while more modest nosh can be had in the Rose Garden nearby (*see also chapter* **Where to Eat**). Vergelegen offers wine-tasting and tours of the winery. There's also an interpretive centre and small souvenir shop. Open 9am-4pm daily (except public holidays), admission is R6 for adults, R4 for children and pensioners. For more info, tel. (024) 51-7060.

Morgenster has been described as one of South Africa's finest examples of Cape Dutch architecture. Built in 1739 by Jacques Malan, it can be glimpsed from the road. On leaving Vergelegen follow the signs to Morgenster and to the left, past the workers' cottages, you will have a clear view of the homestead. Note the typical H-shape of the house and the six near-perfect gables. Opposite Vergelegen is Erinvale, a housing estate developed around a golf course. A compromise between the encroaching suburbs and a desire to preserve the valley's historic character, the original 18th century homestead has been restored and converted into a small country lodge that offers a warm taste of life in the valley. The Gary Player-designed golf course is probably one of the country's finest (*see chapter* **Sport, Fitness & The Great Outdoors**).

One of the great treasures of the valley is the Helderberg Nature Reserve, which consists of more than 150 ha of natural fynbos and is home to nearly 200 different bird species. The views across the valley are spectacular and the walking trails lead past delightful mountain springs and magnificent gorges set high in the Helderberg mountains. Access to the Reserve is off Lourensford Rd. Further along Lourensford Rd, towards the village, is Willowbrooke Lodge. Less grand than Erinvale, it backs onto the Lourens River. Offering elaborate meals in a pleasant garden setting, it also has prettily appointed guest rooms for overnight stays.

Though Somerset West outside the Golden Bowl is pretty suburban, it is home to some of the Cape's wealthiest and most influential citizens. The result is a number of good restaurants, typical of dining in the area. These include L'Auberge Du Paysan, a formal French dining experience in the heart of the vineyards between Somerset West and Stellenbosch; Chez Michel, which offers good, though unspectacular, French cooking, and Die Ou Pastorie, the first of the area's country inns and a source of high-quality South African cooking.

No visit to Somerset West would be complete without a stop at the Strand, the beach town that draws thousands of up-country tourists annually. The Strand would be one of Africa's most idyllic beach spots were it not for the wind, the strong south-easter that blows almost continuously throughout the summer. On a good day or early in the morning before the wind is up, there are few more spectacular places. The water's warm, the waves are gentle and the pristine beach sweeps in a gentle crescent all the way to Cape Point.

A more sheltered spot south of the Strand is Gordon's Bay. A tiny town on the blue sweep of the bay, it offers protection from the wind and a delightful beach, called Bikini Beach, next to a small yacht basin. Surprisingly, at the end of the beach road is the tiny religious retreat End House, protected from the wind, but not from the topless antics of frolicking sun worshippers. The Van Riebeeck Hotel at Gordon's Bay is a local institution. Never really elegant, it nevertheless offers pleasant accommodation and its bar, overlooking the action on the main beach, is a good place to stop for a bite of lunch or a drink.

STELLENBOSCH

Stellenbosch, boasting the country's oldest wine route, lies in the heart of the winelands, a 40-minute drive along the N2 or N1 from

Cape Town. More than 400 wines can be tasted along this well-signposted route, and the historic town (South Africa's second oldest proclaimed town) boasts some of the Cape's most spectacular estates, renowned restaurants, bed and breakfast establishments, hotels, and cultural attractions and antique shops. Set in the valley of the Eerste Rivier (first river), Stellenbosch began as a settlement in 1679, when farms in the area were granted by Governor Simon van der Stel to colonists from Holland, France and Germany. The languages of the European emigrants, combined with those of indigenous peoples and slaves, created the impetus for a common language – Afrikaans.

In 1858 a theological seminary was found here and in 1866 the Stellenbosch Gymnasium was established to prepare students for admission to the seminary. In 1887, the institution was renamed Victoria College (statesman Jan Smuts and writer CJ Langenhoven were among those who graduated here). And in 1918, this academic institution was renamed Stellenbosch University. Since then, it's been the Harvard of Afrikanerdom. The university boasts fine historic buildings as well as the Sasol Art Museum in the Eben Donges Centre, Ryneveld St, which houses the university's permanent art collection. The university's botanical gardens in Neethling St contain indigenous cycads, ferns, succulents, bonsai and orchids. Maps and a key to the bonsai are available at the office.

The best place to begin a walking tour of Stellenbosch is d'Ouwe Werf Country Inn, 30 Church St. One of South Africa's oldest boarding houses, it was built in 1710 on the foundations of an old church and is beautifully restored (*for more info, see chapters* **Where to Eat** *and* **Accommodation**). In the same street, you'll find Coopman House (1713). Ryneveld St contains wonderful historic houses, dating from 1709 to 1850, including Schreuder House (1709), Bletterman House (1789), Grosvenor House (1782) and OM Bergh House (1850). The Dutch Reformed Mother Church in Drostdy St, built in 1863, features typical early settler architecture – thick, lime-washed walls, thatched roof and yellowwood or stinkwood timber work. The family vaults, erected within the ring wall (1734/50) are notable.

To see some of the best displays of historic buildings in South Africa, walk along Dorp St. Its earliest houses were built in 1710. The Theological College (1865), the Old Reading Room, the Old Parsonage, the Old Lutheran Church (now the art museum of the University of Stellenbosch), Stellenbosch Gymnasium, La Gratitude and Voorgelegen can be seen here. For a combination of shopping and historic curiosity, visit Oom Samie Se Winkel (Uncle Sam's Shop). One of Stellenbosch's first general dealers, it dates from the early 1900s and is crammed with traditional food, bric-à-brac, collectables and curios. De Akker pub contains a wine library and the Stellenbosch Information Service. Libertas Parva (1783), also in Dorp St, houses the Rembrandt van Rijn Art Museum and the Stellenryck Wine Museum.

Dorp Street in Stellenbosch, centre of the wine industry and spiritual home of Afrikaner culture.

In Bloem St you'll find the VOC Kruithuis, which was the arsenal for the Dutch East India Company, the Rhenish Institute, the Rhenish Church, which was erected in 1823 for slaves and coloured people, and the Burgher House (1797), which currently serves as headquarters of the Historical Homes of South Africa society.

For more on the history of liquor-making, visit the Oude Meester Brandy Museum, with its stills, bottles and glassware. The De Oude Molen Brandy Museum behind the station covers the history of brandy-making in the area. Die Bergkelder, next to the station, offers tours and tasting. You'll also find the Simonsberg cheese factory with its excellent factory shop in Stoffel Smit St, near the station.

There are some superb hikes in this region, starting with the popular Boland Hiking Trail which offers several two- or three-day hiking options through spectacular mountain scenery in the Hottentots-Holland Nature Reserve. Less strenuous are the walks in the Jan Marais Nature Reserve (in Marais St), some 23 ha of indigenous flora. The Assegaaibosch Nature Reserve is a sanctuary for rare proteas, with a wildflower garden, short nature trails and picnic sites. Or visit the Jonkershoek Forest Reserve, which contains the hatcheries of the fisheries research station.

Opportunities for wine-tasting in this region are considerable. The Stellenbosch Wine Route was inspired in 1971 by the *Routes de Vin* in France and the *Weinstrassen* in Germany. Today, within 12 km of the town there are 28 wine estates and co-operative wine cellars at which wines can be tasted and bought (and

Vineyards outside Stellenbosch.

The Kruithuis (built in 1776) was used as an arms and ammunitions store.

delivered nationally and internationally). An extensive brochure on the Stellenbosch Wine Route is available at the Stellenbosch Tourist Bureau, 36 Market St, tel. 883-3584 or 883-9633, and the Wine Route Office at the same address, tel. 886-4310.

Notable estates include Blaauwklippen, Clos Malverne, Delaire, Delheim, L'Avenir, Morgenhof, Muratie, Neethlingshof, Neil Ellis, Overgaauw, Rust-en-Vrede, Saxenburg, Simonsig, Vredenheim and Zevenwacht. Many of the estates have restaurants and you can enjoy a very good meal at these, or at some of the excellent restaurants in town. *For more info, see chapter* **Where to Eat.** If it's an hotel or guest house you're looking for, you'll find some outstanding establishments, many of them on wine estates. See chapter **Accommodation** or contact the Stellenbosch Tourist Bureau, 36 Market St, tel. 883-3584 or 883-9633 for recommendations.

WEST COAST

The west coast has a rugged wildness and a sense of endless space which makes for very different day trips from the winelands where the beauty is more refined. You'll find deserted beaches, superb nature reserves, mountains, country towns and wine farms. But the area's most renowned assets are wildflowers and whales.

Spring delivers a carpet of wildflowers – more than 2 600 species – to this part of the

Cape. And the flowers, in turn, attract birds, bees – and enthusiastic humans. Because weather conditions make such a difference to what you may see in terms of floral displays, you're advised to call the Flowerline, tel. 418-3705, to find out where the best flowers are to be seen. Similarly, the arrival of whales and dolphins (end June to September) provides another wonderful way to experience the natural attractions of the region.

Travelling up the west coast from Cape Town on the R27 through Milnerton and Bloubergstrand, the first recommended stop would be Koeberg Power Station. It is the only commercial nuclear power station in South Africa and it's open on weekdays and the second and last Sundays of every month. For more information contact the visitors' centre, tel. 553-2133. Continue up the R27 to Mamre where you'll find the Mamre Mission Station and the Mamre Wine Cellar, which stocks some very impressive wines. Travel on up the R307 to Darling and the Darling Flora Reserve, 5 km south of the town, tel. (02241) 2422. Darling is best known for its Wildflower and Orchid Show in September. Visit Baskets for All, a factory where 100 weavers make a variety of baskets.

Yzerfontein, a small holiday and fishing village, has a deserted beach ideal for swimming and surfing. The island in the bay is known as Meeurots (Gull Rock) and is home to a large seagull colony. There is also a whale-watching station – whales and dolphins come to the bay to mate and calve. The best months for whale- and dolphin-watching are end June to September. The Postberg section of the West Coast National Park, tel. (02287) 2-2144, is a must for visitors. It is situated on the sea side of Langebaan Lagoon. Wildflower enthusiasts should head for the reserve between the last week in August and the first two weeks in September when nature decks the fields with pink, purple, white and orange blooms. Call the reserve in advance to check what's blooming. The small village of Churchhaven boasts a long but narrow beach. On the road to Langebaan, the village is popular with watersports enthusiasts and the lagoon's sheltered water makes it an ideal spot for power-boating, sailing, waterskiing, boardsailing and pad-

The beach at Churchhaven, a tiny village on the west coast.

dle-skiing. The birdlife is a delight. The area is also rich in fossils and many of the finds date back to the Pliocene era (four million years ago).

Club Mykonos (*see chapter* **Accommodation**) is situated close to Langebaan and offers self-contained accommodation on the waterfront. There's a modern yacht basin with all amenities. On the northern side of the lagoon is Saldanha Bay, which boasts one of the great natural harbours in the world. The small village of Paternoster has a beautiful, long, deserted beach. The coastline is ruggedly attractive and the cool waters are renowned for their generous yields of crayfish and perlemoen. Visitors have to travel along a dirt road for 9 km to reach the village. Luckily there's the Paternoster Hotel where you can wash down the dust with a cold beer and sample the excellent seafood. Around the corner is St Helena Bay, which was discovered by Vasco da Gama in 1497. It is a commercial fishing area where vast shoals of pilchards, anchovies and mackerel are common. Velddrif is situated at the mouth of the Berg River, finishing point of the strenuous annual 280-km Berg River canoe marathon. A birdwatcher's paradise, the estuary attracts flamingoes, spoonbills, avocets and glossy ibis.

Citrusdal, nestling in the fertile valley of the Olifants River, is one of the largest citrus-growing areas in the country. Visit the fruit estates where the original orchards were planted from seedlings in Jan van Riebeeck's garden in Cape Town, or stop at one of the many roadside stalls to sample some of the country's finest oranges and naartjies (mandarins).

Clanwilliam, spread out at the foot of the Cederberg mountains, boasts several national monuments including the Landdrost's Court and the old Gaol (1808). The Pakhuis Pass just outside town is the gateway to Wuppertal, a Moravian mission village. Bushman rock paintings can be found near Bokwater. Clanwilliam is also famous for its Rooibos tea, an aromatic herbal tea grown from the rooibos (literally red bush) *Aspalathus linearis.*

The west coast also offers its own rugged and hugely enjoyable version of bush cuisine – barbecues of fresh local fish and seafood cooked on open fires and eaten, frequently on paper plates, in the great outdoors close to the ocean. *For a listing of these outdoor eateries, see* **West Coast Fish Barbeques** *in chapter* **Where to Eat**.

There are two fine wine routes on the west coast – the Swartland and Olifants River wine routes. Wine cellars worth visiting include Cederberg Winery, Citrusdal Co-operative Wine Cellars, Klawer Co-operative Wine Cellars, Lutzville Vineyards Co-operative and Vredendal Co-operative Wine Cellar. For information on the area, contact the West Coast Publicity Association, tel. (02281) 4-2058.

SPORT, FITNESS & THE GREAT OUTDOORS

Whether your favourite sport is cycling, swimming, scuba diving or simply watching it happen on TV, Cape Town has plenty to offer.

With its summers and scenery, Cape Town is a sportsperson's delight, and Capetonians, like most South Africans, treat sport with a reverence and enthusiasm normally reserved for religious experiences. The hottest sporting issue is, of course, the Olympics; Cape Town's National Sports Sciences Institute, a sports training and medical institute, is aimed at equalling the USA's great training centres, and Olympic hopes are high.

The big spectator sports are soccer, rugby and cricket, but the annual 105-km Argus/Pick 'n Pay Cycle Tour attracts thousands of participants and spectators, as does the annual 56-km Ohlsson's Two Oceans Marathon.

Thanks to the water and mountains in and around the city and the varied scenery, this is your chance to try everything from snorkelling and cycling to golf and rollerblading.

ANGLING

See chapter **Wet, Wet, Wet**.

ARCHERY

The Protea Club
Main Rd, Retreat, tel. 788-4602.
Archery for able and disabled sportspeople, including coaching every Saturday 2pm-5pm and Sunday 9am-noon. Cost: R8 adults, R6 under-18s.

BADMINTON

Western Province Badminton Association
John Tyers Hall, Myhof Rd, Kenilworth, tel. 61-5233.
Badminton season (Feb-Oct) involves 20 affiliated clubs. For information, call the Association secretary.

BALLOONING

Wineland Ballooning
Tel. (02211) 63-3192.
One-and-a-quarter-hour hot-air balloon flights followed by champagne breakfast at the luxurious Grande Rôche hotel are R740 p/p. (Group bookings for four people are

Sport, Fitness & The Great Outdoors 237

R690 p/p.) Book in advance and leave early – the organisers provide a wake-up call and weather update. Closed during winter.

BIRDWATCHING

Varied habitats and more than 380 species of birds make for rewarding birdwatching. Lion's Head, Kirstenbosch Botanical Garden, the Cape of Good Hope Nature Reserve, Kommetjie, Rietvlei and Hout Bay are accessible and rewarding turf. Captour (*see chapter* **Essential Information**) carries free, comprehensive and indispensable birdwatching guides. You'll also find some excellent books on local birdwatching in stores like CNA and Exclusive Books (*see chapter* **Shopping**).

The Cape Bird Club
Tel. 686-8795.
Information on birding excursions under expert guidance.

Rondevlei Nature Reserve
Cnr Perth Rd and Fisherman's Walk, Grassy Park, tel. 706-2404.
Open: *7.30am-5pm daily.*
Admission: *R3 p/p.*
More than 220 species, including white pelicans, Caspian tern and little bittern, observation towers, hides for hippo-watching, telescopes and a field museum. No barbecue facilities.

The Tygerberg Bird Club
47 Drakenstein Rd, Durbanville Hills, contact Debbie Philogene, tel. 96-8701 (after 4pm).
Club meetings on the third Thursday of the month at the Tygerberg Nature Reserve (take the Welgemoed-Bellville exit off the N1), with birdwatching the following Saturday. Visitors welcome. Nominal charge, depending on outings.

The World of Birds
Valley Rd, Hout Bay, tel. 790-2730.
Open: *9am-5pm daily.*
Admission: *R14 adults, R7 pensioners and under 15s. (Subject to price reviews.)*

One of the world's largest bird parks, The World of Birds covers more than four hectares and features walk-through landscaped aviaries with more than 3 000 birds of more than 350 species. The park is set in beautiful scenery, between Chapman's Peak and Hout Bay.

Also enjoyable is the World of Birds Nature Park & Wildlife Sanctuary at Ocean View (en route to Cape Point). It features an African crane breeding centre, and giants of the bird world. For info, tel. 783-2309.

BOATS: CHARTERS & CRUISES

See chapter **Wet, Wet, Wet**.

Hout Bay Boatyard
Tel. 790-3619.
Storage facilities, charters, boat repairs and servicing, in the appealing oceanfront area of Hout Bay.

BOWLING

Western Province Bowling Association
10th Floor, 45 Castle Street, City Centre, tel. 24-1919.
Open: *9am-noon Mon-Fri.*
Most of the Western Cape's 66 clubs play Tuesday to Sunday. The season runs mid-October to end May. For information, contact the Association.

BUNGI JUMPING

Kiwi Extreme
10 Portadown Rd, Bergvliet, tel. 72-4516.
Open: *10am-5.30pm Sat-Sun and public holidays.*
Fee: *R70 for first jump, R40 for consecutive jumps.*
Bungi jumps at the Gouritz River are the world's highest jumps over dry land. It's around a three-hour drive to get there, but apparently it's the ultimate adrenaline rush. Tours available.

CANOEING & RIVER ADVENTURES

See chapter **Wet, Wet, Wet**.

Western Province Canoe Union
Tel. 551-1770.
Contact the Union for information on canoeing events and clubs.

CRICKET

Western Province Cricket Union
Newlands Cricket Ground, 161 Campground Rd, Newlands, tel. 64-4146.
Open: *8.30am-5pm Mon-Thu, 8.30am-1pm Fri (winter) and 8.30am-5pm Mon-Fri (summer).*
Cricket has been played in Cape Town since British rule, and international and local matches are keenly followed. For information on major events, cricket venues and regular club matches, contact the Union, and watch press for details.

CROQUET

Western Province Croquet Association
Tel. 64-2556.
Visitors' fees at local clubs (including Rondebosch and the Waterfront) are R2-R5 for equipment loan. For information on suburban clubs, contact the Association.

CYCLING

Popular cycling routes include Mouille Point-Bakoven, and if you're energetic, Llandudno, Hout Bay and the spectacular Chapman's Peak Drive.

CYCLE TOURS

Argus/Pick 'n Pay Cycle Tour
Info and application forms, PO Box 205, Newlands, 7725, tel. 461-2390.
Held on the first Sunday of March, the 105-km annual Argus/Pick 'n Pay Cycle Tour is the conclusion of the International Cycle Competition. It combines breathtaking views and breathless excitement and attracts more than 22 500 local and international competitors. Participant's fee: R30-R40. Three days prior to the Cycle Tour, the Argus/Pick 'n Pay Life Cycle Expo at A-Berth Shed, Cape Town Harbour, is the country's largest cycling/health exhibition.

Bikeabout Tours
Tel. 531-3274.
Cycle tours in the mountains, winelands or on roads, with bicycles for hire if needed. A half-day tour, excluding bicycle hire, is R105, a full-day tour is R135. Weekend and long trips available.

The Villager Cycling Club
Brookside, Lansdowne Rd, Claremont, tel. 531-1752.
Regular rides of 40-60 km begin at 7am on Sundays. Visitors welcome.

Mountain Biking Trails in the De Hoop Nature Reserve
De Hoop Nature Reserve, tel. (028) 542-1126 or fax (028) 542-1679.
Open: *7am-6pm daily.*
Accommodation: *R60 per night for up to four people.*
Admission: *R2. Bike entry: R10 per day.*
Three-day trail, limited to 12 cyclists a day, in nature conservation area with rich floral and birdlife. Overnight accommodation includes stove, indoor fireplace, pots and pans. Bring bedding, cutlery and plates and make sure you're reasonably fit.

Western Province Pedal Power Association
Tel. 794-2268.
An excellent source of information on clubs and regular cycling meetings.

BICYCLE HIRE, SALES & CYCLING EQUIPMENT

Mike Hopkins
133a Bree St, City Centre, tel. 23-2527.
Fully equipped mountain bikes hired at R45 per day (incl. helmet). Special deals over long weekends. R350 deposit required.

Sport, Fitness and The Great Outdoors 239

The annual Argus/Pick 'n Pay Cycle Tour, which attracts 20 000 participants and throngs of spectators.

Rent 'n Ride
1 Park Rd, Mouille Point, tel. 434-1122 or (082) 801-5300.
Rollerblades and bikes for hire. ID and deposit required.

DEEP-SEA FISHING

See chapter **Wet, Wet, Wet**.

GO-KARTING

Chequered Flag
Cnr Jean Simonis and De la Rey roads, Parow, tel. 930-1477.
Open: *10am-10.30pm Sun-Thu, 10am-midnight Fri-Sat.*
Admission: *Mon-Fri 10am-5.30pm is R20 for 20 laps. For the rest – R20 for 15 laps.*
Indoor kart-racing complete with driving gear, practice laps, heats and grand finale. No under-12s.

Indoor Grand Prix
Top Level, Coen Steytler Parking Garage, Coen Steytler St, City Centre, tel. 419-5465/6/7/8.
Open: *10am-midnight daily.*
Admission: *R15 for 15 laps.*
Here you go – jostling for position at high speed, heading for the finishing line, or at least the prospect of a drink and something to eat at the on-premises bar and eatery. Indoor go-karting for speed-lovers.

GOLFING

There are a number of beautiful, well-maintained golf courses in and around Cape Town. In addition, you'll find fun clubhouse facilities, albeit of the old-fashioned kind, and Cape golf is generally relaxed and unpretentious.

For a list of the best courses, see the box **Golfing in Cape Town** on the next page.

GOLFING IN CAPE TOWN

Cape Town and its surrounds offer many golfing pleasures. The determining factors are distance and weather, for the summer south-easter can blow away the fun for even the keenest golfer. In winter, the north-wester blows almost as hard but brings the rain in quantities, which will probably scare you off anyway. The wind has also been an important factor in determining the layout and vegetation on most Cape courses. Don't expect the American 'club' experience – you'll be disappointed, since the English-style golf club is the norm here.

Within 15-20 minutes' drive of the City Centre you'll find the **Mowbray** and **Royal Cape** golf clubs, two of the country's oldest and most famous. Both have hosted numerous national championships. They represent good, old-fashioned tests over rather flat terrain, most challenging when there's some wind and somewhat benign on a calm day.

Nearby **Rondebosch Golf Club** isn't in quite the same golfing class, but it's usually in fine condition, especially in winter.

If the weather's fair and the wind calm, however, your best bet is **Milnerton Golf Club**, a true links course that meanders along Table Bay and the Milnerton Lagoon, offering spectacular views of the city and Table Mountain. The four short holes are particularly varied and challenging.

It's a bit further (45 minutes from the City Centre) but a visit to **Erinvale Country Estate and Golf Club** in Somerset West is a golfing must. Recently designed and built by Gary Player, this modern course is arguably the Cape's best. It combines a marvellous setting with varied terrain and has several memorable holes that will entertain and challenge golfers of every level of ability. It's one of the few courses offering full golf cart facilities.

The two winelands courses of **Paarl** and **Stellenbosch** offer excellent golf less than an hour from Cape Town. Set among the hilly vineyards, Stellenbosch rewards the straight hitter, while Paarl's second nine are among the most varied and scenic in the region. Consider a morning round at either, followed by lunch and wine-tasting at a nearby wine estate – golfing heaven.

A 90-minute drive may seem a lot, but if your destination is the **Hermanus Golf Club**, your rewards are various. A spectacular mountain drive through some of the Cape's best scenery, a truly satisfying golfing experience on the heather-lined fairways of an excellent country course, and if you're there in spring – the best time – a chance to watch whales tending their newborn calves in the sheltered waters of nearby Walker Bay.

Closer to town, **Clovelly Golf Club** offers a parkland setting and a short narrow course that's always fun to play and beautifully prepared. Hit it straight here or have a good supply of balls.

A stone's throw from the City Centre is the **Metropolitan Golf Club**, a pretty nine-holer that's ideal if you only have a couple of hours to spare.

All Cape courses welcome visitors, but it's best to phone in advance especially if you need to hire equipment. Green fees are in the order of R60-R80, and most courses have caddies who charge around R40-R50 per round.

Don't miss the most spectacular drive in the country

No golfing trip to the Cape would be complete without doing the rounds at Erinvale in Somerset West, just 30 minutes from Cape Town.

Designed by Gary Player, it is arguably the only true world-class course in the Cape.

Play 9 or 18 holes and enjoy spectacular mountain scenery, luxurious clubhouse facilities or four-star comfort at the estate's own hotel.

To book, telephone (024) 847-1004

ERINVALE GOLF CLUB

The best the country has to offer

Now open for dinner, bed, tees and sandwedges

The Erinvale Estate Hotel stands alongside the magnificent Erinvale golf course and welcomes golfers to 'stay and play' at an all-inclusive price.

The lovingly restored manor house offers a feast for the senses with four-star comfort, delectable food and the most beautiful setting in the country.

For hotel and restaurant bookings, telephone (024) 847-1160.

ERINVALE ESTATE HOTEL ★★★★

Excellence is par for the course

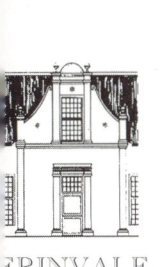

Wind, water and the wonderful sight of Table Bay ... one of the best ways to experience some of the city's pleasures is a cruise.

Sport, Fitness & The Great Outdoors 241

The Western Province Golf Union, tel. 47-8009, has good information, and Captour bureaux (see chapter **Essential Information**) carry comprehensive listings. The clubs listed here are among the Cape's finest but you'll have plenty of options apart from these. For details of opening hours and fees, contact the individual clubs as these vary from club to club and according to season. Make arrangements in advance in summer – the clubs fill up with locals and tourists.

CLUBS

Clovelly Country Club
Clovelly Rd, Clovelly, tel. 782-6410.

Metropolitan Golf Club
Mouille Point Rd, Mouille Point, tel. 434-7808.

Milnerton Golf Club
Bridge Road, Milnerton, tel. 52-1047.

Mowbray Golf Club
Raapenberg Rd, Mowbray, tel. 685-3018.

Rondebosch Golf Club
Klipfontein Rd, Rondebosch, tel. 689-4176.

Royal Cape Golf Club
174 Ottery Road, Wynberg, tel. 761-6551.

GOLF ESTATES

Erinvale
Lourensford Rd, Somerset West, tel. (024) 847-1160.

OUT OF TOWN COURSES

Hermanus Golf Club
Tel. (0283) 2-1954.

Paarl Golf Club
Tel. (02211) 63-1140.

Stellenbosch Golf Club
Tel. 880-0103.

PRACTICE RANGES

Action Golf Centre
1 Port Rd, Waterfront, tel. 419-6767.
Open: 9am-10pm daily.
Virtual reality comes to golf – and brings with it the opportunity to 'play' 18 holes on Dubai Creek, Zell am See and many international 'courses'. Practice your swing, balance and posture. Hire gear available. Can be pricey.

The River Club Function and Conference Centre
Liesbeek Parkway, Observatory, tel. 448-6117.
Open: daily 9am-7pm (summer) and 9am-6pm (winter).
Golf driving range with practice bunkers and target greens. Practice and standard golf balls for hire at R8 for 50 or R15 for 100. Pro-tuition available. The centre also has free parking, security, music, food and lively, if not exactly upmarket, socialising.

GYMS & HEALTH HYDROS

Health & Racquet Club
The largest, best-equipped and by far the toniest gym chain, the Health and Racquet Club is known cynically as the Wealth and Rolex on account of its many fashionable and glitzy members. Temporary monthly membership is R290, temporary daily membership is R30 for guests who are accompanied by permanent members and R50 for guests who are unaccompanied by permanent members. Weights areas, machines, swimming pool, sauna and a variety of high-standard classes, from step to stretch, are included in the fee. If you're using the pool a bathing cap is mandatory, and take a towel if you work out on weights machines.

Health and Racquet Club hours are: 5.30am-10pm Mon-Thu, 5.30am-9pm Fri, 7am-9pm Sat-Sun. The City Centre has different hours: 5.30am-9pm Mon-Thu, 5.30am-8pm Fri, 7am-7pm Sat, 8am-noon and 4pm-8pm Sun.

Health and Racquet Club branches can be found at:
21 Lower Long St, Foreshore, tel. 21-5857.
Constantia Main Rd, Constantia, tel. 94-5010.
Roof Level, Cavendish Square, Claremont, tel. 83-2402/3.
Shop 41, N1 City, Goodwood, tel. 595-3030.
The Point, Bill Peters Drive, Green Point, tel. 434-0750.
Cnr Birkenhead and Pentz drives, Table View, tel. 557-3995.
Shop 8, Drostdy Centre, Stellenbosch, tel. 887-1240/1.
Hume Pipe Rd, Bellville, tel. 946-4261.

Walking along Table Mountain's renowned Pipe Track which offers spectacular views of the city and the Atlantic.

High Rustenburg Hydro
Ida's Valley, Stellenbosch, tel. 883-8600.
Eat too much, smoke too much, stress out too much? Hit High Rustenburg Hydro for a regimen of raw food, hydrotherapy, massage and exercise. Most of the inmates spend hours discussing recipes over the watermelon slice that substitutes for lunch, but the effects of a stay are glorious. All treatments are administered under medical supervision. The best way to do the Hydro is a week (R2 483 all included), but a day (R109), which includes massage, aquacise, hydrotherapy and a good health lunch, is also beneficial.

HANG-GLIDING

Take off from Lion's Head and Signal Hill and Sandy Bay ...

Cape Albatross Hang-gliding Club
Tel. 21-1802 (9am-5pm).
For details on the 29 flying sites within two hours of the city. Hang-gliders for hire (fee negotiable).

Mark Norbury: Hang-gliding Lessons
Tel. 52-3964.
Instruction, including equipment, is R700 for a course that takes a maximum of two months. If in this time you still can't fly, take up diving.

HIKING

Whether you want a pleasant promenade or a serious workout, the Western Cape is hiker's heaven, and one of the most enchanting aspects of Cape Town is the number of mountain, beach and forest walks in an urban environment and practically on your doorstep. An hour to three hours' drive into the country takes you to an inspiring range of nature reserves and hiking trails.

For excellent advice and suggested trails, read Mike Lundy's *Weekend Trails in the Western Cape* and Tim Anderson's *Day Walks In and Around Cape Town*. The Captour Information Office, Adderley St, Cape Town, tel. 418-5202, also has good information on suggested hikes.

HIKES IN AND AROUND CAPE TOWN

For forest walks in the city, try the **Newlands Forest** (Newlands), notably the Woodcutter's Trail. Also wonderful are **Cecilia Forest** (between Kirstenbosch and Hout Bay), an easy route through forest and pine plantations, and the **Kirstenbosch Botanical Gardens** (*see chapter* **The Sights**). The **Silvermine Reserve**, tel. 75-3040, has a terrific range of walks as does the **Tokai State Forest** (Tokai). The Tokai Arboretum, behind Porter School, is less crowded than the Tokai State Forest, and good for peaceful rambling.

For superb views, try the short but energetic **Chapman's Peak Walk** (around 6,5 km) and the renowned **Pipe Track**, which starts at the turn-off to the lower cableway station and follows the contour path above Camps Bay.

For information about the excellent trails on the False Bay side, contact Captour, tel. 418-5202, or the Simon's Town Publicity Association, tel. 786-3046 or 786-2436.

The **Cape of Good Hope Nature Reserve**, some 9 km from Simon's Town, offers magnificent hikes. Comprehensive maps are available at the entrance. For information on the reserve, tel. 780-9526 or 780-9100 (main gate). The reserve is open 7am-6pm daily (summer) and 7am-5pm daily (winter). Try the following Cape of Good Hope Nature Reserve hikes, but a word of warning before you do: if you're disturbed by the local baboons, don't feed them, but if they're determined to rob you of your lunch, *don't* attempt to fight the beasts off – just hand over the grub.

The four-hour Kanonkop Trail includes a gentle ascent through wildflowers and wonderful sea views, and a descent to the beach and an old lime kiln. From the kiln, follow the road back to Bordjiesrif for swimming, picnicking and rock pools filled with anemones, starfish, rock fish and the occasional octopus.

The 10-12-km coastal trail from Groot Blouberg to Cape Point takes about six hours and takes you along the seashore, with possible sightings of buck and zebra. The walk continues along the beach to the Cape of Good Hope and Cape Maclear, via sheltered Diaz Beach.

The Wreck Walk offers magnificent views, crystal clear water and a chance to see the wrecks of the *Thomas T Tucker* and the *Nolloth*.

For interesting ecology, sand dunes and sightings of buck and abundant birdlife, visit the **Koeberg Nuclear Power Station**, tel. 553-2133.

See also chapter **Wet, Wet, Wet** *for the best beach walks.*

OUT OF TOWN TRAILS

There are a number of excellent hiking trails within two hours' drive of Cape Town. Book in advance, arrange a permit, request maps and reserve a bed in the hiking trail huts where available – many of these are extremely popular hikes. The weather is changeable, so take appropriate gear. Don't forget a bathing costume if you're the modest type – natural pools abound.

Arangieskop Hiking Trail
Tel. (02351) 3112.
In the Langeberg Mountains with dazzling farm and valley views.

Boerbok Hiking Trail
Tel. (02351) 3112.
A family hiking trail winding through vines and apricot orchards with overnight accommodation for ten people.

The Boland Hiking Trail
Hottentots-Holland Nature Reserve, tel. (0225) 4301.
Pine plantations, abundant wildflowers, views of the Theewaterskloof Dam and nearby mountains and some rugged, diverse scenery.

Dassieshoek Hiking Trail
Tel. (02353) 3112.
Breathtaking views of Robertson and the Breede River Valley. The route up is around 25 km (nine hours) and the down route is around 15 km (five hours).

Montagu Trails
Montagu Municipality, tel. (0234) 4-1112.
The 16-km Bloupunt Trail and the 12-km Cogmanskloof Trail, both notable for spectacular views, flowers, bird and animal life

(watch out for klipspringers and dassies), can be walked back-to-back for a challenging weekend. The Klipspringer huts (accommodation for up to 12 people) at the centre point have stoves, barbecue facilities, flush toilets and showers. R20 p/p per night.

Other trails to try:
Ceres Hiking Trail, *tel. (0233) 2-1177.*
Helderberg Farm Hiking Trail, *tel. (024) 55-4308.*
Worcester Hiking Trails, *tel. (0231) 71408.*

HIKING CLUBS
Adventure Club
Tel. 683-3227.
Adventures from outdoors to jazz club visits.

The Mountain Club of South Africa
97 Hatfield St, City Centre, tel. 45-3412.
Open: *10am-2pm Mon-Fri; 7.30pm-8.30pm Fri.*
Not for those in search of a picnic route up Table Mountain, this club is geared to experienced climbers.

HIKING ON TABLE MOUNTAIN

The jewel in Cape Town's hiking crown is of course the 1 086-m-high Table Mountain. The variety of routes is massive, both in terms of difficulty and distance. The Captour Information Office, Adderley St, Cape Town, tel. 418-5202, also has good information on suggested hikes. The following hikes are unmissable:

- **Castle Grootkop** on the western aspect of the mountain is a demanding but rewarding 11-km walk that cuts across the Pipe Track.
- **Lion's Head** – 659 m high but accessible and quick to ascend.
- **Maclear's Beacon** – the highest point on Table Mountain – is a 2,5-km walk from the upper cable station.
- **The Newlands side of the Contour Path** is a beautifully shady, almost level walk of about 10 km.
- **Over the Saddle** is 5 to 6 km of hard slog up Devil's Peak.
- **Smuts Track**, named after Prime Minister JC Smuts, is an 11-km track starting at Kirstenbosch Botanical Gardens.
- **The Town End of the Contour Path** offers some 14 km of easy walking, starting at Tafelberg Rd.

HOW NOT TO FALL OFF THE MOUNTAIN

Table Mountain may be in the middle of a city, but that doesn't mean it can't be wild – or dangerous.
- Tell someone where you're hiking and when you expect to return.
- Don't walk alone.
- Stick to paths.
- Take waterproof clothing, hat, strong non-slip shoes, food and water.
- If the weather looks changeable, head home. If you're caught in mist or rain, find shelter and stay put.

Items to carry: water, pencil, notebook, compass, map, magnifying glass for map, small mirror, whistle, penknife, spare shoelaces, instant energy food like chocolate or nuts, torch and matches or lighter.

USEFUL HIKING & WALKING INFORMATION

Cape Nature Conservation
Tel. 418-5226.
The Western Cape's 27 nature reserves are designed to conserve indigenous flora and fauna, and they provide one of the best ways to experience breathtaking views, wildlife (from the rare mountain zebra to the endangered geometric tortoise), cycling, canoeing and hiking.
Besides shorter walks, there are five well-organised national trails. For more adventurous hikers, there's kloofing on the Riviersonderend Hiking Trail and at Salmonsdam Nature Reserve, as well as the Palmiet Hiking Trail, the country's first self-guided wheelchair and visually impaired trail. Affordable, comfortable overnight accommodation is offered at De Hoop, Cederberg and Salmonsdam. For campers, there are well-established sites at Tweede Tol, Cederberg, De Hoop, Salmonsdam, and Grootvaderbosch.

The Hiking Federation of South Africa
Daniel Rousseau, tel. 96-4156 (a/h).
Promotes hiking and provides information on Western Cape trails.

Kommetjie Environmental Awareness Group
Tel. 783-3433.
Two- to three-hour walks, including the Kakapo Trail and Slangkop Mountain, at around R10 p/p. Booking advisable.

The National Parks Board
Tel. 22-2810.
Information on South Africa's national parks, many of which offer good accommodation and excellent trails.

Simon's Town Publicity Association
Tel. 786-3046 or 786-2436.
Information on splendid walks in the Simon's Town mountains and the Cape of Good Hope Nature Reserve.

HIKING & CAMPING EQUIPMENT

See also listing **Sports Gear Stores** *later in this chapter.*

Cape Union Mart
This shop stocks a sturdy, inspiring range of hiking boots and equipment, camping gear, rugged clothing and accessories. For toll-free enquiries, tel. 0800-03-4000. City-wide branches include:
Victoria Wharf, Waterfront, tel. 419-0019.
150 Main Rd, Claremont, tel. 64-2148.
Blue Route Centre, Tokai, tel. 75-8470.
Sanlam Centre, Parow, tel. 930-2420.
Sun Gallery, City Centre, tel. 23-2095.
N1 City, Goodwood, tel. 595-1220.
Corporation St, City Centre, tel. 45-7611.
Tyger Valley Centre, Tyger Valley, tel. 946-2290.

HIKING: GUIDED TOURS

For walks with a difference, get the free *Shipwreck and Lighthouse Guide* from Captour offices (*see chapter* **Essential Information**).

John McDonnell
11 Forest Road, Oranjezicht, tel. 45-2503.
Open: *8am-8pm Mon-Fri.*
Two-and-a-half-hour trip up Table Mountain, including provisions, cable car trip down and certificate to prove you've done the hike. Cost: R50 p/p.

The Mountain Club
Tel. 45-3412.
Training, safety patrols and guides.

Table Mountain Climb Company
606 Heerengracht Centre, Foreshore, tel. 419-2667.
Open: *8.30am-5pm Mon-Fri.*
Guided walks up Table Mountain, along the Platteklip Gorge route or custom-designed trails. Day trips, including cable car down and light refreshments, are R60 p/p.

HORSE-RACING

Kenilworth, Milnerton and Durbanville are Cape Town's major tracks, with races on Wednesday and Saturday afternoons. For info, call the Western Province Racing Club, tel. 551-2110 or 762-7777.

The **J&B Met**, South Africa's premier racing event, begins at 10am on the last Saturday of January at Kenilworth Race Course, Rosmead Ave, Kenilworth. If you don't enjoy horses, go for the upwardly mobile hats and downwardly mobile cleavages. Entrance: R25. Take a picnic or reserve a table, tel. 762-7777.

HORSE-RIDING

For horse-riding trails along the coast, see chapter **Wet, Wet, Wet**.

Winelands Horse-trails
Kruispad, Bottelary Rd, tel. 981-2480.
Open: *8am-5pm Mon-Fri.*
A variety of winelands horse-trails. A full-day visit, including wine-tastings and lunch, is R150.

Riding for the Disabled
Tel. 794-4393.
Call for details of trails and events.

MARTIAL ARTS

British Taijiquan & Shaolin Wu Shu Association
1st Floor, 119 Loop St, City Centre, tel. 439-1373.
Instructors trained at the Shaolin Temple in mainland China teach authentic Chinese Wu Shu (Kung Fu) and Tai Chi. Beginners, intermediate and advanced classes. A serene environment in the heart of the city.

Denis St John Thomson
Ascot House, 2 Pepper St, City Centre, tel. 23-7965.
38 Main Rd, Claremont, tel. 64-2881.
Introductory social evenings and Tai Chi classes in the City Centre and Claremont. R85 per month for up to five weekly classes. Based on Cheng Man-Ching's teachings.

The International Tai Chi Society
Tel. 58-8632.
Branches in Gardens and Table View. Monthly rate: R80 for twice-weekly classes. No charge for introductory class.

National Aikido Association of South Africa
Karate Centre, 67 Mill Park, Milnerton, tel. 511-5311.
A combination of Chi Kung and Aikido at R85 a month for twice-weekly classes. Visitors welcome to join in or watch.

RUNNING

The most popular jogging routes are the Atlantic seaboard – Mouille Point to Bakoven, particularly Sea Point-Clifton, but you can also run along Camps Bay, Chapman's Peak, in the Newlands Forest, or (if you're fit) up and down Table Mountain.

Cape Town Hash House Harriers have a weekly social run on Sunday – free and fun, tel. 701-1621.

The **Ohlsson's Two Oceans Marathon** is run in April and attracts more than 8 000 runners. Participation in this 56-km route: R50 (locals), R120 (foreigners). For more info, tel. 61-9407.

The **Argus/Seeff Gun Run**, run in September, is the city's largest half marathon. For information and application forms, tel. 438-2595.

For details of other races and road-running events, contact the Western Province Road Runners Association, tel. 75-6522.

RUGBY

Check newspapers and book in advance for big matches – South Africans are rugby-mad. Tickets are available at the gate (if you're lucky and happy to stand in line) or at the ticket office of **Newlands Stadium**. For more information contact the Western Province Rugby Football Union, tel. 689-4921.

ROLLERBLADING

Rollerblading is becoming increasingly popular and is particularly good on the Mouille Point promenade. For rollerblade hire, try Rent 'n Ride, 1 Park Rd, Mouille Point, tel. 434-1122. ID documents and deposit are required.

SAILING

See chapter **Wet, Wet, Wet**.

SCUBA DIVING

See chapter **Wet, Wet, Wet**.

SHOOTING

The Cape Handgun Range
Groote Kerk Bldg, Adderley St, City Centre, tel. 45-2277.
Firearms hired out at R50, under an instructor's supervision. Ammunition costs approximately R40 per 25 rounds, depending on gun calibre.

Cape Town Pistol Club
Signal Hill, tel. 24-9030. Phone for road directions.
Pistol instruction and Saturday afternoon shooting. R10 for non-affiliated members. Bring your own firearm.

Clay Pigeon Shooting (Cape Gun Club)
Swartklip Rd (exit 16 on the N2), tel. 797-8787.
Visitors welcome at Saturday afternoon events. R10 for 25 clays, plus R25 per ammo packet.

SPORTS GEAR STORES

See also **Hiking & Camping Equipment** earlier in this chapter.

The Athlete's Foot
276 Victoria Wharf, Waterfront, tel. 21-5717.
Open: 9am-9pm Mon-Fri (Dec-Jan), 9am-7pm Mon-Fri (Feb-Nov), 9am-6pm Sat, 10am-6pm Sun.
Footwear specialists with everything from cross-training to jogging shoes.

Replay Sports
44 Main Rd, Claremont, tel. 64-4222.
Open: 9am-5pm Mon-Fri, 9am-1pm Sat.
A quite extraordinary range of new and used gear, from wetsuits to lacrosse racquets. Equipment to hire, depending on availability.

Logan's Sportsman's Warehouse
34 Klipfontein Rd, Rondebosch, tel. 689-8171.
Open: 8.30am-6pm Mon-Fri, 8.30am-1pm Sat.
The bargain-hunter's idea of heaven – 2 000 square metres of discount sports goods – everything from sneakers and sunglasses to running shoes and equipment.

Sport Unlimited
Constantia Village, tel. 794-3240.
Open: 8.30am-5.30pm Mon-Fri, 8.30am-3pm Sat, 9am-2pm Sun.
Sports clothes, bathing costumes, equipment and tennis racquet restringing.

Total Sports
Shell House, St George's Mall, City Centre, tel. 21-4155.
Open: 8.15am-5pm Mon, Wed and Fri, 9am-5pm Tue and Thu, 8.15am-1pm Sat.
Cavendish Square, Claremont, tel. 61-5643.
Open: 9am-5pm Mon-Thu, 9am-5.30pm Fri, 9am-5pm Sat.
Sports shoe specialists with a large range of clothes, energy products and equipment.

SQUASH COURTS

Constantia Health and Racquet Club
Main Rd, Constantia, tel. 794-5010.
Open: *5.30am-10pm Mon-Thu, 5.30am-9pm Fri, 7am-9pm Sat-Sun.*
No equipment hired; balls can be bought from the shop. No phone bookings.

Cape Town Health and Racquet Club
21 Lower Long St, Foreshore, tel. 21-5857.
Open: *5.30am-9pm Mon-Thu, 5.30am-8pm Fri, 7am-7pm Sat, 8am-noon and 4pm-8pm Sun.*
R50 per game. No equipment for hire, bring your own balls.

The Point Health and Racquet Club
Bill Peters Drive, Green Point, tel. 434-0750.
Open: *5.30am-10pm Mon-Thu, 5.30am-9pm Fri, 7am-9pm Sat-Sun.*
R50 per game. No equipment for hire. No phone bookings.

Monte Vista
Monte Vista Boulevard, Monte Vista, tel. 58-2757.
Open: *8am-10.30pm Mon-Fri, 8am-8pm Sat.*
R4,50 per person per half hour. Racquet hire R4. Balls are free. Phone bookings accepted, but 6-12 hours' notice required.

Western Province Squash Racket Association
Tel. 21-2512.
For information on squash championships, events, venues and coaches.

STEAM BATHS & PUBLIC POOLS

See chapter **Wet, Wet, Wet**.

SURFING

See beach listings in chapter **Wet, Wet, Wet** *for surfing spots and* **Surfing** *in the same chapter for board hire.*

For details of seasonal sporting events like rowing, see chapter **Cape Town by Season**.

Sport, Fitness & The Great Outdoors 249

Western Province Surfing Association
Tel. 64-2972.
Information on events.

TENNIS

Green Point Lawn Tennis Club
Vlaenberg St, Green Point, tel. 434-9527.
Informal, popular courts, close to the City Centre. R5 per game. Balls are available but there's no equipment for hire. Organised social tennis on Saturday afternoon and Sunday, Tuesday and Thursday mornings.

The Point Health and Racquet Club
Bill Peters Drive, Green Point, tel. 434-0750.
Well-maintained courts in a gleaming gym complex, complete with saunas and steam baths.

River Club Centre
Liesbeek Parkway, Observatory, tel. 448-4399.
Bring your own racquet and balls, and phone to check when courts are available, and you can play at the River Club courts at no charge. The centre also has secure parking, food, bars, music and a very sociable vibe.

Rondebosch Tennis Club
Lovers Walk, Rondebosch, tel. 689-2845.
Twelve courts at R1,50 per hour. Balls, but no equipment for hire. Floodlit courts are R19,50 per hour. Book in advance with Dennis Quinn, tel. 689-9768 (a/h) or at the club. Change-rooms and refreshments available 8.30am-4.30pm.

Western Province Tennis Association
Tel. 686-3055.
Information on events and clubs.

WHALE-WATCHING

For whale-watching season, see chapter **Cape Town by Season.** Captour bureaux also carry free whale route guides *(see chapter* **Essential Information***).*

WINDSURFING

Sandvlei, outside Muizenberg, is popular for lake sailing, Big Bay at Blouberg is good for wave-jumping, and there's an annual Boardsailing Marathon in False Bay around March. For details of events, coaching and board hire, contact International Windsurfer Sailing Schools, tel. 797-2824.

YOGA

Ananda Kutir Yoga Centre
24 Sprigg Rd, Rondebosch East, tel. 696-1821.
Weekly and private classes, and a variety of courses and videos. R15 per casual class. Reduced monthly rates.

SURVIVAL

From minor problems to major pains, here are the useful numbers.

EMERGENCY NUMBERS

Air Ambulance, *tel. 948-9900.*
Ambulance, *tel. 1-0177.*
Car Theft Unit, *tel. 1-0111.*
Child Protection Unit, *tel. 592-2601 (office hours) or 1-0111 (a/h).*
Child Welfare, *tel. 761-4128 or 761-7130.*
Crime Stop, *tel. 0800-11-1213.*
Fire Brigade, *tel. 73-1892.*
Flying Squad, *tel. 1-0111.*
Lost Property, City, *tel. 461-7282 ext 258.*
Lost Property, Railways, *tel. 405-4045.*
MedicAlert, *tel. 461-7328 or 461-0000 or 0800-22-2366.*
Missing Persons, *tel. 0800-11-1213 or 461-7282 ext 270 or 274.*
Mountain Fires, *tel. 23-3210 or 790-1045.*
Mountain Rescue, *tel. 1-0111 or 1-0177.*
Police, Caledon Square, *tel. 461-4370 or 461-4326.*
Police Tourist Assistance Unit, *tel. 418-2853.*
Railways Crimes, *tel. 0800-21-0081.*
Rape Crisis Centre, *tel. 47-9762.*
Sea Rescue, *tel. 405-3500 or 1-0111* or 24-hour emergency at the Port Control, Cape Town Docks, *tel. 405-2805 or 405-3666.*
State Mortuary, *tel. 448-4457.*

COUNSELLING & HELPLINES

AIDS Training and Information, *tel. 400-3400 or 400-2682.*
Alcoholics Anonymous, *tel. 24-7559.*
Childline 24-hour Service, *tel. 0800-12-3321.*
Citizens' Advice Bureau, *tel. 461-7218.*
Epicare (support group for epileptics), *tel. 47-3012.*
Gay and Lesbian Support Group, *tel. 21-5420.*
Lifeline Counselling, *tel. 461-1111.*
Overeaters Anonymous, *tel. 794-5593.*
Rape Crisis, *tel. 47-9762.*
Sexually Transmitted Diseases, *Chapel St Clinic (Mon 8.30am-11am), tel. 462-4400* and *Spencer Rd Clinic (Wed afternoon only), tel. 400-2047.*
Tough Love (for families of substance abusers), *tel. 785-1768.*

HOSPITALS

City Park Hospital, *tel. 480-6111.*
Conradie Hospital, *tel. 531-1311.*
Constantiaberg Clinic *tel. 799-2911.*
False Bay Hospital, *tel. 782-1121.*
Groote Schuur Hospital, *tel. 404-9111.*
Jan S Marais Clinic, *tel. 918-1911.*

Karl Bremer Hospital, *tel. 948-1341.*
Khayelitsha Day Hospital, *tel. 361-3470/1.*
Khayelitsha Maternity Hospital, *tel. 361-3480.*
Lentegeur Hospital, *tel. 34-3111.*
Libertas Hospital, *tel. 591-1151.*
Louis Leipoldt Hospital, *tel. 946-1170.*
Mitchells Plain Medical Centre, *tel. 32-3126.*
Red Cross Hospital (children), *tel. 658-5111.*
Red Cross Poison Unit, *tel. 689-5227.*
Tygerberg Hospital, *tel. 938-4911.*
Tygerberg Poison Unit, *tel. 931-6129.*
Victoria Hospital, *tel. 797-8131.*

SUPPORT FOR DISABLED PEOPLE

Cape Town Civilian Blind Society, *tel. 448-4302.*
League of Friends of the Blind, *tel. 705-3753.*
Lighthouse Association for the Blind, *tel. 22-2000.*
SA National Council for the Blind, *tel. 75-3563.*
SA National Council for the Deaf, *tel. 683-4665/6.*
St Giles Association for the Handicapped (temporary wheelchair loan and sporting/social activities), *tel. 689-8328.*
Tape Aids for the Blind, *tel. 689-5983/4.*
Infoguide Kiosk, Waterkant St, City Centre, provides information on business and disabled access.

EMERGENCY PHARMACIES

Cape Town Station Pharmacy, *City Centre, tel. 419-4784.*
Cotton's Owl Pharmacy, *94a Voortrekker Rd, Goodwood, tel. 591-8331.*
Glengariff Pharmacy, *Glengariff Rd, Sea Point, tel. 434-8622.*
Lite-Kem Pharmacy, *Darling St, City Centre, tel. 461-6257.*
Monument Pharmacy, *74 Voortrekker Rd, Goodwood, tel. 591-4164.*
Rustenburg Pharmacy, *52 Beach Rd, Muizenberg, tel. 788-8028.*
Southern Suburbs Pharmacy, *56 Belvedere Rd, Claremont, tel. 61-8444.*

Waterfront Pharmacy, *Waterfront, tel. 21-2255.*
Wynberg Pharmacy, *222 Main Rd, Wynberg, tel. 797-5719.*

DOCTORS & DENTISTS

Consult the phone directory under Dentists or Medical Practitioners.
For dental emergencies, *tel. 61-3634 or 61-2924.*

ALTERNATIVE MEDICINE

See chapter **Services**.

USEFUL INFORMATION LINES

Airport info, plane arrival and departure times, *tel. 934-0407.*
Computer Virus Helpline, *tel. 25-3711 or 25-3773.*
Dolphin Action and Protection Group, *tel. 782-5845.*
Flower Hotline (for information on where to see the best west coast flowers), *tel. 418-3705, daily 8am-4pm Jun-Oct.*
Red Tide Hotline, *tel. 439-4380.*
SANCCOB (for oil- or weather-damaged seabirds), *tel. 557-6155.*
Telephonic wind report for sailing and surfing, Muizenberg, *tel. 788-8226,* Blouberg-strand, *tel. 56-1723.*
Weather forecasts, *tel. 4-0881.*

CONSULATES & EMBASSIES

American Embassy, *tel. 21-4280.*
Argentinian Consulate, *tel. 24-2923.*
Australian High Commission, *tel. 419-5425.*
Austrian Consulate, *tel. 21-1440.*
Belgian Consulate General, *tel. 419-4690.*
Brazilian Embassy, *tel. (012) 43-5550.*
British High Commission, *tel. 25-3670.*
British Embassy, *tel. 461-7220.*
Canadian High Commission, *tel. 23-5240.*
Chilean Consulate, *tel. 21-2344/6.*

Chinese Embassy, *tel. 21-1993.*
Chinese Consulate (visas), *tel. 418-1188.*
Danish Consulate, *tel. 797-1789.*
French Embassy, *tel. 22-1338.*
French Consulate, *tel. 23-1575.*
German Embassy and Consulate, *tel. 24-2410.*
Greek Consulate General, *tel. 24-8161.*
Guatemalan Consulate *tel. 418-2020.*
Israeli Embassy, *tel. 45-7207.*
Italian Consulate, *tel. 24-1256/7/8.*
Italian Embassy, *tel. 23-5157/8.*
Japanese Consulate, *tel. 25-1695.*
Netherlands Consulate General, *tel. 21-5660.*
Norwegian Embassy, *tel. 25-1687.*
Norwegian Consulate, *tel. 418-1276.*
Portuguese Consulate General, *tel. 24-1454.*
Russian Consulate, *tel. 418-3656.*
Spanish Embassy, *tel. 22-2326.*
Swedish Consulate, *tel. 418-1276.*
Swiss Consulate, *tel. 26-1040.*
Uruguayan Embassy, *tel. 25-1847.*

CUSTOMS

Information and advice, *tel. 21-1930.*

STOLEN CARDS

To report stolen bank or credit cards:
American Express, South African and foreign cards, *tel. 080-953-4300 or 418-5600,*
Diners Club, *tel. 686-7880 (Mon-Fri) or (011) 33-5151/2.*
First National Bank, *tel. 0800-0132.*
Standard Bank, (Autobank or Mastercard), *tel. 0800-02-0600.*
For banks and foreign exchange, see chapter **Essential Information**.

LEGAL HELP

Attorney General, *tel. 26-2830.*
Family Advocate, *tel. 26-2830.*
Law Society, *tel. 24-8060.*
Lawyers for Human Rights, *tel. 47-6168.*

CALLING HOME

Two types of easily operated public phone are in use – card and coin operated. Coin-operated phones take old and new denominations and the minimum fee is 30c. Phonecards can be bought from post offices, CNA stores or the Waterfront Information Office.

The Cape Town area code is 021; the Johannesburg code is 011; the Durban code 031; and the Pretoria code 012. Charges depend on the duration and distance of the call; national calls from 8pm-6am are cheapest.

PHONE ENQUIRIES

Local numbers, *tel. 1023.*
Dial-a-conference, *tel. 949-0746.*
Trunk-call booking, *tel. 0020.*
Fixed-time calls, *tel. 1-0216.*
International enquiries, *tel. 0903.*
International bookings, *tel. 0900.*
Emergency international call supervisor, *tel. (021) 948-7171.*

POST OFFICE

Main Post Office, *Parliament St, City Centre, tel. 461-5670.*
Tollfree Customer Careline, *tel. 0800-11-4488.* General Enquiries, Main Post Office, *tel. 461-5670 ext. 2312.*
A poste restante and enquiry desk is situated in the main hall.
Open: *8.30am-4.30pm Mon-Fri, 8am-noon Sat.*

LOST PROPERTY

Property lost on trains or stations, *tel. 405-4045.*
Property lost in the city, *tel. 461-7282 ext. 258.*
Luggage Office, Cape Town Station, *tel. 405-2611.*

The Coon Carnival, also known as the Cape Minstrel Carnival, leads the city into the New Year with such gusto that Cape Town has not one, but two new year's days in which to party, recover and party some more.

A success story which has exceeded even the wildest expectations, the Victoria & Alfred Waterfront attracts literally millions of visitors – for good reason. Head here for eateries, entertainment, shops and craft centres.

WHERE ARE YOU?

Detailed street maps are available from the Tourist Information Bureau, 3 Adderley St, City Centre, newsagents and bookstores.

ELECTRICITY

The electricity supply in South Africa is 220/230 volts AC / 50Hz. United States appliances may need a transformer.

ANIMAL QUERIES

After hours Animal Clinic, *tel. 685-5859.*
Bee removals, *tel. 24-2551.*
Lost pets: descriptions are listed in newspaper classifieds and further information is available from the SPCA, *tel. 705-3757* or Animal Welfare, *tel. 692-2626.*
Snake removals, *tel. 701-9075.*

RELIGIOUS SERVICES

CHRISTIAN

The Anglican Diocese of Cape Town provides details of 50 Cape Town churches, tel. 23-1253 (weekdays).

JEWISH

The Union of Orthodox Synagogues carries details of the City's 11 synagogues, *tel. 461-6310.*

MUSLIM

Cape Town boasts a vast number of mosques. The Muslim Judicial Council has details, *tel. 69-64143 or 69-5150 (9am-2pm).* Worth noting is the Auwal Mosque (founded in 1789), Dorp Street, Bo-Kaap *(see box on the* **Bo-Kaap** *in chapter* **The Sights***).*

MAPS

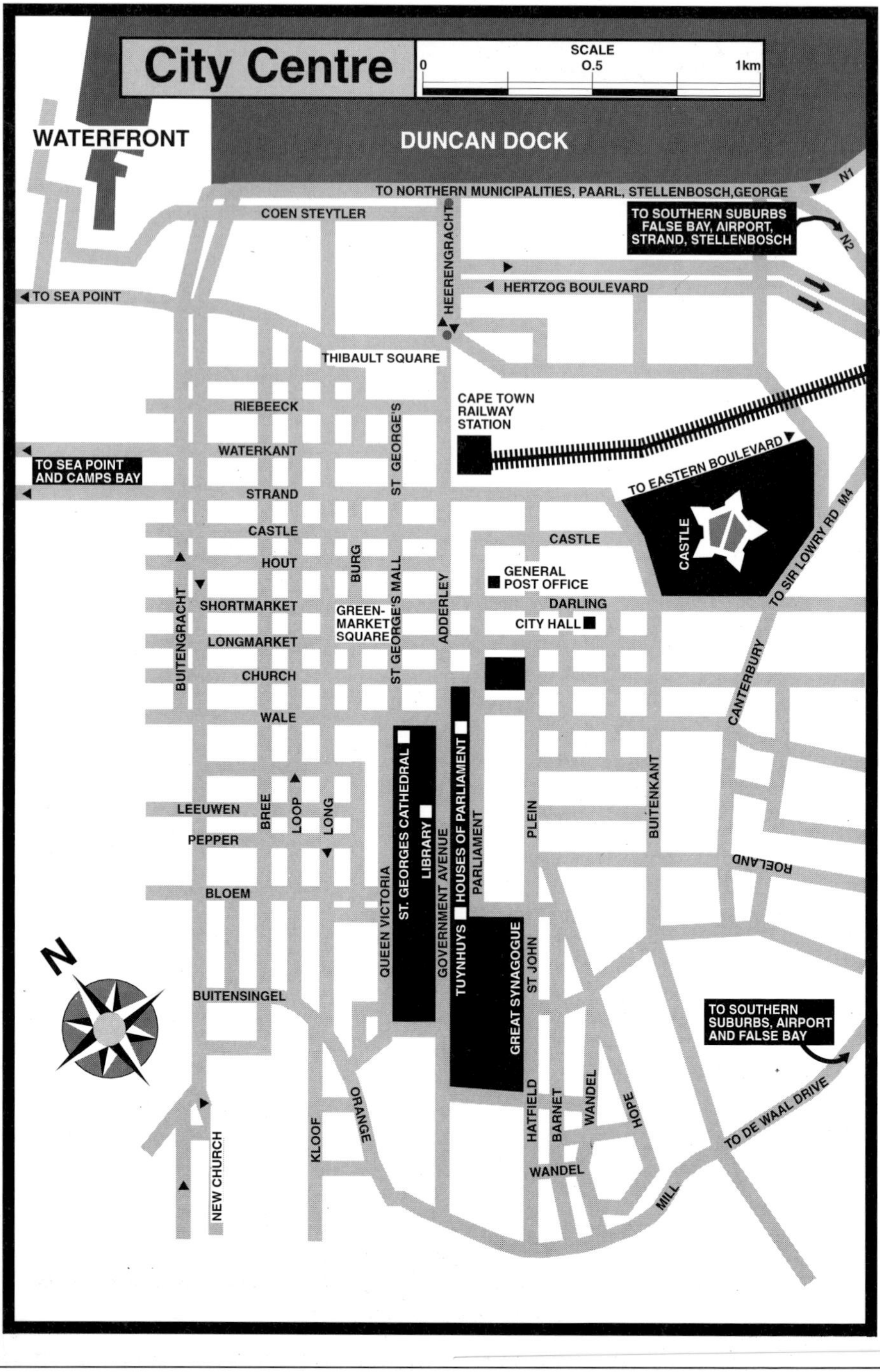

City Centre
SCALE
0
O.5
1km
WATERFRONT
DUNCAN DOCK
TO NORTHERN MUNICIPALITIES, PAARL, STELLENBOSCH,GEORGE
N1
TO SOUTHERN SUBURBS FALSE BAY, AIRPORT, STRAND, STELLENBOSCH
N2
COEN STEYTLER
HEERENGRACHT
HERTZOG BOULEVARD
TO SEA POINT
THIBAULT SQUARE
CAPE TOWN RAILWAY STATION
RIEBEECK
WATERKANT
TO SEA POINT AND CAMPS BAY
STRAND
ST GEORGE'S
TO EASTERN BOULEVARD
CASTLE
HOUT
BURG
GENERAL POST OFFICE
TO SIR LOWRY RD M4
SHORTMARKET
GREEN-MARKET SQUARE
ST GEORGE'S MALL
ADDERLEY
DARLING
CITY HALL
LONGMARKET
BUITENGRACHT
CHURCH
CANTERBURY
WALE
LEEUWEN
BREE
LOOP
LONG
PEPPER
ST. GEORGES CATHEDRAL
LIBRARY
HOUSES OF PARLIAMENT
PARLIAMENT
PLEIN
BUITENKANT
ROELAND
BLOEM
QUEEN VICTORIA
GOVERNMENT AVENUE
TUYNHUYS
GREAT SYNAGOGUE
ST JOHN
N
BUITENSINGEL
TO SOUTHERN SUBURBS, AIRPORT AND FALSE BAY
ORANGE
KLOOF
HATFIELD
BARNET
WANDEL
HOPE
TO DE WAAL DRIVE
NEW CHURCH
WANDEL
MILL

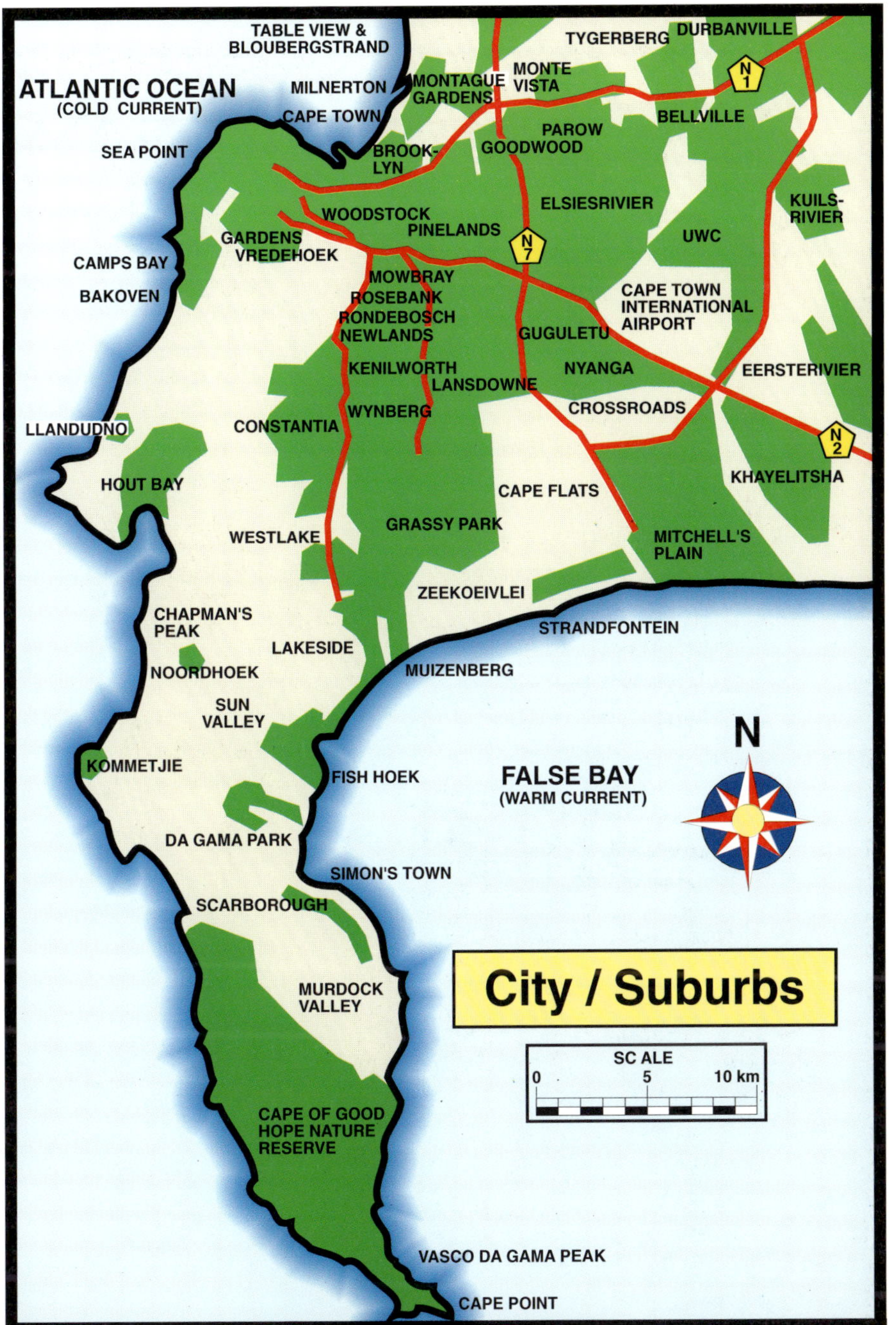
TABLE VIEW &
BLOUBERGSTRAND
ATLANTIC OCEAN
(COLD CURRENT)
MILNERTON
CAPE TOWN
SEA POINT
MONTAGUE GARDENS
MONTE VISTA
TYGERBERG
DURBANVILLE
N1
BELLVILLE
PAROW
GOODWOOD
BROOK-LYN
WOODSTOCK
PINELANDS
ELSIESRIVIER
KUILS-RIVIER
UWC
N7
GARDENS
VREDEHOEK
CAMPS BAY
BAKOVEN
MOWBRAY
ROSEBANK
RONDEBOSCH
NEWLANDS
GUGULETU
CAPE TOWN INTERNATIONAL AIRPORT
KENILWORTH
LANSDOWNE
NYANGA
EERSTERIVIER
CROSSROADS
WYNBERG
CONSTANTIA
LLANDUDNO
N2
HOUT BAY
CAPE FLATS
KHAYELITSHA
GRASSY PARK
WESTLAKE
MITCHELL'S PLAIN
ZEEKOEIVLEI
CHAPMAN'S PEAK
STRANDFONTEIN
LAKESIDE
NOORDHOEK
MUIZENBERG
SUN VALLEY
N
KOMMETJIE
FISH HOEK
FALSE BAY
(WARM CURRENT)
DA GAMA PARK
SIMON'S TOWN
SCARBOROUGH
City / Suburbs
MURDOCK VALLEY
SC ALE
0
5
10 km
CAPE OF GOOD HOPE NATURE RESERVE
VASCO DA GAMA PEAK
CAPE POINT

Stellenbosch Wine Route

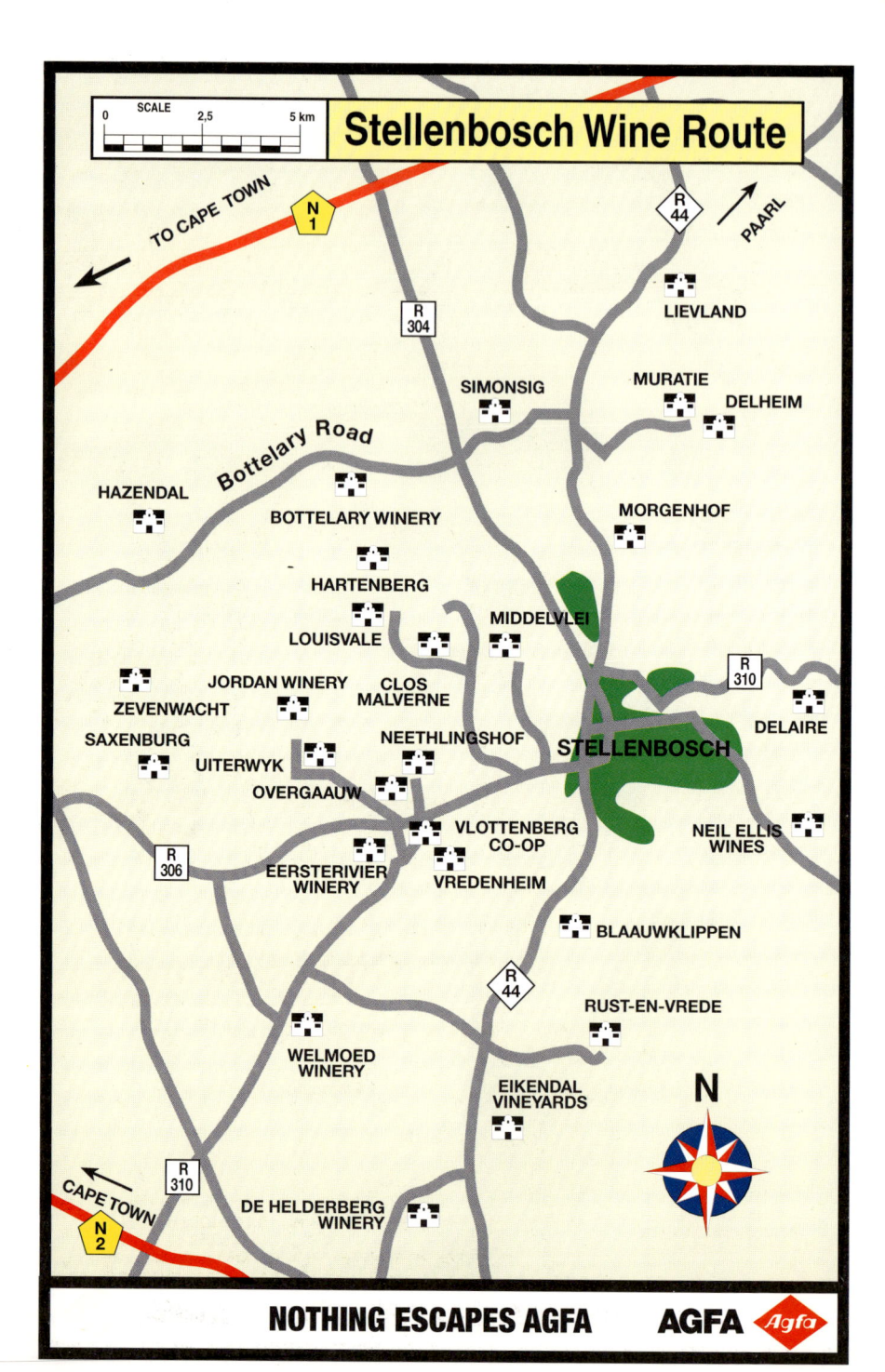

SCALE 0 2,5 5 km

TO CAPE TOWN — N1
R44 → PAARL
R304
LIEVLAND
SIMONSIG
MURATIE
DELHEIM
Bottelary Road
HAZENDAL
BOTTELARY WINERY
MORGENHOF
HARTENBERG
LOUISVALE
MIDDELVLEI
JORDAN WINERY
CLOS MALVERNE
R310
ZEVENWACHT
NEETHLINGSHOF
DELAIRE
SAXENBURG
UITERWYK
STELLENBOSCH
OVERGAAUW
NEIL ELLIS WINES
R306
EERSTERIVIER WINERY
VLOTTENBERG CO-OP
VREDENHEIM
BLAAUWKLIPPEN
R44
RUST-EN-VREDE
WELMOED WINERY
EIKENDAL VINEYARDS
N
← CAPE TOWN R310
N2
DE HELDERBERG WINERY

NOTHING ESCAPES AGFA — AGFA

Paarl Wine Route

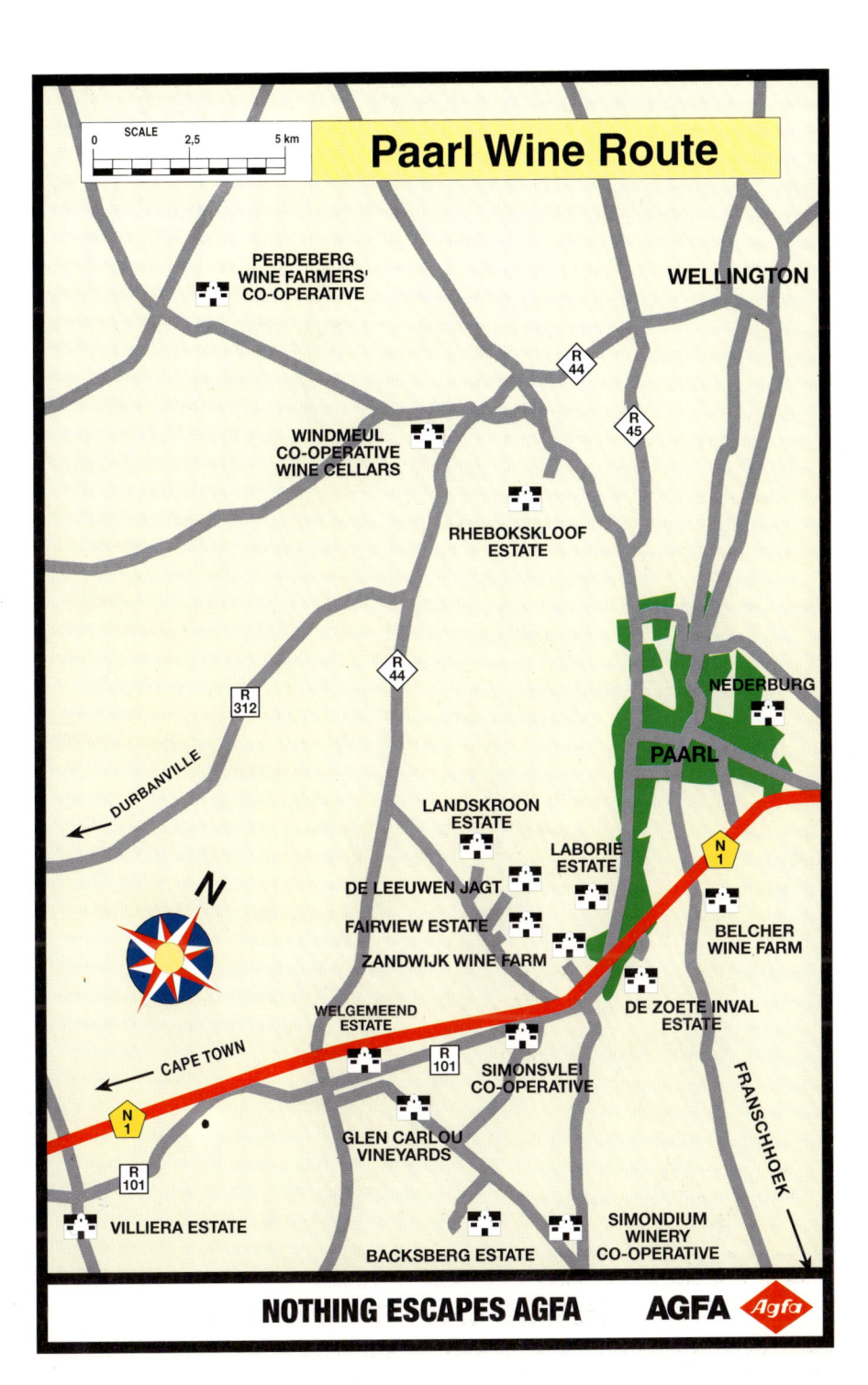

NOTHING ESCAPES AGFA — AGFA

Cape Peninsula

Map

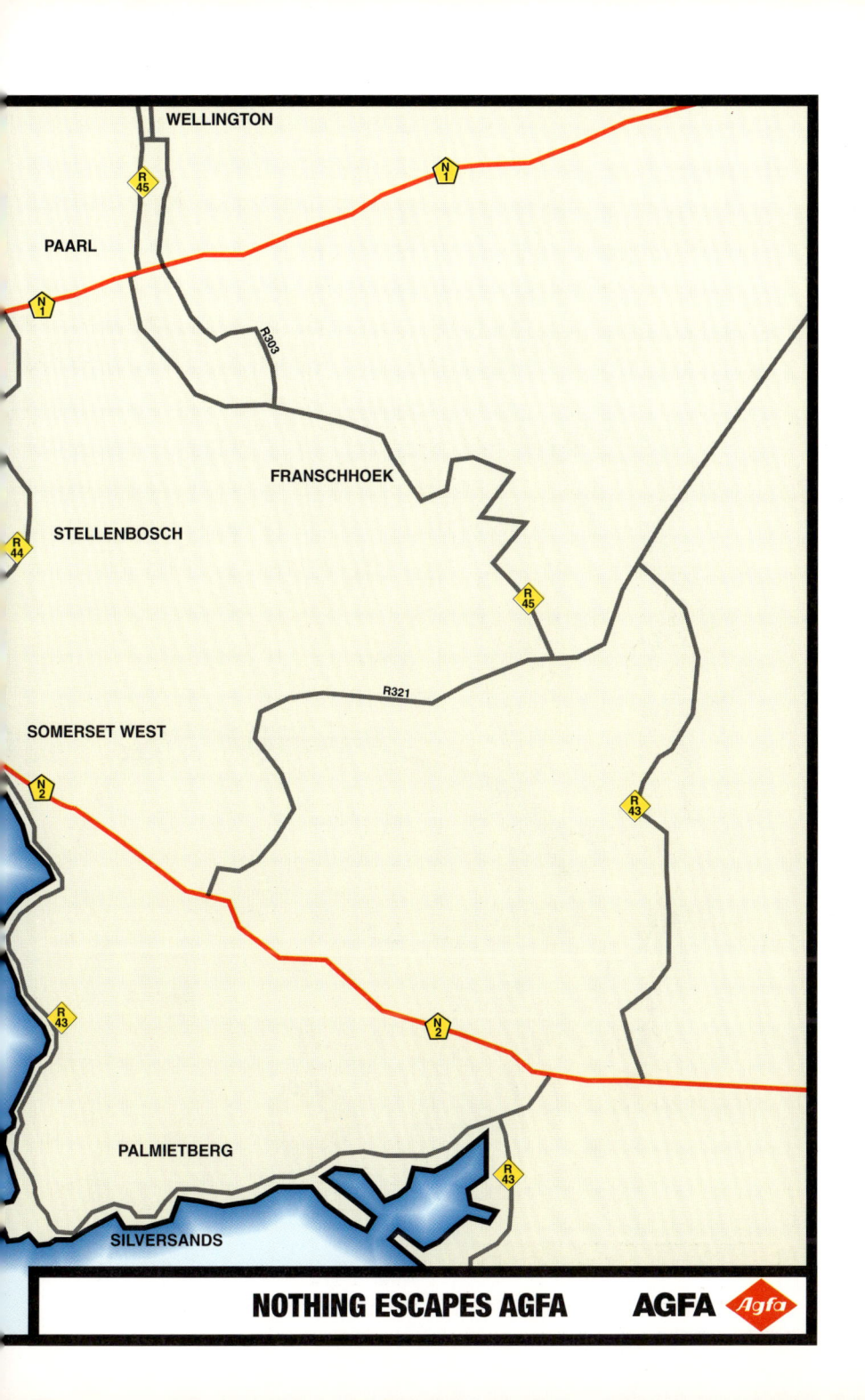

WELLINGTON

R45 · N1

PAARL

N1 · R303

FRANSCHHOEK

STELLENBOSCH · R44

R45

R321

SOMERSET WEST

N2 · R43

R43 · N2

PALMIETBERG

R43

SILVERSANDS

NOTHING ESCAPES AGFA — **AGFA** *Agfa*

Cape Peninsula Beaches

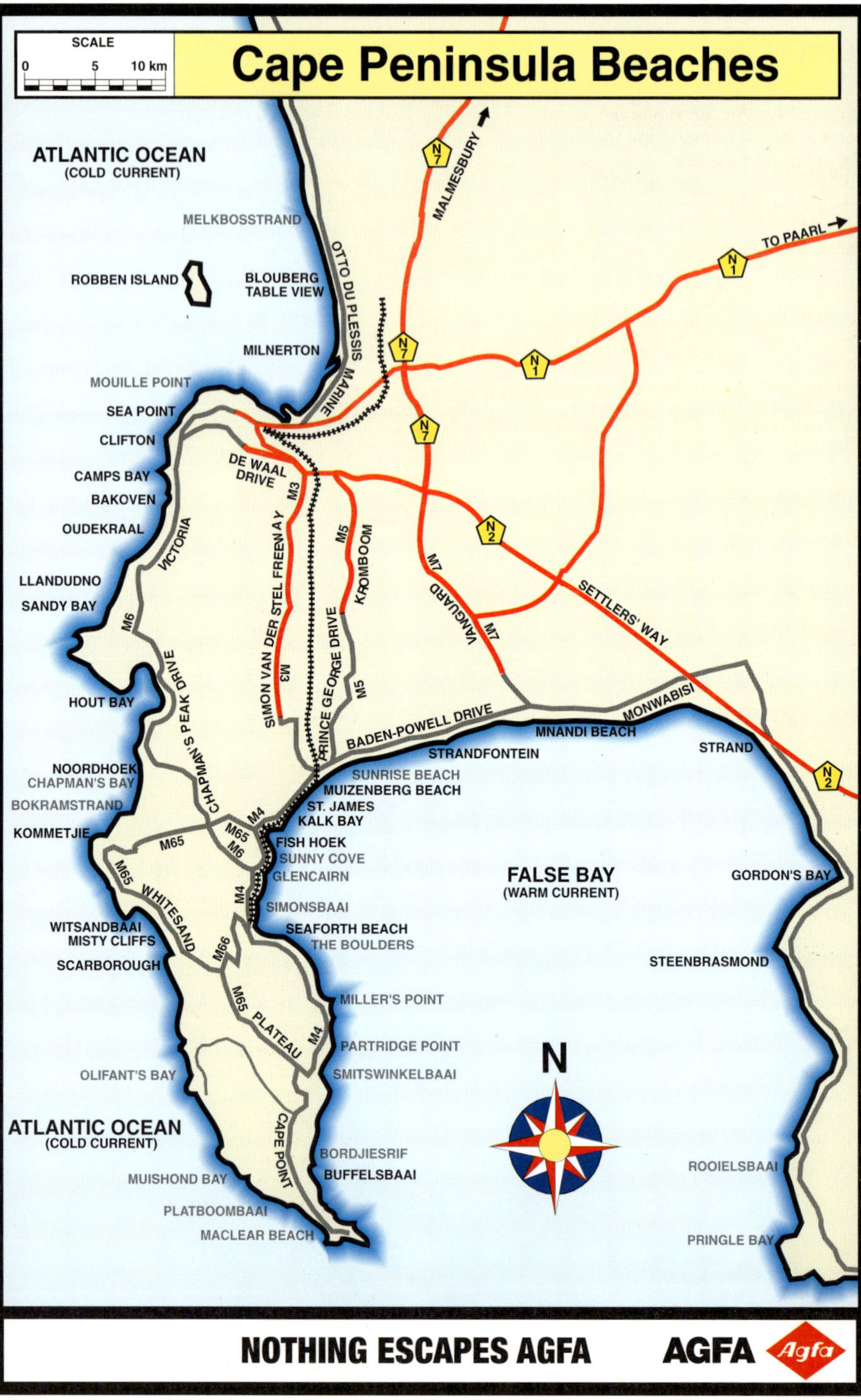

INDEX

Accommodation 13-27
    bed & breakfast accommodation 14
    bed & breakfast associations 14
    booking agencies 14
    booking 14
    budget travellers 192-6
    chains 19-20
    de luxe 14-6
    good 16-8
    guest-houses 13, 20-2
    hostels 195-6
    hotels 14-20
    letting agents 14
    moderate 18-9
    out of town 24-7
    self-catering 22-3
    students 195-6
    women-only 209
Airport 5, 7-8
Alternative health 141
Animal queries 253
Antiques 120-2
Apartheid 37-8, 52, 54, 56
    District Six 56
    history 37
    Mayibuye Centre 52
    Robben Island 60
    St George's Cathedral 54
Aquarium, Two Oceans 55
Architecture 76-8
    Art Deco 77
    Cape Dutch 76
Argus Cycle Tour 29, 238
Art consultants 73
Art Deco walk 61
Art galleries 69-75
    Alfred Mall 69
    Arts Association of Bellville 70
    Atlantic 70
    Chelsea 70
    Kunskamer 70
    New Cape 70
    out of town 72
    Primart 70
    Rose Korber 70
    Seeff 71
    Sembach 71
    South African Association of the Arts 71
    South African National Gallery 54
Auctions 118

Baker, Sir Herbert 54, 76
Banking 1-2
    autobanks 1
    bureaux de change 2
    credit cards 1
    currency 1
    foreign exchange 2

Babysitters 185
Bars 110-3
Beaches 213-20
    Atlantic seaboard 218-9
    beach etiquette 214
    False Bay 213-6
    Gordon's Bay 216-7
    Hout Bay and surrounds 217-8
    public transport 220-1
    surf reports 213
    west coast 220
Beauty clinics 142-3
Bertram House 68
Bo-Kaap
    guided tour 60-1
    museum 45
    karamats 58
    walking tour 61-4
Boat charters and cruises 185, 221-3
Bodyguards 142
Budget travel 192-6
Business 197-203
    computers 199-200
    conference facilities 200
    courier services 200
    phone services 201
    photocopying 199
    property brokers 199
    PR consultants 202
    staff hire 203
    stationery 203
    translators 203
    useful addresses 198

Cabaret 157
Canoeing 223, 238
Cape cuisine 80-2
Cape Education Museum 67
Cape of Good Hope Nature Reserve 47, 215
Castle, the 36, 47-9, 64
Children 180-91
    activities 181-3
    babysitters 185
    creative classes 185-6
    day trips 186
    entertainment 186-7
    hire services 187
    libraries 187
    restaurants 187-8
    services and support 188
    shops 188-90
    swimming 190
    theatre and music 190-1
City Hall 49
Clubs 172-178
    gay 205
    jazz 167
    nightclubs 172
    women's 211
Coon Carnival 29, 169

Computers 199-200
Crafts 122-3
    galleries 74
    markets 139
Cultural History Museum 47
Cycling 238-9

Da Gama, Vasco 33
Da Saldanha, Antonio 33, 54
Dance 161-3
    ballroom 163
    companies 162
    contemporary 163
    gear 163
    Spanish 163
    venues 161
Dentists 251
Dias, Bartolomeu 33
District Six 56
Doctors 251
Drives, scenic 57-8
Durbanville Cultural Society 66
Dutch East India Company 34
Duty-free shopping 5

Electricity 5, 253
Emergencies 250-3
    consulates and embassies 251
    disabled people, advice 251
    doctors and dentists 251
    emergency numbers 250
    emergency pharmacies 251
    helplines 250
    hospitals 250
    legal help 252
    lost property 252
    stolen credit cards 252
    veterinary services 253

Farm stalls 128
Festivals 29-32
Film 158-60
    cinemas 158
    festivals 30, 158
    societies 159
Fishing 223-4
Food and drink 129-33
    alcohol 129-32
    Cape wines 83-4
    delicatessens 93-5
    delivery 143
    farm stalls 128
    fish and meat 132
    health foods 134
    speciality stores 129
Foreign exchange 2
Framers 73
Franschhoek 227
    Huguenot Memorial 227
    restaurants 105

Gardens, the 49
Gay 204-7
    beaches 206
    café's and restaurants 205
    clubs 205
    service organisations 204
    steam baths 206
Gifts 133-4
Golf 239-41
Government Avenue 49
Grand Parade 50
Greenmarket Square 50, 62, 64
Groot Constantia 50, 83
Gyms 241

Hairdressers 145-6
Health
    ambulance 250
    dentists 251
    doctors 251
    emergency pharmacies 251
    hospitals 250
Hermanus 228
    golf 240
    restaurants 106
    whale-watching 31
Hiking 242-5
    clubs 244
    equipment 245
    information 245
    Table Mountain 244
    tours 245
Horse-racing 246
Horse-riding 246
Hospitals 250
Houses of Parliament 51
Hout Bay
    beaches 217
    World of Birds 55
Huguenots 35, 227

Insurance 1

Jewish Museum 67
Josephine Mill 67
    Sunday summer concerts 32

Karamats 58
Khoikhoi 33, 80
Kirstenbosch Botanical Gardens
    history 51
    open-air concerts 32
    tea garden 93
Koeberg power station 56, 243
Koopmans de Wet House 51

Late-night venues 175-8
Laundry 146
Libraries 146, 187, 211
Language 5

Long Street 51
Lost property 146, 252

Mandela, Nelson 40, 49, 60
Mariner's Wharf 52
Markets 139-40
Massage 146
Mayibuye Centre 52
Media 151-3
Michaelis Collection 67
Montebello Design Centre 57
Museums 66-8
    Bo-Kaap 45
    Cape Education 67
    Castle, the 47-8
    Cultural History 47
    Groot Constantia 50
    Jewish 67
    Josephine Mill 57
    Koopmans De Wet House 51
    Mayibuye Centre 52
    Michaelis Collection 67
    Natale Labia 52
    Rust en Vreugd 67
    South African 53
    South African National Gallery 54
    UCT Irma Stern Museum 55
Music 164-71
    classical 164
    folk 171
    jazz 166
    opera 164
    rock and alternative 169-71
Muslims
    Bo-Kaap tours 62
    Cape Malay music tours 62
    cuisine 81
    history 35
    karamats 58

Nature Reserves
    Cape of Good Hope 47
    Helderberg 231
Noon Day Gun 4

Oude Libertas Amphitheatre 32

Paarl 229-30
    restaurants 107-8
    wine festivals 230
Parks and gardens 187
Pets 141, 253
Pharmacies 147, 251
Post Office 252
Public holidays 4
Public swimming pools 221

Religious services 253
Repairs 147
Restaurants 85-113

breakfast 92-6
cheap and cheerful 90-2
children-oriented 187-8
ethnic 97-103
etiquette 81
fast food 104-5
fish and seafood 96-7
haute cuisine 85-6
late-night 175-7
light meals 92-6
moderate priced 86-7
out of town 105-9
steakhouses 103-4
takeout 104-5
trendy and interesting 87-90
vegetarian 104
Rhodes, Cecil John 37, 53, 51
Robben Island 60
Rust en Vreugd Museum 67

Safety 5
Sailing 226
Scuba diving 225
Shebeens 113
Shopping 116-140
    antiques 120-22
    beauty products 118-9
    books 119-20, 152, 210
    cameras 120
    children 188-90
    collectables 120-2
    curios 122-3
    department stores 118
    duty-free 5
    fashion 123-7
    florists 129, 144
    food and drink 129-33
    furniture 127-8
    gifts 133, 144
    interesting and unusual 135
    interiors 127
    jewellery 136-7
    malls 116
    shoes 137-8
    sports gear 245, 247
    stationery 138, 203
Signal Hill 54
Slavery 35, 47
Somerset West 230
    golf 240
    restaurants 108
Somerset, Lord Charles 36
South African Museum 53
South African National Gallery 54
Sport 236-249
    archery 236
    badminton 236
    ballooning 236
    birdwatching 237
    boating 221-3, 237

bowling 237
bungi jumping 237
canoeing 223, 238
cricket 238
cycling 238-9
fishing 223-4
golf 239-41
gyms 241-2
hiking 242-5
horse-riding 224, 246
rollerblading 247
running 246
rugby 246
sailing 226
scuba diving 225
stores 247
squash 248
tennis 249
surfing 113, 119, 226-7
windsurfing 249
St George's Cathedral 54
Stellenbosch 231
    cultural festival 31
    Dorp Street gallery 73
    Oude Libertas Amphitheatre 32
    restaurants 108-9
    university 194
    Van der Stel festival 31
    wine route 83-4
Students 192-6
    accommodation 195-6
    technikons 193-4
    travel 193
    universities 193-4
Surfing 226-7
    board hire 226
    Llandudno 219
    Muizenberg 213
    surf reports 213

Table Mountain 54, 244
Technikons 193-4
Telephones 2, 201-2, 252
    cellphone hire 210
    enquiries 2, 201
    international phone/fax 2, 201
Theatre 154-157
Ticket agencies 150
Tipping 5
Tours
    bicycle 238
    boat charters and cruises 221-3
    coach 58-60
    ecological 59
    green 59
    motorcycle 10, 60
    special feature 59-60
    walking 61-4
    yacht 60

Townships 42-3
    taverns 113
Tourist information bureaux 4
    airport information 5
    Captour 4
    Waterfront 4
Transport 8-12
    bicycle hire 9
    buses 8
    car hire 9
    chauffeurs/limos 9
    disabled travel 12
    helicopters 9
    minibus taxis 10
    motorbike hire 10
    rikkis 10
    rules of the road 5
    taxis 10
    trains 11
Two Oceans Marathon 30

UCT Irma Stern Museum 55
Union of South Africa 37
Universities 193-4
    Cape Town 193
    Stellenbosch 194
    Western Cape 194

Van der Stel, Simon 34
Van der Stel, Willem Adriaan 34, 230
Van Riebeeck, Jan and Maria 34, 47, 60
VAT 5
Victoria and Alfred Waterfront *see* Waterfront
Video hire 148
Visas 1

Waterfront 4, 55, 117, 178
Weather 28
Walking tours
    Art Deco 62
    Bo-Kaap 62-3
    lower city centre 64
Wellington
    restaurants 109
West Coast 233
    fish barbeques 97
Wine 83-4
    shops 129-30
    tours 84
Women 208-12
    accommodation 209
    clubs 211
    organisations 209
    restaurants 211
World of Birds 55

Xhosa phrases 6

Yacht clubs 226